Centennial Conversations

ESSENTIAL ESSAYS IN PROFESSIONAL, CONTINUING, AND ONLINE EDUCATION

UPCEA 1915–2015

Centennial Conversations

ESSENTIAL ESSAYS IN PROFESSIONAL, CONTINUING, AND ONLINE EDUCATION

UPCEA 1915–2015

Edited by

Daniel W. Shannon
University of Chicago

Robert Wiltenburg
Washington University in St. Louis

University Professional and Continuing Education Association
Washington, DC

University Professional and Continuing Education Association
One Dupont Circle, NW, Suite 615
Washington, DC 20036

Printed in the United States of America

Library of Congress Cataloging-in-Publication Data applied for.
ISBN 978-0-9864434-0-4 paperback
ISBN 978-0-9864434-1-1 e-book

∞ This paper meets the requirements of ANSI/NISO Z39.48-1992
(Permanence of Paper).

CONTENTS

Part V. Metrics and Marketing

FOREWORD

In honor of its 75th anniversary in 1990, what was then called the National University Continuing Education Association published a volume entitled *Expanding Access to Knowledge: Continuing Higher Education.* The book was highly innovative in its form. In almost Cubist fashion, *Expanding Access* painted a picture of the origins and evolution of continuing education as a modern social phenomenon by collecting seminal documents and other cultural artifacts: key addresses, congressional testimony, acts of legislation, official reports from regulatory bodies, letters, and critical essays.

In short, *Expanding Access* was, and still is, an indispensable resource for any student of the history of adult and continuing education. As we prepared for the University Professional and Continuing Education Association's centennial year, the question of whether to publish a new book necessarily raised another question: How would a new book complement rather than repeat the same material? *Expanding Access* speaks for itself as the definitive portrait of the first seventy-five years of continuing education, so we decided to create for our centennial a bookend volume dedicated to tracing developments within the past twenty-five years that have not only changed the face of continuing education but also, in a very real sense, helped to reinvent higher education as we know it.

This new collection of essays from the leading thinkers in the field, *Centennial Conversations: Essential Essays in Professional, Continuing, and On-line Education,* maps the ways in which traditional continuing education has morphed in the past two decades into new forms of practice in on-line education, international education, outreach and engagement, and marketing and enrollment management. The essays, edited by Daniel W. Shannon and Robert Wiltenburg into topical conversations, illustrate how the profession served by UPCEA is at once dynamic and transformational, increasingly professionalized and responsive to the ever-evolving needs of our institutions and the public alike.

Why are the conversations in this volume so essential? While many college and university leaders acknowledge the value of serving adult and nontraditional students, it's fair to say that more often than not doing so continues to be marginal to institutional mission, a noble afterthought to the core enterprise of serving first-time, full-time residential students. Universities must reinvent themselves in order to meet the challenges of the twenty-first century, and UPCEA is ready to help provide the leadership and resources necessary to meet the needs of today's students. Indeed, never before has the mission of UPCEA—advancing adult, professional, continuing, and online education—mattered more to our institutions, to the regions they serve, and to our national competitiveness.

I hope that the conversations found in this volume inspire you to join us as we celebrate a century of expanding access to higher education and work together to build tomorrow's universities.

Robert J. Hansen, Ph.D.
Chief Executive Officer, UPCEA
Washington, DC
2015

INTRODUCTION

This year marks the 100th anniversary of the University Professional and Continuing Education Association (UPCEA)—founded in 1915 as the National University Extension Association (NUEA). As the essays in this volume demonstrate, there has never been a time in which the field has been more vital in itself or more important to higher education and to society. Many factors have come together to make this a particularly exciting moment. The changing nature of work means that more people need more education—and more continuing education over the lifespan—than ever before. New technologies make it possible to reach people across the country and around the world—and challenge us to rethink much that we thought we knew about effective teaching and learning. And there is an ever-widening national (and international) commitment to the inclusion of groups—socioeconomic, racial, immigrant, and others—previously excluded from full educational, economic, social, and civic participation. A heady time indeed!

In putting together this volume, we have been delighted to receive the generous and insightful contributions from many colleagues. We have grouped their essays in sections, each of which forms a "conversation" on a key topic, and the diverse viewpoints and treatments often make for interesting and rewarding juxtapositions.

The first section, "The Contexts and Aims of Continuing Education," consists of essays that take broad views of the subject, in national and institutional contexts, examining the individual and social purposes of continuing education. The second section addresses the many aspects—pedagogical, technical, institutional, managerial, and social—of the transformative effect online learning has had, and is having, on the profession. The third conversation takes up a pressing contemporary concern, pathways to degree completion, in terms of national priorities involved and some of the programmatic responses—competency-based education prominent among them—that are now being made. The fourth section recognizes the great diversity of audiences—military, international, immigrant, older adults, donors, and partners, among others—that the contemporary continuing education unit seeks to engage. The final section presents three essays on contemporary marketing and metrics—topics of perennial, and essential, interest to all continuing educators.

Here is a rich banquet of professional experience and reasoning, giving a vivid sense of what the profession is thinking and doing at this centennial moment. Read the book! Join the conversations!

Daniel W. Shannon
University of Chicago

Robert Wiltenburg
Washington University in St. Louis

PART I

The Contexts and Aims of Continuing Education

Continuing education has, of course, a history longer than that of the University Professional and Continuing Education Association. Some of the issues and debates concerning its aims and contexts are perpetual, others relatively new. Each of the six essays in this opening section addresses major concerns of ongoing significance for continuing educators.

Daniel W. Shannon leads off with an essay surveying the historic roots of continuing education in England and America and three key "arcs of activity" (community engagement, international education, and distance education) in contemporary practice. James Broomall examines the classic conundrum: How can continuing education thrive within an institutional framework that values research above teaching? And how can that intrinsic tension be made productive for both? Richard J. Novak traces one of the key developments of the past quarter century—the growing professionalization of the continuing education profession—as the result of several forces and agents, the UPCEA conspicuous among them. Ann M. Brewer analyzes the long-term challenges—social, economic, intellectual, and institutional—to continuing education (or, in her terms, "lifelong learning") and suggests means by which its benefits may be secured for the future. Mary L. Walshok sounds the alarm on the danger of excessive privatization of both means and ends in continuing education, wondering whether in the eagerness to serve the needs of individual students and employers we are in danger of shortchanging the needs of communities and the public good. Robert Wiltenburg examines the long-standing tension between "liberal" and "practical" aims in continuing education and suggests that in the future they will need to be more firmly and deliberately complementary than ever.

A Selective Look at the History and Practice of Continuing Education

▮▮

Daniel W. Shannon

Foundations

American colleges and universities, despite distinctive academic cultures, universally share a commitment to the education of adults. This commitment may be more central to mission in some universities than others, but regardless of centrality to mission, we find someplace in the academic landscape a part of the institution dedicated to the education of adults.

Despite the diversity of higher education institutions and the variability of their program activity in continuing education, who we are and the values that animate our work today grow essentially from several nineteenth-century movements: the British worker education movement, the American Chautauqua movement, and finally, the establishment of the service ethic as a consequence of the creation of the land grant universities with the passage of the Morrill Act in 1862.

The modern movement of adult education in the West begins with changes that occurred in Britain nearly two hundred years ago. While adult education was widespread in England in the late eighteenth and early nineteenth centuries—generally in the form of literary, philosophical, and scientific societies and royal institutes for the middle class and autodidacts among the working class—there was no collective or organized effort to provide adult education for the working class until the Industrial Revolution. Predictably, with the rise of industry came attendant new ideas, attitudes, and needs that drove the organization of adult education from a largely laissez-faire enterprise to one that engaged gov-

Daniel W. Shannon is dean (retired) of the Graham School of Continuing Liberal and Professional Studies, University of Chicago, past president of the UPCEA, 1989–1990, past editor of the *Continuing Higher Education Review*, and a recipient of the Nolte Award.

ernment, universities, and industry in a collective effort to educate the working classes.

B. J. Hake, in his effort to find a narrative structure for the history of adult education, draws attention to several forms of the movement to educate adults in the nineteenth and early twentieth centuries in the English-speaking world. This period of seventy or so years he argues

> witnessed a significant expansion of independent working class forms of [adult education] provision such as working-men's associations, worker's houses, worker's book clubs, worker's travel associations . . . and a diverse range of educational initiatives associated with the Second Communist International. On the other hand [and on balance], there was a range of educational responses to this challenge by conservative and liberal parties. (Hake 2010, 98)

Hake observes that from this expansion many new forms emerged, among them "university extension, university settlements, the arts and craft movement, [and] public libraries" (ibid.).

Roger Fieldhouse, in his *History of Modern British Adult Education*, focuses on the several forces at work in this same period that irretrievably changed the patterns or forms of adult education. First and fundamental was the need for a more skilled workforce "exhibiting a wholly different range of working practices and skills" (Fieldhouse 1996, 2). While employer's needs changed, so did the motivations of workers who saw the acquisition of new skills as increasing employability and mobility. In addition there was a societal need and sense of urgency to acquire new knowledge about the scientific and technological innovations that were driving the industrial machine. These motivations resonate with contemporary needs and interests of adult learners. Out of this mutual interest in continuing education emerged "efforts to bring employers and workers together in continuing education, learning in the workplace, and putative forms of vocational education and training" (Hake 2010, 98).

On the other hand, the radical working class movements, for example, the Owenites and Chartists, in their pursuit of social and political change, defined "really useful knowledge" not in terms of technical skills but as a combination of political knowledge, social science (the principles of social explanation), and labor economics or political economy (i.e., explanations of economic exploitation and why laborers remained poor in the midst of the production of so much wealth). It can be argued that in this atmosphere of free inquiry and the pursuit of socially purposive knowledge, the character of this education greatly influenced "the tradition and even the form of later voluntary, purposive liberal adult education"

(Fieldhouse 1996, 17). One can see in this instance the social and civic purposes of adult education.

In the same period, the 1830s onward, the universities of Britain were under pressure to become more relevant to contemporary educational needs and to extend their limited educational provision to those whose circumstances prevented them from being able to attend the university—a plea for access that is not unfamiliar to current British and American institutions of higher education. Their response to this pressure for engagement was the organization by Cambridge of lecture courses in a limited number of centers away from the university, followed by Oxford almost a decade later. In the words of one historian, university extension had arrived.

In the face of an increasing provision of adult education for vocational ends, it has been observed that in this period

> universities clearly stated the concept of liberal study. In doing so they did not neglect vocational needs of the students, but they insisted that even studies directed to vocational ends should be undertaken in a broad humane spirit, and that the fundamental values and purposes of a human life should be kept steadily in view. (Coles 2010, 9)

More broadly, with the emergence of university extension came a number of different forms intended to "provide educational solutions to the social question(s) of the emergent working class, . . . promoting reformist solutions to widespread concerns with urban housing, family life, working conditions, sanitation and health" (Hake 2010, 98). One can see, for example, the antecedents of the midcentury community development and community service activities in the modern American extension movement.

In America, responding to civic and social needs, a dominant form of continuing education was the lyceum, an organization providing lectures, discussion, and entertainment. The lyceum system, for example, as reported in the *American Review of Reviews* in 1891,

> was of great service in educating the adult population of New England and the North in general to an intelligent understanding of the great political and educational issues of the antebellum period. Both the abolition and the temperance movements were strongly promoted by lyceums. (Adams 1891, 599)

In lyceums and institutes for teachers and mechanics, and with the emergence of the university as a provider of public adult education, the characteristic method of engaging student and instructor was the lecture. Lectures were enormously popular. At the University of Chicago,

> during the first ten years of the [lecture] department's existence the average yearly attendance was 27,296 series ticket holders. The total number of single admissions during that ten-year period was 1,637,802. From San Diego, California, to Tonawanda, New York, there were never more than thirty-four lecturers working during any one year. (Heycke 1989, 7)

In this same period, the late nineteenth century, a distinctly American educational institution found form in the Chautauqua movement. Starting as a church camp for Sunday school teachers in the middle of the nineteenth century, the movement evolved into a nationwide, year-round program of lectures and readings, drawing on the strong impulse of the public to learn. "The Chautauqua experience was critical in stimulating [public] thought and discussion on important political, social, and cultural issues of the day" (Rohfield 1990, 3). It gave life to the notion that learning should be lifelong, that education for adults was both a right and a duty.

It has been observed more than once that the Chautauqua movement was the beginning of the Americanization of university extension, its influence principally being felt through the migration of its leadership to higher education. Most notable among these was William Rainey Harper, the founding president of the University of Chicago. Harper and others brought to higher education the animating values that "adults can learn; education should be extended beyond formal schooling; life is a school; agencies should cooperate in promoting lifelong learning; and education should bring adults into contact with current thought on scientific and social issues" (Stubblefield 1981, 199).

Harper had been a leader of the movement for fourteen years before coming to Chicago, where he imbedded the notion of extension in his educational plans, making it one of the three core activities of the university. The first class taught was an evening class, and when the university opened its doors, it did so with a correspondence study department already in place, contributing the unique notion that correspondence courses should be organized so as to mirror the courses on campus and that credit awarded for courses completed, in a defined number, could be used to meet the requirements for the baccalaureate degree. Incidentally, the award of credit for both correspondence and extension courses distinguished the University of Chicago, and other institutions that followed, as a clear variant from the English system—the first of many divergences from English university extension.

The Chautauqua movement celebrated enlightenment, self-discovery, and liberal learning. By contrast, at the same time, new American universities were being established incorporating an explicit mission of service, focusing on the teaching of agriculture and mechanical arts, "in order to promote . . . the practical education of the industrial classes in the several pursuits and professions of life" (Stubblefield 1981, 203).

This service movement was a consequence of the Morrill Act of 1862 by the Congress of the United States. The Morrill Act established in each state that existed at the time universities that would be known as land-grant universities. Thus began the more than 150-year service tradition of balancing practical education, liberal education, and research. Charles van Hise, the first president of the University of Wisconsin, which was one of the original land-grant universities and remains today among the most prominent, characterized the land-grant university in his remark that "in a broad sense, the idea of culture, the idea of vocation, and the idea of research are held and developed in order that the [land-grant] institution may perform service, and thus the idea of service may be said to be the ultimate purpose of culture, vocation, and research" (Rohfield 1990, 20). It was not until 1914 that an agricultural counterpoint to general extension was established with the Smith-Lever Act, which created the Cooperative Extension Service with the purpose of helping people not enrolled in school to understand and utilize effective practices in farming, marketing, family living, and community development.

These then are three principle roots of modern American extension: the worker education movement and the peculiar expression of that movement in university extension; the Chautauqua movement, demonstrating the need and efficacy of liberal education for a broad public; and the land-grant university's contribution to higher education in the introduction of the concept of service and extension of the university through the application of the intellectual resources of the university to problems and issues of its surrounding community through practical education.

We are, today, the beneficiaries of an important and diverse historical engagement of adults in learning, as expressed through the missions and values of America's colleges and universities.

Transitions to a New Century

From this foundation emerge arcs of activity spanning the twentieth century and beyond, further defining the values, missions, and structures of university adult education and illustrating its nature and impact on America's colleges and universities and the communities they serve. This context is often described in terms of the "social organization of . . . learning in which adults were either organized by others or organized themselves for the purposes of disseminating and acquiring knowledge, skills, and sensitivities" (Hake 2010, 97). The practical purpose of this organized activity was to make knowledge more accessible, while pursuing an "idealistic vision [of] strengthening democracy by helping . . . citizens and government agencies to be better informed and better able to analyze and express ideas in civic discourse" covering relevant social, economic, environmental, and cultural issues of its time (University of Washington 2012, n.p.).

Tracing the arc of activities of American college and university continuing education reveals the presence of a persistent set of attributes or values that have given shape and direction to its programmatic activities and structure as well as defining the fundamental nature of continuing education. Prominent among these are social inclusiveness; a commitment to liberal learning; responsiveness, innovation, agility, flexibility, and adaptability regarding the needs of learners and society, especially in constantly changing environments; pragmatism; and a commitment to assuring the academic value and rigor of its programs. The very nature of these values makes it possible, if not an imperative, to engage in subtle but continuous reinvention.

Arcs of Activity

To appreciate the richness, continuity, and impact of activity associated with American continuing education, what follows are descriptions of several aspects of our work as separate arcs of activity: civic or community engagement, continuing education's international footprint, and distance education and technology. This is not intended as a complete inventory of the programs and services provided by continuing education organizations but rather to illustrate the nature of our enterprise, focusing attention on several of the more important trends and challenges in contemporary continuing education.

While in reality these several arcs of activity are intertwined—much like a weaving, with threads of the warp and woof passing over and under each other, at times disappearing, only to reemerge, creating a new image—through a curated approach to tracing the activities and accomplishments of aspects of continuing education one gets a sense of its growth and changing nature over time. Principally, for generations, continuing education has had a positive impact on the university, the lives of our students, and the civic, social, and economic communities we serve.

Community Engagement: The Social/Civic Agenda

We come naturally to civic or community engagement in the course of our work with the various social, economic, and political communities we traditionally serve. The nature of this engagement is usefully described by David Watson of the University of London, in his *Managing Civic and Community Engagement*, as

> a collection of practices loosely grouped under a policy framework designed to connect . . . a university with its nat-urally constituent community civic engagement presenting a challenge to universities to be of and not just in the com-munity. Not simply to engage in "knowledge" transfer but to establish a dialogue across the boundaries between the university and its community, which is open-ended, fluid, and experimental. (Watson 2007, 3)

This relationship of community and university, in addition to assuring an economic future, makes a "wider contribution. It makes ours a civilized society, develops the spiritual side of lives and promotes active citizen-ship. Learning enables people to play a full part in their communities" (ibid., 6).

In the past one hundred years UPCEA and its member institutions have played an active, if not lead, role in creating structures and programs at our colleges and universities that encourage the linking of community and citizen needs and interests with those of government and business in the pursuit of overarching social, economic, and civic goals. In the Pro-gressive Era, a time of many political reforms—the establishment of direct primaries, the initiative and referendum process, the direct election of US senators, and women's right to vote—the University of Washington created the Bureau of Debate and Discussion to support civic education directed to the achievement of "a more complete and intelligent under-standing of public affairs on the part of the average citizen" (University of Washington 2012, 3). Support came in the form of printed materials, including bibliographies, questions for debates, and outlines for debaters as well as program outlines for high schools, women's clubs, civic better-ment associations, and other organizations. In the same period, across the country, state universities were establishing bureaus of municipal and legislative research, harnessing the research capacities of the university to support collection, cataloging, and dissemination of data to support policy development by community leaders as well as government professionals.

In the same spirit a half century later, universities, including the Uni-versity of Washington, marshaled their financial and economic resources in support of citizens engaged in the identification and solution of civic and social problems confronting the community. The approach of community development to civic, economic, and social problem-solving assumed that education for citizenship, for social good, would best be accomplished by engaging the resident/citizen in the identification of community problems and, with university assistance, research alternative solutions as the foundation for the community decision making—learning by doing. These efforts at community engagement in many universities ultimately foundered as institutional budgets fell prey to legislative mandates for budget reductions.

The civic engagement agenda for continuing education, however, has persisted and may be seen in the annual meeting of UPCEA. For example CONNECT, founded by Extension at the University of California-San Diego in the mid-eighties, has demonstrated the efficacy of engaging individuals, organizations, and the university in the creation of new industry sectors, enterprises, and public policy. Through CONNECT Public Policy its membership achieves a voice in local, state, and federal policy making that drives the innovation economy. UPCEA itself provides a venue for the education of its membership in civic engagement through its Outreach, Engagement, and Economic Development Network. While there exists a strong commitment to and focus on supporting the economic development of our communities through the intellectual resources of the university, we should not forget that continuing education is as well an effective instrument for the building of a strong civic life and an assurance of a civil society.

International Footprint

Many UPCEA institutions have a history with international programs that are decades old, with portfolios predominantly taking the form of English as a Second Language (ESL), study abroad, and international students in campus-based programs. Most of these institutions experienced a decline in numbers a decade or more ago, leading in some instances to the closure of ESL programs. But this setback notwithstanding, international programming has experienced a measurable growth in a variety of initiatives. The original set of activities remain—that is, ESL, study abroad, and traditional international students for on-campus courses—but the diversity of new initiatives or programs is now broader.

One could argue that this reflects the changing international agendas of our mother institutions. And there is much truth in that. In the case of the University of Chicago there are now physical centers supporting faculty and academic programs in Beijing, Hong Kong, Shanghai, New Delhi, Paris, and London. These centers support student and faculty research, study abroad, lectures, symposia, and, importantly, joint programs with in-country universities, all reflecting the institutional interests in a diverse set of international educational and research programs. But continuing education programs have played an important role in furthering their international goals by aligning with the institutional strategy for internationalization. Programmatic opportunities are increasingly available that demand a flexibility in the architecture of our programs.

The opportunities and challenges of engaging in international programming have been diverse. The structures and policies of most of our institutions challenge the ability to meet the expectations of international partners, grounded as we are in its institutional "quality" DNA. This reality has tested, often successfully, the adherence to our values of flexibility, innovation, and academic quality. What has emerged, and is often shared at UPCEA annual meetings over the past twenty-five years, are inventive approaches to partnerships that benefit student, international partner, and home institution. Illustrative are Brown's partnership with IE Business School in Madrid, utilizing blended learning to award an executive MBA; Chicago's partnership with CEU San Pablo Madrid's School of Pharmacy to imbed Chicago's certificate in clinical trials in their undergraduate degree in pharmacy; and Boston University's Metropolitan College collaboration with CEU San Pablo to offer intensive business modules in Spain, with the cohort completing their work for a Boston University certificate on the BU campus.

Distance Education and Technology

Teaching students at a distance has, as already noted, been a remit of continuing education from the final decade of the nineteenth century in the form of correspondence study. With the leadership of the University of Chicago, it distinguished itself from the commercial correspondence schools by attending to the award of credit and accepting a portion of those credits in meeting the requirements of a bachelor of arts. In this competitive environment it was a principal task of the Correspondence Department "to disassociate itself from the odor of chicanery which surrounded the commercial correspondence schools and to prove to a skeptical faculty and to all serious students that the method of study by correspondence was adequate to university subject matter" (Heycke 1989, 56). A testament to its efficacy in reaching and engaging the distant learner is the persistent presence of correspondence study today in the catalog of modes of instructional delivery at many American universities.

In the intervening decades the story of education at a distance has been about the adaptation of emerging technologies to the task of connecting a student to the distant intellectual resources of the university, particularly in support of instruction. Technology not only overcame distance, but also, in many instances, addressed the problem of time:

telephone-supported audio networks in a mode much like a conference call with students at fixed site and time; video-conferencing similarly constrained by locale and time; telecourses employing lectures delivered by television with correspondence study support; cable television utilizing courses developed for open broadcast television; instructional television fixed service (ITFS) employing audio and television for interactivity between the university and students at distant fixed locations; and compressed video utilizing data for high-resolution interactivity audio and video through the web with students at fixed sites.

Even a casual reading of media reporting on higher education today or UPCEA's annual meeting conference program makes apparent the substantial impact technology is having on teaching and learning in American colleges and universities. It is equally notable that there is no consensus among higher education providers regarding the forms, goals, or outcomes of the current nascent efforts at employing technology to support teaching and learning.

The landscape of distance learning that has emerged in the past twenty-five years is similarly as varied as the technologies employed: lecture capture video; audio only podcasts; screencasting; online open courseware; asynchronous and synchronous courses, as well as the channels used, for example, web-only courses, iTunes, online social networks, and TED. This diversity highlights both the challenge of creating a coherent, planned approach to the deployment of technology for teaching and learning and the risks associated with deciding upon a single approach. MIT's decision to adopt an open courseware approach contrasts with the University of Pennsylvania's decentralized, 'nimble' approach to online education with courses on iTunes, Knowledge @ Wharton, and the College of Liberal and Professional Studies offering, at the moment, fourteen full-credit online courses during the summer semester.

These two cases illustrate, as well, divergent approaches to the scale of content creation, where MIT is comprehensive in its offerings, making every course in its curriculum available online, whether in print or video, while the University of Pennsylvania is highly curated, selectively offering courses and mediated works.

Imbedded in these institutional approaches to distance education are notions of the structure of content that align with traditional ideas of the organization of the learning experiences, for example, courses, certificates, and degrees that stand, if successfully completed, as testaments of acquired knowledge. This is a core issue in the current debate regarding the structure of competency-based education. How knowledge is measured in a digital environment is challenging MIT in its MITx program, for example, where authentication and testing are immediate challenges, and in the MacArthur Foundation–funded competition for the design and testing of digital badges and badge systems that can be used instead of traditional structures to prove a candidate's experience and knowledge.

On the other hand, while much of our attention has been focused on the disruptive nature of technology when applied to teaching and learning, we need to recollect that it has in the past twenty-five years had a substantial positive impact on the infrastructure of continuing education. Registration and student information systems, enrollment management, admissions and student communication, and alumni relations all depend upon social media, specialized software, and the web. These technology-based capacities enhance our ability to meet the particular needs of the adult student who does not fit the usual university profile thus eliminating the need for a software workaround to satisfy the needs of the continuing education student. The demand for technology on campus, on the other hand, is almost universal. So continuing education often finds itself competing for resources with other academic technology users on campus, whose interests are more aligned with the research mission of the university, for example, computation in various disciplines and maintenance of data sets in economics, business, social sciences, complex science, and engineering.

The fiscal reality of the competition for technology resources within the college or university and the urgency associated with the adoption of technology for both instruction and infrastructure has resulted in the creation of a new economy of supporting partnerships between colleges or universities and private technology vendors. The partnerships usually involve shared risk but most often frontload the cost of development, leaving the university partner waiting for a substantial period of time for the project to realize a net contribution to continuing education's bottom line. This business model does address the problem of competing with on-campus technology users.

Conclusion

These three arcs of programmatic innovation and responsiveness—community engagement, international relations, and disruptive technology— illustrate as a field and an association how we are challenged to represent the interests of the adult learner and to provide strategic leadership at our institutions in the provision of timely and innovative responses to their educational needs. The form of our response to opportunity and need has varied over time, variously driven by the changing nature and needs of the labor market, shifts in the state and federal policy environment, the needs for social and civic transformation, and alignment with university priorities. Regardless of the source or nature of the demand or opportunity for adult learning, however, university continuing education, with the support of its professional association, will continue to meet the challenge of playing a central role in designing the form and nature of professional and continuing education in America.

References

Adams, Herbert B. 1891. "'University Extension' and Its Leaders." *American Review of Reviews* 3 (July).

Coles, Janet. 2010. *University Adult Education: The First Century in University Continuing Education 1981–2006.* Leicester, England: National Institute of Adult Education.

Fieldhouse, R. 1996. *A History of Modern British Adult Education.* Leicester, England: National Institute of Adult Education.

Hake, B. J. 2010. *Rewriting the History of Adult Education: The Search for Narrative Structures.* Amsterdam: Elseviere.

Heycke, Betty Fackler. 1989. *A History of the Origins of Adult Education at the University of Chicago and of Sixty-Two Years at the Downtown Center.* Chicago: Office of Continuing Education.

"History of UW-Extension." n.d. UW-Extension. Accessed at www.uwex.edu /about/uw-extension-history.html.

Rohfield, R. W. 1990. *Expanding Access to Knowledge: Continuing Higher Education.* Washington, DC: National University Continuing Education Association.

Shannon, Daniel W. 2009. "Continuing Higher Education in America: A Profile." *International Journal of Continuing Education and Lifelong Learning* 1 (2): 19–39.

Stubblefield, H. W. 1981. "The Idea of Lifelong Learning in the Chautauqua Movement." *Adult Education Quarterly* 31 (4): 199–208.

University of Washington. 2012. *Origins of the University of Washington Extension Program.* Accessed at http://www.pce.uw.edu/uploadedFiles/Centennial /1910-1920-uwpce-our-history.pdf.

Watson, David. 2007. *Managing Civic and Community Engagement.* Berkshire, England: Open University Press.

Continuing Education and the Research University

■■

James Broomall

As the University Professional and Continuing Education Association (UPCEA) celebrates its 100th anniversary, it is fitting to reflect that the association's birth followed, but mirrored, that of the American research university. Although coming nearly thirty years after the establishment of the Johns Hopkins University in 1886, UPCEA, then the National University Extension Association (NUEA), comprised twenty-two research universities; of these, eighteen were state or land-grant institutions while the other four were private, highly selective, and urban. From its inception UPCEA's mission and vision as the association to foster extended education and public service was thus intertwined with that of the research university. This essay will review the relationship between the two and suggest an intrinsic tension that has manifested itself in both successes and failures over the past one hundred years. Particular attention will be paid to 1990–2015. While the term *research university* now refers to more than three hundred higher education institutions in the United States, this perspective will be influenced by those one hundred or so that rank highest in research funding, national and international rankings, and the number of doctoral graduates. These universities—due to size, wealth, productivity and influence on public policy and popular attention—set the tone for the discussion surrounding the research and continuing education nexus.

Despite the importance of continuing education in the broader stream of higher education and its record of achievement, its role is often neglected in the professional literature on higher and postsecondary education. For example, in the otherwise encyclopedic compendium

James Broomall is Associate Vice Provost, Professional and Continuing Studies, University of Delaware, and past president of the UPCEA, 2004–2005.

American Higher Education Transformed, 1940–2005, Smith and Bender pay almost no attention to continuing education. Lifelong learning is treated briefly in an essay by former New York University president John Sawhill, reprinted from *Change* magazine. Harping on the historic marginality of adult education, Sawhill offers the cautionary warning that without adequate service—albeit not defined—to the adult and nontraditional student, "lifelong learning could be the scandal of the next decade." The obvious omission of continuing education in the Smith and Bender volume is especially vexing, since its focus is higher education's transformation, with particular attention to post–World War II America. In his benchmark work *The Emergence of the American University*, Laurence Veysey exhaustively examines the internal and external forces that created the American research university. While chapters are devoted to utility and the synthesis of otherwise disparate missions, continuing education is not mentioned. Other thought leaders in higher education, like Henry Rosovsky in *The University: An Owner's Manual* and Derek Bok in *Universities in the Marketplace*, also stand silent on continuing education in the research university.

Within the continuing education literature itself, with reference to its role in the research university, scholarship over the past thirty or more years has centered on organizational structure—centralization versus decentralization. That is, should continuing education be an autonomous organization analogous to an academic college or should it be distributed across the traditional academic structure of colleges, schools, and departments? In part this reflects a reality of academic organization: the continuing expansion and contraction of continuing education units on university campuses. While exploring organizational dichotomy has added to our understanding of continuing education as a structure and function, it has delimited the focus. Rather than viewing continuing education as a university mission, it has explored it as an organized enterprise. Given the expanded importance of lifelong learning motivated by the exponential growth of knowledge and technological sophistication since UPCEA's 75th anniversary in 1990, a broader view is warranted.

This essay owes an intellectual debt to Nicholas Lemann's "The Soul of the Research University," a 2014 article in the *Chronicle of Higher Education*. He suggests that "the two most important developments in American higher education in the 19th century were, arguably, contradictory." He refers here to the Morrill Act (1862), which led to mass higher education in the United States, and just fourteen years later the establishment of Johns Hopkins University. Continuing education in the research university shares this intellectual paradox. It celebrates Ezra Cornell's aspiration to provide any study or body of knowledge to any person. Conversely, the epistemology and method on which the knowledge is based comes from a rigidly monitored process of peer review and selectivity. The inherent tension and its promise and peril will frame what follows.

For purposes of clarity and reader friendliness, this essay will be a "play in four acts." First, it will outline the fundamental ingredients and values of the research university. Second, continuing education will receive the same treatment. Third, the nexus of the research university and continuing education will be considered from one argument-driven perspective. Finally, some heuristic hunches or future gazing will be presented as UP-CEA celebrates its centennial.

The Research University

Although Yale awarded the first PhD in the United States in 1861, the research university took form with the founding of Johns Hopkins and Clark University as primarily graduate universities in the 1870s and 1880s and was enhanced with the founding of the University of Chicago in 1892. Rooted in the ideals of the German university, which provided the training and socialization for many in the professoriate by the 1890s, academic freedom was fundamental to the idea and vision of the research university. Drawn from the German ideals of *Lernfreiheit* and *Lehrfreiheit*—the professor's freedom to explore and disseminate the results of research-based inquiry free from external and, of acute concern, government interference—academic freedom set the process and metrics on which the professor's work would be assessed. If research was the means to identify truth, who best to judge the methods used and the results shared than fellow members of the same discipline. Epistemological validity depended on peer review, and juried publication in specialized journals or at academic conferences became the gold standard. The rise in number and prestige of professional associations and journals governed by academic disciplines solidified this precedent. In essence, the professoriate became an independent and self-regulating body charged with maintaining intellectual rigor free from external demands or requirements. This professionalization of the faculty was expedited as these professional societies and associations were guided by the norms and standards of academic disciplines, not institutional expectations. Larry Cuban (1999) contends that "scholars trumped teachers" to make the research university the centerpiece for American higher education.

Social, economic, technological, and demographic trends since 1990 have served to intensify and institutionalize the place of the research university. Three particular factors are noted here. First, the half-life of knowledge has become reality in light of an explosion in basic research at the university level. While not the only agent charged with the creation of knowledge, the research university has enjoyed special privilege in the form of escalating dollars for fundamental research, particularly from the federal government. This role as arbiter of defining knowledge in its pure form brings with it unique status as a gatekeeper to upward social mobility for those accessing and benefiting from the knowledge discovered and knowledge applied in teaching and learning. Second, globalization and the essentiality of intellectual capital have elevated the American research university to primary status in a worldwide talent competition. Laboratories, classrooms, and seminar rooms increasingly bring an international professoriate and student body to the American research university. In turn, research becomes a common knowledge and language that transcends the traditional divisions among nation states. A third trend—technological innovation—demonstrates the role of basic research. While innovation in the last twenty years has been born in garages and garrets as well as the university, the flow of dollars and accompanying prestige has not exempted the research campus. Technology transfer, intellectual property, and knowledge transformation all are hallmarks. Research universities have become key players in economic development, as is evident in signal achievements like the Route 28 corridor in Massachusetts, North Carolina's Research Triangle, and Silicon Valley.

Continuing Education

Values of intellectual integrity, the discovery of knowledge, and a cosmopolitan worldview set the tone for the research university. Yet, many of those founding UPCEA institutions, while driven by research, also shared a second and equally vital impulse in American higher education—democratization. While democratization was certainly fundamental to public state and land-grant universities, private universities also were obligated to serve the public good. Social trends cited earlier have only exacerbated the demands from multiple stakeholders, including government, corporations, funding sources, and the media, that the knowledge discovered be applied to the needs of a democratic society. Public policy encouraged this egalitarian impulse as well.

The dialogue between knowledge as an ideal and knowledge as utility was most evident in the land-grant and public flagship universities. For the former, the mission statement of its founding charter in the Morrill Act appears straightforward: "to promote the liberal and practical education of the industrial classes in the several pursuits and professions of life." Both the theoretical and the applied are given equal status in these words, but implementation posed a challenge. An early solution was the establishment of the Cooperative Extension System in 1914 through federal legislation. This recognized a reality that between

1906 and 1913 twenty-eight universities had already organized a unit for extension work.

Early efforts at continuing education fell under the rubric of public service—the third element (besides research and teaching) of the three-legged stool of the university. While cooperative extension developed an administrative and programmatic system centered mainly but not exclusively on agriculture and family life, university extension became the catchall for other attempts to apply knowledge to broader social concerns and audiences, in forms ranging from correspondence and evening classes to conferences, institutes, lecture series, and symposia. Continuing education was positioned as a gateway between the university as a fount of knowledge and the general public in whose service this knowledge was to be applied.

Since 1990 the place of continuing education on the research university landscape has become a focus of conflict, cooperation, and compromise. What once was peripheral to the core mission now is under the spotlight from campus administrators, faculty, and constituencies. Why? First, the marketplace for knowledge consumption has broadened. As mentioned earlier, in the well-documented global economy intellectual capital is the driving engine. So, the university competes in an international marketplace. Continuing education becomes the means to meet this reality while still maintaining the boundary between the campus core and the external demand. A second factor, albeit more localized, is the exponential growth of adult learners as a market for continuous education. For the research university this takes many forms, from degree completion to organizational learning. Expectations for accountability and tighter guidelines for professional credentialing are today more pronounced than ever. Finally, financial pressures in an era of dwindling support for the public research university puts continuing education in front as an income generator rather than expense unit.

Continuing education's emergence as a component of traditional academic units is an ever-growing feature of the contemporary research university. In the period leading up to 1990 continuing education was more likely to be defined as an organization with a specific structure and function within the broader academic enterprise. Analysis was limited to the centralization-decentralization debate cited above. Today, continuing education is a means to disseminate, codify, and apply basic knowledge. Professional schools and colleges—whether colleges of business and engineering offering executive and advanced technical education or medical, law, and dental schools presenting state-of-the-art content—have joined the division (or college) of continuing education at the research university. Still, the most common manifestations are in professional fields where the line between basic and applied knowledge is thinnest.

Research and Continuing Education Nexus: Tension and Triumph

At the research university, research as a mission stands with continuing education as a means to meet internal resource needs and external expectations. But increasing concern about the cost of a university education and the concomitant student debt, calls for organizational efficiency from all branches of government and the public, questions of the value of a degree, and the rise of the for-profit university all contribute to creating a confused terrain on which research and continuing education meet in 2015.

What then for the nexus of research and continuing education in the research university? An earlier foray by the Kellogg Commission in 1992 to examine how the university could better serve the commonweal seemed to anticipate this tension, arguing that, while society had problems, universities had departments. Framed by discipline-based inquiry, governed by the norm of academic freedom, and organized into departments, the research university was not structured to respond in a timely and critical way to the external society. Citing as its intentional goal an "engaged university," the commission identified the dichotomy between research as an intrinsic value and its utility that was and remains sobering. Why then this inherent tension?

From federal financial largesse for infrastructure and talent to technology transfer and knowledge partnerships exemplified by the start-up company, research touches the life of its home institution. Over the past quarter century, the search for prestige as measured in dollars, rankings, and reputational status has accelerated the importance of research. As continuing educators in the research university context, it is fundamental to understand the research process and then determine its role in meeting our mission. The challenge is that the research professor as an individual or the academic department as a collective body begins from a different fundamental premise than the continuing educator or continuing education organization.

Research is a quest for discovery through a prescriptively defined and shared process, whether through induction or deduction or, in conventional terms, quantitative or qualitative investigation. It is based on a foundation laid in graduate school and built on the epistemology and methodology set by each discipline or applied field of study in professional fields. The guardians and arbiters are fellow members acting in an almost guild-like fashion. Defining what is of value and meritorious is their exclusive domain. Academic journals, conference presentations, and the gatherings of professional associations and societies enjoy a status hierarchy and can determine a faculty member's career trajectory or a department's ranking. Ideas are exchanged within a tightly defined cohort and sphere of importance. The worth of the research in a marketplace outside this fraternity is of little or no importance and in fact may be a source of academic disdain. A reward system—whether as essential as granting tenure or simply rising in the academic firmament—is predicated on positive peer review, evaluation, and judgment.

What is the role of continuing education in this nexus? If research is evaluated and assessed value in a rigidly defined scope of influence, continuing education operates by definition in an open marketplace defined by market requirements of demand, price, utility, and consequentiality. The social forces of technological sophistication, globalization, and competition have in the past twenty-five years only heightened the market for commercialized knowledge; higher education in general has become a commodity. In the research university this trend often sheds a spotlight on continuing education. With a historical legacy of extending campus boundaries to serve stakeholders (often codified in legislative mandate for land-grant and state universities) and a financially self-supporting business model, continuing education is seen as the appropriate response.

Within the research university there is an implicit tension between the norms of research free from evaluation by "amateurs" and the continuing education mission to serve the general public. Yet, the irony is that for continuing education in a research university to distinguish itself from curriculum and services offered by myriad other providers, it must bring that very research through application to a marketplace. The test for continuing education more often than not is whether market demand is met through enrollment, financial remuneration, or partnerships that will benefit the home institution more broadly. The faculty who create the knowledge with the guiding norm of academic freedom are innately suspicious and often disdainful of subjecting their work to the market decision made by individual customers and organizational and professional clients to "buy" the knowledge. In the nexus knowledge must be transformed to stay both true to its standard and judged as being of value in the marketplace of continuing higher education.

Continuing educators are by temperament and vocation a practical lot. As a state and land-grant, research extensive university with an outreach mission housed in the Division of Professional and Continuing Studies, the University of Delaware faces this challenge: How to bring timely and consequential research to people and organizations? One successful example is a joint venture between the division and the Alfred Lerner College of Business and Economics. Through the Organizational Learning Solutions office, custom-designed programs in leadership, project and technology management, and strategy are presented by research-based faculty to corporate, government, and health-care organizations. In turn, these organizations provide a setting for those same faculty and their graduate students to engage in research. This exchange relationship benefits both parties and identifies a common ground for the application and discovery of knowledge.

Why did this nexus triumph when comparable efforts fell short of the mark? The inquiry process in an applied field like management or business administration, while guided by peer review, is governed by external norms of relevance to professional practice. Tests of consequence in a more general market are a norm. The community of recipients enhances rather than diminishes the researcher's freedom.

Toward the Future: 2015 and Beyond

The social, demographic, and technological dynamics mentioned in this essay and throughout the volume should only accelerate throughout the twenty-first century. With knowledge growing geometrically and technological obsolescence a recurring threat, continuing education will become an even more prominent player in the research university. Not limited to its own organizational domain, continuing education cuts across colleges, departments, and schools. Joint ventures like Coursera and EdX demonstrate the affinity of research universities to cluster together and share their academic resources to provide mass open education. Public and government thirst for intellectual capital as the means to maintain a Western standard of living increases the applied role of research in efforts like technology transfer and university-corporate partnerships.

Still, the research university is subject to the same pressures affecting education at all levels. Three of particular relevance are cost, accessibility, and consequentiality. Cost is driven by the question of who pays. A once seemingly endless flow of federal dollars built the research university. Whether driven by considerations of national defense, as evident in the entrepreneurial university of the Cold War era, or improving health and human welfare, government funding reached an apex in the early twenty-first-century stimulus initiative under the Obama administration. That monetary well is running dry; yet, at the same time, federal regulation and accountability expectations have increased. Continuing education offers an alternative mechanism for revenue generation through sponsored research and its application under market demands and requirements. Those clients, and more significantly those paying, will exacerbate the tension between pure and applied research. Continuing education will become to an even greater degree an individual rather than public good. As early as 1998 Burton Clark foresaw this trend in *Creating Entrepreneurial Universities: Organizational Pathways of Transformation.*

Access to continuing education in the research university raises the question of who benefits. Continuing education's business model is market sensitive, and price can limit the access of those individuals and organizations that could benefit. Public service as subsidized enterprise will become even rarer. Thus, the gap between the educational haves who can afford continuing education and the have-nots is most likely to grow in the research university. Reputational status and limited access may only enhance the prestige of continuing education while serving a more limited audience with a higher socioeconomic and professional/occupational profile. For UPCEA the irony could be that an association with roots in extending knowledge may come to represent a highly selective sector of higher education.

Finally, how will the consequentiality of research-based continuing education be assessed? Will business and economic demands threaten the norms of academic freedom and peer review? The impact of the celebration of STEM education and a de-emphasis on the humanities and many social sciences is already clear. A depressed employment forecast for the traditional academic career and the decline in tenure track faculty positions are daily fodder for the media. In response, continuing education and those who provide its leadership have a moral as well as professional obligation. Especially in the research university, continuing education ought to temper market responsiveness with allegiance to the values that inform the enterprise. The theoretical and the practical informed by basic and applied research inform continuing education. Learning as an end in itself and as an instrument for living can enjoy balance in the continuing education organization.

Continuing education and research enjoy a symbiotic relationship that enriches both. Research is the lifeblood of the programs and services provided to a marketplace which, while receptive to knowledge, is at the same time somewhat suspicious of academic freedom. Yet the creative tension is what makes research university–centered continuing education a unique and signal feature in the complex landscape of higher education.

References

Bok, Derek. 2003. *Universities in the Marketplace: The Commercialization of Higher Education.* Princeton, NJ: Princeton University Press.

Clark, Burton R. 1998. *Creating Entrepreneurial Universities: Organizational Pathways of Transformation.* Bingley, UK: Emerald Group.

Cuban, Larry. 1999. *How Scholars Trumped Teachers: Change without Reform in University Curriculum, Teaching, and Research, 1890–1990.* New York: Teachers College Press.

Lemann, Nicholas. 2014. "The Soul of the Research University." *Chronicle of Higher Education*, April 28. Accessed at http://chronicle.com/article /The-Soul-of-the-Research/146155/.

Rosovsky, Henry. 1991. *The University: An Owner's Manual.* New York: W. W. Norton.

Smith, Wilson, and Thomas Bender, eds. 2008. *American Higher Education Transformed 1940–2005: Documenting the National Discourse.* Baltimore: Johns Hopkins University Press.

Veysey, Laurence R. 1965. *The Emergence of the American University.* Chicago: University of Chicago Press.

Dimensions of Professionalization of the Adult and Continuing Education Enterprise

📖

Richard J. Novak

Is continuing education a profession? Is there a specific body of knowledge, mastery of which determines professional competency? What does one make of attempts to professionalize continuing education? These are among the nagging questions that have been noodled by CE deans, directors, and vice presidents for years. The current context in higher education has intensified the discussion. Apparently, there is no shared vision within the academy as to the role of continuing higher education.

Rather, in a variant of Miles's law, "where you stand depends on where you sit," continuing education is often viewed as a profession by those within it and, at worst, as an avocation or, at best, a service by those outside. Miles himself concluded that, in effect, this is to be expected, as perspective and responsibility change with the change of organizational positions, often resulting in a change of position on issues (Miles 1978). From the seat of this former UPCEA president with thirty years' experience as a CE practitioner, adult education researcher, and graduate-level instructor, an honest reading of a century of CE history tells a clear story: continuing education is a vibrant profession ideally suited to lead higher education into an exciting future of daunting challenges and wide opportunity.

Richard J. Novak is Vice President for Continuing Studies and Distance Education, Rutgers University, past president of the UPCEA, 2007–2008, and a recipient of the Bittner Award.

A Cornerstone of Higher Education

The establishment of UPCEA, even in its the earliest incarnation—the National University Extension Association (NUEA)—included concern for professional standards, instructional methods, and administrative practices, for "their mutual advantage and for the development and promotion of the best ideals, methods and standards for the interpretation and dissemination of the accumulated knowledge of the race to all who desire to share in its benefits" (Knowles 1994, 160). This is the legacy that has been carried forward through one hundred years of existence and thousands of professional development opportunities provided by the association for continuing education professionals.

College and university continuing education, by whatever particular name we call it today—continuing higher education, continuing studies, professional studies, university extension—has reached a point of maturity and can no longer be dismissed as an avocation. At the same time it has become the nexus of various historical developments, societal and cultural changes, and workplace requirements that have created a perfect storm of sorts, where demand is greater than ever. Many of the developments that continuing education has pioneered have become the cornerstones of contemporary higher education. For example, most of university continuing education historically has been self-supporting and revenue generating, operating as an entrepreneurial business unit within traditional colleges and universities. Cuts to state budgets, reduction in subsidies, a weak economy, and greater attention to pricing have all put tremendous pressure on higher education, limiting the growth of tuition, for political and practical reasons. As a result, continuing education and its ability to generate new and diverse revenue streams has been afforded a seat at the table as colleges and universities look to address issues of access and affordability, as well as relevance.

Except for some tenured faculty whose lives have remained largely unaffected, most aware employees in higher education now realize that higher education is big business and is impacted by all that entails (Selingo 2013). Some may embrace that notion, others abhor it; but the truth is that, as the saying goes, the horse is out of the barn. There is no going back; the question is how to deal with this reality. Selingo states that the higher education industry is "beset by hubris, opposition to change, and resistance to accountability" (ibid., x). He calls for significant changes to higher education, which, from the perspective of this continuing education professional, sounds like a call for the adoption of many of the core values long embraced by traditional continuing education.

Continuing Education Core Values and Competencies

The good news for continuing higher education is that some of the traditional core values and competencies of continuing education—strategic marketing, full cost accounting attributing for all revenue and expenses, analysis of return on investment, thorough program evaluation, retaining only the highest rated instructors, new program development based on market demand, investment of margin into future program development—are becoming part of the traditional higher education fabric and indeed part of the solution to many of the problems that higher education faces. Nontraditional adult students, once on the margins, are now in the mainstream and are no longer being labeled as nontraditional. Finally, online learning, once the marginal domain of CE units, has become part of the core, and no institution can expect to remain competitive without online offerings. Granted, there are many more challenges within higher education to address, but this is a healthy start.

At the same time, the challenging news for continuing higher education is that what was once marginal activity is now moving into the mainstream, from the edges to the center. Online learning, for example, has had a dramatic impact on many institutions as it has moved into the mainstream. While providing access to students and revenue to the institution, it has required new technologies and new strategies for instructional design and delivery of student services, to say nothing of the increased regulation from state and federal agencies and from regional accrediting bodies. To put it bluntly, expectations are higher than ever for continuing education to perform, to produce and, in many cases, to lead their institutions through rapid changes and into an uncertain future. At our one-hundred-year mark, that leadership challenge has never been more complex—nor more ideally suited to the insights CE leaders offer.

A brief and high-level summary of continuing education today underscores the wide variety of professional skills, competencies, knowledge networks, and even some personal attributes that are required for the CE leader and the CE unit to be successful. No longer is it sufficient to think of a single market segment, a single product line, and a simplified approach to marketing. All aspects of this enterprise have become multivariate and are constantly changing. Today, for example, the call is for data-driven decision making to maximize resources and determine appropriate return on investment (ROI). Everything is expected to be measured, not just marketing dollars. Data analysis is a key component of any CE leader's workday, and staff expertise in data analytics is highly desired by any CE department looking to succeed and distinguish itself in a crowded and competitive marketplace.

Complex Organizations Pursuing Core Missions

From a structural or organizational perspective, the complexities of to-day's continuing education units can be staggering. For some CE units, agricultural extension and cooperative extension have been merged with continuing education. Other CE operations have achieved degree-granting status, especially for adult students. Many more CE units work with existing traditional academic units to offer the degree to adult students while the CE unit provides exceptional customer service and student support. And to no one's surprise, distance education and online learning emerged primarily and almost exclusively out of continuing education units. This is simply another chapter in the history of continuing education's leadership. Students of the history of adult and continuing education recall that CE advocates began defying distance barriers by developing correspondence programs more than one hundred years ago, and today's wonderfully complex distance learning programs and structures are an organic development of that innovation (Knowles 1994).

Still other CE departments have become experts in global education, creating partnerships and programs around the world, sometimes serving as the focal point for the entire institution's global initiatives. Many CE units have become experts at partnering with third parties, both commercial and nonprofit, for all types of content and services, negotiating contracts, structuring revenue-sharing arrangements, even creating shared intellectual property.

By way of example, my own Division of Continuing Studies (DoCS) at Rutgers University illustrates the complex nature of today's continuing education portfolio. DoCS consists of fifteen unique business units, credit and noncredit, on campus, off-campus, and online. We operate year-round, through the standard terms of fall and spring, winter and summer, but also in special terms for noncredit programs and on-demand learning online. We cover the lifespan with programs for audiences from pre-K through senior adult. In addition, we manage a small hotel and conference center and a fully digital, high-definition broadcast television production studio. This is a far cry from simple university extension and the early days of the Chautauqua movement. The vast majority of our operation is entirely self-supporting and expected to generate a margin that can then be used for reinvestment and to support traditional academic operations that do not cover their own costs.

This complex world of continuing education has required greater sophistication and new skills from both CE leaders and staff. New models have been developed, and continuing education has been able to leverage its inherent strength in partnering to forge new pathways that benefit students. New technologies and new resources have enabled continuing education to operate even more nimbly and with greater precision, basing decisions on data. The expectation for CE leadership is twofold: academic credibility and understanding and business acumen. Strong negotiation skills are definitely a plus. Dealing with space management, negotiating contracts, and developing and interpreting profit and loss statements are all part of the daily routine for university CE leaders today. A review of posted CE leadership positions reveals the demand for such expertise. Moreover, as the university CE model has become larger and more diverse, the discussion is not a debate between profits versus social good but rather about how we incorporate both dimensions in an ethical way. Indeed, there are many decisions related to ethical practice for both adult education instructors and program planners (Imel 1991).

While many have entered the field of adult and continuing education without formal preparation, either accidentally or through a personal commitment, or even as a result of a positive experience as a student, during the past seven decades graduate programs and associations in the field have played major roles in providing for the preparation of practitioners and scholars (Knox and Fleming 2010). Associations preceded adult education graduate programs in providing educational opportunities for the field and, in continuing higher education, have continually matured their level of service and knowledge.

UPCEA's Continuous Education and Evolution

By way of example, UPCEA, in all of its historical iterations over the past one hundred years, has played a major role in the continuing professional development of continuing higher education leaders and practitioners. Throughout its history, programmatic offerings and services have been developed and refined to further the field of practice, to enhance the skills of practitioners, and to engage leadership in discussions and planning for future directions.

Probably the most significant of the programmatic offerings, in terms of numbers, is the annual conference, which draws six to eight hundred CE leaders and practitioners, dozens of industry representatives, and world-renowned speakers. The annual conference is complemented by regional conferences that draw a hundred or more participants from a specific region and specialize in showcasing local talent. For many years, UPCEA offered an executive assembly geared to institutional representatives to the association for an intensive deep dive on a timely topic. A dean and directors program continues to be popular as a separate program, connected to the annual conference. One of the most popular programs after the annual conference is the annual marketing seminar, drawing hundreds of participants, where the critical topic of program marketing in all its dimensions, from market research to digital and social media marketing, is addressed.

More recently, UPCEA partnered with the American Council on Education (ACE) to offer the Summit for Online Leadership and Strategy. The summit convenes key campus leaders and online learning practitioners to help define and develop institutional strategy for online learning. Through the years, other program models have been attempted; some have lasted, others not. For several years UPCEA offered a one-week intensive leadership program in the summer. In addition to program offerings, books, newsletters, online resources, and, most recently, social media have all been used to further the profession. These efforts have become ever more complex as the continuing higher education field itself has diversified.

Developing a Shared Vision

Bierema (2011) notes that the diversity of the field also presents challenges for developing a shared vision for the field. Yet, despite the acknowledged difficulties, she calls for dedication to continued professionalization as a way to develop a shared discourse and language about our practice, teaching, and research; delineate standards of practice; improve practice and create a process to ensure high quality; and rally, preserve, and bolster the status of the field of adult education.

One example of this diversity of the field, even within university continuing education, is represented by the analysis done by Cram and Morrison around social justice. They observe that there is a vigorous debate among university continuing educators in the literature between those who wish to respond to market demands and those who advocate a return to the social justice roots of the profession. As an alternative, they propose to think of social justice as a dialogic process rather than a product. Such an approach, they argue, will enable university continuing education to "remain at the cutting edge of educational innovation and service to society" (Cram and Morrison 2005, 45).

While these ongoing debates within university continuing education are certainly interesting, especially for students of history or philosophy, and sometimes make for engaging spectator sport, more interesting and impactful are the collaborations between university continuing education and external partners.

On the one hand, the university CE community has partnered with more traditional segments of higher education to the benefit of adult students. In 2000, a major institutional collaboration took place between UPCEA (UCEA at the time) and the Council of Graduate Schools to publish the book *Postbaccalaureate Futures: New Markets, Resources, Credentials.* Kay Kohl, executive director of UCEA at the time, and Jules LaPidus, president of CGS, were coeditors, and the book was published by the American Council on Education. Even at the time, this landmark publication was recognized as a significant development in the history of higher education. In the context of this essay, it is emblematic of the professionalization and importance of the continuing education enterprise. It also represents a key collaboration that acknowledges how much the adult student market has become mainstream within higher education and the value that CE expertise brings to the fore.

On the other hand, CE professionals have also increasingly turned to external resources for market intelligence and market research, looking to base programmatic decisions on data and market demand rather than whim or fancy. University continuing and professional education practitioners have been able to use sophisticated tools and services to assist with decision making and planning. Several large education research companies have been used by university continuing and professional education, and many smaller companies and individual consultants also provide university CPE with market intelligence and custom research studies.

Founded twenty years ago, Eduventures, based in Boston, conducts data analysis, research, and advising for higher education. They specifically serve university CPE through their Online and Continuing Education Knowledge Community. They help identify programs to invest in and grow, areas to avoid, and how to align programs with employer interests.

Another leader in this space is the Education Advisory Board, based in Washington, DC. Starting in 1983 with a single membership program for hospital CEOs, the EAB now provides services in fourteen areas serving health care and higher education. For university CPE, they provide a Continuing and Online Education Forum. Like Eduventures, EAB follows a membership model and conducts original research, benchmarking, and member inquiries.

Hanover Research conducts market research, institutional analysis, and grant proposal development. To assist higher education, they address enrollment management, new campus feasibility, tuition management, marketing effectiveness, and brand performance.

There are also research services available through professional associations. UPCEA founded the Center for Research and Consulting in response to members' expressed need for benchmarking and actionable market research. Like other external services, the UPCEA CRC conducts custom research and consulting, national benchmarking studies, and individual consulting projects for UPCEA CRC members.

Reflection and Action

There are many other indicators of the growing professionalization of the field of adult and continuing education, including significant publications from the field itself.

The many editions of the *Handbook of Adult and Continuing Education* stand as "a revealing manifestation of and contributor to a long-running professionalization movement in the field of adult and continuing education" (Wilson and Hayes 2000, 6). However, Wilson and Hayes readily acknowledge the limitations of their own efforts as editors of the *Handbook*, including the fact that their edition was written by academics and not practitioners. They note that academics miss the messiness of practice, including the political, subjective, historical, and contextual perspectives and expertise the practitioners bring to the field (ibid., 669). Life in the trenches and on the front lines is very different than the view from the ivory tower.

The leading and more thoughtful practitioners in adult and continuing education have not been idly standing by while traditional academics analyze their work and issue pronouncements for improvement. More than thirty years ago, Schon discussed the crisis in the professions made present by the inclination to conduct society's business through trained professionals (Schon 1983). The history of the development of the field of adult and continuing education underscores how continuing education has aspired to that same status. Schon's "reflection in action" model has raised the level of discourse among CE professionals as practitioners. Today continuing education's professionals not only battle on the front lines; they also take time to examine the view from the ivory tower, listen to other expert voices, reflect on their own practice, and find ways to improve praxis.

These same thoughtful academic practitioners have shared their insights, conducted and reported on empirical research, and suggested strategies for moving the field forward, largely through two professional journals, *Continuing Higher Education Review* and the *Journal of Continuing Higher Education*, each aligned with a professional association for continuing higher education. The history of these journals has been reported elsewhere. Suffice it to say that these two journals have sustained publication over a long period of time and have attracted a large following. The tenure of these two major journals and the growing sophistication of each is further evidence of the growing professionalization of adult and continuing education, nearing par with developments in other professions that Schon discussed.

There have been other efforts, including the groundbreaking online refereed journal, *New Horizons in Adult Education*, published out of Syracuse University beginning in 1987, moved to Nova Southeastern University in 1992, and picked up by John Wiley and Sons and renamed *New Horizons in Adult Education and Human Resource Development*. Moreover, a study conducted by Syracuse University students in 2003 produced a list of more than forty adult educational journals and organizations (Shablak, Charters, Newvine, Johnson, and Sims 2003).

A Proud Tradition of Opening Doors

There are also key milestones in the history of adult and continuing education that are worth keeping in mind as they precede, align with, or provoke the professionalization of continuing higher education. They are mentioned here as guideposts, not as an exhaustive history. In the United States, in 1862, the Morrill Act created land-grant universities by providing land for the university in exchange for a commitment to extend the knowledge base of the university (Merriam and Cunningham 1989, 31).

Malcolm Knowles, in his succinct and approachable *History of Adult and Continuing Education*, points to Cambridge University in 1873 as the first university-based adult education. Here the term used to describe this initiative was *extramural studies* to highlight the distinction between this effort and campus-based degree programs for traditional students. As this development was transported to the United States, the term changed to *extension*, as in university extension.

By 1914 the university extension mission was furthered by the passage of the Smith-Lever Act and the development of the Cooperative Extension System, focused initially on agricultural matters. Growth was swift, and by many accounts the impact was significant. Of interest to UPCEA was the formation of the National University Extension Association in March 1915. Not long after these developments, the field itself began to experience the push for greater professionalization.

> The beginnings of a movement toward professionalization of the field can be traced to the 1930s, with the greatest growth developing at the end of World War II as part of an overall stabilization of U.S. culture. In the second half of the twentieth century, a focus developed on defining a specialized knowledge base and areas of expertise for the field, on credentialing, on research and the production of theory, and on creating a recognizable and formalized "discipline." (Knox and Fleming 2010, 125)

The timing of this movement toward professionalization coincided with the growth of the professional association. However, since its inception, the professionalization of the field of adult and continuing education has not been universally accepted. In fact, several authors note that there is a dialectical tension created by the professionalization of the field. As Bierema noted, "professionalization helps move the field from a marginal status to one of social influence. On the other hand, the field's absorption into professionalization may create a narrowly conceived field of practice that excludes and marginalizes diverse voices and approaches to adult education" (Bierema 2010, 137) In other words, the main issues surrounding the professionalization debate are whether professionalization truly improves practice or whether it constricts who can practice and how we define "good" practice (Merriam and Brockett 2007).

A Wide Vocabulary for Continuing Education

The term *continuing education* probably derived from the Center for Continuation Study, the first residential facility for adults, established in 1936 at the University of Minnesota (Knowles 1994). Knowles notes that the term spread rapidly after the Kellogg Foundation provided many grants around the country for the construction of continuing education centers, beginning with Michigan State in 1951.

Coterminous with the growth of university adult and continuing education, there were significant developments of adult education in other contexts. Business and industry began actively engaging in continuing education for its workers in the 1920s, and after falling off during the Depression, it picked up in earnest during and after World War II. Part of this growth and development included greater differentiation and sophistication of the employee education enterprise, including closer cooperation with formal higher education. Government agencies, health and welfare agencies, labor unions, libraries, religious organizations, museums, and public schools developed programs, outreach, and expertise that supported the growth of formal adult education (Knowles 1994). Even foundations played a role, most notably when, in 1926, the Carnegie Corporation facilitated the establishment of the American Association for Adult Education (Merriam and Cunningham 1989).

The 1920s also saw the creation of the Department of Adult Education in the National Education Association. These developments and others have contributed to the growth of the field in sheer numbers but also in the sophistication and diversity of offerings and have led to continued professionalization of those engaged with adult and continuing education. These changes have fueled the controversy over whether the field should strive toward greater professionalization and whether the professional associations should develop and administer certification programs (Merriam and Cunningham 1989).

As the field has progressed, diversified, and become more complex, the nature of the work has changed with it. Adult education has continued to be a work-related phenomenon. Much of adult education in the 1920s and 1930s was focused around liberal adult education and self-help, rather than training. By 1969, however, approximately 50 percent of adult education programming was work related, and by 1984 that had grown to 80 percent (Merriam and Cunningham 1989). The dominance of work-related curricula has continued with some minor counterinsurgency efforts, represented by the Osher Lifelong Learning Institutes established at various colleges and universities around the country, funded initially by the Bernard Osher Foundation. Dedicated to the liberal education of older adults, the OLLIs, as they are affectionately called, have developed a strong, loyal, and growing audience and stand as a reminder of the enriching, lifelong impact of continuing education.

University-based work-related continuing education has been amplified and supported by private sector investment, alone and in cooperation with university efforts. Training, one manifestation of adult and continuing education, is viewed as critically important in a competitive world economy. More and more professions have established mandatory continuing professional education as a requirement for maintaining licensure and certification. Less formally, the need to retrain the labor force is a constant refrain in popular and professional literature. Historically, adult education has responded to that need (Merriam and Cunningham 1989). The relevance of continuing higher education and the dominance of work-related activity persists today, as most recently exemplified in President Obama's workforce initiative Skills for America's Future.

Coming Full Circle to Look Ahead

In short, we have come full circle, moving from margin to mainstream, and the requirements for professionalization and accountability have never been greater. Perhaps this is a scenario where the maxim is true: be careful what you wish for. Have we become the victims of our own success and, as a result, now have made our work that much harder?

And what of the future, now that we have achieved a seat at the table, an air of respectability, as our primary audience, adult students, have now become the majority age segment across higher education? What does the future look like? I think the future is bright and our prospects are good, provided we continue to carry on in the best of the tradition of adult and continuing education. We must set the standard and lead by example by investing in our staff to ensure they master both continuing education's core competencies and value continuing education's proud traditions of open access and social justice. At the very least, it seems that we are well served to continue our own professional development, our efforts to advance the work of the field, and our contributions to the professionalism of our work.

To the membership gathered for his presidential address, former UPCEA president Roger Whitaker outlined his program initiatives and asked, "What shall we cause?"—as individuals in our institutions and together as an association. A decade later, in the context of our centennial celebration, it is fitting to ask about our future: "What shall we cause indeed?"

References

Bierema, L. L. 2010. "Professional Identity." In C. E. Kasworm, A. D. Rose, and J. M. Ross-Gordon, eds., *Handbook of Adult and Continuing Education* (pp. 135–146). Thousand Oaks, CA: Sage.

Bierema, L. L. 2011. "Reflections on the Profession and Professionalization of Adult Education." *PAACE Journal of Lifelong Learning* 20, 21–36.

Cram, B., and D. Morrison. 2005. "University Continuing Education Units: Agents for Social Change?" *Canadian Journal of University Continuing Education* 31(1): 29–50.

Imel, S. 1991. *Ethical Practice in Adult Education.* ERIC Digests. Retrieved from http://eric.ed.gov/?q=susan+imel+ethical&ft=on&id=ED338897.

Knowles, M. S. 1994. *A History of the Adult Education Movement in the United States.* Malabar, FL: Krieger.

Knox, A. B., and J. E. Fleming. 2010. "Professionalization of the field of adult and continuing education." In C. E. Kasworm, A. D. Rose, and J. M. Ross-Gordon, eds., *Handbook of Adult and Continuing Education* (pp. 125–134). Thousand Oaks, CA: Sage.

Kohl, K. J., & LaPidus, J. 2000. *Postbaccalaureate Futures: New Markets, Resources, Credentials.* Phoenix, AZ: Oryx Press.

Merriam, S. B., and R. G. Brockett. 2007. *The Profession and Practice of Adult Education: An Introduction.* San Francisco: Jossey-Bass.

Merriam, S. B., and P. M. Cunningham. 1989. *Handbook of Adult and Continuing Education.* San Francisco: Jossey-Bass.

Miles, R. E., Jr. 1978. "The Origin and Meaning of Miles's Law." *Public Administration Review* 38(5): 399–403.

Schon, D. 1983. *The Reflective Practitioner: How Professionals Think in Action.* New York: Basic Books.

Selingo, J. J. 2013. *College (Un)Bound.* New York: Houghton Mifflin Harcourt.

Shablak, S., A. N. Charters, K. Newvine, M. Johnson, and A. Sims. 2003. List of Adult Educational Journals and Organizations. Retrieved from http://library.syr.edu/digital/guides/a/AlexanderNCharters/ms_docs/charters50.pdf.

Wilson, A. L., and E. R. Hayes. 2000. *Handbook of Adult and Continuing Education.* San Francisco: Jossey-Bass.

Innovation for a Future of Lifelong Learning

Safeguarding the Next Generation

■■

Ann M. Brewer

Lifelong learning (LLL) is a social good whose public value needs to be developed further for the future benefit of nations, states, cities, and institutions. To that end, LLL matters to each successive generation of individual learners regardless of educational attainment, employment experience, and professional affiliations.

If lifelong learners (and that is all of us) were marketable commodities, then each successive generation would have to demonstrate considerable advantage in terms of their employability and the value of their contribution to society over the preceding cohort to warrant further investment in their learning. As the innovation of continuous learning has grown, LLL has been converted to a commodity and been increasingly subjected to the vagaries of the marketplace. Consequently, LLL institutions not only compete with each other for learners and revenue but also with all places where learning occurs (e.g., universities, museums, art galleries, bookshop events) as well as learning innovations (e.g., all forms of social media). This has led to many LLL institutions (independent and those affiliated with universities) losing patronage, revenue, and eventually closing down.

However, the sustainability of LLL is less about institutional brand (e.g., the well-regarded research-intensive universities) as it has been in the past and much more about ease of access, flexibility, process and

Ann M. Brewer is Dean of Professional and Continuing Education and Chief Executive Officer, Centre for Continuing Education and Sydney Learning, University of Sydney, Australia.

price of learning so that emerging generations of learners can manage their life's transitions to address their learning needs. Most adults are motivated toward learning when they are intrinsically interested in the subject rather than when it is imposed upon them (Knowles 1984). This is even more so today given the new social media at everyone's fingertips. Learners cocreate and produce their own knowledge using, for example, blogs, YouTube, and other collaborative online tools, creating a participative culture which enhances knowledge and information input as well as creating opportunities for its synthesis. All of these, together with enhanced creativity outputs, go hand in hand and potentially move us toward a "we" economy (Schor 1998).

The aim of this paper is to examine:

- potential challenges for LLL and their implications,

- how to strengthen and widen "engagement" beyond institutions,

- potential "intellectual entrepreneurship" of LLL, and

- the case for and conditions necessary to safeguard LLL through social equality, sustainability, and ethical leadership.

Challenges to LLL

Challenge of Higher Education Structure and Processes

Lifelong learning is challenged first by the vicissitudes of higher education, training, new technology, and the dynamics of the labor market. Globally, the revenue model for higher education has shifted. It can no longer meet the demand for continued learning nor provide access for an expanding diversity of learners across the generations. Governments and sponsors demand quality and yet this is immeasurable. Learning innovation requires continuous investment in information and communications technology (ICT) to provide flexible learning and open up new pathways to the diversity of learners that are upon us. All this contributes to a greater complexity to traverse for LLL providers.

Within universities, working collaboratively with faculties is a challenge often due to a lack of shared and focused points of view about learning, who for, and how to do so. While faculties share a physical and geographical location and an overarching commitment to learning, they are bound by cultural differences arising from diverse disciplines, often preventing greater innovation and unbounded learning between them. At best this impedes any potential interdisciplinary and coordinated curriculum—so often what lifelong learners crave.

Educators charged specifically with leading lifelong, continuing, and professional studies in universities often operate in a haze of poorly articulated expectations as well as pressured budgets and vexed accountabilities, contributing to the variety of conflicting and frequently paradoxical demands, reacting rather than being an equal voice within their own university.

Challenge of Labor Market Dynamics

In terms of labor market supply and demand, nations are concerned about innovation, viewed in light of their investment in human capital, research and development, education, and training as well as policies to forecast and manage a "brain migration"—the loss of citizens to other nations without their skills being replaced, exposing some nations more than others to economic risks. Knowledge loss includes:

- underutilization of accumulated knowledge and skills of experienced early to midcareer residents;

- underemployment of accrued knowledge and skills of older workers, who exit or are forced out of employment (brain atrophy);

- not keeping-pace with midcareer renewal (that is, the potential upgrading of midcareer workers, who may never fulfill their later career potential);

- lack of skill development keeping pace with technological innovation and know-how; and

- under-fueling aspirations of youth, especially those without wide access to further or higher education. Aspirations can be distinguished from expectations, reflecting differences between what the young hope to achieve and what they expect to achieve.

Research in the United States a decade ago, cited by Florida (2005, 109), maintains that "brain circulation" is a more accurate description of the worldwide movement of skilled professionals. Florida questions the extent to which brain circulation works in a nation's favor particularly when the inflow of creative minds appears to be decreasing together with declining university enrollments in science and technology and when shortfalls are not being made up from a nation's internal population. Increasingly limited research funding is invested mainly in medical and engineering and cognate disciplines, with declining funding for both the basic sciences, on which medical and engineering disciplines rely, and the humanities and social sciences, which assist in the translation of all disciplinary research into practice. These challenges make the case for having LLL institutes and divisions deeply embedded in research universities in ways that can assist the pipeline effect of research, providing they can assist in the incubation and application of knowledge as well as translate it into skill development.

This makes the case for the importance of safeguarding the next generation of lifelong learners to defend, uphold, preserve, protect, and sustain them for not only their future survival and well-being but also for that of their nation's talent pool. This is not a short-fix budgetary measure by governments, sponsors, and universities; rather it is a long-term investment strategy. Safeguarding each generation of lifelong learners is not for the fainthearted due to its long lead time for return on investment: ten to fifteen years and an additional ten to twenty years to witness the outcomes beyond this.

Challenge of Twenty-First-Century Learning

The rise of a "participative culture" (Tapscott and Williams 2008) has led to a sense of entitlement, fueling a demand for learning and skill development to be addressed. Educational leaders and current university presidents and deans feel increasingly accountable for this and have long navigated the competing values of government, boards, employers, and professional associations attempting to address the different voices and demands. This is tricky given the multiplicity of worldviews and opinions (Putnam 2007), especially when the purpose and functions of LLL are not always clear to those working within or being served by them.

Notwithstanding this, the problem is exacerbated by the uniformity of LLL institutes, which are roughly comparable to each other within their own countries and states, given the types of programs taught, range of disciplines offered, learning contact hours, qualifications and outcomes, and even fees. Many LLL institutes' missions focus on incremental improvements rather than how to realize a longer-term vision of the sustainability of a generation of lifelong learners of various age/experience cohorts and their changing needs.

Challenges of Creating a Learning Vision

Lifelong learning is challenged by a highly technical and rapidly changing environment that requires teachers, curriculum, and andragogies to be adaptive and proficient. Emerging technology and government policies monopolize attention, often at the expense of other important aspects of learning and student engagement. A vision for learning is required and contains several components, commencing with the learners themselves.

Standing with learners and working from the inside out is the most important and central aspect of LLL, that is, understanding and acting on the facilitators and impediments to learning. Unempathic interventions have an adverse effect on a learner's capacity to engage and result in untimely or an intense release of unfamiliar feelings; an overly intellectual or remote stance of learning distances facilitators from learners, leaving them disempowered, hassled, and interrupted in determining their own learning. And there may be a lag time to realize this disappointment.

Safeguarding LLL is about aiming to create a sustainable LLL generation long into its lifespan by investigating how discipline knowledge can be used to engage learners. Many disciplines are seen as irrelevant today, sometimes erroneously, and the challenge for LLL leaders is to engage researchers, business, teachers, and others in identifying how conventional knowledge can be applied to current issues and debate, as well as popularizing research to inform the general public (Howell 2010, 273). Further it requires publishing research outside of the usual channels. Low and Merry (2010, 203) canvas different forms of engagement such as "sharing and support; teaching and public education; social critique; collaboration; advocacy and activism."

Envisioning sustainability also entails changing incentives for staff promotion and tenure to include extension and community engagement activities; using alumni; and making significant changes in the creation, discovery, and organization of knowledge, as well as curricular and programmatic shifts facilitated by better understanding diverse learning approaches, patterns, and multiple learning practices. However what is blocking this is a mismatch of assessment, incentives, and rewards for staff and students, both seeking to balance workload with personal demands.

Assisting in building collaborations with diverse staff and students is critical. More and more students are studying double degrees, for example, combining science with liberal arts, music with medicine, and law with business. However, many staff are not incentivized to cross their own disciplinary boundaries to work together in a way that would solve problems for the learning demands of individuals, groups, and organizations looking for solutions to complex problems. There needs to be a greater incentive for universities to encourage faculty members, administrators, and students to focus on developing collaborative relationships with each other and with their communities.

A learning vision requires an andragogical strategy that underpins it so as to

- transfer good knowledge and experience including a hands-on approach, reflection and critical thinking, understanding teamwork, and an ability to work with others;

- pose relevant questions about work and influence others to make improvements, rather than resort to the micromanagement of people (Hamel 2009);

- know the strengths and weaknesses of staff and how to manage and develop them to best effect using democratic engagement (Black, Groombridge, and Jones 2011);

- celebrate success and ensure something is learned from failures;

- apply theoretical learning;

- understand work details, while being aware of external influencing factors, including those outside the institution's direct control (Zaccaro and Klimoski 2002; Mintzberg 2009);

- restore degraded policies, procedures, and systems where knowledge can be incomplete, so that learning facilitators understand student histories and the wider context in order to prioritize learning interventions (Maris and Béchet 2010); and

- reflect on learning and teaching and foster development of critical thinking skills.

An Integrative Framework for the Future

A willingness to encourage learning, improvement, and receptiveness to discovering alternative solutions is critical for LLL as the needs of a generation of learners and the external demands change. A dialogue of constructive criticism and informed challenge within a participative community of learning will encourage understanding and improvement (Tourish 2007). To explore the case further, three concepts: social equality, sustainability, and ethical leadership will provide an integrative analytical framework for LLL.

Social Equality

According to the Platonic idea, educators oversee learning and develop responsibilities and rights through participating in ethical learning communities with their students. There are implications for LLL leaders, given a frequent imbalance between program and curriculum versus the tools of learning. If learners cannot access the tools of learning, they are disempowered, especially for self-reflection and assimilation of learning. Stakeholders such as employers, professional associations, and governments also see learning as standardized, compartmentalized, and vertical, bringing with it an inherent hierarchical form that also undermines the power resources of learners and denies them access to the tools of learning beyond the ones they are already using. One way to consider this conundrum is through the concept of curriculum itself, which comes from the Latin word *currere*, meaning "to run," suggesting action and innovation by those who participate in it rather than a given package that learners passively accept; a demotivating and frequently foreign experience for the upcoming generations of learners today (Grumet and Pinar 1976; Pinar et al. 1995).

Sustainability and Voice

Lifelong learning requires integrity in every aspect, including its delivery of learning in the widest sense and is more pronounced and challenging the larger the catchment of learners. The sustainability test ensures the interests of individual learners and groups are protected and conserved. The sustainability test is threefold:

- being with and for students is essential. Acting for rather than with students, the less the leaders can safeguard their own interests and outcomes;

- requiring symmetric participation, properly monitored or, to use Plato's term, guarded; and

- ethically attuned and responsive to the broader humanistic and moral dimensions of LLL practice which could be codified by principles and values.

Sustainability adds to the complexity of leading LLL, balancing fairly the needs and interests of students with special needs groups and others who seek to represent them. The quest for safeguarding is at the heart of LLL today.

Ethical LLL Leadership

Safeguarding the future of LLL requires a standard-bearer, that is:

- a conspicuous frontrunner within the institution and others who stand among learners, not as curriculum experts but rather as coaches or mentors, accessing the tools of learning with them;

- a champion, an originator, an exemplar, and at other times an advocate; and/or

- a curator who demonstrates forbearance, not only caring *for* but also caring *with*, and relishing a relationship involving

mutual exchange, including preserving something for the
next generation.

Ethical bearer-ship goes hand in hand with leading and learning so as
to maximize learners' potential (Maslow 1954). Learning is instrumental
in raising moral consciousness and translating creative ideas into innovation through demonstrating that a humane community is possible only
where learners have equal access to and bear together the responsibilities
and rights that establish it. If some enjoy privileged access over others,
this cannot be sustained as some will be safeguarded and others not. This
is also accomplished by acknowledging that all members of a LLL community are responsible for this not just the appointed leaders.

The Future

LLL Status

Lifelong learning is a privileged learning domain (not just physical
space) from which evolves a set of principles about learning, standards,
and values on which its future can continue to flourish and help address a
nation's needs. LLL has many roles, responsibilities, and functions, most
of which arose with the origin of Western adult education over a century
ago; others are more recent.

LLL institutions and processes stand as both learning banks *of* and *for*
society and are at the interface between our cultural past, the present
as well as the future, with most acting as an unconscious agent across all
these domains. For continuous innovation to occur, LLL institutes will
need to become the agents of learning by way of experimentation and
invention, harnessing and applying creativity as well as learning space
through social interaction emulating the flexibility and diversity of social
media.

Action is central to LLL, for example, skill exchanges through mentoring—conventional (expert to novice), reciprocal (peer to peer), and
reverse (young to wise)—as well as coaching. Matching learner to process
and partnering with appropriate facilitators is key as is a communications
network among the learners themselves. Illich summed this up with his
notion of conviviality, stating that it involves "autonomous and creative
intercourse among persons, and the intercourse of persons with their
environment" (1973, 24).

LLL Learning Spaces

Information and social media have affected the cultural uniqueness of
LLL as well as learners' access to it in terms of affordability and capability

to use it. This has led to a skewed perception and impeded learning for some as well as altering the power balance over knowledge and information. As previously stated people now not only receive information from a wide variety of sources but also instigate and participate in the creation of the information flow and its analysis. They are no longer reliant on fixed places or methods of learning. Increasingly, people are becoming more engaged in developing information and communicating through YouTube, text, databases, webinars, live streaming, and Skype. Information conveys people centripetally toward different parts of the world and different cultures. The effect of these interactive communication devices converts people into ready users and creators of information and knowledge, creating new learning spaces with their own personal access to the tools, depleting the need for institutional learning if it adds little more than accreditation.

Safeguarding LLL

Safeguarding creates and maintains the conditions under which LLL will survive and fulfil social, economic, and other requirements expected of each successive generation. For this to occur, creativity in every sense of this concept has to transpire. Creativity is an ephemeral, challenging state because to reap the value it has to be about translating and implementing the by-products of creativity. LLL institutions are in a good position to achieve this, to integrate learning creativity, behavior, and application (based on Bourdieu 1990).

Safeguarding LLL has to lead to:

1. Establishing innovation as a skill by

   - creating a well-defined set of innovation competencies and embedding them into a competency model that includes ethics and leadership;

   - establishing contexts for creative learning;

   - employing peer mentors and coaches who work with learners to guide their innovation efforts and facilitate their success; and

   - requiring innovation as a learning outcome and attribute success at source.

2. Incubating innovation by

   - conducting idea generation workshops in partnership with external enterprises;

- deploying innovation methods within planning and strategy initiatives; and

- querying established learning outcomes.

3. Leading innovation by

- developing an idea management and tracking capability;

- conducting "clearinghouse" workshops to exploit innovation;

- employing proven innovators; and

- linking innovation to other key processes including financial, commercial, and technical.

4. Creating opportunities for innovation learning by

- hiring internal innovation "subversives" who work around the system to champion new ideas and drive them through to execution;

- sending learners to new cultural contexts to explore and experience different situations: business, education, research, government;

- being open to ideas from outside sources to make nonobvious connections to internal projects;

- experimenting with new concepts; and

- collaborating with like-minded enterprises in diverse industries to source new ideas and trends.

5. Devising innovation as portfolio learning by learners developing a portfolio to demonstrate what they've learned based on evidence such as:

- achievement of performance milestones,

- learning gaps and plans,

- objectives and resources used to meet them, and

- other data related to the field of practice (based on Rees 2011)

There are many uses for learning portfolios, including self-reflection, self-assessment, and critique. Here the learner, novice, professional, or those transitioning to new careers can assess their progress over time, look at and monitor the achievement of objectives, and track other data and learning outcomes. They may be used in an educational manner, providing material for conversations with peers and mentors, allowing for discussion about learning, educational plans, or for monitoring purposes such as formative assessment, quality assurance, or recertification.

Never has there been a time of greater opportunity and challenge than now for LLL. Whatever the reason, the motivated engagement of learners is at the heart of LLL's advancement and a nation's competitiveness globally. North America, the United Kingdom, and Australasia have experienced enormous advantage and diversity of continuing education in the offerings of programs, services, and delivery. LLL is no longer the simple process of finding a course, enrolling, and completing it. Information and communication technological change has altered the landscape forever. Information is now derived from different and unfathomable sources, less filtered and becoming more disembodied from its source. Learners are no longer passive; they participate in the creation of the information flow and its analysis, no longer reliant on places of learning to gain new knowledge and skills. Innovation emerges when hierarchal learning barriers are ignored or relinquished. Only then can risks be taken and important decisions gain acceptance. This requires strong leadership, enabling an innovation culture, which means changing the DNA of LLL.

The structure of LLL, the cultural heritage of which was fundamentally premised on volunteerism, has had to become unashamedly commercialized. Amid this, the challenge is to address LLL's aspirations while not abandoning its historical and cultural roots. The founding generation of LLL had a sense of social justice, democratic participation, and open access, all as relevant for the current and future generations to keep faith with this heritage. What the founding generation built and what the current and future generations are developing together not only meet important social needs but also create economic value for individuals as well as for institutions in which people work or volunteer and the community at large. Everyone benefits. Thus there is great scope for further research in all elements to realize a significant return on investing further into the next generation of lifelong learners.

References

Black, S., J. J. Groombridge, and C. G. Jones. 2011. "Leadership and Conservation Effectiveness: Finding a Better Way to Lead." *Conservation Letters* 4: 329–39.

Bourdieu, P. 1990. *The Logic of Practice.* Cambridge, England: Polity Press.

Florida, R. 2005. *The Flight of the Creative Class: The New Global Competition for Talent.* New York: HarperCollins.

Grumet, M., and W. Pinar. 1976. *Toward a Poor Curriculum*. Dubuque, IA: Kendall/Hunt.

Hamel, G. 2009. "Moonshots for Management." *Harvard Business Review* 87: 91–98.

Howell, S. 2010. "Norwegian Academic Anthropologists in Public Spaces." *Current Anthropology* 51(Suppl.): S269–S277.

Illich, I. 1973. *Tools for Conviviality*. New York: Harper and Row.

Knowles, M. S. 1984. *Andragogy in Action*. San Francisco: Jossey-Bass.

Low, S. M., and S. E. Merry. 2010. "Engaged Anthropology: Diversity and Dilemmas." *American Anthropologist* 51(suppl. 2): S203–S226.

Maslow, A. 1954. *Motivation and Personality*. New York: Harper and Row.

Maris, V., and A. Béchet. 2010. "From Adaptive Management to Adjustive Management: A Pragmatic Account of Biodiversity Values." *Conservation Biology* 24: 966–73.

Mintzberg, H. 2009. *Managing*. San Francisco: Berrett-Koehler.

Pinar, W. F., W. M. Reynolds, P. Slattery, and P. M. Taubman. 1995. *Understanding Curriculum: An Introduction to the Study of Historical and Contemporary Curriculum Discourse*. New York: Peter Lang.

Putnam, R. D. 2007. "E Pluribus Unum: Diversity and Community in the Twenty-First Century." The 2006 Johan Skytte Prize Lecture. *Scandinavian Political Studies* 30(2): 137–74.

Rees, T. 2011. "Creativity Needs Diversity." In *Cultures of Creativity: The Challenge of Scientific Innovation in Transnational Perspective*, Proceedings of the Third Forum on the Internationalization of Sciences and Humanities, Nov. 19–20, pp. 60–63. London: Humboldt Foundation.

Schor, J. 1998. *The Overspent American: The Unexpected Decline of Leisure*. New York: Basic Books.

Tapscott, D., and A. D. Williams. 2008. *Wikinomics: How Mass Collaboration Changes Everything*. London: Atlantic Books.

Tourish, D. 2007. "Communication, Discourse and Leadership." *Human Relations* 60: 1727–40.

Zaccaro, S. J., and R. J. Klimoski. 2002. *The Nature of Organizational Leadership: Understanding Performance Imperatives Confronting Today's Leaders*. New York: John Wiley and Sons.

Everything Old Should Be New Again

∎

Mary L. Walshok

Introduction

I chose the title for this essay after considerable thought. My concern
was where the field of continuing education/lifelong learning began and
where it is today at this, the centennial anniversary of the University Professional and Continuing Education Association. Our roots are in a set of
traditions which I frankly fear have been abandoned in recent years because of the extraordinary financial imperatives and market shifts affecting the world of continuing education. In abandoning these traditions
we are also, I will assert in this essay, in danger of being more a part of
the problems facing American society today than a part of the solution to
those problems.

It is important to remind ourselves that our field of educational practice emerged from a set of social dynamics a hundred years ago that are
not that dissimilar from many of the social dynamics today even though
we live in a world of globalization and advanced technology. Those imperatives included the commitment to providing agricultural, industrial,
business, health, and teaching professionals access to education and
training essential to effective practice lifelong. They included technical
assistance and support to business and enterprises in local communities
in order to contribute to the general economic well-being of communities. Those imperatives grew out of a society that was continuously ab-
sorbing new immigrants and integrating new citizens into the civic life
of their communities. They grew out of a westward migration that led
to the need and the desire to create educational and cultural resources
in developing communities both small and large across America. Those
imperatives were also driven by a fundamental understanding that in a

Mary L. Walshok is Associate Vice Chancellor for Public Programs and Dean of
University Extension, University of California, San Diego.

democratic society built on free enterprise it was essential that all citizens have access to the tools and knowledge they needed to successfully navigate the economy as well as contribute in meaningful ways to civil society. The Wisconsin idea, the early achievements of campuses such as the University of California at Berkeley in dispatching university professors to enhance the skills of high-school English teachers across the state, the ways in which industries as diverse as aeronautics in Oklahoma, mining in Montana, and wine in the Napa Valley of California were enhanced by the connections between practitioners in those industries and the education and research resources of the campuses in their regions cannot be overstated. Continuing education and lifelong learning for many also represented a second chance, an opportunity for adults to return to school for credentialing or to acquire new workplace skills for employment. In this it has also been a force for economic growth and a vibrant civil society. These are the traditions from which we have come. My question in this essay is: Are these the values and purposes we still honor, or have we instead become captive of specific technologies and narrower educational purposes which may have unintentional negative consequences for the society we serve?

What Is the Twenty-First-Century Value of Continuing Education?

At the heart of the question of what is the value and the purpose of continuing education in the twenty-first century is an issue that has concerned me throughout my professional life as a sociologist. That is the extent to which private problems and private good can be balanced with public issues and the public good. The role of higher education in the post–Civil War era, thanks to the Morrill Act of 1862 and the Hatch Act, were animated by a clear sense of public benefits, of economic and social returns to local communities and the nation as a whole. This was realized through research, teaching, and technical assistance enabled by the expansion of land-grant universities across America. This comprehensive view of the value of universities to society is arguably the distinguishing characteristic of American universities. In most other nations, it is unusual to find a higher education establishment that defines its role as deeply and broadly as the architects of America's great public research universities did at the turn of the previous century and throughout most of the twentieth century.

Significant research on the role of universities in regional economies in recent years has underscored the extent to which the public benefits of universities continue to accrue to regional economies in the nation as a whole. A collection of essays recently published by Stanford University Press, edited by Martin Kenney at the University of California, Davis, and

David Mowery at the University of California, Berkeley, reveal from both historical and empirical documentation the critical contributions made by campuses of the University of California to the wine industry in Napa Valley, the semiconductor industry in the Silicon Valley, the medical device industry across Southern California, and the biotech revolution in both Silicon Valley and San Diego as well as the growth of possibly the largest wireless cluster in North America in San Diego.[1] The synergies and complementarities that exist between the curriculum, the research agenda, and the forms of public outreach and lifelong talent development that characterized each of these campuses has been critical to the growth and continued prosperity of unique clusters of economic activity across the state of California.

In my own book, *Knowledge without Boundaries*, published more than twenty years ago, I pointed out many of the critical array of contributions made by various campuses: the University of Wisconsin, Milwaukee, representing the home of the World Affairs Council in that city; the University of California, San Diego, as the home for the important CONNECT organization, which over a thirty-year period has helped incubate more than 1,500 companies across a variety of technology sectors, transforming San Diego's regional economy into one of the most dynamic innovation regions in the Americas; and the role of the University of Tennessee's Public Policy Institute in helping clarify vexing issues faced by the state legislature and informing decision making at the county and state level with data generated by university faculty, shared through forums that educate and network policy makers.[2] These examples were each animated by the values that underlie the land-grant university tradition and the values not only of agricultural extension but of urban extension schools and schools of continuing education across America. All have clearly been centers of adult education through courses, conferences, workshops, part-time degree programs, and certificate programs. However, most throughout the latter part of the twentieth century also provided program content, formats, and connections to communities that address public and social goods as well as individual achievements and credentialing.

However, with the growth of the Internet—and with that the expansion of online learning as a technique, a methodology of delivering valuable education and training to diverse cohorts of young adults and working professionals—the field of continuing education has increasingly been absorbed by issues that connect more directly to private benefits than to the sorts of public and social benefits that have traditionally animated our work. There has always been within our field an interest in what we used to call distance learning—providing education and training in flexible formats, leveraging communication technologies that would assure access to education, credentialing, and lifelong learning to people who could not easily participate because of social or geographic barriers to traditional classroom learning. In the early days of UPCEA, there was a large group of professionals in the field who ran correspondence studies programs, and eventually many of them used television broadcast to remote settings, as ways of delivering education and training. This was one of many foci within our professional association at that time; continuing and professional education associations and publications, while addressing distance learning and the special pedagogical and administrative challenges in education at a distance, were equally engaged in adult continuing and professional education through flexible degree programs, certificate programs, innovative partnerships with industry, learning needs assessments, and customized programming. Additionally, we had a major focus on conferences and institutes through which advanced knowledge and forms of practice were discussed or introduced to key stakeholders in the economy, regionally and often nationally. Ours was a very mixed portfolio of content and delivery mechanisms, and as an association we encouraged and stimulated a broad range of conversations about the uses and value of knowledge in society and the economy and the role of lifelong learning and education as a catalyst and an energizer within our universities for those sorts of services and benefits to the community.

Such discussions have virtually ceased as we move into the twenty-first century, and the association, as well as the field, increasingly has been dominated by the promise and value of new technologies, in particular online learning as a method of delivering content to individual students seeking professional continuing education, degrees, and other forms of credentialing. The focus increasingly is on activities and technologies which can provide enormous personal benefits, but we are paying a price for this frenzied attention to online and distance learning. We have lost touch with the profoundly important social and economic challenges the communities in which our universities reside are facing and with which we as a nation are grappling. We are becoming increasingly irrelevant to the important conversations between the academy and the larger society about the value of knowledge and the diversity of knowledge needs our home universities are being called upon to meet. And in many cases our campuses are complicit in this drift from social and public value to exclusively private benefits, because they too are seeking increased numbers of students and growth in revenues while simultaneously attempting to control costs and achieve efficiencies.

Now that I am a wise old woman in the field I find myself extremely worried that my fellow practitioners are drifting into a primarily market-focused, delivery-focused view of what continuing education and lifelong learning represent. I worry about who on our various campuses will be the keepers of the flame of the continuing value of public service and the importance of intermediary institutions and offices that can connect new knowledge to practitioners and society as a whole. My concern stems from the content of recent national professional meetings as well as the nature of the formal and informal conversations today among deans and practitioners. Increasingly they are focused on techniques and strategies for delivering technology-enabled learning to larger numbers of students rather than meaningful discourse on the community and public service value of what we do.

This growing emphasis on the private benefits of continuing education/lifelong learning is especially manifest in the daily e-mails from associations such as UPCEA, which focus on online education techniques, enrollment strategies, marketing strategies, etc. A stream of webinars, conferences, and reports on online learning dominate the discourse among the associations of continuing higher education today. The content of the national meetings is also more and more about these issues as well. It is clear that there is a large appetite for this kind of information, based on membership numbers and the general response to these various events and programs. My concern, as we look at our one-hundred-year history, is not so much that the innovative and effective ways in which practitioners in our world are adopting and using new technologies to reach important constituencies with education and learning is a bad thing. It is a good thing. My concern is the nearly exclusive focus on these technologies and methodologies and the drift away from serious discussions about the content and competencies practitioners and citizens need in order to adapt to the seismic changes affecting all of our lives as a result of globalization and rapid advances in technologies, all of which are continuously changing the content of work and everyday life.

Is continuing education becoming a field of toolmakers and innovative mechanics, or does it represent a community of ideas, a cadre of knowledge workers who are keeping a pace with substantive changes in the content of work and the trends shaping communities? With emerging technologies that are affecting everything from how we produce goods to how we educate young children, deliver healthcare, and engage in discourse about public issues, it is easy to become technocrats. Our increasing lack of attention to the substantive issues affecting the everyday lives of adult learners across America is what concerns me. We've lost our balance.

Rebalancing the Continuing Education Portfolio

What are the risks of being unbalanced? More than twenty years ago, in *Knowledge without Boundaries*, I made the case that knowledge, not data or raw information, is what reshapes the world and the daily content of all of our lives. When we speak of knowledge, we are referring to more than simply data, facts, and information. Knowledge involves analytical, interpretive, and synthesizing skills. Knowledge takes information from disparate places and organizes it in a manner that honors the context from which it comes and the purposes for which it will be used. Such knowledge can potentially be delivered to people in lecture formats, face-to-face conversations, and roundtable discussions, with online learning tools, and through reading, interactive assessments, testing, and rankings. But all of these are simply methods for delivering and engaging knowledge. They are not about the knowledge per se that can change practice: the areas of knowledge that require integration, the diverse ways in which such knowledge can be validated and effectively integrated into practice. The pressing issue at this moment in time across America is the extent to which companies, social organizations, and political issues can be elucidated and understood through access to this new knowledge and to communities of conversation. Shared values are essential to renewing the prosperity of local communities and to engaging the challenges represented by globalization, worldwide immigration, and environmental hazards. Much is needed to stimulate and empower individuals to be effective members of local school boards, state legislatures, and the United States Congress. The fact that continuing education is disengaged from most of these larger conversations about social change and the role of knowledge, and in particular the role of the university in the development and dissemination of knowledge critical to these challenges, disturbs me as a septuagenarian who has worked in this field for more than forty years.

My motivation four decades ago to leave traditional academic work and to engage in the lifelong learning arena was animated by these sorts of values. However, I find myself without a community of discourse at the end of my career. At the beginning many of my colleagues were activists, engaged intellectuals working in the netherworld of making knowledge accessible and useful to large and diverse publics. Today, rather than focusing on knowledge, we are focusing on courses, credentialing, and certifications for individuals. These are important, but they are not what differentiates us from a growing number of for-profit and not-for-profit entities seeking to serve customers in markets with knowledge needs. In the decades ahead, my hope is that this field of practice will rediscover its unique role in harvesting and integrating knowledge from multiple places and funneling it into important spheres of education and training so that the added value of who we are and what we represent is as educators rather than as toolmakers.

What Needs to Happen for That to Occur?

In order for universities, in particular university-based continuing education and lifelong learning enterprises, to reclaim their legitimate seat at the academic table, there needs to be a renewed focus on three fundamental areas of human activity to which knowledge is increasingly essential:

1. Talent and workforce development

2. Local and regional economic development

3. Civic affairs.

The conversations that need to occur and the initiatives evolving from those conversations cover a wide gamut of substantive arenas, only a few of which I will cite in this essay in order to make the case.

With regard to the substance of the talent development in which we engage, the continuing knowledge needs in our communities run the gamut from K-12 education to learning in retirement. In other contexts I have discussed the importance of more clearly articulating the dimensions of our talent development mission.[3] Clearly, helping develop the pipeline of qualified young adults for college programs and/or apprenticeships and related workforce development programs is on the minds of leaders across America. Expanding the numbers of students attending four-year universities is also important, but even more important is accelerating their time to graduation and assuring that these college grads are ready to put their knowledge to work in practice settings. On both these fronts university continuing education programs have a great deal to contribute because of the outreach capabilities they have and their links to employers and industries from whom practical knowledge requirements can be harvested in a manner that articulates with traditional academic programs, and in helping recent graduates bridge to employment. This is one of the many reasons certificate programs offered through university continuing education and extension programs have become so valuable. Certificate programs for young adults entering the job market, mid-career adults making job transitions, and individuals moving into more complicated positions, as well as supporting mature adults as they transition into retirement and/or volunteer roles, are all critical realities with which we should be engaged.

Across this spectrum the substance of our programs include everything from updating professionals, such as neurosurgeons, bridge builders, and teachers of American history in classrooms, to cross-training professionals, such as history teachers who are now being asked to teach math or electrical engineers who are moving into marketing and management, and retooling professionals because of the ways in which advances in technology have changed the fundamental content of practice, such as laparoscopic surgery or CAD-CAM. All represent education and training for which communities across the United States need some form of further education and certification. These represent the sorts of realms we should be discussing and about which we should be sharing best practices. Also, in a globalizing, technology-based economy there are new and emerging fields of professional practice for which local industries require people not currently certified. One thinks of arenas such as clinical research in the pharmaceutical industry, the explosion of clinical trials management around the world, and the many dimensions of alternative energy, including, in my region, green algae manufacturing practices. And of course there are executive education and leadership programs that require the engagement with assets of the university as well as access to the most up-to-date ideas in the world of professional practice, for example, again in my context, executive programs for scientists and engineers, executive education for museum administrators, focused managing and leading sustainable not-for-profits and arts and cultural organizations in light of changing demographics and increasing fiscal challenges.

On the economic development front, there is clearly a role for our capabilities. However, we cannot deploy them without participating in conversations among ourselves and in our communities about what is needed. Increasingly across America, global competencies as well as scientific and technological literacy are essential to the practice of economic development, to the work of city councils, in county government growth and sustainability, so that individuals can make informed decisions vis-à-vis public policies and strategic investments related to economic development in a twenty-first-century context. In addition, there is significant value in demonstrating to influential groups, professionals, and the lay public many of the valuable social and individual benefits of basic research, for example, a high-level series of lectures on research developments in cancer and the implications of such things as genomics, proteomics, and computational biology for drug discovery, successful therapies, and lives saved drew hundreds. Today, the building blocks of most economies are anchored in research and development, and in particular, innovation and entrepreneurship. As university continuing education and lifelong learning centers on our campuses we have a responsibility to address these issues as part of our portfolio through innovative forms of community engagement and outreach.

Small business development, technology commercialization, and the dynamics of regional business cycles are additionally important substantive issues we can address with education and, in some instances, provide technical assistance. Ninety percent of all new jobs in this country are created by small and high-growth businesses, and ninety percent of those businesses are being driven by either breakthroughs or incremental changes in technology platforms and organizational practices. This means that there is an important role for education in this sector, and one which we can appropriately address. Business and regional economic development professionals should not be the only focus of these sorts of conversations and educational initiatives. However, as the age of suburban living and large shopping malls wanes there are emerging trends in urban planning, inner city redevelopment, design, and community renewal that are knowledge- and data-based. We can provide important information and tools for people grappling with these sorts of issues, whether it is government, not-for-profits, or for-profit organizations. There are also daring and exciting new financing models for building enterprises, assuring the transportation and communication infrastructure a community needs, or launching a health center that serves returning veterans. All of these kinds of initiatives at the community level cry out for access to knowledge and tools to improve practice and maximize opportunity. Why are such issues no longer a part of our central conversations?

The final arena in which we need conversations and programs has to do with civic affairs. More than ever in our democracy there is a need for platforms as well as information that can facilitate civil discourse around major issues shaping regional futures: the shrinking of the middle class, global patterns of immigration, the increasing impacts of environmental change and natural disasters such as floods, hurricanes, and droughts, and the implications of global conflicts such as that between Israel and Palestine for local communities. All of these topics involve significant components of knowledge and expertise and benefit from forums and conversations that help citizens not only understand the facts but explore the implications for their local communities and personal lives. Lecture series focused on World Affairs Councils, public policy, and international affairs can add enormous value to public understanding of complex issues. Structured and even certification programs that enhance competencies of people to run for office or become an effective volunteer, either in their own communities or in rural communities in places such as Africa, represent additional substantive educational needs and opportunities we could and should be addressing.

The Future of Continuing Education

In sum, the need for knowledge lifelong abounds in our communities. We have a history of being linked to those needs and of creating the mechanisms through which many of those needs are served. The creation of innovative education, training, and learning communities is more important today than in our past for many reasons. Nonetheless, as a field, we have become preoccupied with the technology of the moment and less and less connected to these issues, to these communities, and to the important intellectual and substantive issues that should shape curriculum and methodologies for teaching and learning. Have we become servants of private interests rather than the public good? I hope not.

As I reflect on one hundred years of continuing education and lifelong learning, I find myself wanting to say to my colleagues that it is time to sit back and reflect on the priorities we are pursuing at this particular moment in time and ask if they are adequate to the wide range of knowledge needs we could potentially serve. Others may not agree, but from where I sit as a lifelong professional in this field, a professor of sociology, and an individual who continues to do research in communities across America, I perceive enormous knowledge needs that are going unmet by the campuses of which we are a part. A large number of those knowledge needs could appropriately be addressed by schools, colleges, and programs of continuing education and lifelong learning. My hope is that we will reengage with these traditional issues and challenges in a twenty-first-century way. If we do not, we may, like the typewriter, face extinction.

Notes

1. Martin Kenney and David C. Mowery, eds., *Public Universities and Regional Growth: Insights from the University of California* (Stanford, CA: Stanford University Press, 2014).
2. M. L. Walshok, *Knowledge without Boundaries: What America's Research Universities Can Do for the Economy, the Workplace, and the Community* (San Francisco: Jossey-Bass, 1995).
3. Walshok, *Knowledge without Boundaries*; and M. L. Walshok, T. Munroe, and H. Devries, *Closing America's Job Gap* (El Monte, CA: WBusiness Books, 2011).

Liberal and Practical Education in the Twenty-First Century

◨

Robert Wiltenburg

As some will recognize, the title of this essay alludes to one of the founding documents for continuing education in the United States, the Morrill Act of 1862 and its famous general statement of purpose, the aim of the act being "to promote the liberal and practical education of the industrial classes in the several pursuits and professions of life." A broad charter indeed for the future profession of continuing education! And one that, in the more than a century and a half since its articulation, has seen many variations played on both "liberal" and "practical." Recently, some universities have even begun renaming their continuing education units as centers of "liberal and professional" studies—a somewhat more upscale and contemporary version of "liberal and practical."

What the relation of liberal to practical is or should be has never been quite clear. Are they opposites? Certainly many seem to think so, especially today when some parents, students, and politicians consider time spent on liberal subjects (often confused with the humanities) to be wasted, at the expense of practical knowledge that would contribute, so the argument goes, more directly and effectively to workforce development and readiness and to national competitiveness. Or are they complements, and if so, of what kind? One historic view is that they are indeed complementary, based on social class: liberal study for the few, the elite, the governors, the professions; practical study for the everyman and everywoman whose prime concern is to make a decent living for themselves and their family. But the Morrill Act language stubbornly couples the two together, intending both kinds of knowledge for the industrial classes and for all the pursuits and professions one can imagine. In what follows

Robert Wiltenburg is Dean of University College, Washington University in St. Louis, and past president of the UPCEA, 2008–2009.

I will argue that the Morrill language got it right the first time, and that, going forward, the wisdom of coupling these forms of knowledge will be even more important than ever, both to individuals and to society, and finally, that it should be the aim—and obligation—of continuing educators to advocate for the synergies their interaction produces.

As always, when discussing liberal education, one must begin with what it is not. First, it is not a particular set of subjects—despite the origin of the term in the medieval *artes liberalis*, which comprehended grammar, rhetoric, and dialectic plus arithmetic, geometry, astronomy, and music. Nor is it owned by humanities departments—rather, it can draw freely upon virtually all subject areas. Second, it is not a particular list of books or set of experiences. Reading the Great Books or the Harvard Classics or whatever *may* contribute to liberal learning but doesn't necessarily do so. Any liberal instrument may be used in illiberal ways: as the poet John Milton observed, one may even be "a heretic in the truth" if one has not tested and probed and come to one's own authentic understanding of a truth claimed by others. Third, whatever politically minded critics may think, liberal education is not intended to turn people into political liberals—indeed, it sometimes has the opposite effect. And fourth, although it was historically the province of an elite, in a democratic society it aims not for the creation of a particular class but to enable and to elevate a community of full cultural and civic participation for all.

So if liberal learning is not defined by subject, politics, or class, what is it? What can be positively affirmed? Many have tried their hands at this, usually in the form of a list of some kind. One influential recent example is an article by the historian William Cronon, entitled "Only Connect: The Goals of a Liberal Education" (1998). Cronon's list of the qualities of a liberally educated mind include the abilities to listen and hear; to read and understand; to talk with anyone; to write clearly, persuasively, and movingly; to solve a wide variety of problems; to respect rigor as a way of seeking truth; and to practice humility, tolerance, and self-criticism—and above all, taking his motto from the novelist E. M. Forster, to connect disparate areas of experience into the richest whole possible. This is a memorable contemporary restatement of the aims of liberal study, but it doesn't quite replace an older statement, nearly contemporary with the Morrill Act, by the Victorian educator William Cory, of Eton College:

> You go to a great school, not for knowledge so much as
> for arts and habits; for the habit of attention, for the art of
> expression, for the art of assuming at a moment's notice
> a new intellectual posture, for the art of entering quickly
> into another person's thoughts, for the habit of submitting
> to censure and refutation, for the art of indicating assent
> or dissent in graduated terms, for the habit of regarding

> minute points of accuracy, for the habit of working out what
> is possible in a given time, for taste, for discrimination, for
> mental courage and mental soberness. Above all, you go to
> a great school for self-knowledge. (Cory 1861, 7)

Better still, consider the first continuing educator, who was also the first practitioner of liberal learning, Socrates. As depicted in Plato's dialogues, his typical technique, still the best educational practice and the foundation of all liberal learning, was the bait and switch or, more precisely, the bait and add. When young men come to him, in the *Gorgias* for example, hoping to learn the techniques of an irresistible skill in argument, one so strong that they can gain their way in any political dispute or confrontation, he teases them into thinking about justice and a just society—the ends for which all power, and especially the power of persuasive argument, should be exercised.

And we continuing educators very much continue and adapt this tradition: we bait our students with institutional prestige but surprise them with amiability and unpretentiousness; we often bait them with modest prices but then surprise them with the need for a greater intellectual effort than they've made before; we bait them with certificates and degrees but hope to spark lifelong intellectual curiosities and passions; we bait them with the promise of better jobs and incomes but send them away with the skills and sympathies needed by better citizens of a better community.

Continuing educators have always been people of mixed motives—indeed, if we didn't have mixed motives, would we have any at all?—and the challenge is to keep the mix as rich and productive as possible, which means, in most cases, adding liberal elements to our often practically oriented programs. One example: several years ago my unit devised a new certificate in financial services to serve a strong local banking and investment sector. We did the due diligence: assessed the need, hired as program director a recent PhD in economics from our university who worked at the Federal Reserve Bank, surveyed similar programs elsewhere, and consulted with local practitioners. Once we had a draft of the program, we invited—to breakfast before the markets opened!—a distinguished group of industry representatives. They liked what they saw, with one exception: we had forgotten professional ethics! As they pointed out, anyone in the industry soon masters the financial techniques, but what is never fully mastered is the daily ethical struggle to balance your personal interests, your firm's interests, and your client's interests—which may well conflict. The practical elements of this profession had been obvious, and we had provided for them; but we had forgotten the liberal elements that our adult students most needed if they were to live a fully successful life: doing well but also, within their sphere, doing good.

And so it is in all the many pursuits and professions of the twenty-first century. There are no longer any durably square holes for which to produce square pegs. If we are merely practical, we are likely not going to be really practical enough for an economy in which more jobs every day require and reward flexibility and critical thinking. In the knowledge economy and learning society we frequently invoke, both jobs and careers are more often fluid than fixed. Although my own title has not changed, my job as dean is not the same as it was five or ten years ago, and on a given day, my administrative assistant may make a decision regarding, say, an inquiry or a visitor that is more important than any I will make that day. The old distinction between routine and creative work is also outmoded: thanks to word processing, we're all typists now—and all decision makers as well.

Indeed, decision and choice in everything we do is the ground note of life in all developed countries and, increasingly, around the world. Where and how we live, what occupations and ambitions we pursue, what personal style and cultural affinities we embrace, what religious belief we practice, if any, what version of family we create or not: all of these and many other choices are ours to make. And beyond the personal, what kinds of societies embodying what sorts of values and aspirations shall we strive for? These are all practical questions. But to make such choices in the best way we need as many liberal and liberating experiences as possible for the arts and habits and self-knowledge that they provide.

Shakespeare was perhaps the first to fully imagine a world, whether tragic or comic, in which one's choices mattered more than one's circumstances. This was once, and not so long ago, an existential experience and self-conception available only—outside one of his plays—to the occasional king or queen, hero or heroine. But over several centuries the invention and widespread dissemination of ever more powerful technologies—agricultural, political, medical, educational, informational, and many others—has substantially brought that imagined world into being and made it available, at least in principle, to us all. The resulting long-term social and moral revolution in the democratization of choice was news four hundred years ago, is news today, and will be news for many years to come. Its benefits are of course still very unevenly distributed both in the developed world and across the globe, and too many people still live in the iron grip of circumstances that prevent their full flourishing in a life based on choices and choices well made. But the long arc of this development is both unmistakable and irresistible.

We continuing educators are potentially among the most powerful agents of this revolution. Not the only ones of course: the inventors of the Internet have, for example, played a crucial role in recent years! But as the growing edge of higher education we have a special role to play and one of which we should be conscious and proud and deliberate. Not that spreading a four-centuries-old worldwide democratic revolution in morals and manners is in any of our job descriptions—indeed, most provosts and presidents would be shocked at the opportunity costs involved in even entertaining such a thought. But we have both the opportunity and the obligation, I think, to prepare our students for full participation in it just as we wish for their full participation in the job market and in civic life.

One consequence should be our regularly advocating for the most generous understanding of what sort of education continuing education students—now the most numerous of all students—need, an education both liberal and practical that prepares them to make well the many decisions in their own lives and those of their families and of the many communities—local, national, and international—in which we and they share. Our students too should be satisfied with nothing less than the best.

So yes, let's help produce a workforce that can adapt to the many challenges that advancing technologies and changes in the nature of work will bring. And let's help produce the engaged, critically minded citizens who will be needed to control and correct even the best of governments. And finally, let's prepare our students for the dignity and the deep challenge of making, and then living in, a world largely of their own choosing. For that great enterprise, they'll need all the knowledge, both liberal and practical, that they can get!

References

Cory, William. 1861. *Eton Reform II*. London: Longman, Green, Longman, and Roberts.

Cronon, William. 1998. "Only Connect: The Goals of a Liberal Education." *American Scholar* 67(4): 73–80.

PART II

Online Education

The growth in the reach and significance of online learning has not been the only story in professional and continuing education in the past twenty-five years, but many would argue that it has been the most important, and important in several ways. Initially seen as an exciting, if occasionally frustrating, new delivery system that might replace correspondence courses, it soon became clear that the development and refinement of online learning would lead to profound changes in technology, teaching and learning, programming, marketing, recruitment and advising, management, partnership—indeed, in virtually all areas of continuing education.

The eight essays in this section speak to many aspects of this revolution. John F. Ebersole has been closely involved with key innovations at leading institutions and traces how online learning has come to dominate our attention at the same time as the rise of the nontraditional learner as the focus for innovation and driver of change. Rick L. Shearer's account of the movement of online to the mainstream of continuing education focuses particularly on the technical changes that made it all possible. Jay A. Halfond tells the story of how working in partnership with third-party for-profit companies has often been a crucial (and tricky!) stage in enabling university continuing education units to mount online programs. Ray Schroeder and Vicki Cook provide an incisive summary of where we currently stand concerning types and best practices in online education. Karen Sibley discusses the ways in which even private institutions focused on liberal arts education and traditional residential students are now being drawn into online experiments and commitments. Craig Wilson addresses an important new management challenge: establishing and maintaining effective leadership at a distance. Gary W. Matkin engages in some informed, visionary speculation on where both higher education and continuing education are headed in the online age and outlines some of the implications for teachers, learners, and institutions. Jonathan Baldwin reminds us that any remaining skepticism about online learning will be overcome less by describing new technology than by getting excited about what we want to achieve in our teaching and in our students' learning.

Reflections on an Evolution

■■

John F. Ebersole

As leaders of professional, continuing, and online education, we are often consumed by concern for the future. We continually look for opportunities, as well as threats and challenges, that might endanger us or our enterprises. But only by taking time to look back do we get a sense of movement and see the impact of our efforts. That is what I hope to do here. By reflecting on the quarter century that has passed since I came to continuing education and the University Professional and Continuing Education Association, I hope to illustrate how far we have come as a sector of higher education.

In looking at my own path, I certainly see how online learning has come to dominate our attention, in both the credit and noncredit arenas. However, I have also come to see the rise of the post-traditional learner as the focus for innovation and as a driver of change. While I hope there is value in sharing my observations, more important is noting the value the greater academy has come to attach to the long-present expertise of those in continuing and professional education in helping to assure the future of higher education.

The Kennedy Years

Like many in our field, I did something else first. In quick succession, I retired from the Coast Guard and went to work for John F. Kennedy University, America's first institution (established in 1964) focused solely on the needs of the adult learner.

At JFKU, I served initially as an associate dean and faculty member within the School of Management and later as the school's dean. This

John F. Ebersole is President and Chief Executive Officer, Excelsior College, and past president of the UPCEA, 2002–2003.

introduction to higher education was followed by a string of positions in continuing and professional education, as well as international and on-line learning. The common denominator in this, my second career, has always been the adult student, or, as we would later come to refer to them, the post-traditional learner.

An early "aha" moment came with the understanding of the importance time plays in decisions about whether to go back to school and, if so, where. Program delivery models, marketing, and recruitment all must consider this factor if offerings are to attract students. This lesson came early in my continuing education career.

Birth of a For-Profit

Attention to time and convenience have become key factors in an institution's ability to compete in the post-traditional market. This is largely due to one man, John Sperling. During the early 1980s, Sperling used his position as a member of the faculty at San Jose State to launch the Institute for Professional Development (IPD). The University of San Francisco and Saint Mary's of California were IPD's first clients. Under Sperling's direction, these Bay Area schools launched evening degree programs to compete with those of JFKU and Golden Gate University. Higher education would never be the same as a result.

Disputes over program control between Sperling and his client schools' regional accreditor, the Western Association of Schools and Colleges (WASC), would ultimately force IPD out of California. In Arizona, with a different regional accreditor—the Higher Learning Commission (HLC)—he won recognition for his own adult-serving, for-profit institution: the University of Phoenix.

With his HLC accreditation, Sperling returned to California and surrounded San Francisco Bay with satellite, or regional, classroom sites. In keeping with his belief that convenience trumped brand, such facilities were situated near suburban office complexes and mass transit stations. In contrast, the School of Business at the University of California, Berkeley, closed its MBA program in San Francisco during this same period because of faculty objections to commuting into the city in rush hour traffic.

Seeing Phoenix's success with extended sites, JFKU followed suit. By the time I left in 1989, the School of Management had evening programs in Oakland, Walnut Creek, Pittsburgh (CA), San Ramon, and Vallejo. Unlike Phoenix, these were all in borrowed spaces, ranging from hospitals to church basements (not recommended). We even had a site at the California Maritime Academy. All locations were intended to reduce student (not faculty) drive time.

In addition to observing the rise of the University of Phoenix, I had a front row seat in another revolution that was also driven by the adult students' concerns around time—the move to electronic delivery of instruction.

The "Electronic" University

In late 1985, JFKU president Don MacIntyre and one of his neighbors, serial entrepreneur Ron Gordon, met to discuss Gordon's need for an MBA program that could be offered nationwide—via computer. As one of the early officers of Atari, Inc., Gordon had not only gained personal wealth but also the idea of delivering instruction electronically. With a group of investors, he created TeleLearning Systems and its delivery arm, the Electronic University Network (EUN). By the time he met MacIntyre, Gordon had commitments from forty Fortune 500 companies to pay tuition for employees who completed an MBA via EUN. While several colleges and universities, including nearby Stanford, were willing to experiment with individual courses, none were prepared to take on a full degree.

An entrepreneur at heart, MacIntyre agreed to provide the needed MBA, subject to accreditor approval. By now the dean of the School of Management, it fell to me to appear before WASC, the same accrediting body that had caused Sperling to leave California, and make the case for JFKU's entry into the world of online learning. Despite justified skepticism, a pilot program was approved with the expectation that JFKU would file quarterly reports on progress and lessons learned.

Dubbed "Access to Learning," the institution embraced what many, including me, thought was a crazy idea. "Who would want to study in isolation, interacting with a piece of machinery, to complete what looked like an electronic correspondence course?"

As the first ever online MBA went live with marketing and enrollments, a long list of lessons learned was developed for the WASC reports. At the top of the list was the fact that many prospective students didn't have computers nor the modems necessary for connectivity in a pre-Internet world. In response, the university quickly identified a low-cost source for the needed equipment. However, the Korean manufacturer insisted that all shipments had to be made to a single location—the university. Reshipment then fell to the school staff, along with texts and other course materials (at one point the school's offices looked more like a warehouse than office space).

Shortly after the first course packages went out, word came back that employers weren't reimbursing students for the computers and modems. Tuition and fees were their limit. As a result, new enrollments plummeted and withdrawals skyrocketed. In addition, those who remained enrolled found themselves going months between courses as TeleLearning's programmers struggled to create modules, using inflexible templates for lesson construction.

By the summer of 1987, it was clear that neither TeleLearning nor the university had the resources to continue. Shortly thereafter, TeleLearning and the EUN brand were sold. For its part, JFKU attempted to teach our students who had persisted, but took no additional enrollments. President MacIntyre opted to leave JFKU soon after the decision was made to end the Access to Learning program. Having served as provost at the University of San Francisco during its experiment with IPD, he and John Sperling were well known to each other. Thus, there was little surprise that he was asked to be the first chancellor of University of Phoenix's international division. The Access to Learning software, courses, and programming staff went with him to become the nucleus for Phoenix's eventual online presence.

UC Berkeley Extension

I moved to UC Berkeley Extension, one of the nation's oldest and largest providers of continuing education, in 1991. Unlike Kennedy, UC Berkeley Extension offered no degrees, only courses (credit and noncredit) and certificates. In a typical year, it presented hundreds of offerings—in business, various branches of engineering, environmental science, education, and the liberal arts—at multiple locations. Annual enrollments grew to over 60,000 during my years there.

At Berkeley, I had the good fortune to work for, and be mentored by, Associate Dean Gary Matkin, who had been a protégé of Milton Stern, one of continuing education's legendary leaders of the 1970s and '80s. (It is thanks to Gary that I joined UPCEA.) Together with Dean Mary Metz, we continued the effort to move access closer to students, opening sites in San Ramon, Fremont, Redwood City, and Oakland, as well as two large facilities in San Francisco proper.

Initially serving as chair of Continuing Education in Business and Management, I eventually became an assistant dean and director of UC Berkeley Extension's strategic initiatives. I was also tasked with cochairing executive education for the Haas School of Business (Berkeley's chancellor had mandated, much to the chagrin of the Haas faculty, that *all* forms of continuing professional education would be administered by Extension). This provided the opportunity to work closely with traditional faculty and gain insight into factors that impeded innovation, as well as those that aid acceptance. This became the subject of later research.

The two most significant innovations embraced by Extension during my years there were Berkeley Worldwide and UC Online. In the case of the former, Extension leveraged its existing English Language Program

(ELP), one of the nation's largest at the time, to include follow-on credential programs and internships. As a result, the university was able to offer an attractive package of learning to students from around the world—language proficiency, a professional credential, and actual work experience associated with the subject area of the credential (another year spent in the United States, for practical training, came with completion of the Berkeley program as well).

Going Global

Having studied the British credentialing system, and noting the popularity of their diploma in the former Crown Colonies, Berkeley Worldwide developed a series of diploma programs. Each of these required a semester of full-time study followed by an academic internship of an additional four months. Two aspects of these programs are noteworthy—the idea of issuing such a credential was supported by the campus faculty (which was not the case at University of California, Los Angeles) and it proved hugely popular. Students who would never have been admitted as matriculating degree seekers now had an avenue to a Berkeley credential. Demand for entry into these offerings (by way of ELP) became so great that Extension was forced to purchase the former Armstrong College in downtown Berkeley to accommodate growth.

Working with the International Trade Office for the state of California and the US Foreign Commercial Service of the Department of Commerce, Extensions across the entire University of California system came together and developed common marketing materials and joint recruitment operations, which, after a three-year evaluation, were estimated to have brought more than one quarter of a billion dollars annually into the California economy, independent of revenue realized from international degree-seeking students.

The First UC Online

My indoctrination into the world of online learning continued at Berkeley Extension when it received grants from the Sloan Foundation to go online as part of what was initially called the Asynchronous Learning Network (later changed to Sloan-C, and now known as the Online Learning Consortium).

The UC system's Correspondence Course Center was housed at Berkeley under Extension's oversight. Offering dozens of rigorous, highly regarded courses, this center was a perpetual source of deficits. By moving its courses over to an online format it was hoped that their popularity would increase. More important, in the eyes of some, this move online would take place outside of any individual campus. This was critical at a time when online education was seen in a light similar to that of for-profit education today.

Ultimately, Extension received some $2.6 million from Sloan. With this funding, the Correspondence Course Center's inventory was transformed into a series of online offerings, delivered by AOL. Starting with high-demand business courses, but without the expertise of instructional designers, Extension proceeded to transform paper-based correspondence courses into electronic correspondence courses, with the all too familiar read-quiz-read-quiz format. The result, not surprisingly, was that completion rates didn't change. Online study in its original format differed little from study in the nineteenth century except for the manner by which the text arrived.

The importance of marketing, attention to delivery sites and student convenience, the strength of brand, and campus resistance were all points of learning that I would take to my next stop—Colorado State University (CSU).

Colorado State University

Attracted by the opportunity to become an associate provost at a land-grant university, I moved to Fort Collins in 1997. Colorado State University's reputation for innovation and the assurance that continuing education was one of the president's top three strategic priorities were enticing. The late '90s was a time when much innovation in higher education was taking place in and around Denver. Glenn Jones, founder of Jones Intercable, was one of the first to make access to education available through television. His Mind Expansion University originated in Denver with MBA courses provided by CSU and later by the University of Colorado at Colorado Springs. The Colorado State MBA was the first online degree to enjoy accreditation from the Association to Advance Collegiate Schools of Business. Glenn would go on to found the for-profit Jones International University.

Other examples of innovation at work around the Mile High City were REAL Education (later eCollege) with its pioneering learning management system and services to help colleges and universities move online, and National Technological University, which used satellites (the kind in the sky) to deliver graduate engineering degrees using videotaped courses from brand-name institutions. Western Governors University was born here, operating from a former air force base when I arrived in 1997. The fact that satellite broadcasts covered the entire country from Denver, and that it provided easy access to the country's emerging fiber optic network (placed alongside the various railroad rights of way that crossed in Denver), were among the reasons for such a concentration of education providers in one place.

Dealing with Change

In 1997, CSU saw the rise of online learning but was very comfortable with its legacy technologies—two-way interactive, cable, satellite, and pre-recorded video, plus instructors driving to the university's Denver Center for evening and weekend courses. The beauty of these methods was that they did not require special preparation. The same yellowing notes used in classroom lectures could serve as the basis for a distance class. Moving online, on the other hand, required greater effort.

A small cadre of faculty from various schools and colleges were willing to try the online experience but were offered little central support. There were no graphic artists, programmers, or instructional designers for them to turn to. In the area of incentives, continuing education was authorized to pay $1,000 for each course produced. To say that the virtual inventory was disparate would be something of an understatement. It ranged from obviously homemade to acceptable, but with no consistency as to look or format. In most cases, the end product was little more than a variation of a video lecture, now streamed over the Internet, but accompanied by a PowerPoint presentation. While an improvement over the University of California's text-only approach, the early CSU courses were no more interactive.

One of the most interesting findings from research on distance students at the time was that fully one-third withdrew before the third course, most often after the first. Of those who remained, nearly all would complete, and with high GPAs (distance students typically had higher average GPAs than those in the classroom). Motivation, self-discipline, and a lack of alternatives were seen as the contributing factors.

Another eye-opening finding was that the highest concentration of MBA students was in Fort Collins. Apparently, distance wasn't their concern. It was time. John Sperling's emphasis on convenience for working students was again validated, as locals used online access to shift time from specified on-campus class periods to ones of their choosing.

UPCEA

While at CSU I became active with UPCEA. Despite the fact that Colorado State had little involvement in international education, the association allowed me to meet with like-minded colleagues from around the country, sponsored workshops on going international, and printed my monograph on building international programs (*The Global Option: Building and Sustaining International Partnerships*, 1997). From these early efforts, the Global Associates special interest group was formed by the association.

In addition to promoting international education as part of UPCEA's mission, I became a member of the association's board. Additionally, thanks to encouragement from past UPCEA president Cal Stockman, then at Grand Valley State, I deepened my involvement and was fortunate to be elected vice president. At that point in UPCEA's history, holding the office put me on a track that would rotate from vice president to president-elect, president, and immediate past president. These posts provided a unique opportunity to meet members and observe continuing education programs across the nation.

Boston University

In 2000, I accepted an offer to become the dean of Metropolitan College (MET) at Boston University. In addition to the university's adult degree programs, MET was also responsible for Summer Session, a corporate education program with multiple sites in and around Boston and a residential training facility in the White Mountains of New Hampshire. It also operated centers in Israel and Belgium to support graduate diploma and degree programs. Unusual in continuing education, MET had a full-time faculty.

Online, Again

With support from the provost, MET was charged with building an online program for the university from scratch. With the energy and creativity of Jay Halfond (associate dean and later dean of MET) and Susan Kryczka (hired from Northeastern) this happened quickly.

Colorado State, I later learned, had been the very first customer of Embanet, the Canadian software company that eventually created the Online Program Management (OPM) business. Thus, it was not a surprise when Jeffrey Feldberg, Embanet's founder, came to BU with the idea of assisting us in our efforts to go online, and with *no* BU money. Instead, we would share revenue over an agreed period of time to repay Embanet's upfront investment *and* provide a healthy return on investment. From this for-profit/nonprofit partnership came an online program that today accounts for nearly 50 percent of Boston University's graduate enrollment.

The online experience I had gained at three institutions, positive and negative, allowed for a running start at BU. Many of the necessary ingredients for a strong online presence were present—support from senior leadership, an experienced internal team, and an external partner from whom we could learn while developing internal capacity. Most important, however, were the lessons learned on how to involve and obtain buy-in from campus faculty, across the university, not just at MET.

With guidance from the provost, Metropolitan College and its various nondegree programs were reorganized. Jay Halfond became dean of MET, and he and the dean of the School of Hospitality reported to me as the new associate provost. Online learning became a part of the nondegree program portfolio as a service unit, providing support to all of the university's schools and colleges. Revenues earned from online offerings were credited back to the academic department overseeing the offerings, not to the online unit, as were the student enrollments and credit hours taught. Faculty received "overload" compensation for creating and teaching the courses. Ownership was jointly held by the faculty developer and the university. Faculty were free to use their intellectual property as they wished, except in direct competition with BU offerings, should they later move to another institution.

In addition to online education, BU provided an opportunity to develop a range of professional education offerings—including paralegal studies, fund-raising, financial planning, professional investigation, and the always popular project management. Unfortunately, it also needed to downsize and close programs. While technology programs, credit and noncredit, did poorly during the downturn of 2002–2003, other subject areas, such as business and criminal justice, did well. The lesson learned was that a diverse portfolio of offerings is important in times of uncertainty. What sells today may not tomorrow, and today's weak subject areas may be tomorrow's saviors.

The arrival of new leadership at BU and an opportunity for me to lead an institution occurred nearly simultaneously in 2005. I readily accepted the offer to assume the presidency of Excelsior in July of that year. A complication was that I had also been offered a fellowship at Harvard's Kennedy School for that fall. Thanks to the support of my new board, I was able to accept the fellowship, study the issue of resistance to innovation in higher education, and transition into my new post.

Excelsior

Over the eight years that followed, I have been successful in applying some of the lessons of the past to today's environment. Not only has Excelsior entered the online world, it now offers more than 500 courses, in addition to noncredit programs administered by its Center for Professional Development (CPD) which are recognized for GI Bill entitlement by the VA. A source of institutional pride, Excelsior's academic courses now see a 96 percent completion rate, and CPD offerings are experiencing a high volume of repeat customers. Some of the elements necessary for student retention (and returns) are being recognized and now included in instructional design, to good effect.

Serving the Military

Upon arrival at Excelsior, I came to know an institution that I wish had existed in the 1960s—that is, military and adult friendly, willing to accept lots of credit in transfer, as well as multiple pathways to a degree. As a refugee from a Missouri farm, I entered the Coast Guard straight from high school (in 1962). By the latter part of that decade, I had acquired a family and was no longer content with enlisted pay. However, the route to becoming an officer required either an undergraduate degree or substantial prior service, which could be reduced with academic work. My attempts at college began through correspondence courses from the US Armed Forces Institute, or USAFI, as it was more commonly known. USAFI was administered by the University of Wisconsin, under contract from Department of Defense. It was the only way then that someone could go to school while serving in a remote location such as Annette Island, Alaska.

Thanks to USAFI, and other institutions, I accumulated more than 180 semester credits from nine institutions. These came from correspondence courses, classroom instruction (at both two- and four-year institutions), attendance at the US Naval War College and military training evaluated by the American Council on Education. Yet no credential ever resulted from this work. I ultimately qualified for Officer Candidate School by fulfilling the nonacademic service requirements.

Founded in 1971, Regents College, as Excelsior was then known, established a model for adult degree completion that an increasing number of institutions embrace today. Regents, Thomas Edison (NJ), Charter Oak (CT), Granite State (NH), Empire State (NY), Governors State (IL), along with the University of Maryland University College and, more recently, Western Governors University have all come to national attention as "college completion" institutions, focused on the adult learner. These, along with others, serve the military (active and veteran) by aggregating credits, evaluating their source and relevance, and matching them to degree requirements. From this comes a completion plan that shows where there are gaps and how to fill them.

With cost and time to credential as concerns, these institutions offer options that may include more course work (classroom and/or on-line) or test taking, using the college-level subject exams of the College Board (CLEP), Educational Testing Service (DSST), and/or Excelsior (UEXCEL). With free online courses from Open Education Resources and "practice exams" from Excelsior, degree completers can prepare for these assessments at their own pace. Satisfactory completion of one of these exams typically satisfies a course requirement, at little cost ($150 on average).

With access to the Internet, learning is taking place in the air (one of the Stealth pilots involved in the bombing of Iraq in 2003 was quoted as saying that he used the long transit from his home base in Missouri to Baghdad and back to complete an online course assignment), at sea (including aboard submarines, thanks to CD ROM technology), and on land everywhere. One of Excelsior's recent graduates, an active duty Special Forces command sergeant, completed his final course work online while on a mission in Africa. Combat, isolated locations, and sea duty are no longer barriers to the continued learning of our service men and women, thanks to a growing body of online programs. This at a time when military leaders, from former chairman of the Joint Chiefs of Staff Admiral Mike Mullen (Excelsior's 2013 commencement speaker) to the commandant of the Joint Special Operations University's Enlisted Academy SGM Steve Horsley (with whom Excelsior has recently entered into an articulation agreement), have said that a well-educated military is one of our country's strategic priorities. With the continuing, online, and adult education communities as partners, this objective can be realized.

Lessons Learned

As an adult/continuing education administrator and faculty member at five institutions (two public, three private), I have had the good fortune to observe up close the rise of online and for-profit education, the huge international demand for access to Western style learning, and the difficulty of introducing innovation when all stakeholders are not at the table.

From the consumer perspective, I have learned to pay attention to the needs of the learner—time, convenience, and unique support services must all be considered in serving the post-traditional student. From the viewpoint of a program manager, I have developed a deep appreciation for the importance of good marketing and for the application of sound business practices. I have also learned that it is important to have a diversified portfolio of offerings.

Here are the three top lessons I have learned and why we, as continuing education professionals, are well equipped to carry these lessons forward.

Technology has to be sophisticated and consumer demand has to be strong. With the number of traditional-aged students in decline, and the realization that learning really is a lifelong need, how we use technology is critical, especially if we are to maintain a competitive workforce in a rapidly changing world. As technology is increasingly used to reach new student niches, it is continuing education that is being asked to administer the creation and operation of this online learning program. At many institutions, adult degree completion also falls to continuing education, as does international outreach.

Courses need to be engaging and interactive. Over the past thirty years the field of adult education has moved from the periphery of higher education to center stage. Controversial visionaries like John Sperling, Don MacIntyre, and Glenn Jones have helped pave the road for this movement. They saw the need to serve returning adults, and to serve them well, long before established universities did. The University of Phoenix grew to its current size not because of high-quality instruction but because of a combination of smart marketing and attention to convenience. Both are worth emulating, along with high-quality instruction.

Without faculty buy-in and support, programs will not fly. The older, working, post-traditional student has ascended to become the focus of national policy and institutional programming. With this ascent has come greater respect for the role of the adult continuing and professional educator. No longer is continuing education seen as a dead end. Many former continuing education deans have risen to become president or chancellor of institutions and systems. Innovation, the inclusion of faculty in program development, and the ability to produce a financial surplus have long been highly valued concerns of continuing education. Our success, over several decades, is now recognized.

As the traditional student population continues to shrink, and as the connection between education and a competitive workforce becomes clearer, UPCEA's member institutions will see demand for their marketing expertise. Having the world's finest programs is of little benefit if no one knows of them.

The professionals of UPCEA will increasingly find themselves called upon to help their member institutions in an assuredly difficult future. Clayton Christensen's "disruptive innovation" is being driven by opportunities to better serve the post-traditional learners that now make up the bulk of higher education's enrollments. Online learning, MOOCs, adaptive learning, prior learning assessment, recognition of nontraditional learning, and competency-based education all benefit the older, more experienced twenty-five- to eighty-five-year-old student. These are our customers.

From the Margins to the Mainstream

The Shift in Distance Education over the Past Thirty Years

■■

Rick L. Shearer

For most of its existence as a practice and as a field of study, distance education has remained at the margins of institutions in the United States and as such has had the ability to adapt, innovate, and find new ways to meet the learning and educational needs of the adult student. Although there have been many forms of delivery that allowed students to study from a distance, including correspondence courses, educational radio, educational TV, and other forms like audio graphics, it was not until pioneers like Charles Wedemeyer, Desmond Keegan, and others set the foundation for distance education that it became a recognized field of study and an entity within institutions.

In 1971 Wedemeyer highlighted the following in his work on independent study, which outlined the foundation for distance education. Here he defined independent study as

> various forms of teaching-learning arrangements in which teachers and learners carry out their essential tasks and responsibilities apart from one another, communicating in a variety of ways, for the purposes of freeing internal learners from inappropriate class pacings or patterns, or providing external learners opportunity to continue learning in their own environments, and developing in all learners the capacity to carry on self-directed learning, the ultimate maturity required of the educated person. (cited in Diehl 2013, 39)

Rick L. Shearer is Director of World Campus Learning Design, The Pennsylvania State University, and a UPCEA committee chair.

Keegan, in the first edition of his *Foundations of Distance Education* (1996), set forth an operational definition of distance education where he defined the field as having five key attributes. They were:

- quasi-permanent separation of a teacher and a learner throughout the length of the teaching process;

- quasi-permanent separation of a learner from a learning group throughout the length of the learning process;

- participation in a bureaucratized form of educational provision;

- utilization of mechanical or electronic means of communication to carry the content of the course; and

- provision of means for two-way communication so that the learner can benefit from or initiate dialogue. (1996, vol. 1, 111)

Michael Grahame Moore, in his work from 1971 to 1996, conceived of and continued to refine the theory of transactional distance, which stands today as the main underlying theory of the field of distance education (see Moore 1993; Moore and Kearsley 1996). This distance is psychological and can lead to misunderstanding. He also saw distance education as a system where transactional distance was the resultant of the interaction of three key variables: dialogue, structure, and learner autonomy.

These key figures in the field and others formed the bases of the distance education discipline and field and gave a voice to what many in continuing education units had been doing in support of the adult learner at a distance. Further, Wedemeyer, in his book *Learning at the Back Door: Reflections on Non-Traditional Learning in the Lifespan,* described independent study and distance education as "a single great new development in education" (1981, 60). He foreshadowed how the field would have a major impact on higher education.

However, distance education continued to be viewed as a part of continuing education or extension, and as being on the fringe of university operations until online learning through the web began in the late 1990s. So what changed? What caught the conscience of the nation and moved distance education from the margins to the mainstream? This essay will explore technological and pedagogical changes over the past thirty years to highlight key shifts that have led to this awakening. Further, the essay will look at key changes in the educational landscape that have acted as catalysts to propel online and distance education into the mainstream and to the forefront of education.

1985–1995

This period was one of the most exciting for distance educators and instructional designers. A host of technologies were in play, and pedagogically we saw some major changes. In the mid 1980s, we were still using several older forms of distance education delivery systems, including educational television, satellite one-way video, two-way audio systems, audiographics (combination of shared computer screens with an audio phone bridge), computer-based education (CBE) systems like PLATO, and, of course, print correspondence. For the most part these were either mass delivery systems, from one to many, or very individualized experiences, such as CBE. With the exception of audiographics, dialogue between the learner and the instructor was limited and interactions with other students was virtually nonexistent. During this time these delivery systems were what some may consider a resource-based model, which allowed us great economies of scale in delivery, but with large investments in the development of the courses (Inglis 2013).

Also, pedagogically we were still very solidly in the cognitive/behaviorist era (Anderson and Dron 2011). Most of our courses were in the lower divisions, we were looking at the transmission of knowledge/facts, and due to the limited dialogue our goal was not necessarily the construction of knowledge. In those cases where institutions set up learning centers for their students, similar to the Open University in the United Kingdom, then there was the possibility of a heightened amount of dialogue leading to higher levels of attainment.

As we approached 1990, we started to see some very interesting developments in technology that allowed us to improve pedagogically: the emergence of online bulletin boards, systems like FirstClass (a communications platform for group collaboration), and two-way interactive video. These systems allowed for experimentation in our designs and delivery formats and allowed us to move to a classroom-based model where we could provide more learner-instructor interaction, but also student-student interaction (Anderson and Dron 2011). Key at this time were two-way interactive video systems, and we saw widespread adoption of these systems across higher education by both continuing education and extension units, but also by the mainstream portion of the institutions. We also saw the first desktop video teleconferencing systems emerge from AT&T and others.

Also during this period correspondence education was still very popular, and institutions like the University of Nebraska and the Pennsylvania State University had well-established distance education programs that served several thousand students nationally and special populations like those individuals who were incarcerated. While popular with adult learners who did not have many alternatives to obtaining an education, correspondence remained on the margins and was looked down upon due to low completion rates and lack of interactivity. Students in this cognitive/behaviorist mode of delivery had to be motivated and highly self-directed and autonomous learners to complete these programs. Here self-directed, as discussed by Anderson (2013), was related to self-monitoring (cognitive and metacognitive processes), motivation, and control of one's learning, which is slightly different from how Moore (1984) looked at autonomy related to the theory of transactional distance, where it centered on the ability of an individual to be successful with limited dialogue and where the learner determined goals, evaluation, and learning procedures and resources.

1995–2005

Around 1995 we witnessed a major shift in technology that would forever change the landscape of distance education and education overall. About this time the first web browsers that incorporated graphics, like Mosaic's Netscape (introduced in mid-1994), appeared and opened up a wealth of opportunities for new ways to present information and for engagement with others (Digital Research Initiative, n.d.). This also led to the first learning management systems like WebCT, which brought the familiar classroom experience online. While the early online courses were primarily text, as we were still tied to 56k modems for most of our users at a distance, we could start to integrate graphics and animated images into our course designs to help visualize the content for students. Further, this allowed us to shift from a cognitive/behaviorist approach to a social/constructivist pedagogical approach. Students could now easily participate in group work, we could look at problem-based learning approaches, and students could, we hoped, have rich dialogues with the instructor and each other.

During these early years of online instruction, the courses were a blend of correspondence, in terms of narrative written as guided didactic conversation, and the traditional classroom experience (Holmberg 1983). This was a result of two key factors: (1) as mentioned above, we were still tied to an end user who usually had a 56k modem for connection speed; and (2) institutions had to work very hard to get buy-in from faculty to experiment with this new form of educational delivery. Thus, instructional designers strove to have the courses replicate the in-class experience (i.e., typical fifteen-week course, a new topic every week, quizzes, similar assignments, etc.). This is not to say that this form of distance education course and delivery was not successful, just that it was limited in terms of how we thought about the new possibilities of the online world.

As we approached the new millennium and on toward 2005 a major shift occurred again, this time related to the functionality of the web. Web 1.0, a push type of approach to information, graduated to Web 2.0, a collaborative approach to information. Here we can think of the emergence of Facebook (introduced on February 4, 2004), YouTube (introduced on February 14, 2004), and other platforms that today seem commonplace. In the Web 2.0 world experts in the field were no longer solely responsible for producing and distributing knowledge; now anyone could contribute. While this brought up debates about authoritative voice and students being able to discern valid information from invalid, it allowed us to start thinking about how students could collaborate to create knowledge as a socially constructed event.

The Web 2.0 tools and abilities seemed to have caught the attention of faculty in a way that previous technologies had not. Web 2.0 tools were emerging everywhere by the end of this ten-year period, along with feature phones, the precursors to smartphones (the iPhone was introduced in 2007 [McCarty 2011]). Students were showing up on our campuses with these new devices and using these tools, which both excited and probably terrified faculty at the same time. While distance education and online instruction remained on the fringe, they were now on the verge of their own major shift and now in the crosshairs of the government and institutions.

2005–2015

While the first half of this period did not see any radically new approaches, we did witness an avalanche of Web 2.0 tools that continued to expand the ways students could interact with each other both in and outside of class. However, the second half exploded with the idea of connectivism, which was originally introduced by George Siemens and Stephen Downes in 2005 (Kop and Hill 2008). The latter half of this time is a period in which we also saw the introduction and phenomenally quick rise of massive open online courses (MOOCs) through the efforts of Sebastian Thrun at Udacity and Daphne Koller and Andrew Ng at Coursera. Further, occurring at the same time was a dramatic increase in the number of students taking online courses. According to a Babson Survey Research Group study we witnessed a 93 percent increase between 2005 and 2010, with numbers growing from 3,180,050 to 6,142,280 (Allen and Seaman 2011). This increase in students taking online courses, along with the change in the number of personal devices on campuses, started to move the distance education conversation from the margins into the mainstream.

By 2010 we were also starting to see an awakening by state and federal governments and students to the exponential growth in college tuition over the past decade. Higher education was beginning to be out of reach for many, and the debt that students and families were emerging from college with was seen as crippling. In 2012, for the first time, higher education debt in the country topped \$1 trillion, this at a time when the impact of the collapse of the housing bubble had states tightening their fiscal belts to balance budgets, which led to reduced funding for higher education. In addition, the federal government was focused on a new form of financial aid fraud perpetrated around online and distance education. Another factor that was not much recognized during this time period, but whose impact was being felt in many states, was the decline in the number of students graduating from high school (a reduction in students moving through the system).

These factors, combined with reductions in research funding by the federal government in many sectors, had universities starting to take a hard look at their existing structures and operations. The combination of all these factors focused a different light on distance education and online learning. It seems as if overnight online learning and distance education were catapulted onto center stage at many institutions and were now mainstream focuses. They were seen as not just new net revenue producing entities but as a way to grow and/or maintain enrollment levels.

There are obviously pros and cons to moving into a mainstream focus. Some could argue that doing so limits innovation, a hallmark of continuing education and distance education units on the margins. However, a dramatic move like this also stimulates discussion around strategic plans for how online and distance education truly fit within the overall landscape of a higher education institution. Thus, through the recent mainstream focus we have witnessed many more institutions adopting a form of online learning or distance education for their students and the populations of their states. This has led to vastly increased competition for students and a further focus by the Department of Education on online learning (state authorization policies, financial aid disbursement practices, more attention by accreditors, etc.). This regulatory attention, competition, focus on tuition, and dramatic shift from traditional to nontraditional students has also changed the tenor of conversations at universities regarding completion rates and the idea of success within a shorter period of time.

2015 Onward

So what will our world look like in the next ten years? Will distance education exist, will it just be part of the fabric of mainstream higher education, and what impact will this have on adult learners, innovation, and higher education brick-and-mortar infrastructure?

Distance education and specifically online learning have now fundamentally changed the landscape of higher education as Wedemeyer (1981) had predicted. They have opened the door to new possible realities in our near future, which higher education institutions will need to deal with strategically. Already we are hearing stories from some institutions of more than 50 percent of traditional resident instruction students attending remotely during the summer. We are witnessing a resurgence of interest around master-based and competency-based approaches to learning, along with an increased interest in prior learning assessment (PLA) as means to address the cost of higher education. We also have a critical conversation emerging around credentials, and what our world might look like if we move to microcredentials (badges). Fundamentally we are at a point where we, as academics, administrators, government, and industry, must answer the question, What do we want a higher education credential to represent? One would like to think that an education is more than just a collection of credits around discrete topics. Further, it should be more than just preparing someone for a particular job.

If we move aggressively into online formats for our traditional resident instruction students and work to do more with PLA, transfer articulation agreements, and competency approaches, what is the balance we must maintain between lower division and upper division courses to maintain institutions financially as we think of them today? Or are we moving past some point of no return? Pedagogically we will also be challenged to integrate the ideas of connectivism into our social/constructivist models and determine authoritative voice and how to capture and promote the construction of knowledge. New course models will need to appear that take us beyond the replication of the traditional classroom experience and truly take advantage of the technology at our fingertips.

Distance education, online learning, and the new Internet of Things have opened the door to a new world. It is up to us, the continuing education, distance education, and extension professionals who have worked in these areas for years at the fringe, to help our institutions think about the new world and how best to adapt as the fringe is now mainstream. Then it will be up to us to once again imagine what lies ahead as we once more innovate on the fringe of new possibilities.

References

Allen, E., and J. Seaman. 2011. *Going the Distance: Online Education in the United States, 2011.* Babson Survey Research Group, Babson College.

Anderson, T., and J. Dron. 2011. "Three Generations of Distance Education Pedagogy." *International Review of Research in Open and Distance Learning*, 12, no. 3.

Anderson, W. 2013. "Independent Learning: Autonomy, Control, and Meta-Cognition." In M. G. Moore, ed., *Handbook of Distance Education*, 3rd ed. (pp. 86–103). New York: Routledge.

Diehl, W. C. 2013. "Charles A. Wedemeyer: Visionary Pioneer of Distance Education." In M. G. Moore, ed., *Handbook of Distance Education*, 3rd ed. (pp. 38–48). New York: Routledge.

Digital Research Initiative. n.d. "The Story of the Netscape Browser." Accessed at http://ibiblio.org/team/history/evolution/browser.html.

Holmberg, B. 1983. "Guided Didactic Conversation in Distance Education." In D. Stewart, D. Keegan, and B. Holmberg, eds., *Distance Education: International Perspectives* (pp. 115–122). New York: St. Martin's Press.

Inglis, A. 2013. "The Changing Costs of Delivery of Distance Education." In M. G. Moore, ed., *Handbook of Distance Education*, 3rd ed. (pp. 507–520). New York: Routledge.

Keegan, D. 1996. *Foundations of Distance Education*, 3rd ed. London: Routledge.

Kop, R., and A. Hill. 2008. "Connectivism: Learning Theory of the Future or Vestige of the Past?" *International Review of Research in Open and Distance Education* 9. Accessed at http://www.irrodl.org/index.php/irrodl/article/view/523/1103.

McCarty, B. 2011. "The History of the Smartphone." The Next Web blog. Accessed at http://thenextweb.com/mobile/2011/12/06/the-history-of-the-smartphone/.

Moore, M. G. 1984. "On a Theory of Independent Study." In D. Stewart, D. Keegan, and B. Holmberg, eds., *Distance Education: International Perspectives* (pp. 68–94). London: Routledge.

Moore, M. G. 1993. "Theory of transactional distance." In D. Keegan, ed., *Theoretical Principles of Distance Education* (vol. 1, pp. 22–38). New York: Routledge.

Moore, M. G., and G. Kearsley. 1996. *Distance Education: A Systems View.* Belmont, CA: Wadsworth.

Wedemeyer, C. A. 1981. *Learning at the Back Door: Reflections on Non-Traditional Learning in the Lifespan.* Madison: University of Wisconsin Press.

When You Reach a Fork in the Road

Critical Moments in Distance Education

■■

Jay A. Halfond

As Fate Would Have It

Were I looking out on a clear night sky that fall of 2001 I might have seen the stars align. After the bursting of the dot-com bubble and the fall of World Trade Towers, we could not have anticipated the profound effect these mega-events would have on enrollments at Boston University's Metropolitan College. Or the critical juncture we were about to reach. New to my deanship, I was invited to participate in a conference call with a fledgling company called Embanet, spun off from the University of Toronto's executive MBA program (hence its name) and from a somewhat more established distance learning firm called Compass.[1] With less than ten employees, this start-up pitched a new and compelling model for online education and suggested we take our tiny criminal justice master's program online.

Their approach addressed several immediate dilemmas. I was anxious to enter the online market (foolishly believing we were late in doing so), but faced the quandary of how to manage the risk of launching any effort. Boston University also confronted a challenge unique to its criminal justice program. Thanks to the Quinn Bill, Massachusetts police officers automatically received pay raises when they received degrees. This generated a slew of "cop shops"—degree programs of dubious academic integrity that exploited this demand. It was far from clear how Boston University could possibly compete in this congested arena of local academic suppliers. As I listened to the proposed revenue sharing model, my

---

Jay A. Halfond is Associate Professor, Administrative Sciences, and Educational Leadership and Policy Studies, Boston University, and a UPCEA Senior Fellow, Center for Online Leadership and Strategy.

thoughts drifted to the solution—one that was uncommon in part-time, continuing education at the time: leapfrog over the now saturated Boston market and go national.

We benefited from naïveté—and from the benign neglect of university leaders in an era before online education was at the forefront of their consciousness. We could not fully fathom the plunge we were taking or how potentially transformative this could be. Academe can be especially unforgiving. Had we failed, it is unlikely that further online initiatives could have been undertaken. Had we forecasted the explosive growth about to occur, we might have been paralyzed by its sheer magnitude. The online criminal justice master's program was an immediate success and lulled us into thinking it could now proceed smoothly. The MCJ degree catapulted us into distance learning (and Embanet as well) and provided resources to bolster our faculty talent and our confidence to introduce another dozen online degree programs over the next five years. With a paucity of competition, each new program was immediately able to dominate its market.

As local on-campus enrollments plummeted, especially in computer science, we more than offset declines each year with even greater growth in adult learners across the nation. From the start we proudly proclaimed that we had more online students from California than Massachusetts. We experienced net enrollment growth annually—with a student profile that served BU well and provided even greater financial margins. Continuing education deans at other institutions could not grasp why we focused on those beyond our catchment area. Because Boston is a small, academically dense environment, rather than offer online options to our existing student base, Metropolitan College chose to be as cosmopolitan as it was metropolitan. Fellow deans at BU began to work with us to launch their online degree programs as well.[2] We took "distance" literally and sought students who could not otherwise commute to BU. By doing so, we could isolate the growth that easily justified the faculty and staff positions needed to support these new students. We had stumbled onto the virtuous cycle to propel our college forward.

I was soon able to announce with pride that the majority of our students were in programs that had not even existed a few years earlier. But I was also keenly aware of the counterfactual reality that, had we not innovated when we did, we could easily have become a ghost town. Such a decline would have been ugly and messy. Instead, through serendipity as much as strategy, Metropolitan College's enrollment and stature grew. MET's veteran faculty courageously embraced the challenge of teaching online, and newly recruited faculty were immediately enlisted to engage students asynchronously.

From an early point, we confronted a nagging concern about our deepening dependency on one for-profit company. We gradually insourced key functions and diversified our partnerships.[3] We renegotiated each program contract to bring instructional design in-house (in our view, an important academic function and one we could do as well and more economically). On the other hand, we decided that recruiting students nationally was not a skill we were internally equipped to develop. We also stipulated in the contracts our right to negotiate for students directly through businesses, BU alumni, and foreign academic institutions. Boston University began to partner with other fledgling online service providers in order not to be beholden to any one company. These moves improved our financial returns and raised our comfort level with corporate partnerships.

Our programs grew throughout the decade, generating about $40 million of annual revenue (most as contribution margin) and about 40 percent of MET's enrollments, 8 percent of BU's total student head count, and the majority of those part-time students seeking master's degrees at Boston University.

These were the days before distance learning had achieved respectability. I still found myself confronting campus naysayers daily. The final phrase in each conversation with my provost was always his admonition not to become the University of Phoenix. The registrar resisted much-needed systems changes because she thought online courses would be a short-lived fad. I bought many beers for arts and sciences faculty colleagues who needed to be persuaded that online learning wasn't the work of the devil. I would do the math to demonstrate how much more opportunity online students had to communicate asynchronously than those in-class students seeking a few minutes of precious airtime.

It was all worth the fight. This fundamentally changed our profession as continuing educators and our place on our campuses. Having a school like Metropolitan College on campus helps generate a deep dialogue about pedagogy. Continuing education deans need to be able to speak the language of academe and of the business world—and represent the values of their university with the fire in the belly to pursue initiatives far beyond conventional academic imagination.

As I think back to that fateful 2001 phone conversation, I realize now that this was the beginning of a conspiracy of internal and external entrepreneurs. Although we redefined and reduced the role of for-profit partners, I pay homage to the instrumental role they played. That might be my major lesson learned: we probably could not have succeeded without the intervention of a few start-up companies. While these online service providers even now support only a small share of America's academic institutions and a miniscule portion of US academic degree programs (even those online), their impact has been pivotal. To appease those in academe, they set the bar high for this emerging movement. They were the catalysts that brought a new modality of instruction to otherwise recalcitrant institutions. They helped earn respect as much as financial reward for distance learning.

When the definitive history of online distance learning is written, a critical factor in that success will be from those outside the academy, in it for the money as much as the mission—who taught us to innovate in ways we were, frankly, incapable of doing ourselves.

A New Model Emerges

What allows third-party companies like Embanet and Deltak to convince universities like mine to enter the distance learning market?

They provide the impetus to act, in particular, the upfront market research and capital needed to launch a new distance learning program. It can take a year or more to court universities, negotiate revenue-sharing contracts, add staff, develop the first few online courses, and recruit the first group of students—and then several more years just to recoup that investment. Few companies have the patience, capital, and respect for academic values to play this role.

They aggressively seek a high volume of mature, admissible students on a national scale. Academic quality may be the university's imperative, but high volume is the key nonnegotiable in this business model. If this partnership falls short of its potential, the company's financial forecasts and commitments suffer. With only a small portfolio of institutions and programs, this shortfall can be fatal.

These service providers engage and support full-time faculty (who become the main authors of the online courses) and, by doing so, help soothe the skeptics and technophobes. Significant upfront investment occurs not only in recruiting students but in working deferentially with faculty.

Remarkably, for-profit companies helped create a now common national curricular foundation for delivering online programs. Through an ever-rotating carousel of online courses, offered consecutively in half-semester terms, students can start their studies at six points during the academic year, taking one course at a time. (Prerequisites and electives were discouraged as complicating this simple and smooth course cycle.) This lockstep carousel helps retain students by keeping them on track—and makes course design and delivery predictable.

By developing and offering the lowest number of courses possible, with the highest allowable volume, and then sectioning these large courses into small clusters of about a dozen students, overseen by instructional facilitators, this model became immensely scalable and efficient. The master's curriculum can be prescribed and concise, with a small set of courses developed with high production values. MET was able to modestly grow the size of its full-time faculty and leverage them over ever-increasing student enrollments. The part-time master's degree emerged as the sweet spot for this escalation of quality distance learning, which anticipated the national trend

From the first point of inquiry the online student experience was intended to replicate and even elevate that of the typical part-time evening student. Fully online students paid on-campus tuition (perhaps even a premium) and received comparable access to advisors, instructors, and services. In contrast to pre-Internet distance learning, where remote students were marginalized viewers of the physical classroom, this model set the gold standard for allowing busy, accomplished students to feel like equal citizens in a new mode of learning. We in turn learned a great deal about how to market, recruit, respond to, analyze, and serve students, online and otherwise, by watching the efforts of our corporate partners. Online students soon had far greater connection to Boston University than typically isolated part-time evening students.

I soon appreciated that we were now seeing a very different species of student. I would point out to faculty that although they encountered more students online, I met face-to-face with many more than they ever could. I invited current distance learning students to alumni events in cities I visited and grilled them on their backgrounds, motivations, and impressions of the particular program in which they were enrolled. Distance learners were far more likely to attend graduation events and seek out their faculty and fellow students in person. We also conducted biennial student surveys on who they were and what they thought of their program.

These students, we learned, were older, more accomplished and discerning, and led far more complicated lives than those we typically saw on campus. They equated rigor with value. Their educational journey was as important as the outcome: these students valued the intrinsic learning experience even more than the extrinsic, transactional aspect of gaining another credential. Although they had access to schools in their own region, they wanted education on their terms. Distance learning programs gave them that control—within a nationwide cohort of similar online students. This was revolutionary for part-time learners, who were previously dependent on limited local opportunities to be with others from their region. They could now join a geographically dispersed and diverse virtual student community.

I also began to see a new self-consciousness and excitement develop among the faculty about the art and science of teaching, which rejuvenated those who had been conducting the same courses the same way year after year. Though intentionally only a small part of MET, online distance learning now permeated everything we did and had become.

Through one singular, somewhat innocent foray into distance education, a model emerged that allowed us to recruit students nationally, deliver high-quality online courses, and reap the financial rewards that helped to underwrite the growth of a college. This changed the profile of part-time students and the education they experienced. This also helped elevate the role of continuing education deans and of those faculty who participated, who were now appreciated as pedagogical innovators by their peers throughout the university. This ecosystem beautifully blended the business and academic facets of a new model for part-time higher education. And it was created, remarkably, by for-profit firms working in close collaboration with deans and their faculty—initially in an otherwise skeptical era.

'Til Teach-Out Do Us Part

On a day-to-day basis, though, these partnerships have been far from the turnkey relationships we were promised. In our innocence, we thought this would just happen through the gentle management of our partners, who would tell us what they needed on a prescribed schedule. In fact, we soon became painfully aware that these relationships were complex and labor intensive, often volatile and frustrating, fundamentally challenging, and constantly in need of nurturing.

Universities are built to last centuries, while growing companies are built to be sold every few years. As each service provider grew, ownership changed, and we would have to adapt to a new regime. The intricacies of building rapport between organizations constantly demanded protocols, oversight committees, weekly conference calls, summits, and sometimes even delicate lobbying and mediation. We had to hire staff just to work with their staff.

Over time, these service providers developed their own critical mass of in-house professionals who could share their expertise and pursuit of innovative tools and techniques. However, this concentration of staff became a double-edged sword: while promoting continuous improvement, these companies also became more complex and bureaucratic, and partners were forced to learn more names, navigate more mazes, and become more assertive in getting attention and resources.

We were always in search of the right metaphor or label to characterize our ties to outside service providers. They are something less than true partnerships but more than conventional vendor relationships. The university and the corporation have different vested interests—and it is imperative that the university exert the upper hand in defining the message, standards, and attributes of its academic programs. Academic leaders must be willing to assume a significant, persistent watchdog role when they outsource critical and visible mainstream components of their public presence. Unlike other vendor agreements, universities are ceding more than just narrow, marginal activities of campus life. Every marketing piece, every conversation with a prospective student, every interaction with current learners, and every facet of the academic experience reflects on the reputation of the school. An online degree program makes a bold statement in the academic marketplace. The stakes are high and require constant vigilance.

Quickly, many of our online degree programs were copied by others. With enrollments on the rise, we could be less involved in the operations of our partners. But when numbers began to ebb in a more-competitive marketplace, this became a wake-up call that BU had to be more engaged in marketing strategy. One frustration was that these service providers never moved much beyond North America. I hoped that our virtual community of adult learners would extend globally as well. Most of MET's tuition dollars come from employer tuition reimbursement, and until corporate tuition benefits become more universal, adult higher education will not be nearly as prevalent abroad. But the maturation of the market shattered the mystique of the online service providers and forced many of us to challenge their marketing savvy. They in turn pointed the finger back at us to further differentiate our programs through new courses, concentrations, and tracks. Through this tension and these growing pains both organizations were forced to look critically at themselves.

Occasionally I would hear the metaphor that these academic/business distance learning alliances were "marriages." They are, at best, open marriages. With so few companies in this business, these firms found that their ambitious financial model required nonexclusivity to pursue many schools with potentially overlapping programs. Their ability to rationalize program differences was matched by our paranoia that we were losing students to other universities supported by the same company. Despite the claims of internal firewalls, faculty simply could not believe that two similar degree programs could be marketed ethically by the same for-profit.

Some naively assumed these corporate partnerships would be easy to reevaluate and even exit, but the reality is that there would be a long teach-out tail to any nonrenewed contract. It takes several years to see those in the pipeline through to graduation. The financial risks of enrollment decline during any transition could be devastating. As a result, these online program alliances have an innate inertia—which, in retrospect, made these potentially long-term, perpetual decisions even more consequential.

Another facet of entrenchment was the need for ongoing faculty commitment to distance learning. Early on, online teaching fatigue began to set in. We had grossly underestimated the time required to build quality online courses and revise them before each iteration. We realized that scalability was somewhat of a myth: there were diminishing returns the larger courses became. Students did not respond as favorably in course evaluations when class size was too high and the head of the course too remote. But building in enrollment caps meant offering even more courses. To alleviate faculty strain, we invested far more in instructional support. Our innocence had foisted us onto a path we had barely understood.

In the first era of nationwide, fully online distance learning, companies like Embanet, Compass, Deltak, and 2Tor (now 2U) were almost undetectable catalysts in enabling college deans to take the leap into e-learning. Their "white label" concealed their identity from the public, but not their impact on campus. In this pre-strategic period, deans could not anticipate the roller coaster ride they had launched.

The End of the Beginning

For-profits have found several vacuums to fill within the academic landscape. In the first decade of the twenty-first century, for-profits were most visible and controversial in the dramatic surge of proprietary universities. These for-profit schools rose from a negligible presence to having more than 10 percent of the market share of the nation's students in less than ten years. They were fueled by the power and reach of the Internet, a willingness to exploit federal aid for those who succumbed to predatory recruiting tactics, and the neglect of traditional nonprofit universities to accommodate the rising student demand for accessible higher education.

When massive open online courses (MOOCs) burst upon the scene, the perception of online education flipped dramatically in the often superficial perceptions of the popular press, university boards of trustees, and even senior university leadership. Prognosticators now claimed they could foretell a future in which online technology would resolve all that ails higher education. Online education went from its former rogue status to being fashionably mainstream, from subterranean to strategic. Ivies-come-lately now dabbled in noncredit online courses and partnerships with even newer third-party start-ups, and overshadowed decades of unsung heroes who had built substantial online learning opportunities for their students, especially at community colleges and comprehensive public institutions, without the resources and visibility now common.

Ironically, the now-mature market for true distance learning degree programs—always a small subset of total online course enrollments—has flattened out in recent years and become more competitive and less hospitable to newcomers. A glut of similar online degrees has emerged, with participation from universities much higher in national rankings. The differentiation of programs, the prestige of the institution, and the quality of the online experience itself have become critical to success in distance learning.

University leaders have been hearing the message from their boards and peers that they need to stake a position in this brave new world, which for many of us did not seem terribly new and required far less bravery. The for-profit online service providers began shifting their conversations from deans to provosts and presidents, from their focus on individual degree programs to enterprise-wide roles.

The university has a long history of engagement with for-profit publishers whose clients were individual faculty. Now as the industry evolves and combines curated content (such as textbooks) with professional services (such as those offered by Deltak and Embanet), its relationship has shifted from faculty members adopting texts to senior university leaders launching distance learning programs, and the focus has shifted from individual courses to major cross-institutional efforts. Ideally, deans of professional and continuing education will continue to insinuate themselves into these alliances on their campuses as they propel their institutions forward.

We are now in a phase of more self-conscious, cautious evolution than the revolution touted frequently in the rhetoric. Universities are scrambling to formulate some internal structure that will facilitate the integration of digital technology. Those with a longer history in online education tend to have stand-alone, all-purpose units dedicated to producing and delivering instruction through the web. Those with less experience are tapping existing units to share their resources or well-regarded faculty to head this virtual effort before putting an infrastructure in place.

The range of functions and facets of online management span advocacy on campus, entrepreneurial initiative, oversight of student services, faculty support, and the technologies needed to deliver quality instruction. Deans of professional and continuing education, some of whom might have had opportunities like mine at Boston University to share their efforts across colleges, are now in an even stronger position to play a more strategic and visible role within their universities.

This is a critical inflection moment in the professional position and stature of continuing education deans. Will they respond successfully to the leadership vacuum created by online education? Or will they revert back to their previous, more comfortable marginality on campus? As an explicit professional role for online management emerges on America's campuses, continuing educators can either rise further or fall in stature. The UPCEA is itself at a similar inflection point—and can capture a key place nationally as a leading professional association in online education.

In retrospect, I have come to appreciate the instrumental role third parties play in provoking change. The first decade of this century drove many of us out of our complacency and into a more dynamic and less familiar realm. While for-profits and nonprofits might have some inherently incompatible features, these are neither universal nor unmanageable. With different goals and structures, they can share in projects like distance learning and make the otherwise impossible occur.

Are outside for-profits necessary in academe? I would suggest the answer, at least from my vantage point and experience, might very likely be yes. Universities rarely have the will or wherewithal to be innovative without some infusion of outside assistance. Increasingly, start-up companies address specific internal and external needs of the academic community—from international student recruiting to the integration of digital technology. There are at least one hundred start-ups and consultancies, as well as major players, just in the Boston area dedicated to finding niches in student recruiting, fund-raising and alumni relations, and educational technology and services to address critical challenges we all face—with creativity, agility, and risk capital not often found in academe. The question for the future will not be whether or not to work with for-profits, but when to do so and how best to manage those relationships.

That memorable 2001 conference call with one such start-up set Metropolitan College on an exciting path, changed my professional fate, and allowed what had been the university's night school to blossom into its entrepreneurial hub.

Notes

1. This fateful discussion was convened by then Boston University associate provost John Ebersole, who served as UPCEA's president in 2002–2003 and now presides over Excelsior College. Along with Metropolitan College, I also acquired those units that previously reported directly to John when he departed in 2006, including the Office of Distance Education, which supports all of BU's online certificate and degree programs.
2. Metropolitan College is one of sixteen degree-granting entities at Boston University and functions as a multidisciplinary university within a university. MET possesses its own degrees and full- and part-time faculty but also collaborates with BU's other schools and colleges.
3. Embanet went through four ownership changes in our first decade working together—including a merger with Compass (once its rival) and a recent acquisition by Pearson Education. Boston University also worked briefly with Datamark and more recently with Deltak (also acquired by a major publisher, John Wiley and Sons), along with several other companies, particularly MindMax, which supports MET's online noncredit certificate programs.

Online Continuing and Professional Education

Current Varieties and Best Practices

■■

Ray Schroeder and Vickie Cook

How Did We Get Here

Several elite public and private universities, including the Pennsylvania State University, the University of Chicago, and the University of Wisconsin, introduced distance education in the form of correspondence courses, or "home study," in the United States in 1892 (Chaloux and Miller 2014). This innovation was followed, over the next one hundred and twenty years, by an evolving array of mediated modes for the delivery of continuing education content. Each delivery system exploited a new technology or imaginatively adapted an existing technology. The lineage of distance education systems, or technologies, includes newspapers, radio, audio and video recordings, instructional television fixed service (ITFS), statewide audio networks, compressed video systems, cable television, satellite delivery, and computer technology. The ultimate utility of each mode reflects an assessment of cost effectiveness, adaptability to course content, ease of interactivity, propinquity of students to each other and to the instructor, and learning effectiveness.

In the immediate past we have observed a heightened engagement with distance education at institutions of higher education, a consequence of the ubiquity of and incredible capacities associated with computer technology, with the associated promise of improved learning. And,

Ray Schroeder is Associate Vice Chancellor for Online Learning, University of Illinois, Springfield, and UPCEA Director of the Center for Online Leadership and Strategy. **Vickie Cook** is Director of the Center for Online Learning, Research and Service, and Research Associate Professor, University of Illinois, Springfield.

importantly, the revenue potential imagined from the perceived cost effectiveness of media-supported instruction. In each of the periods of mediated course or program development spanning the last century and a quarter, continuing and professional education at America's colleges and universities has been a key player, if not the leader, in the application of technology to educational provision.

Penn State and the University of Wisconsin, along with the University of Illinois, helped lead the way in using the Internet to deliver professional and continuing education to distant learners. With the support of the Alfred P. Sloan Foundation, initiatives were seeded across the country through the Anytime, Anyplace Learning Program (McGuire 2013). Many of these early initiatives had a focus on professional degree and certificate programs offered through the use of fully online delivery systems.

Where We Are Today

Economic pressures on institutions and students are driving higher education to become more responsive to effective and cost-efficient use of technologies in teaching and learning (Viacave, Fitzgerald, and Smith 2014). Online continuing and professional education in today's competitive environment in higher education requires the strength of partnership and collaboration among key constituents. It is vital that these partnerships between course developers and instructors share a strong understanding of the audience for whom the professional development is being designed. Creating quality online continuing and professional learning experiences takes time to plan and execute the creation of strong learning objects.

Professional development is available on a variety of different platforms. Those seeking professional development in a wide variety of fields need only do a quick Google search to find courses offered in an array of formats and instructional styles.

The Blended Classroom

By way of example, one such instructional style is the blended classroom. This classroom provides a combination of online and face-to-face instruction. The teacher who uses this form of instruction most effectively allows the content and the learning needs of the student to dictate which sections of the course work occur online and which components are provided face to face. The learning needs of the student may be met through flexible access to lectures and content that can be reviewed outside the classroom. Precious class time may be devoted to learning activities and practice problems to assist students with synthesizing and applying their learning. This approach is important for those time-pressed students who are working professionals and are capable of doing much of the reading and preparation for the class prior to the first class meeting. Adults enrolled in continuing and professional education typically hold a foundational knowledge of the content and, as such, are prepared for class discussions, simulation projects, or hands-on training to occur during the face-to-face component of the blended classroom.

The Flipped Classroom

The flipped classroom is a popular version of the blended classroom. In this instructional model, students listen to lectures, watch videos, and read content materials prior to coming to classroom meetings. By participating in the more passive activities of learning outside the classroom, students are allowed additional time for engagement and more active learning while in the physical classroom. The actual classroom time may be used to do assessment activities, labs, videos, audio lectures, and hands-on learning activities that indicate the student's competency or mastery of the content area. This model is especially good for learners who take a mature approach and personal responsibility for learning content. Blended learning or a flipped classroom approach exhibits more pros than cons for educators. The advantage of this approach is that the use of online learning allows students to engage content from an individualized approach. Then classroom time is spent in a community of learners that deepens the learning experience. The drawbacks of this approach are usually identified as being related to the lack of technology in a student's home setting. Low bandwidth or inadequate access to computing devices can create a situation where a learner may quickly fall behind the class (Hertz 2012).

Asynchronous, Synchronous, or Mode-Neutral Learning

Considerations and approaches to asynchronous and synchronous models have long been debated. If we look back, we discover that correspondence courses were completely asynchronous, that is, the instructor and student did not engage in real-time interaction. For example, in correspondence courses students may wait a week or more for responses to questions or assessments from the instructor. Online courses using asynchronous models are characterized by much shorter delays, measured in minutes and hours rather than days and weeks. Many of those who are enrolled in continuing and professional education appreciate this approach and enjoy the asynchronous models of online learning today. Those instructors who utilize Twitter feeds and other social media to extend learning outside of a physical classroom setting are engaging students through asynchronous connectivity (Rhode 2012).

However, there may also be a significant instructional rationale behind including a synchronous component to a continuing education course. When webcasting, online chat, and Skype are used for electronic office hours, live-discussion sessions can add value and spontaneity to interactive online learning. Synchronous models can be quite effective in assisting students with confusing or complicated assignments or skills that need an immediate answer. If skill set mastery is dependent upon immediate feedback, then a synchronous component may be the best option for the distance learner. Additionally, synchronous models may be used to build a sense of community within a course of study.

A new approach in continuing and professional education allows the instructor to be located at a distance to teach to co-located students. This type of grouping may take place formally or informally. Courses are held in a variety of locations through various distance technologies. One such example is the Minerva Project (www.minervaproject.com). The Minerva Project provides students with residency in major cities, where they live and learn together. Each term, the students move to another city to learn in a new environment while taking their next term of online classes (Rivard 2013).

Additionally, there are mode-neutral classes. Mode-neutral classes allow the learner to be in control of the space in which they learn. Mode-neutral classes combine face-to-face, online, and blended classrooms in such a way that the student can decide which mode of delivery works best for them at any time during the semester. This student-centered approach allows for the optimization of faculty time, while giving the student control over how they will engage with content, faculty, and fellow learners (Smith, Reed, and Jones 2008). For example, students may begin a class face to face and, at any point in the term, choose to move to the online or blended delivery section of the course.

Prior Learning and Competency-Based Learning

Many universities have offered prior learning credit for decades. More recently, these prior learning programs are offered in an online mode to students at a distance. Professional and continuing education students commonly have competencies developed through work, military, and volunteer experience. This often involves a faculty assessment of a portfolio of activities that previously took place. Universities offer a limited amount of academic credit for the demonstration of competencies acquired.

Western Governors University was chartered in 1996 to begin offering a competency-based learning approach to awarding credit for degree completion. This collaboration among nineteen governors of western states was one of the first competency-based, large-scale initiatives (Western Governor's University 2014). This approach has come to be included in an increasing number of online programs. The US Department of Education announced in 2013 that it would approve the offering of financial assistance to students in competency-based programs—notably the large and growing program at Southern New Hampshire University (Fain 2013). The benefits of competency-based education are that it can decrease the time in which a student completes a degree and decrease the cost of the degree. The challenges include motivating students to stay on task to complete each set of competency-related assessments.

Teaching Consideration

At its core, as Larry Ragan stated, "good teaching is good teaching" (Ragan 1999, par. 4). Ragan provided context for this statement in his article regarding teaching at a distance. Some instructors excel in a face-to-face environment, while others are superstars in an online environment. Good teaching strategies are necessary to provide the roadmap to success for participants in the continuing and professional education arena. Participants learn best through varied media. One may learn best through listening; others do better watching video or reading graphs or tables. Some need kinesthetic involvement, which must be built into the online class through activities that will encourage hands-on learning to occur. Some learners need social engagement outside of the online course, which requires assessments to include interviews or observations of groups related to the field.

Connecting course work to a level of thinking skills is important. Using Bloom's taxonomy (Bloom 1969) or a newer derivative such as the "Online Tools and Taxonomy Resource" (University of Central Florida Center for Distributed Learning 2014), consideration must be given to providing foundational thinking, allowing for review and reflection of the material, and substantive evaluation or analysis of the content to be reflected through assessment or project work. Extending learning by providing for a professional community to develop after the class officially ends is one way to add value to the continuing and professional education needs for working adults. This can be done through blogs, professional learning communities, and collaboration with a variety of web tools. These learning opportunities eventually may be built into personal learning networks that can be used for professional development throughout a career.

Teaching online requires a team, not just an individual. While face-to-face teaching may be a singular effort, online teaching includes a multitude of technical, pedagogical, environmental, and associated considerations that requires a team of experts. The team determines who the learner is and what characteristics are needed to ensure the material addresses immediate and relevant needs for the learner seeking continuing and professional education. Some fields are more likely to use specific types of technologies than others. Providing a level of comfort or stability in course offerings is important when assessing the needs of the learners. Identification of specific teaching strategies are needed to best engage the learner with the content material.

Those who follow best practices in online teaching and learning do not simply add documents that they have used in face-to-face presentations to an online classroom. The team of experts analyzes and recommends the best way to present concepts to help students fully understand the theory and application related to their content area. This can be done with a variety of tools, including video, audio, PowerPoint presentations, music, lectures, podcasts, calendars, work schedules, handwritten comments, web pages, quizzes, tests, and a variety of web-based tools. Quality assurance is an active and ongoing process in online learning.

Course Quality

There are several tools that the team of experts can use to determine overall course quality in online learning. Quality Matters (www.qualitymatters.org) is a recognized leader in providing a peer-reviewed approach to assessing the content and design of online learning courses. Quality Matters takes a continuous improvement approach by engaging instructors in the review of online courses, providing professional development to assure consistency in the review process, and maintaining a recognized standard of quality in the field of online learning.

In order to connect effectively with the continuing and professional education participant, it is necessary that the instructional design team understand what connections must be made as they design and assess the effectiveness of the continuing and professional education course. This connectivity to the participants is key for the design team to consider during the development and teaching of the course. Working professionals who want to learn new skills expect high-quality courses and strong networking opportunities. Garrison, Anderson, and Archer (2000) viewed online learning as a process. Their work on creating a "community of inquiry" within the online course provides a strong framework for building teaching and learning.

Continuing and professional education courses that use the community of inquiry approach deliberately seek to engage the participants with content, the participants with each other, and the participants with the instructor. As this community of learning is built, the learner becomes skilled in the content area through a social-constructivist approach to learning. The learner connects with the content, the other students, and the instructor to build skill level and expertise.

By merit of having classes delivered in a digital, online format, this kind of learning offers a rich array of data that cannot be collected in the face-to-face environment. Students in the online classroom can be monitored every minute and by every action taken. The detailed data of how much, how long, how well, how many times, and so on, is available for analysis, interpretation, and action. This data can be used to improve the class as well as provide effective interventions for struggling students. It is this data-centric approach upon which the future of online learning will be built.

The Future of Online Continuing Higher Education

Corporate engagement in education has flourished in some ways and declined in others. At its peak two years ago, the for-profit universities were flourishing, funded by high tuition paid by federal financial aid. But more recently federal and state regulators have joined accrediting bodies in holding for-profit universities accountable for the relatively low success rates of their students and graduates. At the time of this writing, for-profit universities are sustaining substantial losses in profitability, and some are even moving to become private nonprofit universities (Fain 2014).

In the complex context of higher education in 2015, there are some interesting experiments that may point to the future of professional and continuing studies in higher education. In the past few years, massive online classes have emerged to reach hundreds of thousands of students at a time. Universities have begun "giving away" their product in massive open online classes (MOOCs). Many of these are produced within the schools of professional and continuing studies. Now more than a thousand MOOCs have been produced by some of the largest and most successful universities in the United States. They have reached huge audiences of students, mostly located outside of the country. The completion rates have been low, but the public relations impact has been high. A more recent development is the advent of learning hubs to support students taking MOOCs. The US State Department has built hubs around the world to sustain distant students on other continents, and Coursera has begun an initiative to install learning hubs in libraries and other sites around the country. In effect, these hubs turn MOOCs into blended learning experiences with both online and face-to-face support components. Through the MOOC experience, universities continue to conduct learning research that has resulted in the development of tools and techniques that will impact our field broadly in the future. As MOOCs evolve, we will see even more efficient models of teaching emerge.

Notably, we look to the experiment by Georgia Tech, Udacity, and AT&T to offer an online masters in computer science using MOOC designs (www.omscs.gatech.edu). This initiative, begun in early 2014, offers the degree, which carries a price tag of $42,000, for less than $7,000, a reduction made possible by economies of scale and subsidies from industry. As this program rolls out, the goal is to serve up to 10,000 students in a limited-entry program that will be self-sustaining over time. If the massive open online approaches of Coursera, EdX, Udacity, and others succeed, we will surely see this model replicated for other online graduate degrees—often offered through schools of professional studies—at other universities.

Udacity continues to press the envelope in professional studies. The most recent effort, being closely followed, is the self-paced "nanodegree" (www.udacity.com/nanodegrees). Once again in collaboration with AT&T, Udacity is rolling out a series of professional development courses. Using a unique pricing model of $200/month for as long as it takes the student to complete the sequence (anywhere from three to twelve months), the nanodegree promises that the student will have the skills and knowledge for an entry-level position in the industry. Selecting areas of high demand for and low supply of qualified prospects, this approach to professional development is industry driven. If it succeeds, we will surely see university professional and continuing studies programs adopting the model of self-paced, adaptive learning offered on a pay-as-you-use basis.

It is clear that consumers are seeking value in higher education in terms of jobs and careers. Traditional universities have lost their monopoly on education; competition has arrived in the form of MOOCs and corporate-led learning. Yet, in the midst of these challenges for higher education, there exists within our universities the bright prospect for change and a shift in focus. These changes are already in place in the departments, schools, and colleges of professional and continuing studies. They are at the core of our commitment to serving the adult learner with quality, relevant, just-in-time learning.

The University Professional and Continuing Education Association is leading the effort to ensure quality and flexibility in online professional education. As this centennial report is released, UPCEA is developing Hallmarks of Excellence, drawing upon our collective expertise and vision to prepare a roadmap for the design and implementation of excellence in schools, colleges and departments of continuing and professional education. Dr. Jay Halfond, senior fellow for the Center for Online Leadership and Strategy, is coordinating the efforts of leaders across the field to further develop standards for excellence in the field of online learning. This blueprint will guide us into the next century of leadership in our field.

The values that have led our efforts are the same that are driving change across all of higher education. Those of us in professional and continuing studies are prepared to lead our institutions through the disruption that awaits us.

References

Bloom, B. S. 1969. *Taxonomy of Educational Objectives: The Classification of Educational Goals. Handbook I: Cognitive Domain.* New York: McKay.

Chaloux, B., and G. Miller. 2014. "E-Learning and the Transformation of Higher Education." *Leading the E-learning Transformation of Higher Education* (pp. 258). Sterling, VA: Stylus.

Fain, P. 2013. "Beyond the Credit Hour." *Inside Higher Ed.* Accessed at http://www.insidehighered.com/news/2013/03/19feds-give-nudge-competency-based-education - sthash.g6LMqIgw.dpbs.

Fain, P. 2014. "Dropping Profit." *Inside Higher Ed.* Accessed at http://www.insidehighered.com/news/2014/07/17/few-profits-have-become-non profits-despite-regulatory-environment.

Garrison, D. R., T. Anderson, and W. Archer. 2000. "Critical Inquiry in a Text-Based Enviornment: Computer Conferencing in Higher Education." *The Internet and Higher Education,* 2, nos. 2–3: 87–105.

Hertz, M. B. 2012. "The Flipped Classroom: Pro and Con." Accessed at http://www.edutopia.org/blog/flipped-classroom-pro-and-con-mary-beth-hertz.

McGuire, R. 2013. "Sloan's Frank Mayadas on the Early History of Online Ed." Accessed at http://www.skilledup.com/blog/sloan-frank-mayadas-early-history-of-online-ed/.

Ragan, L. C. 1999. "Good Teaching Is Good Teaching: An Emerging Set of Guiding Principles and Practices for the Design and Development of Distance Education." *Cause/Effect* 22(1).

Rhode, J. 2012. "Best Practices Teaching with Twitter." Accessed at http://www.jasonrhode.com/twitterinedu.

Rivard, R. 2013. "The Minerva Moment?" *Inside Higher Ed.* Accessed at http://www.insidehighered.com/news/2013/04/05/minerva-project-plans-different-kind-online-education-sthash.j7broCb1.dpbs.

Smith, B., P. Reed, and C. Jones. 2008. "'Mode Neutral' Pedagogy." *European Journal of Open, Distance and E-Learning.* Accessed at http://www.eurodl.org/materials/contrib/2008/Smith_Reed_Jones.htm.

University of Central Florida Center for Distributed Learning. 2014. "Online Tools and Taxonomy Resource (OTTR)." Accessed at http://teach.ucf.edu/pedagogy/ottr/.

Viacave, D. F., S. Fitzgerald, and K. M. Smith. 2014. "Growing Pressure Evident in Fiscal 2013 Public University Medians." Moody's Investors Service.

Accessed   at   http://saportareport.com/wp-content/uploads/2014/10
/Public-University-Medians-FY-2013.pdf.
Western Governors University. 2014. "The WGU Story." Accessed at
http://www.wgu.edu/about_WGU/WGU_story.

Traditional College Education Meets the Twenty-First Century

██

Karen Sibley

Continuing education units, professional schools, and summer session divisions have been centers for the development of online initiatives that serve nonresidential students, experiment with new technologies, and support pedagogical innovation. On campuses where there is currently significant online content being developed and delivered, initial stages of this activity can often be traced back to the continuing education area or to professional schools providing courses for working adults. Continuing education and summer session leaders at many liberal arts institutions with strong focus on traditional age undergraduate students have watched their peers at land-grant and large private institutions develop quality online educational offerings for the past ten or more years. Participation in professional associations active in the assessment and improvement of online education, most notably the University Professional and Continuing Education Association (UPCEA) for this group of higher education professionals as well as Sloan Consortium and Educause, brought knowledge of current best practices and successful projects at peer schools. During the past decade these academic leaders, even at institutions with little drive toward online activities, have been able to build small initiatives, pilot projects that enabled faculty to test new teaching models and developed organizational capacity to support additional projects as the online evolution continues.

At liberal arts colleges and universities where highly regarded residential undergraduate education is considered a sacrosanct core of activity very little engagement with online education had occurred until just within the past two years. For these four-year degree programs comprised

Karen Sibley is Dean, Brown University School of Professional Studies, and past president of the UPCEA, 2013–2014.

of relatively small numbers of students living in a campus environment and taking courses from highly ranked faculty, online education has been viewed as something of an oxymoron. Why, then, has there been something of a rush to action and eager attention paid to online efforts at these places of late?

Commentary on this topic in this article is based on research interviews with campus leaders at five highly ranked liberal arts institutions: Brown University, Tufts University, Yale University, Washington University in St. Louis, and Wesleyan University. Interviews with senior institutional officers and others directly responsible for online activities at these institutions provided insights about what activities are being undertaken and the motivations, hoped-for outcomes, and lessons learned from just a few years of engagement.

Since the early years of the century, significant strides in online education and growing acceptance of this mode of instruction have occurred. Excellent pedagogic quality and even enhanced teaching tactics for subject mastery and learning outcomes have been demonstrated at schools like Carnegie Mellon, Massachusetts Institute of Technology, and Stanford, as well as in many professional schools at excellent institutions across the country and the world. Still, fear and doubt have persisted at many top-tier institutions and made them reluctant to engage in this mode of instruction. Evidence of the rejection of online quality is demonstrated in policies that refuse credit transfer for online courses in undergraduate degree programs and block the creation of courses taught online for matriculated undergraduates. Often the number of online courses a student is permitted to count toward degree completion are capped, preserving the essentially residential nature of the undergraduate experience.

Adoption of online instruction at top-tier undergraduate institutions, priding themselves on the quality of their four-year, primarily residential experience, has lagged far behind the development of this form of course delivery at the major public institutions in the United States. While flexible access to courses without the need to be on campus at a specific time has become a key component of many undergraduate degree programs across the country and is especially popular in programs for midcareer professionals, the traditional plan of four years in residence with classes scheduled MWF and TuTh, interspersed with student activities, athletics, and campus social life has remained the model of education for Ivy League and other highly regarded colleges and universities.

This status quo is experiencing gradual impact from the broadening acceptance of online instruction, with a sudden burst of urgency brought about by the MOOC mania of 2012–2013. A belief in the value of campus-based instruction has a firm hold on these institutions still, as likely it should given the high numbers of undergraduate applications schools in this tier of higher education enjoy. But talk of "disruption" of the sort

Clayton Christensen points to in industries turned inside out by the impact of technology and innovation has begun to resonate in higher education circles. Add to this an ever increasing concern about the cost of education, political pressure on cost, quality, and financial aid, and the continuing impact of the 2008 financial crisis and we see higher education being driven toward innovation and less complacent about the longtime model of campus functionality.

Prior to the current moment, the view toward online engagement at residential institutions seemed to consist of sentiments like "we don't need to engage with online," "that's not what this campus does," and "residential education and online study is incompatible"; even for students engaged in study abroad or internships the sense was that they should be "fully immersed in the experience and not taking a campus course online at the same time." Only a few years ago senior academic leaders did not hesitate to say "we will never offer online courses for credit."

Research and reports from experiments in the use of technology in teaching and learning at Carnegie Mellon, Stanford, MIT, and other respected institutions over the past decade have brought new respect and attention to this sort of instruction and prompted some faculty on liberal arts campuses to experiment in their own classes. The installation of learning management systems (LMSs) on most campuses to aid in delivery of course content, instructor-student communication, calendaring, assignment submission, grading, and other course activities has sparked faculty interest and the development of a new level of facility with technology across faculty ranks. It is now typical for central information technology units to offer faculty support in adoption and use of technology and in the application of "best practice" technologies to achieve individual faculty teaching goals. In addition, many campuses have opened offices or centers aimed at cultivating good pedagogy and assisting faculty in course design and instructional planning. All of these now common features of most campuses have served to make the use of technology more comfortable and accessible for faculty.

Some would say that many, if not most, faculty teach "online" now; they just don't know it. Faculty using the campus LMS and other interesting technology tools to facilitate new ways of teaching their students in campus classrooms could be described as engaging in blended online instruction. Recent attention to experiments in flipped classrooms, online courses individual faculty members simply offer on their own, and bold new degree programs like the masters in computer science at Georgia Tech, as well as experiments taking place in high schools, have prompted discussion and inspired more individual attempts at course redesign on many campuses.

At the end of the first decade of the twenty-first century, it was really the impact of 2tor (now 2U) at the University of Southern California and Udacity and Coursera, both out of Stanford, that focused attention across the country on the potential for online education to significantly alter the traditional mode of face-to-face instruction. Media coverage was huge. Faculty teaching MOOCs were describing excitement about teaching courses with worldwide reach and amazing enrollments, some well into six digits. Suddenly alumni were looking at Coursera to see if their alma mater had courses posted. Alums and board members were asking campus leaders about this new development. Whether an individual campus chose to produce any MOOCs, to partner with an online design and support enterprise, or to hold back to see what these efforts produced elsewhere, all needed to spend time in strategy and consideration of the potential impact to their campus and the traditional residential model of instruction.

Reflections from campus administrators indicated a period of activity in developing online content that was not driven by careful strategy but was rather more reactive and experimental. While small trial efforts had been happening on a few campuses, such as some fully online summer term courses, noncredit courses for precollege students, or streaming video of campus courses for alums, high-level comprehensive plans for action had not been developed prior to 2012. Emerging interest in teaching with technology and delivering content fully online was a topic of discussion but not an urgent action item. Fast action from top-tier schools across the country joining Coursera in 2012–2013 and creating courses for massive enrollment, media buzz about this and other broad impact online projects, questions from key institutional stakeholders, and often urging from trustees all combined in the same brief period to force leadership action. The result was a series of experiments that have produced valuable understanding and continue to cause interest, discussion, and more structured planning. In some cases new leadership positions (vice president, associate provost, etc.) have been developed. New offices with titles like "pedagogical innovation" or "laboratory for educational innovation" have been created, and committees comprised of faculty and administrators charged with keeping abreast of developments in online instruction and recommending initiatives for their campus have been launched.

On many campuses, and indeed on each of the five I looked at for this piece, the unit responsible for continuing education or summer session became the lab for early efforts. In addition to offering courses for campus undergraduates in summer session or special certificate programs, these units serve populations of students who are not matriculated (for example precollege, local adults, or visiting undergraduates) or students in graduate programs while still maintaining employment (like teachers who need continuing graduate credits or enroll in masters programs in their disciplines or other employed professionals). These campus divisions could engage in experiments outside the policy-constrained core and had small programs where a few courses could be developed as trials. They often had been engaged in early efforts inspired by their peers at other institutions and so had staff with skills necessary to support such projects and the infrastructure required to build, market, and enroll for new programs. Conducting experiments in such a unit would not distract other campus areas from supporting traditional programs. Directing flexible trial programs is a common experience for continuing studies and summer session offices. A safe lab for experimentation existed.

Some might say that in 2014 we recovered from MOOC mania. No longer is the emergence of Udacity, Coursera, and 2U a call for alert and concern among academic leaders. But the call to action these entities and their bold initiatives created persists, and more serious considerations of the application of modern technology in teaching and learning has joined other key strategic topics for senior administrators. Lessons learned from both observation and early activities have demonstrated that experimentation is important and that building capacity for action is essential. In some cases, such capacity has been distributed in multiple areas, including information technology, teaching and learning centers, summer programs, and continuing education. In other cases it was developed on the fly in order to capture content for web streaming or to develop MOOCs. New recognition of essential requirements, including instructional design support, videography and editing skills, and administrative services for online initiatives, has emerged from early trial efforts. While such capacity might be best lodged in different campus areas, for example, professional schools often have their own staff for such work, there is recognition that collaboration and a ready talent pool is necessary for continued experimentation and to avoid the extremely costly effort of attempting to ramp up capacity on short notice. In some cases, the effort of building new projects on short timelines, maintaining quality standards and facing high risk due to massive exposure, created strain and opportunity cost of unanticipated proportions. Lacking some degree of readiness leaves an institution far behind and facing a steep challenge when new developments worthy of emulation surface.

A consistently noted outcome of this period of small experimental efforts is renewed interest in and even excitement about teaching on the part of faculty. Respondents interviewed for this article regularly described individual faculty who had agreed to teach in new online formats and came away from the experience extremely pleased with what they had achieved in student development and what they learned about their own teaching. Comments included the value of teaching in the massive open format of the MOOC, which was both daunting and exciting on the basis of sheer numbers but also brought an amazing array of new and differently informed perspectives to the class. Faculty identified broader learning for all of the students and new ideas and angles on material and teaching tactics they themselves discovered. Faculty teaching seminar courses online or producing short instructional segments identified new understanding of lecture segments (high impact of short and intensive lectures with activity-based learning between lecture segments), group work, and highly engaged discussion activities that can occur online. Participation from all students and improved quality of engagement, especially in asynchronous courses, which allow time for reflection, was also a valued outcome of online teaching. Student engagement and regular attendance was found to be equal to, and in some cases to outperform, face-to-face classes. The refreshed excitement about teaching expressed by these faculty can ignite new discussions about teaching across a campus and raise expectations for this faculty responsibility. In particular, the voices of faculty seen as "not particularly techie" or from humanities and other disciplines viewed as less engaged with technology carry significant influence in the faculty conversation about technology in teaching, online instructional potential, and quality learning outcomes.

Instructional design support offered by experts in continuing education divisions and at professional schools on campus is named as key to these efforts. Faculty consistently identify and value the quality of this support and the high value of engaging conversations with people who care about teaching, are interested in the content and goals for the course, and have great expertise with technology. They describe this experience as rare in their professional experience, very exhilarating and valuable to both online and face-to-face pedagogy.

Another value particular to the MOOC model is the potential to gain far broader insights on content and projects from a worldwide, multigenerational, widely experienced student population. Courses offered to students on a single campus who share common experience (even if they are from diverse backgrounds), who are typically eighteen to twenty-two years old and thus have limited world experience, can result in rather standard and perhaps less innovative learning outcomes compared with courses that include more experienced learners who don't share the common campus experience. This, of course, is commonly understood in continuing education courses and programs where students have always brought a wide diversity of life experience to the classroom. Faculty teaching these students often comment on the excitement of having their ideas challenged by older students with varied academic and professional experience and the value of this both in the classroom (residential or online) and in continuous improvement of the course and faculty pedagogy. If online courses and the potential of engaging in both campus-based and MOOC instruction in combination can bring this experience to the residential classroom, great strides in student learning and more complex global understanding may be achieved.

While such revelations from faculty who gained experience in online teaching are consistent and passionate, administrators on all campuses still recognize a prevalent distrust of online education among faculty. They identify early adopters and willing converts as still small in numbers. More broadly, faculty advocate for the familiar and traditional classroom instruction, enhanced with technology tools, but demonstrate less interest in fully online teaching. In fact, the 2U consortium effort in which Washington University participated was disbanded after the faculty at Duke and then at Washington University voted against the project.

Perhaps the lack of a student audience in need of online instruction at schools with an unwavering pipeline of residential students diminishes faculty motivation to explore online teaching. Students (and their parents) select residential colleges for the traditional undergraduate experience they offer. Students may indicate that they don't want online offerings, though to some degree they cannot know this since they base their preferences on their current experience. Our undergraduates (and alumni) can be more passionate about maintaining the status quo of their experience than anyone else in higher education. But as secondary school experiences change, and if new opportunities to enhance college education and career prospects through experiential learning opportunities away from the campus setting or other ideas for innovation emerge, perhaps future cohorts of students will find value in the flexibility of online course opportunities.

In some cases, distrust of online initiatives also stems from a fear of homogenization of teaching across the country, imagined as massive introductory classes taught by "star faculty" from a few campuses while multitudes at other campuses enroll online. If such a model were ever developed, it threatens to shrink the demand for faculty and even reduce the number of academic departments any one campus would need to support. On the other hand, such a development could ensure consistency of basic disciplinary understanding delivered through courses with broad quality approval, enabling faculty to spend more time teaching at higher levels within their discipline rather than in the often disliked service courses. In any case, without faculty buy-in new initiatives in teaching will not take hold.

In addition to the positive impact of these activities in provoking renewed focus on teaching, it is believed that online efforts serve to promote the institution. Well-designed and well-executed MOOCs highlight the quality of the faculty and teaching at institutions that are already highly regarded within their regions, nationally, and by their peers but may be less well known farther afield. Many also identify the potential to involve alumni continuously in more academically engaged ways, further expanding institutional reputation, reach, and the potential for engagement with activities beyond the campus. In particular, the Coursera platform enabled smaller schools with limited marketing budgets to attract attention and build their reputation for particular strengths with a far distant audience.

Administrators also named an expectation that following generations of students will bring ever-improving technological skills and the expectation that modern technologies will be used in their learning experiences. While the use of online education has not been widely embraced at the secondary school level, many expect that this evolution will occur. Secondary schools have already begun to employ flipped classroom models and the use of LMSs for student-faculty and student-student communication on assignments and projects. Research information and learning support is commonly sought out on the Internet and from platforms like Khan Academy, HippoCampus (chemistry), Saylor Academy, YouTube, and other online resources. Communications, writing, graphic display, and project tools continue to evolve and gain broad popular use in education, work, and life in general. Expectations of working with such technology tools are becoming the norm across education, as they have become common across the industries that will employ our graduates. Given this certain evolution, higher education must stay current and advance experimentation in technology-enhanced teaching and in preparing our students, of all ages, for the highest levels of performance as they complete degrees and other specifically designed learning programs at our institutions.

In similar fashion, new generations of faculty will find the use of technology in their academic professions to be a given. In fact, an additional demand felt in higher education is to support the development of digital literacy, technology facility, and the most current teaching skills for our graduate students who aim for academic careers.

It is early still to understand the potential for online education and the impact this change in the education landscape may eventually have on the traditional residential model of education for students going directly from high school to college and seeking top-ranked liberal arts degrees. It may be that changes in this particular sector will continue at comparatively slow evolution, though it is highly likely that teaching with the most current practices and flexibility in degree programs, providing opportunities for a variety of learning environments, will continue to pressure, influence, and produce innovation in this segment of higher education.

No longer are senior academic leaders comfortable predicting a steady state and rejecting online developments as passing fads. Experienced educators on our campuses note more change in the past three years than in the decades prior to 2010. Having experienced a rush of challenge and call to action, it seems more openness to change has taken hold and more strategic attention is being paid to the value and potential of online projects.

Although the core campus may experiment slowly and evolve only when provoked by necessity, it appears that the continuing education units on these campuses will remain in the lead in online initiatives and experimentation. The value of these units has grown as their capacities have been ready when needed, their "lab environment" easily deployed to experimentation, and new student populations and revenues developed.

Practical Leadership in
Online Team Environments
What Really Works

Craig Wilson

As more higher education institutions seek to move educational programs to online environments, leadership of personnel and management of resources must adapt in ways that will bridge local and remote locations. Continuing education units are widely known for being very entrepreneurial thinkers with respect to relevant and forward-edged educational programming, delivery modalities, and tailoring education and training solutions to specific audiences, and opportunities loom for units that can capitalize on new, remote markets by leading and managing personnel from a distance. What's more, online leadership can reduce operating costs, while providing quality service to customers. While the concept is not new—it is used by airlines, technology companies, and others—its use in higher education is in the early stages. That stated, some leadership and management practices could be reexamined and adjusted to fit the online space. Leaders will need to develop virtual fluency in this new work mash-up that incorporates many of the tried and true leadership and management theories and translates them to an environment that seamlessly melds the physical space with the online space. This four-part essay is designed to serve as a primer for readers who lead online learning programs with team members geographically dispersed or who plan to lead one in the near future.

Craig Wilson is Associate Dean, Division of Continuing and International Education, Head of School for the University of Miami Global Academy, an online middle and high school, and a UPCEA committee chair.

Step One: Communication

As with all leadership endeavors, the critical first step in creating a high-performing team is establishing clear communication channels. The challenges of misunderstanding or misinterpretation are all too real. In traditional face-to-face settings we tend to rely on nonverbal and visual cues to support verbal communication as part of the information-sharing process. And in that setting, if miscommunication arises, it can be resolved in a relatively simple manner because leaders are able to set in-person follow-up meetings quickly and work through misunderstandings with the added benefit of eye contact and body language.

When leading an online team, it is good practice to assume there will be gaps between transmission and reception of information. This assumption is based on several factors, including varying geography, time zones, technology, and meeting preparedness of the team. Informal lines of communication should be reimagined because geographically dispersed team members don't benefit from the spontaneous synergies found in chance meetings at the water cooler or in the hallway. Further, depending on the distance at which team members are located from one another, even "sync-socializing" (e.g., synchronized duplex communication via telephone, FaceTime, Google Hangouts, Skype, etc.) to share the in-the-moment atmosphere surrounding national events like breaking news or sporting events would be a challenge without prior planning due to time zone differences.

Time zones, a seemingly minor detail, can be a point of friction in online team meetings. Here is why. A prescribed meeting time may be convenient to some team members and a struggle for others. Online team meetings tend be scheduled around the nexus of operations or where the leader is geographically positioned. This means all team members need to be aware of the time zone for which the meeting will be held, and this needs to be clearly communicated to all team members. (This may also be an opportunity to rotate meeting times and allow team members to help plan and/or lead an online team meeting.)

Technology plays a significant role in online meetings. It stitches together data and ideas from team members around the country and globe into a cohesive quilt of information. That stated, assume the inevitable—technology will fail! You can bet technologies used for online team meetings (e.g., the Internet, video conference software and equipment, virtual presentation software, etc.) will fail or be seriously degraded just before or during an important meeting with your online team. Once you have embraced this eventuality, planning alternate forms of communication becomes a bit simpler. Cut out the fluff and ask yourself what are the informational items that must be shared and what is the lowest technological approach to relaying that information?

Once this analysis is done, you may come to realize that a telephone and e-mailed presentations using backup commercial e-mail accounts like Gmail and Outlook.com will allow you to continue the meeting. As a matter of last resort, you may need to reschedule the meeting. If so, reach out to all team members as soon as possible and inform them of the new date and time.

Meeting preparedness is necessary to maximize information sharing and productivity outcomes for online teams. It encompasses setting a clear agenda, keeping meetings concise, and managing conflict.

· Having a clear agenda will help alleviate confusion. Set and reinforce ground rules about civility and collegiality in the online space.

How long is too long for an online meeting? Think about attention spans during face-to-face meetings. Now, imagine having to compete with what's going on locally at each team member's location. Next, sprinkle in some web surfing and an errant text message, and a picture of your meeting's competition for attention quickly crystallizes. Keeping meetings concise will increase team focus and sends the message that their time is valued.

This also means managing conflict via long distance. In an online space, as previously mentioned, there are multiple opportunities for misinterpretation of communication leading to degraded team interaction and, ultimately, productivity. Recognizing a team member's affect, reaction, and behavior during team communications (video or audio) helps inform the leader how engaged each person is with the meeting's content. The astute online team leader will have to quickly recognize conflict among team members and between team members and the leader. Once recognized, the leader will then need to address it right away. This will mean investing extra time in gathering facts surrounding the conflict, scheduling follow-up meetings (preferably via video) with the affected team member, and keeping a conflict resolution log to record friction points and strategies used to arrive at a solution(s). That log will help with future conflicts and may also serve as a baseline of accountability for corrective action.

Additionally, leaders should make a habit of recording audio and video of online meetings (a common software feature) and provide a way for team members to access the contents, remotely. This allows them the ability to double-check discussion that might have been unclear and provide a baseline of accountability for goal and task clarity.

Step Two: Autonomy (Measured and Managed)

Online team members need to function with degrees of autonomy. This means your online team should be comprised of members you can rely on to complete tasks and objectives, ultimately helping the team accomplish its goals. They are remotely located from home base for a variety of reasons—local talent is scarce, they are managing existing clients at a distant location, or new opportunities exist for your organization at a distant location and it's more cost effective to have someone work remotely to gauge feasibility—and your organization values the ability to leverage their knowledge and skill set with minimum overhead costs. Coming to terms with the reality that there is a large amount of autonomy organically afforded your remote team members due to geography may be a bit unnerving to an online leader. Acceptance of this autonomy is necessary for your team to function. To function well, however, autonomy needs to be measured.

Measured autonomy can be achieved in a variety of ways, including team member updates during and between meetings, contact with clients, and the use of cloud-based project management tools. The level of reporting and sophistication these tools employ is remarkable and provides the team leader with a real-time, bird's-eye view of all team projects to aid with understanding the full "battlefield," revealing where chokepoints may be hindering progress, and providing talking points for meeting agenda formation. Using customer relationship management (CRM) software to keep track of the customer contacts all of your team members have, whether by e-mail, web-based communications, or telephone/video notes from conversations, is also helpful. To go a step further, you can use a cloud-based dialing software package that stores telephone calls for later review of content and process improvement.

Leaders manage autonomy of online team members best when they are proactive and highly engaged with them. They must strive to ensure communication lines are open, information is flowing, and maximum support is provided to each member of the team. What happens when a team member shows signs of missed deadlines, time management challenges, or struggles with customer communication? Or when, through a series of measuring autonomic performances of a team member, a leader identifies concerns with a team member's performance at a remote location? That's when the other side of managed autonomy comes to light. One of the first things the leader should do is gather multiple streams of information to develop a fuller view of the situation. Matching data provided by the autonomic measuring devices with a team member's affect, reactions, and behavior in meetings as well as outside communication received from customers and/or vendors can quickly inform the leader. The leader should also schedule one-on-one meetings with the struggling team member to determine if there is something beyond the workplace that may be impacting performance. This combined quantitative and qualitative approach helps provide a fuller view of the situation for the leader to determine next steps.

If corrective action is deemed necessary, having a policy that details steps to help the team member get back on track is essential and would be utilized. If the team member cannot get back on track and needs to be replaced, several factors that could impact the rest of the team should be considered before replacing the team member. These factors include, but are not limited to, the following:

- Lost productivity while a replacement is sought

- Costs to recruit and train a new replacement

- Potential disruption to team chemistry

- Potential disruption to customers the replaced team member was responsible for serving

This does not mean the underperforming team member should not be replaced; it means that the totality of the replacement should be considered when making the change.

Step Three: Accountability

Teams need to know they can rely on each other to exhibit professionalism, complete tasks and assignments, and respect each other. Online teams must maintain these attributes despite distance from each other, and they must do so in inventive ways. These critically important areas of accountability are a must-have for an online team to be a high-performing team. In general, modeling these areas of accountability come from three sources: the organization's existing culture, supporting employee policies, and the online team leader.

Online leaders should consider establishing an online environmental standard for the team to use on and off webcams. For instance, inform your team to sanitize their viewing areas when on camera by being mindful of wall art and other displayed items that could be considered controversial or culturally offensive. Family members and pets should not be in view or to within earshot. Also, urge your online team get used to donning professional or business casual attire at all times, even when not on camera. The reasons are simple. First, being dressed up to work from home helps set the mind up for a day of productivity (sorry, no pajamas or fuzzy slippers!). And second, you never know when a client or someone from the corporate office might need an immediate video call with a team member.

Step Four: Connection (Online Team Building and Maintenance)

One of the under-spoken truths about online teams is the feeling of isolation. Autonomy, as previously mentioned, should be embraced and measured by online leaders. However, there is a point where autonomy should be balanced with interdependent activities that require online team members to interact with each other regularly. Whether they are called group projects or collaborative projects, these types of activities cause team members to communicate, combine efforts, and share resources and insights, and they enhance team cohesion and help with online team building. It is important to develop team cohesion early in the lifecycle of an online team because there is a tendency for members to develop individualized work habits that may not be team-oriented. And a team member's focus may be more on her or his local environment and less on the overall team. A savvy online leader will orient all online team members to the culture and expectations of the organization and balance that with the unique perspectives each team member brings to the team. Finally, rotating who convenes each meeting gives team members a chance to lead, share their unique perspectives based on location, and provide diversity of thought to the decision-making process.

Maintaining a healthy online team requires planning, sensitivity, and creativity. Providing a sense of connection beyond working hours can go a long way toward maintaining the online team's health and keeping engagement levels high. Showing concern for team members' work-life balance helps connect the leader to team members on a human level that transcends geographical distance. Remembering birthdays or other personal milestone events (e.g., completing a marathon, being recognized in the community for volunteer work, etc.) helps team members see and appreciate each other as the multidimensional beings we are.

One novel way would be to encourage team members to be involved in their communities and allow time for showcasing at a quarterly meeting. Another way would be to provide a link to their social media page (e.g., Facebook, Google+, etc.) where their contributions would be chronicled by multimedia wall postings. If you are looking for a low-tech approach to maintaining the health of your online team, try sending a periodic newsletter to the team that covers the hobbies and outside interests of team members. An online office party is also a fun way to help connect your team. Using video conferencing software as the communication link, try selecting a theme—"College Day," for example. Using this theme, all team members could wear t-shirts from the college they attended and stream their alma mater or fight song to see if there are any commonalities. Or, encourage each team member to dress in local customary attire and discuss the cultures they live in while streaming cultural music and socializing during the online office party.

The leader of an online team has a unique opportunity to connect team members, and soliciting input from the team on ways to improve team cohesion may prove to be the best approach.

Another Word on Technologies Deployed for Virtual Teams

The technologies typically used to lead and manage virtual teams are comprised of teleconference software, videoconference software (with screen sharing and remote whiteboard capabilities), project management software, and CRM software. Each play a significant role in communication and information distribution, and as software programs advance, some functionalities will overlap. However, a good rule of thumb is to rely on each program only for the primary purpose for which they were designed.

Technologies like those listed require advance planning to set up usernames and passwords for each team member. Additionally, although each software service has extensive tutorials, it is considered good practice to have team-centric and mission-focused training of all technologies used for team operations. Consider conducting several dry runs to ensure proficiency with these software tools. The added benefit of having a dry run is the opportunity for it to aid the online team bonding process.

Foundation: Trust

Trust is essential to leading an online team. Its importance cannot be overstated and is the foundation for any successful organization or team. Without trust, no number of steps will provide a pathway to success for a team. That stated, trust becomes even more important in online teams. Trust must permeate the entire team, in full duplex, from the organization's home base to the online leader, from the online leader to the online team, and between online team members.

As in any relationship, personal or professional, trust is organic and builds over time. Trust can start with simple things like following through on tasks, keeping deadline commitments, mutual respect, and how team members are treated when they leave the team, whether voluntary or not. Online team members also gauge trust levels by how other teams (online and on the ground) are treated by the organization and leader. If they observe behaviors that are deceitful, undermining, or unprofessional, it becomes difficult to believe similar treatment will not be directed to them at some point.

A great way to establish a baseline environment of trust is to have the online team meet in the same physical space at the beginning of the project if at all possible. Although this may appear to be a financial burden at first blush, it is best seen as an investment in the team's success and ultimately the project. And in most online team configurations, expenses tied to the initial meeting period will be easily made up via savings in lower overhead costs. Once the initial in-person team meeting is complete, deploying team members will have a physical presence to tie to the online presence, providing an analog-to-digital context for future online meetings. A good rule of thumb is to have an on-site meeting once a year (or biannually if possible) to continue to nurture team trust and keep members connected to home base.

After investing time and resources to establish a foundation of trust for the online team, its preservation is key. Create a trust maintenance plan to ensure the team trust isn't taken for granted. For example, one way to accomplish this is for the leader to stand up for the team during home base negotiations or in meetings with other team leaders. When your team knows you have their back, it provides a level of camaraderie and esprit de corps that allows them to innovate, problem solve, and push themselves further in an effort to make the team excel at the highest levels. In sum, trust is the foundation of an online team and without it the likelihood of team success is zero.

Conclusion

It is highly likely that the use of online teams will continue to increase in many areas of higher education, including academic and business operations. As colleges and universities continue to expand their reach beyond regional and national boundaries, team members will need to be geographically dispersed, whether academic programming is online or provided to a distant site. This essay has examined key issues that occur regardless of configuration and has sought to provide real-world solutions.

Global competition for student enrollment means that it would be wise for continuing education units to incorporate online team building into strategic planning and allocate resources to support the endeavor. This includes leadership training for the online leader that speaks to the nuances and challenges of leading an online team. Further, training and orientation should be provided to individuals who will become the online team. Ensuring communication channels and associated technologies are established and that all team members are comfortable with their use is very important to achieve early in the team's formation. Setting clear expectations and providing accountability measures will help the online leader manage the team as it moves through challenges and arrives at solutions.

The role trust plays in online teams cannot be overstated. Geographical distance and associated time zones are a natural barrier for an online team. Establishing trust in each other by following through on tasks, observance of deadlines, and a team culture of support for one another will help ensure the team completes its goals and overall project. As online teams evolve and team members change, the leader needs to treat each situation with professionalism because this also helps with team stabilization and overall trust.

Finally, there has never been a better time for continuing education units to deploy online teams. The depth of available information on the topic has increased, as well as the acceptance of online teams as a new norm. This, coupled with advances in communication and accountability technologies, makes online teams a very attractive option.

Resources

Cunha, M. M., and G. D. Putnik. 2006. *Agile Virtual Enterprises: Implementation and Management Support.* Hershey, PA: Idea Group Publishing.

Duarte, D. L., and N. T. Snyder. 2001. *Mastering Virtual Teams: Strategies, Tools, Techniques That Succeed.* San Francisco: Jossey-Bass.

Edwards, A., and J. R. Wilson. 2004. *Implementing Virtual Teams: A Guide to Organizational and Human Factors.* Burlington, VT: Gower Publishing Company.

Klobas, J. E., and P. D. Jackson, eds. 2008. *Becoming Virtual: Knowledge Management and Transformation of the Distributed Organization.* Heidelberg, Germany: Physica Verlag.

Nemiro, J. E. 2004. *Creativity in Virtual Teams: Key Components for Success.* San Francisco: Pfeiffer.

Shapiro, D. L., M. A. Von Glinow, and J. L. C. Cheng, eds. 2005. *Managing Multinational Teams: Global Perspectives.* San Diego: Elsevier, Inc.

Shellenbarger, S. 2012. "Pants Required: Attending Meetings When Working from Home." *Wall Street Journal.* Accessed at http://blogs.wsj.com /atwork/2012/05/16/pants-required-attending-meetings-when-working -from-home/.

Taormina, T. 1996. *Virtual Leadership and the ISO 9000 Imperative.* Upper Saddle River, NJ: Prentice Hall.

Whitcomb, C., and L. Whitcomb. 2013. *Effective Interpersonal and Team Communication Skills for Engineers.* Hoboken, NJ: John Wiley and Sons.

"Working in a Virtual Team: Using Technology to Communicate and Collaborate." Mind Tools. Accessed at http://www.mindtools.com/pages /article/working-virtual-team.htm.

Universal Access and the Technological Imperative

How to Think about Higher Education Today and Tomorrow

■■

Gary W. Matkin

There are two major drivers of change in higher education (HE) and continuing education (CE). They are the inexorable advance toward universal access to education and the technological imperative that enables that advance. Understanding these two concepts provides a useful structure to describe the many changes that HE and CE are facing today. They also point the way to the future, to the students and instructors of the future, and to the new structure of HE institutions and their CE units.

Universal Access

In 1973 Professor Martin Trow of the University of California, Berkeley, wrote a series of papers that established a framework for the study of HE for the next four decades. He described the worldwide movement from elite higher education (10% of secondary school graduates going on to college) to mass higher education (30% or more). This helped explain and place in context a complex of changes that were sweeping through HE around the world. In these essays Trow also described the beginnings of what he called "universal access," a concept that was growing quickly, descriptive of what was happening in the realms of both formal and infor-

---

Gary W. Matkin is Dean, Continuing Education, Distance Learning and Summer Session, University of California, Irvine, on the UPCEA Board of Directors, and a recipient of the Nolte Award.

mal education. Universal access anticipated the expansion of motivation for learning, an increased diversity of educational providers, a decrease in the distinctions between education and "life," a decrease in the cost of education, and a real-world orientation toward learning that ultimately would compete with formal HE and its institutions. Trow believed that technology would be a driver of universal access through the "use of videocassettes and TV's and on computer and other technological aids to instruction."[1]

This essay will extend Trow's concept to today's world where universal access is defined as the opportunity for anyone to learn anything, any time, anywhere, for free. Technology is pushing us closer to that goal. Universal access is even more visible as the headlines discuss MOOCs and new, more efficient formats to help people learn. True to Trow's prediction, these innovations appear threatening to formal education, open the door to new educational providers, require shifts in faculty roles, and portend a major shift in the roots of HE finance. But more important, these innovations hold the promise of educating nearly one billion people who otherwise would not have access to a meaningful education.

Technology as Imperative: A Break with the Past

New technology and its application are and will be the most important drivers of change in HE and CE. After more than twenty years of experience with online education and its continuing increase, there are still those who dispute this hypothesis or resist the evidence to the contrary (MOOCs, for instance). Until the 1990s, no major technological advance had much of an impact on the way education was carried out.

Trow described the relationship between universal access and the technological imperative:

> information technology now forces a revision of our conception of the conditions making for universal access. It allows, and becomes the vehicle for, universal access to higher education of a different order of magnitude, the courses of every kind and description available over the Internet in people's homes and workplaces. That involves profound changes in both institutional structures and attitudes regarding higher education.[2]

How to Think about the Present and Future of HE and CE

Understanding universal access and the driving influence of technology provides a lens for administrators to view and filter the daily onslaught of both encouraging and discouraging news and events and, importantly, a method of placing the present in relationship to the future. Universal access is both a goal and a driver of all change. The imperative of techno-logical change and developments in teaching and learning are primary enablers of universal access. While it can and is being used by many insti-tutions for higher-quality education and expanded access, technological advancement has a life of its own and is not controlled by HE and CE administrators.

What follows is the application of this structure to four major issues facing HE and CE to show the validity of this framework for analyzing and understanding what is happening. For each issue the problem is identi-fied, its general dynamics are analyzed, and then the concepts of univer-sal access, open educational resources (OER), and the technology imper-ative are used to place the problem and its possible resolution in context.

Understanding the Dynamics of Higher Education and Its Publics Today

An interconnected set of dynamics exists among the major issues facing HE. Authors have exploited these dynamics, writing about the problems of HE, how HE needs to change and why, and who should lead those changes. One major strand of criticism is that, unlike many other sec-tors of society, HE has not become more productive on any measure, in-cluding, for instance, graduates produced or the quality of the education graduates are receiving. This lack of increased productivity, so the logic goes, leads to higher costs. Higher costs, in turn, expose a failure on the part of administration to accept change and innovation, produce calls for greater accountability, and open the door to nontraditional provider competition, including global competition.

The Higher Cost of Education

The Problem   There is evidence that the inflation-adjusted cost per student has not actually increased in the last thirty years.[3] However, the share of the cost paid by students and their parents has risen considerably. Costs in private universities have floated to market rates because most private universities serve the wealthy. In 2012–2013 the number of institutions charging over $50,000 per year increased from 123 in the prior year to 149.[4] At elite private universities over 80 percent of students come from the top 20 percent of family income distribution.[5] In public institutions, higher costs to students are the result of the decrease in state support of public higher education. Between 1982 and 2012, state support of higher education per $1,000 in personal income declined from $10.06 to $5.89

(41%).[6] While average four-year public higher education in-state tuition for 2012–2013 was a relatively modest (in relation to private university tuition) $8,655 per year, total per year cost including on campus housing was $22,261, still a considerable burden for families even in the upper middle income brackets.[7]

General Dynamics   The increase in costs to students and their parents creates a number of dynamics, which reveal themselves in many ways. One result of higher costs is the rapid increase in student debt, which exceeds $1 trillion (more than consumer debt) and is approaching an average of $30,000 per debtor graduate. This heavy debt burden, combined with a sluggish job market, has placed a huge economic burden on our society. Naturally, HE constituents (board members, politicians, students and parents, pundits and commentators) look to the root cause of this debt, often focusing on the underlying financial structure of institutions and university systems. Since governing boards consist of business people, cost containment and ways to increase productivity are typical responses. Reductions in force, particularly at the administrative level, higher teaching loads for faculty, larger class sizes, and year-round use of the physical plant are all natural business-oriented reactions to cost pressure. Politicians often ignore the root cause of tuition increases at public universities—the reduction in state funding—and blame institutions for rising student costs, offering the same remedies that governing boards are prone to propose.

Analysis   By July 2011 the stock of OER and OpenCourseWare (OCW) had increased dramatically. MIT had produced 1,800 open courses, and the members of the OCW Consortium (now the Open Education Consortium) had produced more than 20,000 open courses. YouTube had hundreds of thousands of video-captured lectures, and iTunes U was also accumulating thousands of courses. Open repositories such as MERLOT and Connexions had thousands of open learning objects easily available for downloading. Yet very little of this material was recognized or being used. Then in July 2011, Stanford's two artificial intelligence MOOCs hit the mainstream media. The overwhelming response to this free and open material (more than 160,000 signed up for the two courses), combined with Stanford's reputation, caused open education to catch the attention of the public. The notions of free (open), high-quality (Stanford), public acceptance, and extensive inventory (OCWC, YouTube, MERLOT) came together and produced some surprising and troubling responses. Symbolic of these responses was the bill proposed in the California state legislature in March 2013 that would require public institutions of higher education to give credit for MOOCs under certain conditions.[8] The logic of the bill was as inevitable as the proposal was unworkable; that if the content of a course were free, then the total cost of education should become less. After opposition from institutions, SB520 was not put forward, but the consequences of MOOCs did not end. The possibilities of using online education to reduce costs persisted to the point that the governor earmarked $10 million per year for the University of California budget (with similar amounts for the California State University and community college systems) to produce online courses that students from one campus in the system could take from other campuses.

Resistance to Change and Innovation

The Problem   In most industries, increased productivity has come from new technologies and their application. It is clear that new technology has been adopted by higher education to great effect. University libraries are quite different than the libraries of even ten years ago. They serve much more as electronic portals to information and places for groups of students to study than as repositories. There are many additional examples of how the teaching and learning processes are becoming more effective through the use of technology. However, a clear relationship between the use of new technology and increased productivity has not been established.

General Dynamics   Measuring productivity in HE is a complex problem. Many measures commonly used are number of graduates produced, time to degree, completion rates, and student satisfaction. Yet the most important outcomes, the impact of the university experience on student's lives and on society in general, are impossible to measure. The one metric that is measurable is the personal income difference over a lifetime of a college graduate compared to those with only high school diplomas. The aggregate data (which show that there is a significant difference) hides the fact that for many students there is no noticeable economic benefit to attaining a degree, particularly when student debt is factored in. Accrediting agencies are struggling to have institutions define desired student outcomes and then measure them in graduates, often months or years after graduation. However, this lack of acceptable metrics for measuring changes in productivity does not stop those who see change and innovation as the key to productivity gains.

Analysis   Again, boards of directors and politicians often see their role as demanding change and the use of new technologies to achieve greater productivity. Take the case of President Theresa Sullivan at the University of Virginia (UV). In June 2012 the university's board of regents voted to remove her from office. While at first the reasons for removal were unclear, it came to light that several members of the board were disturbed by the slowness with which the university was adopting new instructional technology and online education.[9] With support from faculty and students, Sullivan was reinstated. It is not surprising then that UV was one of the first sixteen institutions to join Coursera and produce MOOCs.

There are echoes of this around the country. In 2010 the president of the University of California was urged by the regents to initiate a system-wide effort to create online courses that could be offered both to UC students and nonmatriculated students. UC, despite its public and land-grant status, had produced less than a handful of online degrees while other major state systems were producing hundreds. To remedy this, the regents authorized a $9 million loan to the project. The project failed to attract nonmatriculated students, but it did change UC faculty attitudes toward online education, opening doors for the slow development of online education.

In the short term, involvement with MOOCs or free education became the means by which institutions demonstrated their willingness to adopt new technology and experiment with new forms of education. While a number of institutions are rethinking their policies and involvement with MOOCs and OER, others are inventing new ways to use MOOCs and OER to serve deserving populations, increase institutional reputation, and serve students. MOOCs or their derivatives are expanding and will become a permanent part of HE.

Belying the criticism that HE is unwilling to change or accept innovation, note that the major player in the OER movement in 2001 was MIT (with funding from the William and Flora Hewlett Foundation), and the initiator of the MOOC movement was Stanford. It is HE, not the private sector, from which innovation in open education springs. While Coursera, EdX, Udacity, and other private firms have taken the headlines, all these private organizations depend on universities to continue to supply the content that is the substance of the MOOC and OER movements. Since most MOOC business models depend on a free or low-cost supply of content, this will continue to be the case.

Accountability

The Problem   As the efficiency of HE came into question, the demands for accountability rose. Accountability wears many hats—accountability for cost efficiency, for educational and research results, for compliance with hundreds of laws and regulations, for integrity in all dealings, and for contributions to regional economic development. Of course, accountability comes with a cost and is one of the drivers of higher-cost education.

General Dynamics An axiom of accountability is that what is measured is paid attention to. Where accountability does not align with institutional purposes and aspirations, distortions occur: deviation of resources from strategic and aspirational goals toward secondary purposes. The dollars spent on accumulating and reporting data take resources away from the central activities of new knowledge creation, teaching, and learning.

Another axiom of accountability is openness. Data must not only be accumulated and reported, it must be publicly available. This openness, while necessary and logical, places HE and its institutions at risk of misinterpreting the data.

Analysis Openness is one of the levers that pushes OER into the accountability equation. Another lever is the potential that OER has for opening the heart of the educational enterprise to public view. Online and open education requires the expression of the entire learning content for a course or full curriculum. The mistakes, faculty foibles, errors, and chances for misinterpretation that fall quickly by the wayside in a classroom-based course are manifest and evident in online education. If online education can be made open, then why not require such openness of all faculty members? Sound far-fetched? Maybe not. For example, the Texas state legislature passed a law (HB2504) requiring public institutions (except medical and dental schools) to post a public website for every undergraduate course.

Competition

The Problem Online education has changed the competitive landscape for HE and CE. This change has several dimensions. First, because the cost barriers to entry are relatively low, institutions of all kinds can now, through boundless online education, expand their market reach efficiently. Second, educational institutions other than those in higher education, including professional societies, museums, and private sector firms, are queuing up for their part of the market share. Third, the power of the brand now pushes high-level competition into every corner of the country. Institutions now have the capability to enroll thousands of students from everywhere to capture large market share in specific subjects, draining potential students from local, less well-branded institutions. Increased competition has an international aspect as well, with national boundaries no longer the barriers they were to cross-national education. Policy developments in the United States and in Europe with EU coordination are beginning to remove policy barriers to competition.

General Dynamics The power of universal access is evident in this increased competitive nature of the market. While keeping track of market share is important for examining competitive shifts, the market is growing as people recognize that they have to learn to maintain their standard of living and that learning is available at no or very low cost. The most important competitive elements of HE and CE are content, convenience, quality, and price. Through the use of online education the variety of content and convenience increases and becomes ubiquitous. By removing the constraints of time and place from learners, quality and price become more important as competitive advantages. The brand will continue to be the primary indicator of quality, and the public will rate online education just as they have rated traditional educational programs.

Analysis Prior to the coming of MOOCs the public had mixed reactions to OER, and rightly so. Before MOOCs, the quality of OER was uneven, displaying both the best and the worst of what OER could be. The first instances of MOOCs demonstrated that OER could be high quality, thus opening the door wider to the notion that OER could legitimately begin to address the issue of the high cost of education. Early MOOCs were developed at very high costs, reported in some cases to exceed $50,000 and running as high as $1 million. Development costs at this level are simply not sustainable, but the public gained an image of what education could be.

Early MOOCs set a standard across all types of online education, including instructor-led courses where the quality of the offering is primarily dependent on the instructor. MOOCs have contributed to a sharper focus on what online quality really is as defined by its efficiency in producing learning outcomes. OER and MOOCs have directly influenced the price of higher and continuing education. They have revealed the very high margins produced by normally priced degrees, increasing pressure on colleges to lower their tuition.[10]

The effect on CE is likely to be greater. Price sensitivity in CE is higher, particularly in corporate markets. These markets are now clearly targets for major MOOC players. In September 2013, Udacity announced the launch of the Open Education Alliance.[11] This was followed in June 2014 with Udacity's announcement of the nanodegree or modularized format for employee training.[12] Coursera is also entering this market with its course sequences and its "always open" delivery mode. This turn from degree-based education to workforce development and corporate training reflects a certain desperation among MOOC providers to reach new markets. How can university CE units compete with these very low-cost providers? CE units will have to adopt the MOOC delivery mode, offering free courses but, as with the private MOOC providers, charging for learning assessment and certification. They will have to tie free courses to fee-bearing course sequences, led by qualified instructors and at very high quality. Few of the private MOOC providers of today will last without offering their own learning certification and establishing their own legitimacy independent of their university partners. In this they will act very much like CE units. CE units will have to meet and face down this challenge.

What Today's Learners Tell Us about Tomorrow's Learners

For some, in examining the first MOOC participants, a surprising result was their high level of educational attainment. This is confirmation that the more educated a person is, the more likely he or she will consume more education. This holds true at all levels of education. In a reversal of classical economics, demand for education is increasing because of the huge supply of learning objects that are available, quickly, easily, and for free. We are faced with many more learning projects, learning what we need in order to live our lives productively. Most of these projects demand that we learn quickly, efficiently, and sufficiently to achieve at least a minimum proficiency.

Studies of MOOC participants reveal more about today's learners. First, for many, learning offers intrinsic satisfaction, often dissociated from any practical concern. Very few of the thousands who enrolled in Princeton's MOOC The History of the World since 1300 expected to use that knowledge in any practical way. When asked, learners say they are taking the course for fun or for a very general purpose of self-improvement. Second, among those taking a MOOC, levels of engagement vary from viewing the video parts to taking the full course with all of its assignments. For traditionalists, this variation indicates a failure on the part of MOOCs to engage students and produce more acceptable completion rates. For those interested in human learning, this variation offers an opportunity to explore the ways in which people choose learning projects and define what they want for those projects. Today's students clearly want to choose their own level of engagement, from a light review of a subject or deep engagement in only part of the offering to full academic assessment and academic credit.

Third, as Trow predicted, learning is merging with work, family life, entertainment, and other ways we spend our time. The convenience of the learning process is still paramount for most students. The advent of mobile devices and the learning applications being developed for them are a major recent development in this merger. HE institutions underestimate the impact of this. But most online providers are making sure their learning materials are mobile-friendly.

Fourth, this merging is partly the cause of the trend toward chunking of learning materials into shorter segments. Students need education delivered to them in smaller bites or modules to accommodate both shorter attention spans and busy lives.

Fifth, the period between learning and application is being shortened. In traditional education the trend toward project-based education is evidence of the merger of learning and application. Increasingly CE learners have the opportunity to time their learning so that they can immediately employ what they have learned. For instance, Coursera used the cohort model exclusively for its course offerings but has recently added the "always open" or independent study option so that learners can get what they need "just in time."

Sixth, the social aspects of online and open learning are becoming more important and available. Social learning is central to a new trend in education: learner as creator rather than consumer. Real-world projects requiring group project work with a defined deliverable are being embedded in course assignments. Interaction among students is becoming a part of the instructional design of courses, with social networking employed for group work on projects. Learning social networks are evolving, becoming more sophisticated, and are capable of being monitored and directed by instructors. In open education social learning is accomplished through peer assessment where students grade each other's work. And now learning hubs, where students in open courses can come together in face-to-face meetings, are sprouting up.[13]

Finally, instructional design is pushing into adaptive learning and supplemental learning. In adaptive learning the course design automatically discovers gaps in student knowledge and understanding and directs students to the learning materials needed to gain mastery of the concept. This promises the customization of learning to fit individual needs on a massive scale, helping to focus the attention of the student and the instructor on elements of the learning process where it is needed. Supplemental learning takes place outside the normal classroom work and its assignments. It includes what happens in study groups, in studying for tests, and in the individual student organizing the time and methods for learning. Instructional design is beginning to address this important area of learning, providing supplemental material and offering more help in organizing study time. For some this detracts from the need to have students take responsibility for their own learning. For others, this is a natural extension of the guidance students need and deserve to master a subject.

All of the features of today's learners are evident and can be extended into the future. Soon we will begin to know much more about the learning that will be employed to improve human learning. This research may go beyond current pedagogical practice into the realm of the biological bases of learning and retention, the psychological states necessary for effective learning, and the increasing of the capacity to learn through iterative practice. The infancy of MOOC research gives us some hints at what might be possible. The quality of MOOCs, how students engage, the international character of participation, and the possibility of conducting statistical testing with large populations all promise to yield much information about human learning. The revolution in learning will have its roots in evidence-based examination of human learning rather than institutional change.

The Future of Higher and Continuing Education

The examination of the current state of higher and continuing education leads to some predictions that have a high degree of probability of realization.

Faculty as Learning Architects   Change in faculty roles will be at the heart of the changes over the next ten years. Faculty will enlarge their scope of teaching to include more elements of instructional design. It is they who must set the learning context for the learner. They will have available to them and will use more information and methods about learning and technology to foster human learning. They will go well beyond being content experts to being learning experts, possessed of an understanding about how to select content and learning assets, sequence them, tie them together, adapt them to the collective and individual needs of the students, and extend all this into the full life cycle of the learning experience of the student, including supplemental learning and subsequent application. The term *architect* is appropriate in many ways in that the faculty of the future will be central in building the learning context for students, who often will have quite varied backgrounds. Institutions will have to support this new role through training, infrastructure development, instructional design resources, and, most important, cultural shifts that honor the role of learning architect.

Research-Driven Continuous Improvement   As the learning research enterprise becomes more extensive and sophisticated across institutions, it will begin to have an effect on how the teaching role is carried out. Content will become less of a distinguishing feature of learning among institutions as quality, value, and accessibility of learning material increases. Those institutions with the most effective continuous improvement processes will gain a competitive quality advantage.

Quality as Defined by the Market   Increased accountability will push all institutions toward quality standards defined more and more by market forces. Where institutional and market standards diverge, the movement will be toward market values. Student employability measures will be a market preoccupation whereas human development will remain an institutionally valued outcome. Universities will likely serve this demand by adjusting curriculum, pedagogy, and programs to create a more workforce-ready graduate.

Technology across the Spectrum   "Technology as imperative" will continue, increase, and be expressed in every part of teaching, learning, and institutional life. HE institutions, CE units, and faculty will have to remain open to technological innovation and change, able to employ technology where it truly assists learning, and willing to evaluate new technology for its effectiveness. Administrative and instructional technology will merge to include data about students both collectively and individually. Student life situations will become a part of the equation more directly than is imaginable today. Learning efficiency will be correlated with health, psychological, and attitude data, first for traditional students and then later for adult students.

Institutions as Bundle of Services   The traditional services provided by institutions are unbundled in today's marketplace. The online and OER movements have played a role in this unbundling. Libraries now are portals rather than repositories. It is common for online courses to be produced by outside organizations or for one institution to vend to another institution. The increasing costs and sophistication of online and open courses requires that professionals other than faculty members be involved in the course production process. Open courses of very high quality are available for free or low cost, much lower than the production cost. As MOOCs came into play, the evaluation and certification of learning became the role of the MOOC purveyor or an outside agency (such as American Council on Education). The pressure on institutions to provide some form of credit for open courses will increase, and institutionally acceptable ways for dealing with this pressure will emerge.

Open Education as Norm   Current experience clearly indicates that every major university will be both a producer and a user of open education. Institution's reputations will rest in part on the quality and amount of open material they produce. It has become an expression of public service for institutions to make these contributions that serve their own students and institutional purposes. The production of open material is more consistent with institutional culture than is the use of OER. Universities are burdened by the not-invented-here syndrome—if we didn't come up with it, how good can it be?—and by the practical exigencies of trying to create a coherent learning context from different sources. But OER and MOOCs (in their evolved state) are a permanent feature of worldwide higher education.

Conclusion

These six predictions are meant as challenges to today's HE and CE administrators. They may be used as examples for the application of the concepts of universal access and the technological imperative to make predictions. Are these valid lenses through which to view the future? One conclusion should be clear. We are not experiencing a revolution. We are experiencing the evolution of learning and a historical turning point that will determine the future of the world. Will we meet the demands of almost one billion people who want and need higher education? The answer is in our ability to harness the power of that demand to the new technologies and new understanding of human learning. Can we meet the challenge? The answer is simple: we must, and will.

Notes

1. M. Trow, "Problems in the Transition from Elite to Mass Higher Education," in *Policies for Higher Education, General Report of the Conference on Future Structures of Post-Secondary Education* (Paris: OECD, 1974), 9.
2. M. Trow, "From Mass Higher Education to Universal Access: The American Advantage," *Minerva* 37 (Spring 2000): 1–26.
3. G. C. Fethke and A. J. Policano, *Public No More: A New Path to Excellence for America's Public Universities.* Stanford, CA: Stanford University Press, 2012.
4. "Colleges that Charged $50,000 or More in 2012–13," *Chronicle of Higher Education, Almanac of Higher Education, 2013–2014*, 48.
5. J. Quiggen, "Campus Reflection," *Chronicle of Higher Education*, May 12, 2014. Accessed at http://chronicle.com/article/Campus-Reflection/146431/.
6. "State Fiscal Support for Higher Education per $1,000 of Personal Income, FY 1961–2012," *Chronicle of Higher Education, Almanac of Higher Education, 2012–2013*, 45.
7. "Average College Costs, by Institutional Type," *Chronicle of Higher Education, Almanac of Higher Education, 2012–2013*, B51.
8. L. Gardner and J. R. Young, "California's Move toward MOOCs Sends Shock Waves, but Key Questions Remain Unanswered," *Chronicle of Higher Education*, March 14, 2013. Accessed at http://chronicle.com/article/A-Bold-Move-Toward-MOOCs-Sends/137903/.
9. J. Stripling, "Teresa Sullivan Will Step Down as UVa's President after Two Years in Office," *Chronicle of Higher Education*, June 10, 2012. Accessed at http://chronicle.com/article/Teresa-Sullivan-Abruptly/132205/.
10. G. Blumenstyk, "Starbucks Plan Shines Light on the Profits of Online Education," *Chronicle of Higher Education*, June 27, 2014. Accessed at http://chronicle.com/article/Starbucks-Plan-Shines-a-Light/147395/.

11. C. Shen, "Announcing the Launch of the Open Educational Alliance," Udacity Blog, September 9, 2013. Accessed at http://blog.udacity.com /2013/09/announcing-launch-of-open-education.html.
12. E. Porter, "A Smart Way to Skip College in Pursuit of a Job," *New York Times*, June 17, 2014, B1. Accessed at http://www.nytimes.com/2014/06/18 /business/economy/udacity-att-nanodegree-offers-an-entry-level -approach-to-college.html?_r=0.
13. T. Lewin, "U.S. Teams Up with Operator of Online Courses to Plan a Global Network," *New York Times*, October 31, 2013. Accessed at http://www.nytimes.com/2013/11/01/education/us-plans-global-net-work-of-free-online-courses.html?hp&_r=2&.

"Against the Natural Order of Things"

Why E-Learning Refuses to Take Off

■▌

Jonathan Baldwin

I've come up with a set of rules that describe our reactions
to technologies:
>   Anything that is in the world when you're born is
> normal and ordinary and is just a natural part of the way
> the world works.
>   Anything that's invented between when you're fifteen
> and thirty-five is new and exciting and revolutionary and
> you can probably get a career in it.
>   Anything invented after you're thirty-five is against the
> natural order of things.
>
> —DOUGLAS ADAMS, *THE SALMON OF DOUBT*

The Pace of Change

I recently attended a talk by someone who enthusiastically told the audience about all the "new" things technology would soon allow us to do and
how it would transform education. He pitched it not just as disruption,
which can be a positive, but (rather gleefully) as destruction; e-learning,
he told us, sounded the death knell for universities as we know them.

There were distinct groups in the audience. When he predicted we
would soon be embracing tools such as Twitter in our teaching, I could
tell many in the room had, like me, been using it as a teaching tool since
it first appeared and were somewhat surprised that it was still worthy

---

Jonathan Baldwin is Director of Teaching and Learning, Institute of Continuing
Education, University of Cambridge.

of being called "new." However, there were some in the room who had clearly never heard of Twitter, never mind used it.

I have been to several talks like this over the past fifteen years or so, and they never seem to get much further than predicting how technology will make everything we are doing now look silly. The message is the same; only the technology they use to project their predictions on the screen changes: in the early days they used slides on a carousel, then overhead projection, then data projectors dragged around in a suitcase on wheels, and more recently transmitting images wirelessly to a large screen.[1]

I find myself wondering why e-learning is still seen as new, despite the fact that I and many others have been doing it for nearly two decades or more. I couldn't quite believe that one audience member admitted at the end of the talk that he had never heard of MOOCs and I was shocked that the idea of using an iPad to hold a video call with a student on the other side of the planet was still seen as revolutionary. There is a large group of educators who remain outside the bubble and who are almost blissfully unaware of what is going on. When told about it, they respond in the same way as if they'd been told that their favorite brand of washing detergent had a new, improved formula: polite but mildly annoyed.[2] But there is another group for whom the basic concept of e-learning is still the subject of intense debate and rather a large amount of FUD (fear, uncertainty, doubt) gleaned from articles about plagiarism (students just copy their essays off Wikipedia!), high dropout rates (nobody finishes an online course!), heavy workloads (I'll have to assess three thousand students!), and plots to do away with academics altogether (if I put my course online, the university won't need me anymore!). All these arguments, in one form or another, have followed me throughout my career as a lecturer, manager, and advocate of technology-assisted or technology-facilitated learning.

Technology has changed drastically since I started teaching. In 1999 there was no broadband, most monitors were 256 colors at 640 × 480 pixels, Apple was about to go out of business, AOL was most people's idea of what the Internet was, and getting your e-mail meant dialing up on a very loud modem, grabbing your messages as quickly as possible, and then disconnecting before your phone bill mimicked the national debt. But the debates surrounding e-learning have hardly changed at all. We are still experimenting and wondering if any of this will ever catch on when, by Douglas Adams's maxim, the vast majority of academics should be more than comfortable with technology in teaching and learning.

In this essay I want to explore why it is that e-learning hasn't taken off in quite the way many have predicted at various times. Is it because of an inbuilt Ludditism among academics? Or overpromising on the part of enthusiasts? Or is there, as I suspect, a fundamental problem with the way technology is talked about?

Two Anecdotes about the Future from the Past

A former colleague worked in computing back in the days when a computer was supposed to take up a large part of a room. He worked for a firm that was producing computers that could, in theory, sit on the corner of a desk.[3] That was quite radical. But they discovered that in order to sell them, they had to put a concrete block in the computer casing so that it was extraordinarily heavy.

In 2013 I sat in a packed cinema to watch a 1965 science-fiction movie. The hero takes apart a mind-controlling device and, poking around among wires and large transistors, describes it as "highly sophisticated." The audience burst out laughing. But I remember watching that same scene on TV as a child in the 1970s and being rather horrified by it. At some point between 1965 and 2013 that scene went from awe-inspiring to laugh-out-loud funny.

Why did early personal computers need to be heavy to be accepted, and why did an electronic mind-controlling device go from being horrific to comical?

I'll return to these questions later.

Innovators versus Luddites

Looking back, I was both cursed and blessed to be born when I was. Blessed because of all the new inventions coming out, but cursed because I seemed to work with people who could not see their potential.

For my first job interview as a layout artist, I arrived with a portfolio full of leaflets I had created in the new Aldus PageMaker on an Apple Macintosh SE. The man interviewing me entered into a long lecture on how I had wasted my time and that what he needed was someone who could use a scalpel and cow gum. As far as I know, he was out of business eighteen months later.

A few years later, in an attempt to persuade the FTSE 100 company I worked for that they should take this new thing called the World Wide Web seriously, I demonstrated a site I had created in my spare time. Our finance director dismissed the idea, stating that the amount of money we would need to spend on it (a few thousand pounds) would never be recouped, and the Web was a fad that would never replace traditional stores. Today that company's website makes more money than all its stores put together.

It was shortly after this that I made the move into education to help set up an online course. The year was 1999—in technological terms it might as well be a hundred years ago—and the idea of online learning had a whiff of science fiction about it.[4] The stumbling blocks I ran into have remained the same to this day: fears that this was a way of getting rid of teachers, protestations that people could not learn without face-to-face interaction, suggestions that while it might work for other disciplines, it would not work for [insert any discipline here].

This reaction to technology, particularly among people whose way of life or jobs are potentially disrupted, is nothing new. In Britain during the nineteenth century, textile workers reacted strongly to the invention of new machinery that threatened to turn their skilled labor over to unskilled people who were much less expensive and increase the supply of cloth, making their product easier and therefore cheaper to obtain. This group gave their name to the largely pejorative term *Luddites*, which has come to mean anyone resistant to change.

The Five Stages of Grief

Reactions to technology could be compared with the five stages of grief: denial and isolation, anger, bargaining, depression, and finally acceptance. However, the idea behind the five stages is that people move through them, meaning that when it comes to e-learning, the deniers should eventually become accepting of change. But while I've witnessed a lot of denial and anger during my careers in both design and education, in my experience the educators who display those responses do not eventually accept or even embrace it—the anti-e-learning and the indifferent are quite distinct groups from the enthusiasts.

The Diffusion of Innovation

Responses to e-learning are not following what the textbooks tell us to expect. Everett Rogers's (2003) conceptualization of the "diffusion of innovation" will be familiar to many. It breaks down the adoption of new ideas, products, or services into a process that moves through the population via distinctive groups:

Innovators (2.5%)

Early adopters (13.5%)

Early majority (34%)

Late majority (34%)

Laggards (16%)

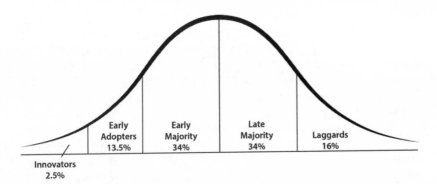

Innovators
2.5%

In this model, a new product has to be taken up by the innovators who give it something of a shakedown and, hopefully, evangelize to their friends, who potentially become the early adopters once it has become more widely available and cheaper. The laggards are the last group to catch up and are, in the words of Simon Sinek, author of *Start with Why* (2011), the kind of people who only bought touchtone phones because they stopped making phones with dials. By the time the laggards have adopted something, everybody else has already moved on to something else.[5]

While the diffusion model is useful, something odd seems to be happening when it comes to e-learning. Despite the fact that some of us have been involved in e-learning for twenty years or more, we don't seem to have moved much beyond the early adopters. My guess is that only around 16 percent of educators in the United Kingdom are actively embracing e-learning.

Predicting the Future of Technology

At the time of writing, YouTube has a growing collection of videos about predictions of the future going back to the 1920s (see the General Motors ride at the 1964 World Fair for one example: www.youtube.com /watch?v=2-5aK0H05jk). One such video, from Microsoft (www.youtube .com/watch?v=9V_0xDUg0h0&feature=youtu.be), gives an end-of-century view of the smart home of the future. Time has not been kind and the things they got right are lost among the things they got wrong (wait for the scene with the pocket PC).

A more recent video is a live presentation at the Consumer Electronics Show of Samsung's home of the future (www.youtube.com/watch?v =mEzSF29EBgI). This shows a number of devices that at the time were close to being available, but rather than use a family setting, the focus here is a professional single woman in her thirties.[6]

Another video produced by NTT (Nippon Telephone and Telegraph) is well worth a few minutes of your time. It shows how they think technology will be used in a variety of situations such as remote conferencing, education, disaster relief, and medicine (www.youtube.com/watch?v =GpJ36KzHJG4). This is a typical example of the corporate prediction genre, which typically groups together quite disparate ideas under a (very) loose narrative.

A fourth video is rather more famous and dates from 1987: Apple's Knowledge Navigator, created for a presentation to higher education managers (www.youtube.com/watch?v=9bjve67p33E). Apple's video directly addresses the future of education and the ways technology would change it. Given the audience for the video, it focuses not on teaching but on an academic checking his e-mail, doing research, and video conferencing with a colleague in another country.[7] The video slowly began to attract a lot of attention, leading Apple to produce another in 1988 focusing on students, with various speakers predicting the future of computers in the classroom (www.youtube.com/watch?v=VWlA_cDE5RU &feature=youtu.be). Two minutes into the video a child gives a presentation about volcanoes to his peers using what we would now identify as an iPad. The video is full of predictions that turned out to be accurate, but also a few misses.[8]

Why Technologists Are the Wrong People to Predict Future Technology

For the first seven minutes, Apple's 1988 video seems rather prescient. The things it shows are things we now take for granted. But then something odd happens. A woman is designing a new aircraft engine on screen using computer visualizations to model the effect of different nozzle shapes. This kind of thing certainly happens today. But she is talking to the computer, asking it to make the changes, instead of directly manipulating the designs using a pen or mouse. For this viewer at least, there is something of a problem here, and it's not because I'm a Luddite; it's because this prediction goes against the way design is done.[9]

Microsoft's "home of the future" video also contains things we either accept today or are looking forward to in the near future. But the video leaves me cold, not because of the technology, but because of the relationships. Microsoft's video is a prediction of the home of the future, when what it really needed to be was a prediction of the family of the future. Technology should not be the thing that defines family interaction; it should be the thing that enables it. This requires social scientists, not computer scientists.

Samsung's presentation eschews relationships entirely and focuses on the idea of saving time. All the home's gadgets are automated and controlled remotely. But the ideas themselves are unappealing because, at the end of the day, all that happened was the user got home and fell asleep alone on the sofa. That is not a life to which many would aspire. Like Microsoft, they are selling the technology, not the life.

To explain why the Apple video stands out for the wrong reasons, it is worth thinking about the success and failure of educational games. Gabe Zichermann, in a potted history of gamification, points to the 1980s educational game Where in the World Is Carmen Sandiego? and calls it "the first and last time that parents, teachers, and children all agreed that a game was good for them" (http://youtu.be/6O1gNVeaE4g). But it is also, argues Zichermann, "the first and last time that an educational game was a good game." Why? "Because parents and teachers got involved in the design of edutainment titles. Kids can smell that s*** a mile away. It's not fun anymore. It's work." Carmen Sandiego was a good game because it was made by people who understood games. And that's key: let family specialists explain how families work, let gaming specialists create games, and let educators figure out what to teach and how, adapting tools to help as they see fit.

In the Apple video, up until the point where the designer starts telling the computer to change her concept, the people whose ideas were being realized on screen were educators expressing ideas of which they had direct experience. Those bits worked—they understood how people learn and interact. But the section on how computers would revolutionize design was a non sequitur arising from one contributor's belief that voice input was far superior to keyboard input. He was talking about words—dictating text; for some reason the video's director interpreted this in a field of which, I would wager, he knew little: design. Imagine featuring an artist of the future creating a portrait by instructing the computer to "add hair, make it shorter, more wavy, make it flick across the left eye" or a writer creating a novel not by dictating the words she wants the computer to transcribe but by telling the computer to "add more suspense."[10]

Designers *think* with their hands and articulate their thoughts through visualization and by making physical prototypes, not by speaking. This is why my first job interviewer was wrong: he was rejecting a new tool, believing it was an attack on his craft. But tools don't do anything—they still need to be mastered and applied in appropriate situations.

This helps to explain why many predictions of the future fail: not because the technology itself will not materialize, but because the people doing the predictions are not experts in the situations or domains they are aiming to affect. They develop tools without watching the way people work.[11] This is why their visions strike us as funny, odd, or even offensive. And it's why, when a technologist tries to tell a designer, a doctor, or a teacher "you will work like this in the future," they laugh.[12]

To use Douglas Adams's explanation of why some people refuse to accept technology in their lives, it is "against the natural order of things." But while Adams focused humorously and self-deprecatingly on age, the slow adoption of technology in teaching is less about how old the teachers are (I witness acceptance and rejection equally across all age groups, some of it Ludditism, but much of it not) and more about the nature of the thing being changed.

For those who are focused on teaching in universities, it is often the human interaction that is important. But many people working in universities did not become academics to teach; they are focused on research. As Terry Pratchett puts it: "Many things went on at . . . University and, regrettably, teaching had to be one of them. The faculty had long ago confronted this fact and had perfected various devices for avoiding it. But this was perfectly all right because, to be fair, so had the students" (1994, 21).

So telling someone that technology can replace the need to actually talk to students may be greeted more enthusiastically by those who are not focused on teaching than by the teachers.[13] But showing the teaching enthusiasts how technology can *enhance* rather than replace the things they value is a far better approach than effectively insulting and threatening them, which is how many evangelists come across, because they are evangelizing technology, not teaching (or, put another way, they are evangelizing the "e," not the "learning"). As long as e-learning resides in the purview of school and university IT departments or in technology companies, it will never get past the educational innovators and early adopters, who are operating largely independently anyway.[14]

The Problem with Hype

All of the above demonstrates why visions of the future fail to engage if they are proposed by technologists, rather than actual users. Apple's video is the only one of the videos cited that appears to use experts but even it fails to include teachers or students, except as characters. Students and teachers are, to borrow from sociology, actors, not characters. Technologists who ignore the difference are doomed forever to predict things, but never meaningfully change anything.

These videos are somebody else's vision, and the further removed it is from reality the less enticing it becomes. A kind of "uncanny valley" is in effect.[15] Microsoft's family of the future seems not to have any fights; it has a family room, an entertainment room, and a music room—almost, but not completely, unlike my home or that of anyone I know. The kitchen is spotless. Is yours? And because I reject the scenario, I reject the things that apparently create it. Similarly with Samsung's presentation: if the future means I'm rushing to work in the morning so desperately late that, while I can remember to put a single shirt in the wash, I forget to turn on the machine or turn off the air conditioning, and then I get home so late I don't even have time to eat before I fall asleep, drooling onto the sofa—that's not a great vision. I reject it. As for NTT's video—it seems to be promising a glorious future in which we all get to attend extraordinarily dull meetings while sitting isolated in our cubicles. Reject.

The Hype Cycle

This rejection is predicted in another model, Gartner's "hype cycle" (www.gartner.com/technology/research/methodologies/hype-cycle .jsp). Gartner has applied this cycle to many sectors, including education (Lowendahl 2013). In this report, Lowendahl shows technologies such as education tablets, "mashware," and affective computing as being on the rise; gamification, MOOCs, and adaptive learning as being at the peak; and e-textbooks, cloud e-mail, and virtual environments as sliding in to the trough.[16] Meanwhile, lecture capture, retrieval tools, and open-source repositories are climbing the slope, with e-book readers and self-publishing entering the plateau.

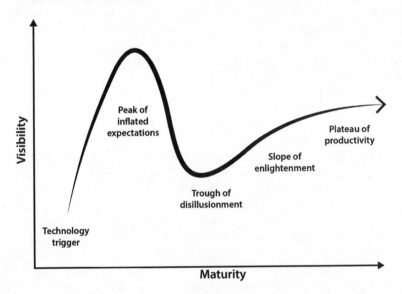

There is something about the idea of the hype cycle that is instantly recognizable. In particular, the notion that technology hits a peak of inflated expectations rings uncomfortably true. But does it explain why e-learning doesn't seem to be following the traditional diffusion of innovation? Why is it stuck with the early adopters?

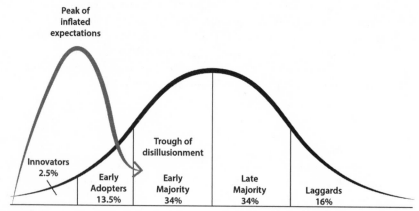

If you overlay the hype cycle on the diffusion of innovation, the trough of disillusion comes right at the point where the early adopters connect to the early majority. And the slope of enlightenment does not occur because the innovators have already moved on to the next big thing. In other words, the reason why e-learning in all its various guises has failed to get beyond that initial 16 percent is because of the hype. There's a disconnect between the promise and the reality, largely because the people doing the promising are unfamiliar with the practical realities of the situation they are seeking to change.

I think there's a simple explanation for this. Think back to the two stories that opened this essay: the desktop computers that had to have concrete inside them and the mind-control device that was scary in the '60s and '70s but funny in 2013.

The desktop computers my colleague sold in the early 1980s had to be heavy because while our minds could comprehend something as big as a room being reduced in size, we have a harder time imagining that it would be portable. Particularly at those prices. "Always be wary of any helpful item that weighs less than its operating manual" (Pratchett 1998, 178).

The mind-control device in the 1960s movie could have been depicted as a box of pulsing lights (as it might be today), with the same narrative effect, but with no emotional effect. It was depicted using exactly the same type of things that you would see if you opened any radio or TV of the day.[17] That is what made it believable and, as a result, scary. My radio can control my mind? That's terrifying.[18] By 2013, of course, the "sophisticated" electronics were dated, and so the idea the audience was supposed to focus on—mind control—was smothered by the way the message was communicated. But the point is that *at the time* the idea made sense because it was in the hands of a storyteller telling a story in a way that made sense to audiences at the time, not a technologist pitching an idea about the future to which nobody can relate.

And this is what happens when we talk about the future of technology in education—good, potentially revolutionary ideas are lost because the people with the message cannot tell good stories and often know little about their audience.

We have certain expectations in life, and we hold certain values and beliefs. To convey a complex or new idea, it is usually best to position it within those expectations or connect it to those values. It may come across as dated in the future, but that's not a problem if your task is to make a difference today. If you want e-learning to take off, don't tell someone a story about somebody else in the future; tell a story about them and their students today. The innovators and early adopters occupy two overlapping camps: those who love technology (and so will give anything a go) and those who enjoy an adventure and a bit of risk. The next group, the early majority, like a good story too—but they want others to write it for them and no risk.

Revolutions do not start with a PowerPoint presentation or slick video and a ridiculing of the audience; they start with a belief held *by* the audience and an urge to use that belief to enhance or change something. E-learning will only get beyond the innovators and early adopters when it stops being pitched as revolutionary in itself. Technology is not the revolution, education is. And we need to get excited again about what we want to achieve in our teaching and in our students' learning before we get excited about the technology.

This Will Cheer You Up

I wanted this essay to be positive. E-learning offers us so much, and I consider myself an advocate of its use, not just in enhancing existing provision but in widening access to excellent educational opportunities to those who currently do not, or cannot, access them. That is as much the shop worker in Anytown, USA, or the United Kingdom, as it is the stereotypical teenager in a developing country.

I cited a few videos about the future—now let me cite a couple about the recent past that will simultaneously amuse and distress you: use a search engine to find "Kids react to old computers" and "Kids react to typewriters." Douglas Adams missed a line about anything invented before you were born.

Notes

1. Even as the technology changed, two other things didn't: presenters filling the screen with bullet points they then read out to us as we silently

mouthed along; and almost always standing in front of the screen and having their presentation projected onto their shirts.

2. The insinuation that there was anything wrong with the old formula being a fact unsupported by peer review.

3. A large, reinforced desk

4. It also had the ability to attract phenomenal amounts of money, most of it wasted. The project I was involved with was linked to the UK government's "University for Industry," which led to nearly £1 billion being spent on a network of "learndirect" centers and a bunch of missed targets.

5. I once had a colleague who didn't "do" e-mail. He would type a document and attach it to a blank message. Unfortunately his word processor of choice was QuarkXpress, which isn't a word processor and which only his colleagues on the graphic design faculty had. In the end people gave up and just assumed that if anything he sent was important, he'd eventually come and visit in person to ask why they hadn't replied to it. (Ironically, he refused to use QuarkXpress to do actual design, preferring scalpel and glue.)

6. Families are so last century.

7. The video is set in September 2011 and features an intelligent virtual personal assistant that responds to voice commands. The idea was ridiculed at the time. In real life, in September 2011 Apple launched Siri.

8. Among the things it predicted: interactive whiteboards, tablet computers, and that the United States of the future would still not have embraced the metric system.

9. I realized when typing this that I was in danger of sounding like the man who interviewed me for the layout job I described at the start. Bear with me. I think I get away with it.

10. On reflection, this does explain much of Dan Brown's work.

11. This is an important point. When teaching design, I would emphasize to students the importance of empathy—of observing users in situations, questioning them, including them in the design process. I've had students who have accompanied police on patrol to develop protective gear, spent time with a family in the evening to redesign social housing, and even sat through major surgery to help develop new tools for surgeons. You can't do that by sitting in a studio, and especially not by talking to a computer.

12. Or punch them in the face. That has undoubtedly happened.

13. Let's call this Baldwin's E-learning Paradox: the less interested an individual or organization is in teaching, the more interested in e-learning they will be.

14. That, incidentally, is not a criticism of IT departments, who are often as surprised as anyone that they are suddenly seen as experts in how people teach and learn.

15. The uncanny valley is a theory from human computer interaction that says, "the more lifelike a creation, the more likely it crosses the line from cute to creepy" (Eveleth 2013). Here I am suggesting that the more "perfect" a scenario is, the creepier it becomes.

16. Affective computing refers to devices that evoke and respond to emotions. Adaptive learning refers to educational materials that can be adapted to the particular circumstances of the learner. And regarding virtual environments, I've sat through, at the last count, twelve talks and demonstrations about using Second Life in education, but only one that seemed to achieve anything.

17. Much to my father's dismay, I frequently did that sort of thing.

18. The TV series on which the movie is based, *Doctor Who*, made great play out of rendering the ordinary scary: statues and shop window mannequins, to give just two famous examples.

References

Adams, D. 2012. *The Salmon of Doubt: Hitchhiking the Galaxy One Last Time.* London: Pan.

Eveleth, R. 2013. "Robots: Is the Uncanny Valley Real?" BBC Future, September 2. Accessed at http://www.bbc.com/future/story/20130901-is-the-uncanny-valley-real.

Lowendahl, J.-M. 2013. "Hype Cycle for Education, 2013." Accessed at https://www.gartner.com/doc/2559615.

Pratchett, T. 1994. *Interesting Times.* New York: HarperCollins.

Pratchett, T. 1998. *Jingo.* London: Corgi.

Rogers, E. 2003. *Diffusion of Innovations.* New York: Free Press.

Sinek, S. 2011. *Start with Why.* New York: Portfolio.

PART III

Pathways to Completion

Driven by debates associated with the standing of the United States in educational achievement internationally and that standing's impact on policy development, by assessments of the value or benefits of higher education, often framed in terms of access to higher education, and by the utility of alternative routes or pathways to degree completion, the following essays explicate the challenges and impacts associated with these policy issues.

In the opening essay, Jeff Rosen focuses our attention on the contending frameworks of access and completion in higher education, asking important questions about the impact of each perspective in the context of the public good. Kay J. Kohl directs our attention to issues associated with a changing workforce and the impact these changes will have on professional and continuing education, particularly competency-based education, shifting demographics, the importance of collaborations, and the role of technology. David Schejbal provides a practical primer on the development and implementation of a competency-based education structure through an explication of the experience of the University of Wisconsin. Patricia A. Book focuses our attention on how informal learning or learning that occurs outside the classroom can be translated into a currency that articulates with the academic awards, that is, credit, associated with formal learning. And finally, Cathy A. Sandeen returns us to the issue of the international standing of the country regarding academic attainment, including certificates, as well as two- and four-year degrees, with an argument for the innovative steps needed to reposition the United States vis-à-vis other developed countries.

The Completion Agenda and the Public Good

■■

Jeff Rosen

Public policy debates about higher education today are increasingly divided between two opposing poles that once presented a unified front. Past unity was expressed in broad agreement that society benefited from increased access to educational opportunity, a value extending from the Morrill Act of 1862 to contemporary support for expanding the role of community colleges. We might refer to this movement as higher education's "access agenda," a pledge to make higher education available to all as much as a promise to future generations that they would inherit an educated citizenry. After World War II, this agenda served the interests of what used to be called nontraditional students: adults with some college, underrepresented minority groups, the military, the disadvantaged, and the poor. The present contention stems from the conflict of this historic commitment to college access and affordability with the new "completion agenda," the drive to dramatically increase college completion rates in the United States.

The value of a higher education has never been stronger: reams of economic data show that college graduates earn more over their lifetimes and experience fewer job losses than those without a college education, results that have been confirmed by numerous nongovernmental agencies and think tanks.[1] The conclusion that America needs to catch up to the advances of other countries hinges on accepting that it faces global competition to produce the largest number of baccalaureate degree holders as a measure of its economic viability, and the breathlessness with which these facts are reported suggests there's no time to lose. President Obama elevated the college achievement goal to national prominence

Jeff Rosen is Vice President for Accreditation Relations and Director of the Open Pathway, Higher Learning Commission, and a UPCEA committee chair.

in his 2011 State of the Union address as a challenge to lawmakers to invest in the country's future. Private foundations like Lumina and the Bill and Melinda Gates Foundation joined the president and others in this groundswell of concern, setting ambitious targets for the attainment of college credentials nationwide as a measure of promoting America's economic fortunes, global competitiveness, and national pride.

But in shifting the focus to college completion over access, an imbalance has also occurred in public discourse and policy making, one that tosses aside long-standing problems like the uncomfortable question of how well or how poorly students have been prepared to succeed in college or the increasing burden of student financial aid. In their place, the public agenda now focuses on ways to produce college credentials for the largest number of people, using the least costly path and shortest duration possible. Fundamentally lost in this determined effort to increase the number of college graduates is the way society can actually achieve this goal in an era of diminished resources. In order to pursue this goal and maintain their budgets, public and private institutions now increasingly rely on part-time and non-tenure-track faculty, deliver their programs of instruction online, and focus almost exclusively on job preparation and skills, frequently as defined by employer needs and often at the expense of other programs of study that lack immediate economic returns or an explicit career focus.

Many good reasons explain these trends. For example, professionals in many fields introduce real-world experiences into classrooms when they moonlight as college instructors, and their valuable insights can often balance a highly theoretical curriculum. Digital platforms, online learning resources, and free open courseware make it possible for students to study any place at any time, and maximize enrollments at less cost to institutions. And when employees are well prepared to succeed at work, employers spend less time training workers, productivity is improved, and our economy hums along more efficiently. These trends admirably meet the postsecondary needs of most students today, particularly those that function in sync with students' mobile and digital lives and feed their appetite for practical knowledge.[2] But it is also apparent that in addressing these concerns colleges and universities have shifted their priorities to workforce demands and economic efficiencies, the two chief drivers that inform the completion agenda. How did this shift take place, and to what extent are possible negative consequences for both students and the academy overlooked in the process? A brief overview is helpful.

Commercial Interests

In 2003, prior to the rise of the completion agenda, two former university presidents wrote well-regarded books that presented accumulating evidence about the growing influence of commercial interests in higher education. Both raised cautionary flags about the effect of a marketplace mindset on the academy. Derek Bok, former president of Harvard University, began his study of commercialization in higher education with the observation that "during the past twenty-five years, universities have become much more active in *selling* what they know and do to individuals and corporations."[3] And in his study of the public university system, the former president of the University of Michigan James J. Duderstadt devoted an entire chapter to market forces, noting that "governments at the state and federal level have increasingly accepted the argument that a college education should be viewed less as a public investment in an educated citizenry and more as a *consumer good* of primary benefit to the student."[4] Both authors wrote that universities typically relied on extension and continuing education units to meet emerging demands from students and employers, test new programs, and foster innovation and technological change but noted their influence also extended across campuses in response to market forces.

Commercial interests, Bok wrote, shift the university's attention away from its core mission to focus instead on selling and competition, on filling its lecture halls and athletic stadiums, on outpacing the number of applications for admission it receives annually in comparison to its aspirational peers, and on using its popularity to climb national rankings and gain status. As evidence of Bok's prescient caution, during the past decade we have witnessed the transformation of college admissions into "enrollment management" and the extraordinary elevation of its role in administrative hierarchies. Enrollment management rationalizes student recruitment by collecting data and analyzing demographics to yield predictive models about the incoming student body. But if the great sociologist C. Wright Mills were writing today about the influential white-collar businesses of our time, he'd surely replace his iconic "IBM-Man" of the 1950s with the data-obsessed enrollment manager, proud emblem of the rational university.[5]

Market forces, wrote Duderstadt, have encouraged a diverse array of products, services, and providers to serve higher education, particularly the online learning marketplace, offering new technologies and learning platforms to institutions that otherwise would have no experience in these areas. In order to obtain market share or remain competitive in a particular market segment, many institutions today have outsourced a portion of their educational product, allowing third-party providers to deliver these services, especially through e-commerce. In exercising its role to protect consumer interests in the face of growing business involvement with higher education, the federal government through the secretary of education regulates all such outsourcing and expects regional accreditors to oversee the extent to which colleges and universities comply with those regulations.[6]

If Bok and Duderstadt are right about a college education having become a consumer good that is merchandized to increasingly fragmented market segments, what has become of its larger identity as a public good? Does teaching and learning take a backseat to satisfaction and scalability? Will academic majors that yield lower starting salaries suffer at the expense of high-salary fields? Will the importance given to economic efficiencies and workforce development actually yield higher graduation rates? The sections that follow address these questions, examining recent research to evaluate three emphases of the completion agenda: (1) the reliance on part-time faculty, (2) the growth of online delivery, and (3) the emphasis on job-related curricula. At stake is what kind of educational system the completion agenda would have us create and what impact these changes will have on higher education as a public good.

Part-Time Faculty

Certain fields of study, like engineering and fine art, have long been defined by the knowledge and skills gained from professional practice. When they emerged as academic disciplines, these fields historically drew upon the expertise of practitioners to define their curricula, establish learning goals, and set proficiency standards.[7] Indeed, college and university engineering laboratories and studio art spaces in which hands-on applications are practiced attempt to re-create the professional world of the engineer and the artist; technical oversight, creative guidance, and field experience are cornerstones of the learning activities that take place in these facilities. In order to educate students effectively, these disciplines have long employed professionally trained adjunct faculty.

Contemporary engineering education in America is complicated by the need to study math and science, engineering principles and physics, materials and energy, and technology and design. Yet it was not until the Morrill Act that "the dominant pattern of engineering education shifted from shop floors to classrooms."[8] In the transition, programs struggled to balance theory and practice while broadening education to include the humanities and social sciences. Today, the Carnegie Foundation for the Advancement of Teaching has addressed the lingering gulf separating theory and practice in professional and technical education by proposing a "cognitive apprenticeship" model that assigns equal weight to academic knowledge, skills-based practice, and ethics and social responsibility.[9] Nevertheless, at many leading universities, like Johns Hopkins Whiting School of Engineering, professionally trained part-time faculty form the core of their professional engineering programs; at Whiting, part-time faculty outnumber full-time faculty by almost four to one. In states like Illinois, where engineering is a regulated profession, adjuncts who teach in professional programs are expected to hold the professional engineer (PE) license. In general, studies have shown that students gain valuable insights from the adjunct faculty corps about the engineering workplace, as adjuncts tend to emphasize important skills like communication, presentation, and fulfilling customer needs.[10]

In studio art programs today, adjunct faculty members play an equally important role in the education of artists, in large part stemming from the professionalization of the field in commercial areas like graphic design, fashion design, interior design, and digital media, as well as the extensive influence of the fine art marketplace, which has affected the nature of art making as much as its exhibition and sale to the public. The most recent influential manifesto about art education, *Art School (Propositions for the 21ˢᵗ Century)*, argues that universities actually shortchange students when they employ faculty whose experiences are limited only to those they acquired *in* the academy and who lack the hard-won practical knowledge born of taking risks *outside* the academy: "We . . . need to stop hiring faculty artists who have no field experience—artists who have jumped from their BFA to their MFA without blinking and have very little to offer students other than textbook ideas and textbook art."[11] To many, education in the arts cannot be reduced to a single curriculum or assessed by contemporary notions of learning outcomes. As John Baldessari asserts, "Art schools are unlikely bedmates with universities"; what students must learn, he insists, is that "art is not orderly: you don't go A, B, C, D and end up with art."[12]

For the disciplines of engineering and art, then, adjuncts play an essential role, offering skills and practical knowledge central to preparing students to work as an engineer or artist. Schools of business have also included adjunct practitioner faculty in areas like entrepreneurship, management, and leadership when they developed new programs for part-time adult students, midcareer managers, and senior executives, and they increasingly relied on the practical expertise of working professionals to teach these groups during the evenings and on weekends. Yet the role of specialized accreditors of business programs soon divided the field, pushing accredited programs to employ full-time faculties who possessed advanced degrees and who gave equal time to teaching and scholarship. According to Jay Halfond and Thomas Moore, these measures "shifted the emphasis in accredited business schools from practice to theory and from professional to academic credentials."[13] Ironically, over the past decade, in order to preserve their relationship to part-time instructors, universities developed exempt degree programs in areas like professional studies, leadership, administrative studies, and organizational development specifically to skirt the rules of specialized accreditation. Often taught by specialists lacking MBA degrees, these programs avoid those restrictions on research productivity and the role of part-time faculty. Universities knowingly erect a split-level house in their midst when they assign full-time faculty to the accredited program and part-time faculty to the exempt program, thereby reinforcing differences in learning outcomes and status.

But as fiscal constraints have increasingly impinged on college and university budgets, a large corps of non-tenure-track faculty has come to dominate all faculty members nationally and now represents 75 percent of all new hires among nonprofit institutions. Moreover, according to the American Federation of Teachers, approximately 66 percent of all faculty members employed nationally are ineligible for tenure.[14] Among public institutions, part-time or adjunct faculty members form the largest sector of the untenured ranks: in 2012, the National Center for Education Statistics reported that part-time faculty deliver almost 70 percent of all instruction at community colleges; at comprehensive four-year colleges, almost 46 percent.[15] At private, for-profit colleges, nearly all faculty positions are untenured, with more than 88 percent of them part-time.[16] Aside from financial considerations, institutions explain the growth of the part-time instructor as a necessary consequence of dealing with unexpected enrollment demands, of bringing real-world experience into classroom teaching, and as a way to build community relations, particularly for community colleges.

But because part-time instructors are compensated on a per course basis, their economic lives are unstable. Traveling to multiple campuses, they often lead transient lives. Having minimal contact on campus, their influence is marginalized. And with little opportunity to interact with academic peers, they are isolated and unknown, even at their own institutions. As a group, they are also increasingly invisible. After 2003, when funding for the National Study of Postsecondary Faculty ended, so too did broad understanding of their working conditions and how that status affected their teaching. In the absence of national data, several independent groups created volunteer surveys to poll part-time instructors directly. These studies consistently report the following working conditions: inadequate time to prepare classes, with unpredictable course loads; no offices in which to advise students, as well as uncompensated office hours to meet student demand; exclusion from departmental faculty meetings; and insufficient resources for professional development or to attend college meetings.[17]

Not surprisingly, when student contact is minimal, learning consequently suffers. But part-time faculty members also report being cut out of campus-wide discussions about academic governance, including modifications to the curriculum, assessments of student learning, evaluations of student achievements and difficulties, and analyses of rates of retention and completion. In short, the dominant teaching corps on many campuses appears to be increasingly isolated from the core areas that assure quality. Consequently, student retention and graduation rates have been shown to decline as the numbers of part-time non-tenure-track faculty increase.[18] This trend suggests that the goals of the completion agenda are not well served when the part-time faculty outnumber the full-time corps.

Online Education

Since the federal government began collecting data in 1996 on the delivery of online education by postsecondary institutions, the number and kinds of institutions involved, courses offered, degree programs approved, and students enrolled has grown steadily each year. In 1996, NCES estimated that 753,640 students were enrolled in courses online during the previous academic year; in 2013, the Sloan Consortium reported the number taking at least one online course surpassed 7.1 million.[19] In response to this exponential growth, William Bowen proposed that online technologies could help solve the "cost disease" in higher education by reducing instructional expenses over time.[20] Yet it is striking that throughout this period colleges and universities repeatedly justified their online investment in similar ways: to provide students with flexible schedules; to provide increased access to nontraditional groups; to make more courses available; and to increase student enrollment.[21] In short, online education fueled their drive to seek competitive advantage with each other and demonstrate relevancy to students as they vied for enrollments.

The meeting of market-driven competition and new technologies helped disrupt traditional higher education, which has widely expanded the range of educational providers, pedagogical approaches, modes of assessing student learning, ways to record and analyze student engagement, and the kinds of credentials offered. We now have a heady blend of crowd-sourced and peer-taught curricula, open learning resources, technologies informed by big-data and adaptive learning platforms, MOOCs offered in long and shortened varieties, and a wide array of badges and certificates from which to choose. Anya Kamenetz and others have celebrated this wide assortment of educational choices as if it truly empowers learners, but she confuses consumer choice for citizen participation and the entrepreneurial spirit for the public good of higher education.[22]

If 2012 was "the Year of the MOOC," the following year saw that rage fizzle as studies revealed most enrolled students struggled to stay engaged in learning and persevere to the end of the course.[23] This disappointing trend matched new analyses about the learning patterns of typical online students pursuing traditional degrees, particularly those enrolled in community colleges and employed adults working asynchronously. These findings disclosed that online students are significantly more likely to fail or withdraw than students in traditional "on-ground" classes, according to Columbia University's Community College Research Center; in fact, one of the center's five-year studies completed in 2011 tracked 50,000 students and found that those who enrolled in higher proportions of online courses were less likely to earn degrees or transfer to four-year colleges.[24]

Because evidence shows that highly motivated self-starters are best equipped to succeed in online programs, Harvard Business School's decision to enter this marketplace in June 2014 came under close scrutiny. Unmoved by Bowen's concerns for college affordability, two of Harvard's faculty celebrities considered the university's decision to take its business program online as if it were simply a question of risk management, that is, whether it was better to risk devaluing the on-campus brand for which a tuition premium was paid, or whether failing to go online could potentially leave the university vulnerable to external competition. Harvard ultimately decided to create a program for a carefully nuanced market segment; this choice pleased neither professor, however, because each believed Harvard was attempting to retain its competitive advantage but refusing to disrupt its existing business model entirely.[25] Ironically, online MBA programs offered by less-influential universities have been forced to declare their own value proposition, grasping to find their way in a cluttered online marketplace that has commoditized its own product.[26] These trends have contributed to a sense of inevitability about the continued growth and legitimacy of online learning. Indeed, as Paul LeBlanc has claimed, "while many nonprofit institutions are just now catching up with online programs, often entering that market because of economic pressures, online learning is already well understood, well established, and well respected by those who genuinely know it."[27]

Nevertheless, a gap in perception still exists between advocates like LeBlanc and the public at large. For example, in 2011, according to Public Agenda, less than a third of American adults thought online programs were equal to or better than classroom-based learning, and in 2012, only half said an online degree "provides a similar quality of education as compared to traditional colleges or universities."[28] The same survey indicated employers recognized a niche for online education for older students and that many valued the discipline students acquired from those programs, but at the same time they also remained largely unconvinced about the quality of the educational experience they received. Online programs have indeed expanded access, lowered costs, and made educational opportunities possible for many individuals for whom it would be otherwise unattainable. But it rewards only the most self-motivated students and still has yet to convince a skeptical public about its value and quality.

Workforce Development

One of the central tenets of the completion agenda is the claim that America's employers are seeking individuals who are college-prepared as a condition of their employment. Another is that higher education should equip students to succeed in today's knowledge economy, our technology-rich and globalized world, where hydra-like supply chains have replaced local manufacturing and where commercial success depends upon workers' agility in adapting to changing environments. Yet another claim is the familiar demand for college graduates to possess basic critical thinking, problem solving, and computational skills.[29] Indeed, in 2002, the Association of American Colleges and Universities (AACU) report *Greater Expectations* noted that a college education often produced "inconsistent results," which "lead employers to question higher education's effectiveness and wish that its degrees, like technical certification, ensured documented levels of accomplishment."[30] To compound this problem, business leaders report a gap now exists between employers who have jobs to fill but cannot find those who possess the right skills to perform these jobs. In 2013, for example, the Business-Higher Education Forum reported that "the number of job openings in the United States has grown to nearly 4 million, with many going unfilled for long periods of time because approximately half of employers now claim they cannot find employees with the competencies, skills, and degrees they need."[31]

To help solve these problems, foundations have allied with business and industry to help answer the education-to-employment challenge. In 2012, for example, McKinsey Global Institute reported that by 2020, employers worldwide could face a shortage of 85 million high- and medium-skilled workers and that higher education must help by redesigning curricula, meeting employer needs by

> moving away from traditional lectures and the lecture-home-work-exam format to a student-centered format, which engages students through active learning with business partners providing business-relevant, real-world projects, guest lectures, or course co-development, matching more closely the classroom experience to the professional setting and motivating students to actively apply their coursework.[32]

McKinsey's ideas have significantly influenced the Lumina Foundation, as evidenced by its McKinsey-sponsored publication, *Education to Employment*, which calls for using online education to develop a standardized curriculum "to supplement faculty and spread consistent instruction at a modest cost"; to use technology "in the form of 'serious games' and other kinds of simulations"; to provide "practical experience to large numbers at a comparatively low cost"; and to offer incentives to employers that "combine customization and scale by offering a standard core curriculum complemented by employer-specific" additions.[33] Similarly, in 2012, the Bill and Melinda Gates Foundation dispensed $9 million in grant funding "to provide more students with an affordable opportunity to receive a high-quality postsecondary credential with labor market value."[34]

Innovative programs that lead to sub-baccalaureate credentials like badges and certificates promise to meet this demand and help satisfy the economic imperative.[35] So too do new competency-based programs, whose advocates imagine learning as the only viable academic currency for today's "post-traditional learners," who can now be liberated from seat time and the credit hour, traditional college measures that accounted for the time that students spent on their studies and the unit value assigned to each class.[36] For example, Southern New Hampshire University's College for America was created with employers serving as curriculum advisers to provide real-world guidance to academics on how to set up the competency-based tasks that form the basis of the associate's degree conferred by this institution. Created for working adults who possess some college but who lack a degree, students complete 120 competency-based tasks to earn a credential that demonstrates preparation to succeed in the workplace.[37] The university's development of an accelerated, three-year, integrated, competency-based bachelors degree accomplishes the same objectives by saving a fourth year of tuition and providing "a set of competencies that would make its graduates more attractive candidates for employment."[38]

While preparation to succeed in the working world has always been a tacit objective of obtaining a college education, the emphasis today on skills development and job preparation is extreme and threatens to eclipse other reasons to pursue higher education, like providing students a foundation for how to learn and think analytically, understand the experience of others, value material culture and human expression, and plan for the future. Indeed, even when it recognized employers' frustrations with ineffectively prepared college graduates, AACU's *Greater Expectations* still promoted the virtues of a liberal education. "As an educational philosophy rather than a body of knowledge," the report noted, liberal education "asks students to grapple with complicated, important issues"; as a result, its students are transformed and become "intentional about learning and life, empowered, informed, and responsible."[39] And while competency-based education promises to use andragogy and practical experience to condense courses in the humanities and social sciences into performance-based tasks and assignments, its roots originate in cognitive models of job training and its reliance upon evidence-based presentations belie its vocational origins, at least for postsecondary learners.[40]

Although studies reveal that alumni of science and engineering programs (the so-called STEM fields) initially earn greater compensation than others, a recent long-term study of college graduates holding degrees in the liberal arts and sciences revealed they also "earn middle-class salaries, make progress in their careers, and close earnings gaps with those who hold baccalaureate degrees in professional and preprofessional fields."[41] Economists ever since Adam Smith have asserted that liberal arts and sciences enrich the social life and economic framework of society.[42] Yet in spite of these facts, liberal education is truly absent from the completion agenda. In order to reach its college completion goals, for example, the Lumina Foundation proposes instead devoting resources toward developing "learning-based approaches—including competency-based courses and degrees, open or low-cost courseware, accelerated learning models, credit and degree aggregation, course redesign, and assessment of prior learning" to create "postsecondary credentials based on transparent recognition of skills and knowledge, including those required by employers. This approach will contribute to the creation of an aligned system for delivering high-value credentials to millions more learners."[43]

Accreditation and the Public Good

When college graduates themselves were asked about the value of their college experiences in a 2014 Gallup-Purdue University study, they reported that a professor's personal contact with them—as a supportive and caring individual, mentor, or advisor—was instrumental to their success and emotional well-being when they were enrolled and that they felt this positive impact many years later, long after graduation.[44] There would appear to be significant dissonance between this key finding and Lumina Foundation's "learning-based approaches" model described above, where, in the name of cost-savings and economic scalability, employer-based benchmarks and individualized, self-paced models are called upon to replace the personal contact of professors. At the state level, of course, public higher education has been increasingly defunded while performance-based budgetary models have gained ascendancy, but colleges and universities are not compelled to promote business-oriented fields at the expense of the liberal arts and sciences or to invest in adaptive learning technologies and online delivery platforms over full-time faculty to fulfill their educational missions.

Indeed, higher education accreditation expects colleges and universities to educate students broadly as evidence of their service and commitment to the public good. The Higher Learning Commission, the nation's largest regional accreditor, unambiguously affirms the importance of higher education as a public good; indeed, accreditation is awarded in the name of civic responsibility. In 2012, the commission affirmed the following as core elements as essential to its "guiding values":

Because education is a public good its provision serves a public purpose and entails societal obligations. Furthermore, the provision of higher education requires a more complex standard of care than, for instance, the provision of dry cleaning services. *What the students buy, with money, time, and effort, is not merely a good, like a credential, but experiences that have the potential to transform lives, or to harm them.* [emphasis added] What institutions do constitutes a solemn responsibility for which they should hold themselves accountable.[45]

This fundamental value is reiterated in the Higher Learning Commission's standards by which it holds all accredited institutions accountable, known as its *Criteria for Accreditation*: "The institution's mission demonstrates commitment to the public good" (1.D), along with its clarifying subcomponent, "The institution's educational responsibilities take primacy over other purposes, such as generating financial returns for investors, contributing to a related or parent organization, or supporting external interests" (1.D.2).[46] Every accredited institution is expected to provide evidence that support these expectations.

Higher education serves the public good in numerous ways, and many factors may influence how policy makers think about its impact as a powerful economic engine, a producer of new knowledge and research, and/or an agent of democracy, intellectual integrity, and civic engagement.[47] But as Bok and Duderstadt cautioned many years ago, a competitive and consumer-based service model has threatened to take hold of many institutions. Instead of promoting college readiness for all students, for example, attention now focuses on the attainment of workforce-created sub-baccalaureate credentials, as companies like Udacity create so-called nanodegrees to compete with universities' certificates. Like goods purchased from a mail-order catalog, each credential can be used independently or "stacked" and assembled in portfolios, an approach duplicated by universities.[48] Rather than devising new ways to enhance meaningful contact between professors and students in real or virtual classrooms, technologies that atomize individuals even more into their laptops and cell phones are normalized and their widespread use seem inevitable.

In the name of economic necessity, political imperative, and global competitiveness, today's advocates of the completion agenda have inflated consumerism into a kind of noble cause, accepting nothing less than "increasing the proportion of Americans with high-quality degrees, certificates, and other credentials to 60 percent by the year 2025."[49] In the name of technological innovation, they portray the core values of accreditation as out of touch or as obstacles to this goal.[50] But in the name of completion, they have supported the growth of contingent and part-time faculty, promoted the growth of adaptive technologies to deliver instruction, and elevated the importance of job skills and training over other kinds of knowledge. For the majority of students, however, these developments have been shown to decrease their retention in academic programs rather than increase it, and ironically, college completion suffers as a result. Accreditation may not be able to change these trends, but it fulfills its public role by focusing on the student experience and the transformative value of higher education, reminding the public that credentials are evidence of a student's academic success, not consumer items purchased in the marketplace.

Notes

1. Organisation for Economic Co-operation and Development, *Education at a Glance 2013: OECD Indicators* (Paris, France: OECD Publishing, 2013), accessed at http://dx.doi.org/10.1787/eag-2013-en; Katie Zaback, Andy Carlson, and Matt Crellin, *The Economic Benefit of Postsecondary Degrees: A State and National Level Analysis*, December 2012, accessed at http://www.sheeo .org/sites/default/files/publications/Econ%20Benefit%20of%20 Degrees%20Report%20with%20Appendices.pdf; Lumina Foundation, *A Stronger Nation through Higher Education: Visualizing Data to Help Us Achieve a Big Goal for College Attainment*, 2013, accessed at http://www .luminafoundation.org/stronger_nation_2013/downloads/pdfs/a -stronger-nation-2013.pdf .

2. Arthur Levine and Diane R. Dean, *Generation on a Tightrope: A Portrait of Today's College Student* (San Francisco: Jossey-Bass, 2012).

3. Derek Bok, *Universities in the Marketplace: The Commercialization of Higher Education* (Princeton, NJ: Princeton University Press, 2003), vii [emphasis added].

4. James J. Duderstadt and Farris W. Womack, *The Future of the Public University in America: Beyond the Crossroads* (Baltimore: Johns Hopkins University Press, 2003), 75 [emphasis added].

5. C. Wright Mills, *White Collar* (New York: Oxford University Press, 1951).

6. See the US Code of Federal Regulations 34 CFR 668.5(c).

7. In art, the classic study is Nikolaus Pevsner, *Academies of Art: Past and Present* (Cambridge, England: Cambridge University Press, 1940); in engineering, see the *Journal of Engineering Education*, created in Chicago at the World's Columbian Exposition of 1893 by the Society for the Promotion of Engineering Education.

8. Bruce E. Seely, "Patterns in the History of Engineering Education Reform: A Brief Essay," in National Academy of Engineering, *Educating the Engineer of 2020: Adapting Engineering Education to the New Century* (Washington, DC: National Academies Press, 2005), 115.

9. First introduced in 2005 by Sherri Shepard, "Preparation for the Professions Program: Engineering Education in the United States," in *Educating the Engineer of 2020*, 132; and later in William M. Sullivan and Matthew

S. Rosin, *A New Agenda for Higher Education: Shaping a Life of the Mind for Practice* (San Francisco: Jossey-Bass, 2008).

10. Joan P. Gosink and Ruth A. Streveler, "Bringing Adjunct Engineering Faculty into the Learning Community," *Journal of Engineering Education* 89, no. 1 (2000): 47–51.

11. Steven Henry Madoff, ed., *Art School (Propositions for the 21st Century)* (Cambridge: MIT Press, 2009), 7.

12. "Conversation: John Baldessari and Michael Craig-Martin," in *Art School (Propositions for the 21st Century)*, 45.

13. Jay A. Halfond and Thomas E. Moore, "Academe Makes for Strange Bedfellows: How Continuing Education and Schools of Management Collide and Cooperate," *Continuing Higher Education Review* 73 (2009): 84.

14. Jack H. Schuster and Martin J. Finkelstein, *The American Faculty: The Restructuring of Academic Work and Careers* (Baltimore: Johns Hopkins University Press, 2006), 324; American Federation of Teachers, *The American Academic: The State of Higher Education Workforce, 1997–2007* (Washington, DC: American Federation of Teachers, 2009); Adrianna Kezar and Sean Gehrke, "Why Are We Hiring So Many Non-Tenure-Track Faculty?" *Liberal Education* 100, no. 1 (Winter 2014), accessed at http://www.aacu .org/liberaleducation/le-wi14/kezar_gehrke.cfm.

15. National Center for Education Statistics, *Integrated Postsecondary Education Data System* (Washington, DC: US Department of Education, 2012).

16. *AAUP Contingent Faculty Index* (Washington, DC: American Association of University Professors, 2006), accessed at http://www.aaup.org /sites/default/files/files/AAUPContingentFacultyIndex2006.pdf. See also Andrea Kezar and Daniel Maxey, *An Examination of the Changing Faculty: Ensuring Institutional Quality and Achieving Desired Student Learning Outcomes* (Washington: Council for Higher Education Accreditation, January 2014), 5.

17. Center for Community College Student Engagement, *Contingent Commitments: Bringing Part-Time Faculty into Focus (A Special Report)* (Austin, TX: University of Texas at Austin, Program in Higher Education Leadership, 2014); House Committee on Education and the Workforce, Democratic Staff, *The Just-In-Time Professor: A Staff Report Summarizing eForum Responses on the Working Conditions of Contingent Faculty in Higher Education*, January 2014, accessed at http://www.mpsanet.org/Portals /0/1.24.14-AdjunctEforumReport.pdf; Coalition on the Academic Workforce, *A Portrait of Part-Time Faculty Members*, June 2012, accessed at http://www.academicworkforce.org/survey.html; Center for the Future of Higher Education, *Who Is Professor 'Staff' and How Can This Person Teach So Many Classes?* August 2012, accessed at http://www.insidehighered.com /sites/default/server_files/files/profstaff%282%29.pdf.

18. Kezar and Maxey, *An Examination of the Changing Faculty*, 7.

19. US Department of Education, Institute of Education Sciences, Na-

tional Center for Education Statistics, *Distance Education in Higher Education Institutions* (1997), table 10, accessed at http://nces.ed.gov /pubs98/98062.pdf; I. Elaine Allen and Jeff Seaman, *Grade Change: Tracking Online Education in the United States*, Babson Survey Research Group and Quahog Research Group (2014).

20. William G. Bowen, *Higher Education in the Digital Age* (Princeton, NJ: Princeton University Press, 2013).

21. US Department of Education, Institute of Education Sciences, National Center for Education Statistics, *Distance Education at Degree-Granting Postsecondary Institutions: 2006–07* (2008), table 13, accessed at http://nces.ed.gov/pubs2009/2009044.pdf.

22. Anya Kamenetz, *DIY U: Edupunks, Edupreneurs, and the Coming Transformation of Higher Education* (White River Junction, VT: Chelsea Green, 2010); this consumerist perspective is critiqued by Henry Giroux, "Neoliberalism, Corporate Culture, and the Promise of Higher Education: The University as a Democratic Public Sphere," *Harvard Educational Review* 72, no. 4 (Winter 2002): 425–463.

23. According to the *New York Times Education Life* Supplement, accessed at http://www.nytimes.com/2012/11/04/education/edlife/massive -open-online-courses-are-multiplying-at-a-rapid-pace.html?_r=0; Laura Perna et al., *The Life Cycle of a Million MOOC Users*, MOOC Research Initiative Conference, University of Pennsylvania, 2013, accessed at http://www.gse.upenn.edu/pdf/ahead/perna_ruby_boruch_moocs _dec2013.pdf.

24. Community College Research Center, *What We Know about Online Courses* (New York: Teachers College, Columbia University, April 2013), accessed at http://ccrc.tc.columbia.edu/media/k2/attachments/online -learning-practitioner-packet.pdf.

25. Jerry Useem, "B-School, Disrupted," *New York Times*, June 1, 2014.

26. Srikant M. Datar, David A. Garvin, and Patrick G. Cullen, *Rethinking the MBA: Business Education at a Crossroads* (Boston: Harvard Business Press, 2010).

27. Paul LeBlanc, "Thinking about Accreditation in a Rapidly Changing World," WASC Concept Papers, 2nd Series, January 2013, accessed at https://wascsenior.app.box.com/s/b07qq706a36inujpfoqg.

28. "Not Yet Sold: What Employers and Community College Students Think About Online Education," Public Agenda (2013), 3, accessed at http://www.publicagenda.org/files/NotYetSold_PublicAgenda_2013.pdf.

29. The Economist Intelligence Unit, *Closing the Skills Gap: Companies and Colleges Collaborating for Change*, Lumina Foundation, 2014, accessed at http://www.luminafoundation.org/publications/Closing_the_skills_gap.pdf.

30. American Association of Colleges and Universities, *Greater Expectations: A New Vision for Learning as a Nation Goes to College*, 2002, 8, accessed at http://www.greaterexpectations.org/pdf/gex.final.pdf.

31. *The National Higher Education and Workforce Initiative: Forging Strategic Partnerships for Undergraduate Innovation and Workforce Development* (Washington, D.C.: Business-Higher Education Forum, 2013), 3, accessed at http://www.bhef.com/sites/g/files/g829556/f/201308/2013_report_playbook.PDF.

32. McKinsey Global Institute, *The World at Work: Jobs, Pay, and Skills for 3.5 Billion People,* June 2012, accessed at http://www.mckinsey.com/insights/employment_and_growth/the_world_at_work.

33. Mona Mourshed, Diana Farrell, and Dominic Barton, *Education to Employment: Designing a System That Works* (McKinsey Center for Government, 2102), p. 21 , accessed at http://dl.njit.edu/mnj/Education-to-Employment_FINAL.pdf.

34. Bill and Melinda Gates Foundation, "Gates Foundation Announces $9 Million in Grants to Support Breakthrough Learning Models in Postsecondary Education," press release, June 19, 2012, accessed at http://www.gatesfoundation.org/Media-Center/Press-Releases/2012/06/Gates-Foundation-Announces-Grants-to-Support-Learning-Models.

35. This is a major initiative of the conservative American Enterprise Institute; see Andrew P. Kelly and Mark Schneider, eds., *Getting to Graduation: The Completion Agenda in Higher Education* (Baltimore: Johns Hopkins University Press, 2012).

36. Sally M. Johnstone, Peter Ewell, and Karen Paulson, *Student Learning as Academic Currency,* American Council on Education Center for Policy Analysis (2010), accessed at https://bookstore.acenet.edu/products/student-learning-academic-currency-2010-pdf; Louis Soares, "Post-Traditional Learners and the Transformation of Postsecondary Education: A Manifesto for College Leaders," American Council on Education (2013), accessed at http://www.acenet.edu/news-room/Documents/Post-traditional-Learners.pdf.

37. According to Paul LeBlanc, president of Southern New Hampshire University's College for America (CfA): "We have targeted CfA at the lowest 10% of wage earners in large companies, adults who have zero to few college credits and who need a degree to improve their skills, retain a grip on their employment, seek better employment, and move up the job ladder within their organizations. We work with large scale employers like ConAgra Foods, McDonalds, Panera Bread, Partners Health, the City of Memphis, Anthem Blue Cross-Blue Shield, and others. Many of these employees are making minimum wage, often not making family sustaining wages." Paul LeBlanc, *Written Testimony to the Committee on Health, Education, Labor, and Pensions* (October 2013), accessed at http://www.help.senate.gov/imo/media/doc/LeBlanc.pdf.

38. Martin J. Bradley, Robert H. Seidman, and Steven R. Painchaud, *Saving Higher Education: The Integrated, Competency-Based Three-Year Bachelor's Degree Program* (San Francisco: Jossey-Bass, 2012), 68.

39. AACU, *Greater Expectations*, 25.
40. Terry Hyland, "National Vocational Qualifications, Skills Training and Employers' Needs," *Journal of Vocational Education and Training* 48, no. 4 (1996): 349–365; Sandra Kerka, "Competency-Based Education and Training," ERIC Clearinghouse (1998), accessed at http://www.calpro-online.org/eric/docgen.asp?tbl=mr&ID=65.
41. Debra Humphreys and Patrick Kelly, *How Liberal Arts and Sciences Majors Fare in Employment: A Report on Earnings and Long-Term Career Paths* (Washington, DC: Association of American Colleges and Universities, 2014), 20.
42. Jacob Soll, "The Economic Logic of the Humanities," *Chronicle Review*, February 28, 2014, B4–5.
43. Lumina Foundation, *Strategic Plan 2013 to 2016* (2013), 19, accessed at http://www.luminafoundation.org/advantage/document/goal_2025/2013-Lumina_Strategic_Plan.pdf.
44. Gallup, Inc., *Great Jobs, Great Lives: The 2014 Gallup-Purdue Index Report* (2014), 7, accessed at http://s3.amazonaws.com/content.washingtonexaminer.biz/web-producers/GallupPurdueIndex_Report_2014_050514.pdf.
45. Higher Learning Commission, *The Criteria for Accreditation*, "Guiding Values," accessed at https://www.ncahlc.org/Criteria-Eligibility-and-Candidacy/guiding-values-new-criteria-for-accreditation.html.
46. Higher Learning Commission, *The Criteria for Accreditation*, revised and made effective January 1, 2013, accessed at http://policy.ncahlc.org/Policies/criteria-for-accreditation.html.
47. Tony Chambers and Bryan Gopaul, "Decoding the Public Good of Higher Education," *Journal of Higher Education Outreach and Engagement* 12, no. 4 (2008): 59–91.
48. "Efficient, Accessible, Affordable Online Program Will Help Job Seekers Get High-Demand Technical Skills: AT&T and Udacity Launching Business-Led Nanodegree Based on Real-World Needs," press release, June 16, 2014, accessed at http://www.marketwatch.com/story/efficient-accessible-affordable-online-program-will-help-job-seekers-get-high-demand-technical-skills-2014-06-16.
49. Lumina Foundation, *Strategic Plan 2013 to 2016*, 1.
50. Accreditation's perceived resistance to innovation has been a consistent rallying cry of advocates of the completion agenda, where the term is used as shorthand for new educational approaches that rely on technology to deliver instruction or assess learning. So-called disruptive innovation is a hallmark associated with Clayton M. Christensen's book, *The Innovative University* (San Francisco: Jossey-Bass, 2011). For an effective rebuttal of the mandate to innovate, see Jill Lepore, "The Disruption Machine: What the Gospel of Innovation Gets Wrong," *New Yorker*, June 23, 2014, 33–36.

Ensuring More Working Adults Can Pursue Higher Education

■■

Kay J. Kohl

What will tomorrow's workforce look like? And what could it portend for professional and continuing higher education?

Since the Great Recession, the country's economic recovery has been inching ahead slowly. It is apparent that many legacy industry jobs have vanished. Still new jobs are being created and employers are hiring today. Yet labor economists are cautioning that within a few years employers may not have a sufficient supply of qualified workers with postsecondary education to fill their workforce needs.

To be certain, at many colleges and universities, professional and continuing higher education experienced a surge of enrollments during the recent recession. At the same time, changing higher education demographics together with the widespread diffusion of digital technologies have challenged higher education institutions' long-standing instructional practices, credentialing, and budgetary models.

What are some of the key trends affecting professional and continuing higher education's responses to the changing workforce? And how might they influence the directions in which traditional higher education evolves?

Staying Competitive Requires Raising US Educational Attainment

Currently, millions of adults—spanning a wide age range—are pursuing a baccalaureate or postgraduate degree on either a full-time or part-time basis in the United States. Many students hold down a job while pursuing

---

Kay J. Kohl was the UPCEA Chief Executive Officer, 1984–2010.

their studies in order to afford to pay their college fees. Therefore they graduate later than their counterparts in other developed countries. The average student in the United States is thirty years old when awarded a baccalaureate degree, and two-thirds will have accumulated nearly $30,000 in student loan debts.

According to the latest estimates, by 2025 the United States will need to produce an additional twenty million college-educated workers. That breaks down to fifteen million workers with a college or postgraduate degree, plus another five million with at least one year of postsecondary education.[1] For the last several years, however, the supply of US college graduates has not been in tandem with the economy's demand. Often there has been a mismatch between labor force needs and the qualifications of the job seekers.

Looking ahead, the opportunities for economic mobility appear robust both for young adults who acquire the vocational education and training that prepares them for an advanced manufacturing setting and for those adults who earn baccalaureate degrees in high-demand fields such as business management, engineering, and health care. Maintaining a successful career in the case of both groups is dependent upon being able to access ongoing education and technical skills training. Some employers who are eager to build a qualified, innovative workforce are prepared to take it upon themselves to make substantial investments in the development of relevant education for their employees. A number of individual workers also can foresee that an investment in obtaining a higher educational credential would be their best opportunity to advance their career prospects.

The change in education requirements for a professional license can be a powerful motivator for working adults to enroll in a degree program. Licensed registered nurses (RNs) are one group now feeling pressure to earn a baccalaureate degree or higher.[2] The Affordable Care Act (ACA), launched in 2014, brought many more patients into the US health care system and introduced new pay-for-performance standards. As a consequence, hospitals and other providers are compensated based on patient outcomes. Hospitals with a high percentage of baccalaureate-prepared nurses rank better than those with fewer, according to research. Moreover there is an increased demand for specialized geriatric nurses and nurse practitioners who hold postgraduate degrees and for certified nurse midwives. Taking into account the anticipated growth in demand for nurses and the replacement of all those projected to leave the profession, it is estimated that there will be well over a million job openings for nurses by 2022.[3]

Accredited, online university nursing bachelor's degree programs are especially popular. A big part of the appeal of online programs among registered nurses is that this mode of study makes it possible for nurses to earn a degree without any interruption to their employment.

Competency-Based Education Attracts Renewed Interest

All too frequently part-time adult students' progress toward a four-year degree can be derailed when they attempt to transfer to a four-year institution. A recent national study by two scholars at the Graduate Center at the City University of New York revealed that 58 percent of students were able to transfer all or most of their credits from a community college when transferring to a four-year institution, whereas 42 percent of the students lost between 10 and 89 percent of their credits.[4] Not surprisingly, credit leakage during the transfer process was found to be the most influential factor determining whether or not a student earns a baccalaureate degree.

In an attempt to slow credit leakage, some community colleges are creating articulation agreements with professional and continuing education units in public and private universities. It is common for these agreements to rest on program-specific accreditation as a way of ensuring that departments in both institutions adhere to the same standards. Elsewhere a few state legislatures have mandated that community colleges and local public four-year institutions create programs to ensure that students at two-year colleges are able to transfer as many credits as possible when they enter a four-year college.

Also, more and more employers are alert to the impending talent gap and are willing to help subsidize their employees' education. The opportunity to earn a competency-based college degree and pay only a fraction of the price of a traditional course-based degree has become an attractive option for some students and employers. A degree model that requires students to follow a structured pathway as they master a set of prescribed competencies (in lieu of credit hours) holds a certain appeal. Employers like the idea that their employees will be mastering specific competencies, many of which have a direct application in their workplace. The fact that regional accreditors recently have given the green light to a few colleges that have introduced competency-based degrees can be viewed as further validation of the option.

Yet another type of competency-based education that has attracted renewed interest is prior learning assessment. These programs are especially suited to midcareer adults who may already have a community college degree but have yet to earn a four-year degree. Upon enrolling in the university, students are given a chance to earn additional credits toward a degree by paying for an intensive in-person assessment. Students who can successfully demonstrate their knowledge and skills in person to faculty assessors stand to earn a number of credits toward their degree and realize a substantial savings of time and tuition. Competency-based programs do not eliminate classroom and online courses. The programs recognize the work and life experiences that adults bring to their studies and seek to minimize the bureaucratic hurdles that can impede students' progress.

There is no single best model for an accessible, part-time degree program for working adults. What is important, as one foundation report stated, is for colleges and universities "to ensure that all students who seek the opportunity are able to complete a high-quality, affordable post-secondary education that leads to a sustaining career."[5]

Demographic Shifts Challenge Workforce Assumptions

Workers age 55 and older comprise the fastest growing segment of the US labor force. By 2020, older workers will account for 25 percent of the US labor force, compared to only 13 percent in 2000. The baby boomer generation that joined the labor force in the late 1960s tends to be on average healthier, better educated, and more active than previous generations. This explains in part why many baby boomers are choosing to stay in the workforce past retirement age. In fact, the labor force participation rate of those 55 and older was slightly higher in 2013 than in either 2007 or 2010.[6] Where there has been a decline in US labor force participation during this period is among workers of a much younger age.

There is no doubt that the Great Recession prompted people to revisit their retirement plans. Many older workers subsequently postponed withdrawing from the labor force in order to accumulate additional savings for their retirement. Others have elected to remain in the workforce a few years longer, simply because they enjoy working and being productive.

Interestingly, the baby boomer generation has spawned a strong subset of entrepreneurs. It would be easy to conclude, based on frequent media reports about young high-tech CEOs, that the 20-to-34-year-old cohort is where the country's entrepreneurial talent is concentrated, but that would be incorrect. The highest rate of entrepreneurship in the United States has shifted to the 55–64 age group. According to the Kaufmann Foundation, people over 55 are almost twice as likely to found successful companies than those between ages 20 and 34.[7] Among older baby boomers there appears to be a substantial number who are keenly interested in creating their own business and, moreover, possibly willing to invest some of their own savings in an entrepreneurial venture.

At present, a few elite universities offer working professionals an opportunity to enroll in a flexible advanced study program on an unmatriculated, nondegree basis. Typically, participants in such programs design their own curricula and set their own pace. And often their employers are willing to underwrite participants' customized study programs.

Economic Imperatives Foster Collaborations

Employment of computer software developers is projected to grow 22 percent in the coming decade.[8] The growth is happening because industries are finding ever more uses for computer software. Mobile technology, health care systems, computer security systems, and consumer electronics are just some of the major drivers of demand for trained computer talent. It makes for an environment where competition among employers for new talent has become intense. And this explains in part why a top US university engineering school and a for-profit educational organization offering massive open online courses (MOOCs) decided to collaborate on the creation of an affordable online master's degree in computer science. The low $7,000 cost of the master's degree also proved so attractive that a major telecommunications corporation was persuaded to provide a generous initial program subsidy for the project.

The university and the MOOC organization that are collaborating on the low-cost online master's degree in computer science anticipate that the project will realize the benefits of scale and be revenue-producing for both parties at least by the third year.[9] By that time they expect to have completed the major upfront investments and have in place the large corps of course managers and teaching assistants required to support a rapidly scaling program. In the first year of operation, the average age of the students enrolled in the program was 34, as compared with 23 in the university's residential program. A number of the applicants accepted already possess advanced degrees and view the master's program as an opportunity to update their credentials.[10] These data suggest that developing high-quality content for an affordable online degree program delivered via a MOOC could be a productive business model for a top-flight university that wants to deliver highly sought-after master's degree programs to widely dispersed populations of midcareer adults in the United States and possibly also abroad.

Higher education has shifted from a public good to a largely private one in the United States, especially following the precipitous decline in state appropriations to public institutions in recent years. Inevitably, climbing tuition fees and student debt have made students of all ages far more cost-conscious consumers. For instance, they expect their colleges and universities to offer both online and face-to-face classroom courses in most programs. Students want the flexibility of mixing courses accessed via different delivery modes because, apart from convenience considerations, it may enable them to earn a credential faster and so save money.

Online Higher Education Becomes the "New Normal"

Prior to the Great Recession, online degree programs at many universities were largely the province of professional and continuing education units. Today many university leaders view the expansion of online programs as a promising institution-wide strategy that has the potential to furnish a substantial revenue stream for a financially strapped institution.

As colleges and universities have sought to expand online enrollments, their attention has focused on the promotion of collaborations and elimination of duplications. A number of large state university systems have built extensive portfolios of online degree programs simply by uniting the dozens of existing online degree offerings developed by individual campuses under a single university system brand and placing management of the system in a central office—one that is often led by professional and continuing education personnel. The online degree programs available in state university system portfolios tend to target working professionals, practitioners, and managers in growth occupations. This emphasis is a response to market demand and also offers universities an opportunity to highlight the value of their institutions' online degree offerings to the economic success of their state.

The conversion of classroom courses into quality online programs rarely reduces costs. However online programs do yield valuable student data that, when subjected to large-scale measurement analysis, can help an institution assess how well different instructional approaches work. Securing resources to pay for this kind of research and the infrastructure needed to effectively support large enrollments in university online programs tends to be a perennial challenge. It is one of the reasons why many universities choose to partner with a for-profit provider of online education services. Among the services that especially interest universities with substantial online portfolios are marketing, student support, student analytics, and adaptive learning. Some for-profit service providers offer program development as well. However the practice of ceding academic control to a commercial company provokes considerable controversy. Most universities maintain that program development must be a responsibility reserved for their own faculty and are unwilling to contract out the function.

While a few years ago employers were inclined to question the legitimacy of an online degree, attitudes have changed rapidly in the interim. Now many universities that have online degree portfolios are forging collaborations with large employers. Recently, a large state university struck a deal with a major international corporation to provide discounted tuition to the company's huge low-wage workforce.[11] Under the terms of the agreement negotiated, all workers in the company will have a chance to earn a degree at a discounted rate. Insofar as many of the workers qualify for federal Pell grants, that financial aid in addition to the discounted fees will flow to the university. Moreover, the university may eventually realize substantial benefits of scale from this new collaboration. For its part, the company stands to attract better workers and enhance its corporate brand. What sets the program apart is not the size of the benefits offered. Many companies offer their employees substantially more generous educational benefits. Very few employers, however, offer educational benefits to their low-wage employees.

Employers Prefer Technically Savvy Professionals

It was not so very long ago that US workers could expect to have perhaps four or five jobs during a work life, whereas today the norm is around twelve.[12] As for careers, having four or five different careers today is not unusual. Technological change has automated jobs in many industries. US employment in manufacturing is now less than 10 percent, and the services sector accounts for almost 80 percent of all jobs.[13] The jobs that are not easily automated are those that are not routine and which require specialized knowledge and the flexibility of human workers to make complex organizations effective. As computers have suffused the workplace, both the knowledge and the skill sets required for jobs have also risen.

There is a widening wage gap between workers with a college degree and those with a postgraduate degree. This wage differential is attributed to the different skill sets and jobs of postgraduates and college graduates.[14] A recent study by economists Joanne Lindley and Stephen Machin found that when computers were massively diffused in the workplace, postgraduates were found to have higher levels of numeracy, specialist knowledge, and ability to analyze complex problems, compared to workers with a baccalaureate degree.[15] This explains in part why many employers favor postgraduates who possess qualifications that correlate with the heightened use of computers to perform complex tasks in their organizations and are willing to pay the salaries required to recruit talented postgraduates.

Still, employers may not be able to attract critical talent with wage increases alone. When it comes to recruitment, some of the most successful organizations are those that can demonstrate a commitment to employee career development by offering generous ongoing training and career development opportunities together with coaching and mentoring. Because the critical skills required tend to be continually changing in the face of new technology and shifting global markets, employers must not only attract workers with the skill sets that support an organization's current strategy but also seek to engage individuals who are continuing learners eager to update their knowledge.

An increasing number of organizations are personalizing their educational benefits in an effort to avoid losing critical talent. This stems from recognition that gender and generational differences can also be expected to influence the appeal of alternative educational perks. Sometimes employers are willing to offer a sabbatical to a valued worker who wants the freedom to pursue a passion. Offering such a sabbatical can be immensely important to the employee and ultimately also of value to the employer.

Currently, a few private elite universities in the United States provide postgraduate professionals an opportunity to enroll in a flexible advanced study program on an unmatriculated degree basis. Participants in such programs typically design their own curricula and set their own pace. Their employers often underwrite the participants' customized study programs.

Professionals Earn Certificates to Stay Ahead in a Changing Job Market

University professional education units frequently are the first to offer accredited certificate and master's degree programs in emerging fields such as cybersecurity, sustainability management, astronautics, and sequence analysis and genomics. This is one of the field's signature contributions. Moreover it is a service that appears to have considerable growth potential in light of the expansion of online education nationally and internationally. History suggests that good jobs are bound to appear in a new sector from time to time even as they disappear in another. For the professional who wants to take advantage of new opportunities, a certificate and/or master's degree from a recognized university may be the key to advancing or changing careers. Also, there are professionals who already have earned a couple of postgraduate degrees but who still harbor an insatiable curiosity or professional need to gain new knowledge in a niche area. A rigorous, multicourse certificate program of the kind offered by many university professional education units can be the ideal educational response.

Demand for specialized technical skill sets has given rise to new, non-university "just-in-time" continuing education competitors.[16] These education organizations operate in a few major US and foreign cities. They target a wide range of professionals, including career changers, prospective entrepreneurs, and college graduates preparing for entry-level jobs. The emphasis is on teaching relevant twenty-first-century economy skills such as mobile app development, user experience design, and data science.[17] Instruction is offered via online and on-demand courses, in workshops, and in part-time as well as full-time immersive program formats. Instructors are practitioners and entrepreneurs.

Looking Ahead

Ongoing education has become essential to remaining employable in today's rapidly changing economy. University professional higher education is a primary source of quality higher learning for many workers who want to enhance their professional qualifications or prepare for new occupations, and it is a role with substantial growth potential. But change often happens fast in the work world. This means that university professional education must be able to keep up with employer demands and changing credentialing requirements in professions. When professional education units and employers forge effective collaborations, these can be critical to securing the resources required to develop timely, relevant, affordable programs for their far-flung constituencies.

The United States needs to ensure that a greater number of working adults earn high-quality postsecondary credentials that can lead to a sustaining career. Degree completion programs offered by continuing higher education provide clear pathways to credentials that are essential to many adults' futures. Currently, nearly three out of four college students are not enrolled full-time. Ensuring that these part-time degree students complete their studies takes on added urgency in the face of projections that the US labor force will require at least fifteen million additional baccalaureate and advanced degree holders by 2022. Moreover the socioeconomic benefits that accrue to families wherein one or more parents have earned a college degree are often significant. And given that many part-time adult students happen to be immigrants, studying for a higher education degree can help facilitate their integration into US society.

Colleges and universities can expect *flexibility* to be the byword when urged to revisit their policies on prior learning assessment. There is renewed interest in this approach because it has been found to be well suited to working adults and especially midcareer adults who already have a community college degree and are pursuing a four-year degree. Giving adult students an opportunity to demonstrate their knowledge and skills successfully to a faculty assessor can serve to validate their life experiences, encourage their academic progress, and also often reduce the time to degree.

Technological change can be counted upon to exert a large impact on the workforce and on professional education. Already there is intense competition among employers for trained computer software developers and technically savvy talent in knowledge industries. In response to student demands and employer preferences, many more professional master's degree programs may integrate segments on computer-aided problem solving in their curricula. Digital technologies such as mobile technology, health care, computer security, and consumer electronics will inevitably introduce new skill requirements for workers and at the same time suggest exciting new opportunities to entrepreneurs. Consequently, there may be both an expansion and an increased differentiation of the providers of technology-related education for adults.

National boundaries will continue to recede in importance for universities in an increasingly interdependent world. It is a world where knowledge transmission is being dramatically changed with the diffusion of information technology, where there is a worldwide competition for human talent, and where global networks of institutions are working collaboratively to find solutions to urgent environmental, social, economic, and health problems.

The explosive growth of higher education graduates in developing countries and emerging economies during the last decade has profoundly altered the distribution of the talent pool among countries. Graduates from Europe, Japan, and the United States are no longer predominant according to the Organisation for Economic Cooperation and Development (OECD).[18] Meanwhile, the strong demand across the globe for professionals in knowledge-economy fields suggests that earning a high-quality master's degree from a relevant online US university professional education program could be a fruitful strategy for workers seeking to distinguish themselves in a very competitive labor market.

Globally, the importance of highly educated workers to a knowledge economy is widely recognized. Also, there is a growing appreciation of the value of investing in human capital. More and more employers and workers are coming to the realization that education rarely ends with the earning of a postsecondary credential. And investing in ongoing higher learning is seen as critical to future social and economic well-being.

Notes

1. Anthony P. Carnevale and Stephen J. Rose, *The Undereducated American*, Georgetown University Center on Education and the Workforce, June 26, 2011.

2. The Institute of Medicine has called for "an 80 percent baccalaureate-prepared nursing workforce and a doubling of doctorates held by nurses by 2020." Institute of Medicine, *The Future of Nursing: Leading Change, Advancing Health, 2010.*

3. US Department of Labor, Bureau of Labor Statistics, Economic News Release, table 8, accessed at http://www.bls.gov/news.release/ecopro .t08.htm.

4. David B. Monaghan and Paul Attewell, "The Community College Route to the Bachelor's Degree," *Education Evaluation and Policy Analysis*, March 19, 2014.

5. Accessed at http://www.gatesfoundation.org/What-We-Do/US-Program /Postsecondary-Success.

6. Alicia H. Munnell, "The Impact of Aging Baby Boomers on Labor Force Participation," Center for Retirement Research at Boston College, February 2014, no. 14-4.

7. Testimony of Dane Stangler, vice president of research and policy at the Ewing Marion Kauffman Foundation, testifying on February 12, 2014, before the US Senate Special Committee on Aging and the Senate Committee on Small Business and Entrepreneurship, 113th Congress, 2nd session "In Search of a Second Act: The Challenges and Advantages of Senior Entrepreneurship," accessed at http://www.kauffman.org/waht-we-do/research/2014/02/the-challenges-and-advantages-of-senior-entrepreneurship.

8. John E. Sargent Jr., "The U.S. Science and Engineering Workforce: Recent, Current, and Projected Employment, Wages, and Unemployment," Congressional Research Service, 5-6-3013, accessed at http://digitalcommons.ilr.cornell.edu/cgi/viewcontent.cgi?article=2170&context=key_workplace.

9. Zvi Galil (dean at the Georgia Tech College of Computing), "Proving Grounds for a New Model for Higher Education," *Huffington Post,* September 29, 2014; accessed at http://www.huffingtonpost.com/zvi-galil/proving-grounds-for-a-new_b_5899762.html.

10. Currently, students are able to fine-tune their master's degrees in computer science with specializations such as computational perception and robotics, databases and software engineering, high-performance computing, interactive intelligence, machine learning, networking, social computing, and systems.

11. "Starbucks Degree Program Not as Simple as It Seems," *Washington Post,* June 19, 2014; accessed at http://www.washingtonpost.com/business/economy/2014/06/19/b154fce0-f7e9-11e3-a3a5-42be35962a52_story.html.

12. According to the Bureau of Labor Statistics, "nearly half of these jobs were held from ages 18–24." See http://www.bls.gov/home.htm.

13. Table 2.1 Employment by Major Industry Sector, Bureau of Labor Statistics, US Department of Labor; see http://www.bls.gov/home.htm.

14. Joanne Lindley and Stephen Machin, "The Rising Wage Inequality and Postgraduate Education Premium," IZA Discussion Paper 5981, September 2011, Institute for the Study of Labor, Forschungsinstitut zur Zukunft der Arbeit, 1–55 (available from the Social Science Research Network).

15. Ibid.

16. The term *just-in-time education* was coined by John Katzman, founder of the *Princeton Review.*

17. See https://generalassemb.ly/new-york-city.

18. According to the OECD, "if current trends continue, China and India will account for 40 percent of all young people with a tertiary education in G20 and OECD countries by the year 2020, while the United States

and European countries will account for just over a quarter." Organisation for Economic Cooperation and Development, *Education Indicators in
Focus—2012/05* (May); accessed at http://www.oecd.org/edu/50495363
.pdf.

Competency-Based Education

A Natural Extension of Continuing Education

■■

David Schejbal

Change does not come easily to higher education. One of the oldest institutions in the world, higher education evolves at a very measured and careful pace. There have been a few historical exceptions. In the United States, the GI Bill following World War II is perhaps the most notable. Recognizing the need to repatriate returning soldiers, most of whom left the country as boys and returned as battle-worn men, the US government provided extensive resources so that higher education could be used to help make the transition to civilian life smoother and more productive. To accommodate the new student needs, alternative models of higher education became common at many institutions, including night classes, summer classes, new degrees and disciplines, and continuing education.

In the 1960s and early 1970s another wave of change came across higher education, and states like New York, New Jersey, Connecticut, Wisconsin, and others established alternative schools or institutions to address the needs of adult and nontraditional students who didn't fit easily into the well-worn structures of existing campuses. For example, New York established Regents College to award degrees to teachers and nurses outside of the existing colleges and universities in the state system. Today Excelsior College replaces the Regents College name, but its mission remains true to its origins. Connecticut opened Charter Oak State College in 1973, "designed to provide adults with an alternate means to earn degrees that are of equivalent quality and rigor to those earned at other accredited institutions of higher learning."[1] New Jersey opened the doors of Thomas Edison State College in 1972, and like its counterparts in neighboring states, it too focused on meeting the unique needs of adult students.

David Schejbal is Dean of Continuing Education, Outreach and E-Learning, University of Wisconsin-Extension, and president of the UPCEA, 2015–2016.

In 1971, Wisconsin established University of Wisconsin-Extension as an independent institution within the newly created University of Wisconsin system. Unlike Excelsior, Charter Oak, and Thomas Edison, however, UW-Extension was not set up to be a degree-granting institution. Instead, UW-Extension was charged with representing the outreach and continuing education functions of all institutions of the UW system and to be the embodiment of the Wisconsin Idea: to extend the resources of the university to all residents of the state.

Well before Clayton Christensen began writing about disruptive innovation and the extreme challenges of change from within, Connecticut, New York, New Jersey, Wisconsin, and many other states recognized that it was necessary to build new institutions because existing colleges and universities either could not or would not change. Interestingly, Regents, Thomas Edison, and Charter Oak were early pioneers of competency-based education and each also served as an aggregator of students' prior learning: administering proficiency exams, compiling credits, and awarding degrees based on the knowledge and learning that students accumulated before coming to those institutions.

Each of these alternative degree-granting institutions remained relatively small, niche schools. Over time, they developed processes and structures that tied directly into nationally established practices regarding credits and credit transfer, accreditation, financial aid, and so on. Today, they continue to focus on the audience for which they were created, adult and nontraditional students, and they continue to provide an alternative model for how adult students can earn degrees while using knowledge and learning acquired through channels outside of higher education. For lack of a better expression, they are continuing and professional education campuses.

In the 1990s a new wave of building alternative institutions ensued. Most of it focused on online instruction, and like previous efforts, most of it was directed at the underserved adult student market. The most notable developments came in the growth of for-profit higher education, with corporations like the Apollo Group, Corinthian Colleges, and others expanding very rapidly to capture a significant share of the higher education market. Nearly all of the for-profit institutions were modeled on traditional higher education; the main differences were in their business model and target student populations. One very different institution, forged by nineteen governors and chartered in 1996, emerged as Western Governors University.

A completely competency-based, online, private, nonprofit university located in Salt Lake City, Western Governors University began to accept students in 1999. For more than a decade, WGU escaped the attention of the majority of the higher education establishment. Then it began to generate significant interest in 2010 when Mitch Daniels, governor of Indiana, brought a branch of Western Governors into that state. The following year, WGU established branches in Washington State and Texas and has since added campuses in Missouri and Tennessee. Today, Western Governors University enrolls more than 40,000 students in competency-based programs. It is the largest competency-based institution in the country and growing quickly.

Competency-based education is no longer a peripheral approach to higher education. The US Department of Education is focusing considerable effort on it, the Obama administration has expressed strong interest in it, and more than 130 higher education institutions (at time of writing) have developed or are in the process of developing competency-based degree programs.

A number of factors are leading to the surge in competency-based programs. The recent recession highlighted the rapidly rising costs of higher education and the increasing indebtedness of students; advances in technology have made content and access to learning nearly free; the need to continually reeducate oneself to remain well employed is now a routine requirement; and the relative decline of the United States in global competitiveness necessitates an increasingly educated workforce. In brief, the old model isn't good enough to keep up with the new social and economic pressures impacting higher education. We need new models, not to replace the old ones but to add to them—to grow the pie at a scale that the traditional model of higher education can't achieve.

Perhaps the single greatest impetus for competency-based education, however, is the call for greater accountability in higher education, just as there has been in K-12 education for some time. As things cost more, people want to know what they are getting for their money. In particular, employers, politicians, students, and parents want proof that a college education is worth the cost. They want evidence that graduates have knowledge and skills that they can actually use and apply in practice to get good jobs that make the initial investment worthwhile.

Competency-Based Programs

The call for greater accountability naturally leads to outcomes-based education. The conversation in higher education about outcomes is nearly the same as it has been in K-12 education since the early 1990s.

Regional and state policy-making bodies (along with the president and state governors), in the 1991 National Goals for America's Schools, demanded improved student outcomes and placed them at the center of major efforts to improve all aspects of schooling: curriculum, instruction, assessment, attendance, credentialing, accreditation, and accountability. Major examples include legislation in Kentucky, Michigan, Minnesota, and Washington. This emphasis on improving student learning and demonstrating student success is mainly the result of stringent criticisms that have been heaped on the public schools by a host of business people, legislators, and journalists. Successful outcomes are now both the starting point and the bottom line of educational policy thinking and action in both the United States and Canada.[2]

Although the focus on outcomes in higher education has followed a similar path, it has been a bit slower in the making. The issue is summarized well in Amy Laitinen's 2012 report *Cracking the Credit Hour.*[3] In the report, Laitinen identifies the same kinds of issues that critics of K-12 education have touted for some time: lack of adequate knowledge and skills after graduating, inability to use what students have learned effectively, and general lack of preparation for life after graduation.

A 2006 study by the US Department of Education's National Center for Education Statistics found that the majority of graduating college students lacked the basic skills necessary to summarize opposing newspaper editorial arguments or correctly compare credit card offers with varying interest rates.[4] This study found alarming deficiencies in three key areas: document literacy, prose literacy, and quantitative literacy. Only 25 percent of college graduates had the document literacy necessary to understand and use information from noncontinuous texts, like interpreting a table about age, blood pressure, and physical activity. The results weren't much better when it came to prose and quantitative literacy since only 31 percent of college graduates could take away lessons from a complex story or perform computations like comparing the cost of food items per ounce using numbers from printed materials.

The particular challenge in higher education, as Laitinen argues, is the use of the credit hour as a measure of learning. Never designed for this purpose, the credit hour evolved into the semistandard measure of student learning that it is today.[5] However, using the credit hour in this way is problematic because it is a measure of *time spent* learning and not a measure of how much a student has learned. Although the US Department of Education has tried to separate credit hour from clock hour, it repeatedly defines the former in terms of the latter: "Semester Credits— Must teach a minimum of 15 lecture hours to award 1 semester credit hour (divide lecture hours by 15). Quarter Credits—Must teach a minimum of 10 lecture hours to award 1 quarter credit (divide lecture hours by 10)."[6]

In theory, colleges supplement the credit-hour count of how much time students have spent being taught with an objective measure of how much they have learned: grades. But here again, the picture is troubling. Although grades are supposed to objectively reflect learning, it is hard to reconcile today's grades with the research suggesting poor learning outcomes are widespread. Almost half of all undergraduate course grades are A's (in 1961, only 15 percent of grades were A's). Grade inflation is cited as a serious problem in higher education by nearly two-thirds of provosts and chief academic officers at undergraduate institutions in the United States.[7]

Enter the focus on outcomes and the natural move to competency-based education. For those interested in clear evidence of student learning, competency-based education is very attractive because in competency-based programs, the evidence of student learning occurs through clear demonstration of learning via authentic assessments. Students take assessments constructed in ways that require students to apply their knowledge and to show that they are able to use what they learned. Moreover, when focusing on competencies, the emphasis is on student achievement and not on the time that students spend learning. This difference is critical, because it again reinforces demonstration of mastery and not on the time that a student has spent in the learning process. Put differently, simply spending time learning in no way indicates successful learning; demonstration of successful learning comes from passing relevant assessments that require the application of learning in various contexts.

How Competency-Based Education Works

Just as there is no clear uniformity in how institutions teach and assess students in traditional courses, there is no uniformity in how institutions administer competency-based programs. The model described here is more or less approximated by institutions involved in competency-based education. The most common elements in competency-based education are demonstration of learning, separation of teaching and learning, and self-paced instruction.

When writing about competency-based education, language can get in the way. Competencies are outcomes, and there is confusion about the use of terms such as *competency, outcome, mastery,* and so on. The distinguishing features of most competency-based programs as opposed to outcomes-based programs in general is that competency-based programs uncouple teaching from learning and learning from assessment. In addition, competency-based programs allow students to progress at speeds that not only vary by student, but vary within a student's academic program relative to how quickly he or she is able to demonstrate competency. For example, we would expect a student who is good in English and poor in math to be able to demonstrate competency in written communication more quickly than in algebra or symbolic logic. However, to graduate from a competency-based program, students are expected to demonstrate competency in all parts of the curriculum.

Curriculum Design

The curriculum design process in competency-based education differs from curriculum design in most traditional programs. When designing a standard credit program, the typical design process entails faculty coming together around a discipline, identifying courses that comprise the curriculum, and then assembling the courses from introductory to advanced in a building-block fashion. In most cases, students are able to choose from a menu of courses which are grouped into categories that meet certain program requirements. Students must then successfully complete a set number of courses from each category. For example, students majoring in English might have to complete three courses in the social sciences, four courses in math-related disciplines, four courses in the natural sciences, and so on, with most of their courses in English.

In traditional curriculum development, faculty typically act as individual content experts, and their domains are their own courses. Most faculty do not spend time with fellow faculty exploring the content of each other's courses to minimize redundancies or to create seamless transitions for students from one course to the next. When this does happen, it happens within a discipline; it almost never occurs between disciplines. For example, in an economics department, faculty might work together to ensure that students who have taken Economics 101 are prepared to take Economics 201 and 301 by talking about what each faculty member is teaching in her or his respective course and ideally treating the courses as segments of one large class. However, this process almost never extends beyond the academic parameters of individual departments. It is extremely rare for faculty to work together across departments to hone their classes in the effort to create a unified and reinforcing learning environment for students. That level of curricular fine-tuning simply does not occur at most institutions.

As students progress through traditional curricula, they accumulate credits required for graduation (usually 120 semester credits for a bachelor's degree). To pass each course, students must earn a grade of D or better, and to graduate, students usually must have a C or better grade point average. Grades are determined by faculty who evaluate students in whatever ways they believe are appropriate for the courses that they teach. Faculty do not evaluate students for knowledge outside of their courses. Most would consider that inappropriate and unfair, even when students are expected to have disciplinary knowledge from lower-level courses. At the end of a degree program, students are not assessed for comprehensive learning, and there is no requirement to demonstrate skill or mastery in anything. In a few disciplines such as accounting, students must pass industry exams after graduation to demonstrate comprehensive mastery and competency in the discipline. Similar processes occur in law and medicine. However, these industry requirements are the exceptions and not the rule.

Competency-based curricula are developed differently. In a competency-based program, the curriculum is envisioned first at the macro level by identifying the program competencies that students must master to graduate. Those competencies are broad and program-wide. They might include things like "has demonstrated the ability to communicate complex ideas across divergent audiences, in various formats, and in multiple contexts" or "has demonstrated the ability to think critically and to apply critical reasoning in discipline-specific contexts and across contexts that extend beyond the discipline" or (in a business curriculum) "has demonstrated the ability to use and apply business concepts, practices, and standards effectively and efficiently to achieve business goals." In a course-based curriculum, these competencies would be called program outcomes, but the main difference is that in the competency-based program, students must clearly show that they really are able to use and apply the outcomes in various contexts and in multiple ways in order to achieve mastery and graduate.

A typical competency-based program might include three to five program competencies. Once articulated, these broad program competencies are deconstructed into their constituent parts or smaller competencies all the way down to foundational ones. Graphically, this looks like a pyramid in which the apex is the program competency, and each level below the apex represents a more specific set of competencies. The base of the pyramid represents the foundational competencies for that particular program. For example, for a program-level competency pertaining to communication ("has demonstrated the ability to communicate complex ideas across divergent audiences, in various formats, and in multiple contexts"), a foundational competency might be "is able to write clear and concise sentences and paragraphs," and a competency in the next level just above that might be "is able to write well-constructed and grammatically correct expository essays conveying information clearly."

Once program competency pyramids are established, it is important to identify redundancies and overlaps. For example, the demonstrated ability to think critically is likely to be as much part of a communication competency as it is to be part of a technical competency. As redundancies are identified, the next step is to determine which redundancies are important to reinforce essential program goals and which redundancies should be eliminated to help students move through the curriculum more expeditiously. Graphically, this takes the two-dimensional pyramids representing program competencies and combines them into a single, three-dimensional curriculum pyramid that shows the inter-relationships between the various competencies. At the apex of the three-dimensional pyramid are the program competencies in their interrelated states. For example, "has demonstrated the ability to think critically and to apply critical reasoning in discipline-specific contexts and across contexts that extend beyond the discipline" and "has demonstrated the ability to use and apply business concepts, practices, and standards effectively and efficiently to achieve business goals" might be brought together so that the student has demonstrated the ability "to think critically and apply critical reasoning to effectively evaluate business concepts, practices, and standards to achieve business goals."

Quality Assurance

In traditional programs and in competency-based ones, quality assurance happens at the assessment level; it does not happen at the point of instruction. After all, there is no way to know if students are learning in a classroom unless they are able to demonstrate what they have learned through some kind of assessment, be it a test, project, paper, clinical assignment, or some other result. The same principle applies in competency-based programs. The main difference is that in competency-based programs, the entire focus of the program is on assessments and demonstrations of mastery, while the focus of traditional programs is on teaching as the process for facilitating learning with assessments being secondary.

The Student Experience

One of the most common complaints among students in traditional programs is that they find courses or parts of courses in their programs either redundant or unnecessary because they already know the materials. Except for prior learning assessments, traditional programs do not have mechanisms in place to enable students to move through classes or parts of classes faster than the set pace of the course.

In competency-based programs, instruction is divorced from assessment, so students are able to take assessments without having to repeat learning if they already know the material. Since quality control happens at the assessment level, academic integrity is maintained by requiring all students to pass all assessments, regardless whether they also participate in formal learning. Hence, a student who has been a bookkeeper for ten years, for example, and who is working on an accounting degree should be able to pass foundational accounting assessments without having to engage in the instructional part of accounting classes. The student then engages in new learning when needed, that is, when he or she can't pass any more assessments.

There are several significant benefits to students in competency-based programs: they can move through the program at their own pace without having to repeat learning what they already know, thus saving time and money; they are free to learn from whatever source they learn best, regardless whether it is formal or informal learning; and they end up with demonstrable and documented competencies that they can share with employers.

Competency-based education is not for all students. Those who need a lot of structure in their studies or who have very little prior knowledge to bring to their program might be better off in traditional formats. However, for students who are motivated and already have learned a bit in a discipline, competency-based education works well.

Administration

The administration of competency-based programs differs considerably from traditional, credit-hour programs. Most competency-based programs are structured as team efforts: faculty have one role, instructional designers have another, student coaches have a third, and so on. The educational enterprise becomes more specialized and integrated to reduce costs while focusing on facilitating positive student learning outcomes. The process is not unlike that of health care. Twenty or thirty years ago, physicians provided most patient care. Today, patient care is done through teams of caregivers arranged in a hierarchy from case managers to nurse practitioners, physician assistants, internists, and specialists. Care for patients is provided by individuals at a level appropriate for a need. When patients have the flu, for example, they might see a nurse practitioner, but when they have abdominal pain in the area of their appendix, they would see an internist who, after examination, might refer them to a surgeon.

The team structure of competency-based education works similarly. Because of the decreased focus on routine instruction and the increased focus on the demonstration of learning, the role of faculty changes from the proverbial sage on the stage to the guide on the side. Faculty continue to be content experts and to oversee the curriculum. They determine program competencies, and in many programs they also write the assessments. However, faculty do not need to administer the assessments, and they don't need to advise or counsel students. Those tasks can be handled by specialists in those areas. In some programs faculty serve as tutors for students, but the level of tutoring might be stratified so that students learning at introductory levels would be supported by non-faculty tutors, and faculty time would be focused primarily on advanced students who need a more advanced level of expertise. In some programs, faculty grade assessments; in others, such as Western Governors University, for example, professional graders grade assessments, thus removing familiarity with students from the grading process and making the process more objective.

A commonality among most competency-based programs is their very clear focus on students' academic success. Students are shepherded by professional advisors who act as guides, coaches, and advocates. An advisor or coach proactively works with students, regularly monitoring their progress to ensure that they are succeeding. When students struggle, the coach connects students with the resources they need to get over whatever hurdles they are experiencing so that they can continue their studies. Although imperfect, the analogy with health care is useful here. Ideally, the long-term well-being of patients is the primary objective of modern health care, and preventive medicine is an important strategy to both reducing costs and improving patient health. Similarly, in competency-based education, student mastery of learning is the primary institutional goal, and the role of each member of the academic team is to support students in the achievement of that goal. Since students must increasingly return to higher education throughout their working lives to learn new skills and new knowledge, the education teams often work with students for long periods of time.

The Challenges of Novelty

Although some institutions have been delivering competency-based education for many years, for most institutions this is a new endeavor. Because as described above, the model is different from traditional term-based, classroom programs, institutions must develop new structures and processes to administer competency-based education. For example, at time of writing, no off-the-shelf student information system was available to handle competency-based education well. Banner, Peoplesoft, and other enterprise systems are not designed to adapt to an individualized and time-agnostic format. Furthermore, none of the enterprise systems and no other solutions currently exist to automate financial aid processing for direct assessment competency-based programs.

Direct Assessment

On March 19, 2013, David Bergeron, then acting assistant secretary for postsecondary education at the US Department of Education, released a *Dear Colleague* letter in which he specified how institutions can apply to award financial aid on the basis of direct assessment. Until 2013, all accredited higher education institutions awarded financial aid on the basis of the credit hour. However, there was a provision (section 8020) in the 2005 Higher Education Reconciliation Act to allow the awarding of financial aid in programs in which students are provided with the means to demonstrate achievement of specific competencies identified as necessary to complete a program and earn a degree or other credential. . . . An increasing number [of these programs] are not offered in credit or clock hours, and many of the institutions offering such programs want them approved for participation in the title IV, HEA programs. . . . HERA provided that instructional programs that use direct assessment of student learning, or that recognize direct assessment by others of student learning, *in lieu of measuring student learning in credit hours or clock hours,* may qualify as eligible programs if the assessment is consistent with the institution's program's accreditation.[8]

Unlike credit-hour based programs, however, Bergeron adds that approval for awarding financial aid on the basis of direct assessment must come directly from the secretary of education.

Southern New Hampshire University was the first institution to gain permission to award aid on the basis of direct assessment. A handful of other institutions applied for direct assessment permission after that, and to date only two have received approval to do so. At time of writing, my own school, the University of Wisconsin, is awaiting a ruling from the Department of Education in response to our application.

Because of the newness of awarding aid on the basis of direct assessment, institutions are not set up to do this. Hence, each institution awarding or preparing to award aid on the basis of direct assessment is using mostly clunky manual processes until more automated solutions come to market. To date, those solutions have yet to appear.

Experimental Sites, Demonstration Sites, and Other Ways to Get Around Regulations

Jamie Merisotis, president of the Lumina Foundation, said to me recently that federal regulations are about fifteen to twenty years behind where higher education is in its evolution. He is right. We are now at a point in higher education where, despite the glacial pace of change, parts of the enterprise are no longer in sync with federal regulations governing higher education, especially as it pertains to the distribution of title IV funds.

Recently, and under pressure from the White House and some members of Congress, the Department of Education has begun to try to adapt its regulatory processes to the changes in higher education. David Bergeron's *Dear Colleague* letter was one step in that direction. However, in the end, the letter requires institutions to connect their direct assessment processes to credit and clock hours, thus significantly limiting the ability to innovate and develop new models of higher education.

In recognition of the shortcomings of the letter and under pressure from political and higher education leaders, the Department of Education recently announced opportunities for institutions to engage in experimental sites, highly structured exceptions to select regulations, in order to try new ways to award financial aid. Always concerned about fraud and protecting taxpayer dollars, the Department of Education will closely monitor institutions participating in experimental sites and require them to report extensively on how their experiments (trials to award aid in otherwise unsanctioned ways) are working. Although this process will be slow and cumbersome, it is essential to help realign federal regulations with developments in higher education and to maintain access to higher education for students who otherwise cannot afford it. Ideally, positive results from the experiments will be used to inform the reauthorization process for the next iteration of the Higher Education Act.

Experimental sites are not the only ways in which federal regulations governing title IV funds can be changed. Another option open to Congress is demonstration sites. Demonstration sites are similar to program pilots in which Congress directly sanctions the Department of Education to allow select institutions to award aid in new ways. At time of writing, there is discussion in Congress about demonstration sites, but it is unclear if it will result in actual legislation.

Ultimately, Congress has the power to change legislation governing financial aid. However, the complexity of the process coupled with grave concerns about abuse of public funds makes that change process very slow and labored. It is not unlike changing the tax code. It can be done, but the political will and understanding must exist to do it.

Concluding Remarks

Institutions considering developing competency-based programs should consider very seriously their willingness and ability to do so. In addition to the expense, the culture, systems, and bureaucratic structures at most schools are aligned against change. As Clayton Christensen points out, the business environment of most established industries does not allow them to pursue disruptive change because their value networks do not put enough emphasis on disruptive innovation to warrant sufficient investment to pursue it. This is exactly the case in most universities. In addition, most higher education institutions are, if not resource starved, certainly not resource rich, and they are risk averse. Hence, making investments in educational models that feel foreign or uncomfortable is not something that they like to do. This is not the case, however, with new start-ups. New businesses or institutions have different value networks, so they are able to focus on the disruptive innovation as their primary focus.

Hence schools that choose to pursue competency-based programs must decide whether to invest internally and go against the direction of their own momentum or set up new institutions that from the beginning are competency-based and thus unfettered by history. Examples exist on both sides of this dichotomy. Southern New Hampshire University built the College for America as a separate institution developing competency-based programs. The University of Wisconsin has chosen to build its competency programs within its existing structures. There are trade-offs either way. Setting up a separate institution is challenging and expensive, and it is likely to garner significant criticism from established faculty. In addition, it becomes open to charges of lower quality and lesser value since by design it is divorced from the already proven quality metrics of the established institution. Building from within is also very challenging and perhaps more so because the product of the internal process is unlikely to be true to the original concept once it runs the gauntlet of established practices. Regardless of the way in which an institution moves forward, however, it is imperative to plan for the inevitable challenges from the beginning, anticipating pitfalls and learning from the experiences of others.

Finally, it is interesting to note that like many innovations in higher education before, most competency-based education is aimed at adult and nontraditional students, thus furthering the broad mission of continuing education. It is this effort to extend the resources of the university and to make the institution more accessible to students that makes the work of continuing education units both forward-thinking and critical to the evolution of American higher education.

Notes

1. "Mission Statement," Charter Oak State College, accessed at http://www.charteroak.edu/aboutus/mission.cfm.
2. W. G. Spady and K. J. Marshall, "Beyond Traditional Outcome-Based Education," *Educational Leadership* 49, no. 2 (October 1991): 67.
3. A. Laitinen, *Cracking the Credit Hour*, New America Foundation and Education Sector, accessed at http://higheredwatch.newamerica.net/sites/newamerica.net/files/policydocs/Cracking_the_Credit_Hour_Sept5_0.pdf.
4. Mark Kutner, Elizabeth Greenberg, and Justin Baer, "A First Look at the Literacy of America's Adults in the 21st Century. NCES 2006-470," *U.S. Department of Education National Center for Education Statistics* (2006), accessed at http://files.eric.ed.gov/fulltext/ED489066.pdf. See also Laitinen, *Cracking the Credit Hour*, 6.

5. The credit hour, also known as the Carnegie unit, was developed by the Carnegie Foundation as a unit of measure of faculty workload in order to make it possible to determine if faculty worked enough to qualify for pensions.

6. Accrediting Council for Continuing Education and Training, "Credit Hour and Clock Hour Policy," document 15, accessed at http://docs.accet.org /downloads/docs/doc15.pdf.

7. Laitinen, *Cracking the Credit Hour*, 6.

8. David Bergeron, "Dear Colleague Letter," DCL ID: GEN-13-10, March 19, 2013, accessed at http://ifap.ed.gov/dpcletters/attachments/GEN1310 .pdf.

Credible Currencies in the Continuing Education Realm

▌▌

Patricia A. Book

Introduction

Continuing educators have been at the forefront of capturing learning that happens in informal or noncredit venues for decades. The opportunity for leadership in continuing higher education in the future is in the integration of formal and informal learning to develop learning pathways to meaningful credentials for adult learners. Tackling the need for a common language and currency around informal learning that imparts value that is recognized across postsecondary education sectors is at the heart of this integration (Roberts 2014a, 2014b). Learning can occur in the workplace, while serving in the military, or through volunteer work, for example. Translating this learning into a credible currency that can be articulated with formal learning is the most pressing challenge. By attending to this challenge, continuing educators can create affordable, timely pathways to credentials for adult learners.

Traditional pathways have taken the form of degrees comprised of credit courses made somewhat more accessible to working adults through evening and weekend programs, accelerated formats, off-campus locations, and online delivery. These efforts to extend access to adult learners have followed the course-centric, credit-based formats familiar to postsecondary education. Transfer credit, especially from career-oriented programs, or even credit recommendations such as those from the American Council on Education's (ACE) credit for military training or experience or workplace experience were typically given short shrift, counting as

---

Patricia A. Book is Leadership Fellow, Western Interstate Commission for Higher Education (WICHE) Cooperative on Educational Technologies (WCET), and past president of the UPCEA, 2009–2010.

electives at best or not at all at worst, thus frustrating learners, policy makers, and employers alike.

Continuing educators used market research to determine labor market needs for education and training, yet the readiness, willingness, or capacity of academic departments to extend their degrees were often the determinant for which needs were met and how well. Continuing educators created new formats to accelerate time to degree for adult learners by compressing semesters, operating year-round, and offering classes closer to home, work, or online, but in general, even these units have not given much credence to prior informal learning of working adults to enable degree completion in an even more reasonable timeframe. In some cases, independent colleges within universities were formed to provide a continuing education unit with the flexibility and authority to develop its own degrees and requirements to meet unique needs given the reticence of academic departments, but these often met with concerns about internal competition. Approaches that structurally separated continuing education units from the main academic enterprise tend to be vulnerable to leadership changes and faculty concerns while those that retain faculty ownership of curriculum in academic departments seem more sustainable long term. As academic entrepreneurs, yet with the responsibility of being stewards of existing university academic policy, continuing educators also sought to expand opportunities to consider what adult students already know before requiring them to take courses on topics in which they were knowledgeable.

Continuing educators also pioneered the noncredit continuing education unit (CEU) as a method to document continuing professional education for many fields of practice. However, this measure placed emphasis on attendance (clock hours) rather than assessment of learning.

So, what is in store for the upcoming decades if ambitious goals for increased education attainment in the United States cannot be met by current approaches? What innovations are likely to take hold in whole or part that can prepare students and working adults for greater success in the workplace and better satisfy employers with the return on their investment in higher education? Which of the current disruptions in the traditional distance education and credit-based models will contribute most to increasing access to meaningful credentials, including degrees, contribute to increased education attainment, and address issues of affordability? Will the Carnegie unit continue to define learning accomplishments (Laitinen 2012)?

The Education Attainment Goals

The goals for educational attainment in the United States as of this writing are bold. The Lumina Foundation is unique among the foundations to have articulated what they call an "audacious" goal: "To increase the proportion of Americans with high-quality degrees and credentials to 60 percent by the year 2025" (Lumina Foundation 2013).

The nation's goal is equally ambitious, articulated by President Obama in a joint address to Congress February 24, 2009. President Obama said that the United States "should once again have the highest proportion of college graduates in the world by the year 2020." The United States is perceived to be falling behind globally. To reach this goal, the US Department of Education (USDE) projects that the proportion of college graduates will need to increase by 50 percent nationwide by the end of the decade (US Department of Education 2011). Many analyses have shown that this level cannot be reached at current education attainment rates, given our current educational models. The American economy requires more highly skilled workers. The ability of Americans to contribute to the workforce and society and provide for themselves and their families depends on continuing education. This has been true for decades, but its importance now cannot be overstated.

Drivers of Reform

The drivers that set the stage for the future for continuing educators are tied to the need for a more highly educated workforce, yet current perceptions from employers are that significant skill gaps persist in graduates. A skill gap coupled with painfully slow economic recovery from the 2008 recession has fueled calls for reform in higher education. Jobs finally reached prerecession levels in 2014, after some six and a half years, the longest recovery since before World War II. The lagging growth has been too slow to absorb emerging workers or older adults who lost high-paying jobs in the recession. Some seven million additional jobs would need to have been added during these six and a half years to absorb labor force growth, thus we remain in a hole in the US labor market. This job deficiency negatively affects consumer demand and causes further drag on US economic growth. Many economists predict a long period of slow growth for the US economy.

Emerging workers with university degrees in hand are saddled with unacceptably high education debt due to ongoing higher education price escalation caused by states' disinvestment. Those adult incumbent workers who lost good jobs have had to settle for lower-paying or part-time jobs and adjust their living standard downward.

In a survey of 343 executives in the United States conducted by the Economist Intelligence Unit, "the overwhelming consensus among employers is that too many graduates lack critical-thinking skills and the ability to communicate effectively, solve problems creatively, work collaboratively and adapt to changing priorities" (Labi 2014, 3). Labi goes on to say that "in addition to these 'soft skill' deficits, employers are also finding that young people lack the technical, or 'hard' skills associated with specific jobs" (ibid., 3). Dane Linn, vice-president at the Business Roundtable noted: "Colleges and universities think they are adequately preparing students for the workforce. You couldn't have a more stark difference of opinion from industry" (ibid., 7). Industry says they want to engage with colleges and universities but they question the return on investment. Students saddled with debt and unable to find good paying jobs question the value of their degree. Given this context, policy makers' goals for higher education are driven by issues not only of access, but completion, affordability, quality, and relevance (McCarthy 2014).

Focus on Learning

An overriding issue for the coming decades for continuing educators as they seek to integrate informal and formal learning for working adults is going to be precisely a focus on learning: What do graduates know and how do we know they know it? Can they apply what they know in different circumstances? Can we be more transparent in how we define, assess, and document what our graduates know? Delivering credit courses, particularly when they result in a certificate or degree, has been a successful business model for continuing education. The question increasingly on the minds of employers, students, parents, and policy makers alike relates to whether or not the investment in higher education is worth it. The price of higher education has lost its elasticity, so continuing educators can't count on continued price increases to cover cost inflation and to increase their net revenue, the latter often seen as their primary value to their institutions. Graduates young and old face a poorly performing labor market and are bearing debt levels that they cannot repay and cannot discharge in bankruptcy. Yet more education—not less—is demanded of current and future jobs. Higher education has to become more affordable, completion rates have to climb, and better assessments of competency, in fact, mastery, have to be the norm.

MOOCS, PLA, CBE, and Badges

Today, the environment is characterized by many alternative learning assessments—and providers—adding massive open online courses (MOOCs), competency-based education (CBE), and badges to long-standing models of prior learning assessment (PLA) (Ewert and Kominski

2014). These innovations are currently perceived as disruptions with the potential to address the broader goals for higher education. MOOCs were the disruptive darlings of 2012–2013, largely due to their breathtaking scalability. The new CBE models continued to include credit-based, course equivalency models pioneered by Western Governors University but suddenly added the new direct assessment models truly untethered to the credit hour model. CBE is an antecedent to credentialing through yet another innovative mechanism for validating attainment of knowledge and skills, that is, badges, which are seen as a new currency for continuing professional development.

MOOC Mania

The current mix of alternative credentials, or credentialing, pushes the envelope further and challenges continuing educators to help their institutions participate effectively in reform initiatives. Over the past few years with the advent of MOOCs, continuing educators have come to be seen as providing "traditional" distance education largely because online education has not significantly reduced the cost of education, nor increased affordability for students. Continuing educators certainly increased access for working adults and place-bound learners. MOOCs were hyped in the media as solving the affordability crisis in higher education. They were free and offered by top-tier universities in the United States as well as abroad. Literally millions flocked to the MOOCs although virtually no advertising was done. It was media-fueled by design with the added appeal of elite brands.

MOOCS are in essence noncredit continuing education experiences, although uneven in pedagogical quality, enriched beyond measure by the global participation of learners. MOOC instructors offer their courses through user-friendly course platforms developed by faculty computer scientists at Stanford and MIT under either for-profit business enterprises (such as Coursera and Udacity) or through a nonprofit consortia model (such as EdX). Faculty inexperience in online delivery is evident in MOOCs as course pedagogy has not benefited from decades of now standard good practice in what makes a quality online experience. The mini-lecture format prevails in MOOCs—bite-size lectures by talking heads—coupled with minimal assessment, if any. Some institutions, such as San Jose State, have used MOOCs in a flipped classroom where students watch the MOOC videos online outside of class—the equivalent of a lecture though more palatable due to their brevity—and classroom time is spent on discussion. Yet, MOOCs proved what no distance education program had yet done and that was scaling access to education to massive audiences. The MOOC mania has now peaked and the inflated expectations have perhaps been tempered, but perceived barriers to access and affordability have been significantly altered by these developments, along with technology-enabled components to build upon, including intuitive course hosting platform design and scalable assessment such as peer and machine grading.

The essence of MOOCs is similar to what continuing educators have been doing for decades in developing credit and noncredit certificates, often packaging existing courses into a sequence of defined competencies. These can be at the entry or pre–associate degree, prebaccalaureate, or postbaccalaureate levels. Some institutions have stacked these certificates so that they can become part of an undergraduate or graduate degree program. Community colleges have also included apprenticeship training as components of technical associate degree programs. The American Council on Education's CREDIT review includes credit recommendations for several apprenticeship programs, obviating the need for internal review by institutions themselves. ACE CREDIT review also has reviewed some MOOCs for academic credit recommendations, and MOOCs have been experimenting with offering a few courses that carry ACE CREDIT recommendations as well as courses that carry a noncredit certificate-like imprimatur, for example, Certificate of Accomplishment from the course hosting platform or Verified Certificate awarded jointly by the course hosting platform and university offering the course. The certificates do not carry academic credit but appear to be highly valued by participants. Some MOOC providers have developed relationships with employers to serve basically as employee recruiters through highly technical MOOC course offerings in high-demand areas needed by industry.

Prior Learning Assessment

Prior learning assessment (PLA) has been around since the end of World War II when the American Council on Education (ACE) was asked to create general educational development (GED) tests for returning soldiers so that they could take advantage of the new GI Bill. ACE added a credit recommendation service for military training and experience to its portfolio around the same time. In the 1970s ACE added credit recommendation reviews for education and training that occurred outside the formal classroom in industry, government agencies, social service organizations, and other entities. Around this same time, the Council on Adult and Experiential Learning established the portfolio assessment model to permit students to document their learning for credit equivalency.

Thousands of adult learners have transcripts from ACE documenting that they have taken training that is the equivalent to what they would have been taught in a typical college classroom. While less prevalent, portfolio credit recommendations are also significant. The problem is that many universities do not accept ACE credit recommendations or externally validated portfolio assessments, or if they do, they only accept them as electives so they don't satisfy major requirements to accelerate time to degree.

National exams are the most commonly accepted form of prior learning assessment by campuses. The College Level Examination Program (CLEP), Defense Activity for Nontraditional Education Support (DANTES), and Excelsior College exams are prominent among these forms of PLA.

Greater understanding and acceptance by campus faculty of the process behind these academic credit recommendations, which are conducted by teaching faculty at institutions across the country, would contribute significantly to student persistence and education attainment goals. PLA could help institutions and accrediting bodies implement some of the new models as well, such as competency-based education.

Competency-Based Education

Competency-based education (CBE) is the newest darling of the media and remarkable for the intensity of investment and innovation going on. CBE models have been described as either course-based with credit equivalency or direct assessment (Book 2014). The course-based model ties to the Carnegie unit. Institutions translate competencies into courses of the appropriate length and complexity (Johnstone and Soares 2014). The other model, referred to as direct assessment, is untethered from course material, seat time, and the credit or clock hour. Learners demonstrate competencies, with particular emphasis on mastery, at their own pace, typically online, and progress through academic programs when they are ready.

Direct assessment of student learning refers to a measure by the institution of what a student knows and can do in terms of the body of knowledge making up the educational program. These measures provide evidence that a student has command of a specific subject, content area, or skill or that the student demonstrates a specific quality such as creativity, analysis, or synthesis associated with the subject matter of the program. Examples of direct measures include projects, papers, examinations, presentations, performances, and portfolios. Some of the current competency-based education programs offered are noted below, with only three approved by the USDE for Title IV federal financial aid eligibility for this direct assessment approach as of this writing (Book 2014). All the others are converting to a course-based, credit equivalency model in their competency-based education programs.

Course-based/CreditEquivalency

Western Governors University, www.wgu.edu

Kentucky Community and Technical College System (Learn On Demand), http://learnondemand.kctcs.edu/

Northern Arizona University (Personalized Learning), pl.nau .edu

Texas A&M-Commerce, South Texas College (Texas Affordable Baccalaureate [TAB] Program)

Direct Assessment

Southern New Hampshire University (College for America), collegeforamerica.org

Capella (Flex Path), www.capella.edu/online-learning /flexpath

University of Wisconsin (Flexible Option), flex.wisconsin.edu

These CBE programs provide certificate, associate, baccalaureate, and graduate degrees. Some programs provide stackable credentials that build upon one another. The programs are characterized by their affordability, flexibility, and subscription tuition model, providing students with the ability to pace their learning. Both regional accrediting bodies and the USDE have approved these approaches as required by federal policy. Presently, there are a large number of institutions experimenting in this space, with many consulting with Western Governors University on their model. The USDE and foundations are investing heavily in experimentation to further the higher education goals articulated earlier.

Badges

Badges are part of an emerging pedagogy, and like CBE, they focus on defined competencies and demonstration of those skills and abilities. They are awarded by education providers, employers, community organizations, and even individuals documenting, through an evidence-based assessment, that the badge holder has attained articulated competencies (Derryberry 2013). Badges may conjure up in our minds fun at summer camp or scout troop badge collections, but not so much as being relevant to an academic credential or evidence of learning. In fact, badges are not rewards; rather they are being developed and offered for credit or noncredit courses as well as other informal learning opportunities and training opportunities within higher education today.

Purdue University's Passport to Intercultural Learning (PUPIL) is a tool to assist faculty and students in assessing and documenting student learning outcomes in human cultures, global citizenship, and social responsibility and intercultural knowledge and effectiveness. Instructors can create and award digital badges to reflect evidence of learning. Students can earn up to six specific knowledge, attitude, or skill badges and a seventh capstone badge when completing all six specific badges.

The University of Alaska Southeast Educational Technology program is in its infancy in offering badges to indicate competency in the International Society for Technology in Education's (ISTE) Standards for Coaches (formerly NETS). Badges are awarded for nongraded assignments that demonstrate mastery of competencies in leadership and accomplishment related to the NETS-C Standards for Technology Coaches. As noted on the UAS Educational Technology website, teachers and professionals may include these badges in portfolios and other professional documents (http://uasedtechbadges.wordpress.com). These badges recognize and value work that is not easily captured in grades and other course assessments. They are all based on what students do with the knowledge they have gained, and UAS recognizes this knowledge at different levels of mastery (Lee Graham, personal communication, June 15, 2014).

The University of California Davis has incorporated badges into the sustainable agriculture and food systems undergraduate major. The focus is on learning outcomes in areas like systems thinking, experimentation and inquiry, understanding values, and interpersonal communication, precisely the skill gaps that industry has identified as lacking in current graduates. UC-Davis's use of badges focuses on higher-level competencies (Buell 2013).

Concordia University of Wisconsin (CUW) is putting together perhaps the most ambitious program of all using badges. CUW is planning to create an entire master's degree that is based around earning badges rather than completing traditionally structured courses (Nate Otto, personal communication, June 16, 2014). There would be some seventy competency badges removed from the course format, allowing students ultimately to earn the master's degree through the earning of badges. Full implementation will require regional accreditation approval (Bernard Bull, personal communication, June 16, 2014).

All this experimentation at public and private universities involves faculty training and faculty engagement in defining competencies. Badges provide a more meaningful way for participants and graduates to provide evidence of what they know and can do. Grades on transcripts can't do this as well. Also participants can show increasing mastery and have something to add to their resume even before they finish the course or program (Bull 2014). Participants can share these badges with employers or on their professional social networks. Bernard Bull points out that use of badges is helpful in altering social or professional perceptions of students' capabilities.

Hickey (2014) recently published an interim report on the Design Principles Documentation (DPD) Project providing principles for recognizing, assessing, motivating, and studying learning in digital badge systems. This work is based on research with thirty organizations awarded grants to develop badge content in the 2012 Badges for Lifelong Learning Initiative supported by the John D. and Catherine T. MacArthur Foundation in collaboration with the Mozilla Foundation. Badges for Vets, Pathways for Lifelong Learning, Peer 2 Peer University (P2PU), and the UC Davis project were among the recipients.

The UC Davis project is the most promising digital badge system because it validates experiential learning within a formal institutional context at the undergraduate level. It is unique in that it bridges learning in and out of the classroom. To address the transparency issue desired by learners and employers alike, the UC Davis badge system identifies competencies so that learners can better communicate their skills and competencies to a broader audience, including employers. Better yet, the badges are integrated into the student's formal degree curriculum. Michael V. Reilly, executive director of the American Association of Collegiate Registrars and Admissions Officers (AACRAO) likes what he has heard about the UC Davis program. Reilly was quoted in *Inside Higher Ed* as being in favor of efforts to capture students' experiences outside the classroom, including through badges. "The transcript is pretty limited in what it does," Reilly says (Fain 2014). This is a significant statement of support from the likes of the AACRAO.

There is opportunity for continuing educators to work closely with faculty to better understand and use alternative assessments of learning, whether they be MOOCs, PLA, CBE, or badges. Can they be potentially relevant credentials integrated into a college degree pathway, as at UC Davis? Whether the assessments cover learning that occurs in informal or formal learning environments is not as important as how well we can document and support what graduates know and can do, both as they enter and exit a program. Garnering faculty engagement in this process could be a valuable key to further accelerating the pathway to a credential or degree for adult learners.

The Role of Policy in Facilitating Innovation

I would be remiss if I didn't give a nod to policy issues at this juncture, as they can facilitate or hinder innovations in educational reform movements. Continuing educators, as practitioners, are often not well informed about the higher education policy environment and tend to operate in a fee-for-service business model as opposed to seeking grants to support new initiatives. This makes them less likely to be aware of policy issues behind federal funding initiatives or foundation grants. Familiar refrains heard on campus have created barriers to entrepreneurship. Statements like: "accreditation won't allow it" or "our specialty accreditation prohibits that" or "our Title IV funds will be jeopardized if you do that" have been heard by most continuing educators. Higher education reform, however, is a hot topic at the federal and state level and within accreditation bodies, so it behooves CE leaders to be informed, keeping in mind the national goals to address ongoing issues of access, completion, affordability, quality, and relevance to the nation's needs.

There is an increased interest in providing opportunities to test new innovative models using CBE and alternative credentials to the traditional degree. Initiatives of note that are fueling experimentation and innovation include the US Department of Labor's 2009 Trade Adjustment Assistance Community College and Career Training (TAACCCT) Grant Program, implemented in partnership with the US DE. The federal government is investing $2 billion over four years in this grant program, which entered round four in 2014. It is designed to improve programs of two years or less that prepare adults for high-skilled jobs. Many of the funded projects have focused on CBE programs, engaging employers in defining needed competencies in the curriculum.

In 2013, the US DE published a notice in the *Federal Register* inviting ideas for the Experimental Sites Initiative for those institutions that participate in the federal Title IV student assistance programs. David Nagel reported on a subsequent event held by the US DE, asking the higher education community, among others, for ideas on how to allow students to use federal financial aid for credit for prior learning, for example, and most interestingly, ideas on "combining traditional calendar-based and competency-based courses into a single program of study" (Nagel 2014). This is further evidence that the federal government is serious about fostering reform that addresses the issues of affordability, completion, and relevance. And it reinforces my advice to continuing educators that their leadership contribution in the coming decades should be to integrate informal and formal learning in pathways to meaningful credentials.

In addition, the Higher Education Reconciliation Act of 2005 (HERA) amended the Higher Education Act (HEA) of 1965 and established the eligibility of direct assessment programs to participate in the Title IV HEA programs. Specifically, HERA provided that instructional programs that use direct assessment of student learning or that recognize the direct assessment by others of student learning in lieu of measuring student learning in credit hours or clock hours may qualify as eligible programs if the assessment is consistent with the institution's or program's accreditation (Bergeron 2013).

Accreditation bodies have also stepped up to support institutions in taking advantage of the direct assessment competency-based models afforded for in the HERA. In 2013, the Higher Learning Commission (HLC) of the North Central Association was among the first to approve four institutions to offer competency-based degrees. The HLC application for "direct assessment competency-based programs" is considered a substantive change application. While direct assessment is to be untethered from the credit hour, HLC's application asks that institutions "describe the number of semester or quarter credit hours, or clock hours, which are equivalent to the amount of student learning being directly assessed for this program" (Higher Learning Commission of the North Central Association 2013, 8). Institutions are further asked to describe the methodology for determining the number of credit hours. The way faculty are used in the proposed program is also to be contrasted with traditional, credit-hour based programs. So much for untethering! Reconciling CBE approaches with Title IV eligibility requirements is equally challenging as financial aid policy is tied to the academic year, enrollment status, and satisfactory academic progress. This is why the Experimental Sites Initiative to enable change is so important. Nonetheless, these innovative approaches are being taken into account in federal policy and funding and in accreditation policy and championed by major philanthropic entities such as the Lumina Foundation, John D. and Catherine T. MacArthur Foundation, and the Bill and Melinda Gates Foundation.

Conclusion

The future continues to hold great promise for the entrepreneurs and innovators who make up continuing higher education. The nation's goals, our citizen's social and economic well-being, and higher education can continue to be positively influenced by the work of our colleagues in this dynamic field. Continuing education has the opportunity to work collaboratively with faculty to create new models that focus on learning and integrate informal and formal learning, recognizing alternative credentials that matter. Fostering faculty engagement and critical assessment of reform movements is more critical than ever to ensure that all learners persist and succeed. Together, continuing educators and faculty can carry on the great outreach work of our public and private universities to give Americans the second chance they deserve and, at the same time, continue to be relevant to societal needs.

References
Bergeron, David. 2013. "Dear Colleague Letter," DCL ID: GEN-13-10, March 19. Accessed at http://ifap.ed.gov/dpcletters/attachments/GEN1310.pdf.

Book, Patricia A. 2014. *All Hands on Deck: Ten Lessons From Early Adopters of Competency-Based Education.* Boulder, CO: WICHE Cooperative for Educational Technologies (WCET). Accessed at http://www.wcet.wiche.edu /wcet/docs/summit/AllHandsOnDeck-Final.pdf.

Buell, Courtney. 2013. "Using Badges to Quantify Learning Outcomes at UC Davis," edcetera blog, August 30. Accessed at http://edcetera.rafter.com /using-badges-to-quantify-learning-outcomes-at-uc-davis/?utm _source=dlvr.it&utm_medium=twitter&utm_campaign=using-badges -to-quantify-learning-outcomes-at-uc-davis.

Bull, Berhard. 2014. Mozilla Badges Community Call. Accessed at http://etale .org/main/2014/06/01/10-promising-practices-possibilities-for-using -digital-badges-in-your-courses/.

Derryberry, Anne. 2013. *Badges, Credits and Accreditation.* WCET, October 10, WCETblog. Accessed at http://wcetblog.wordpress.com/2013/10/10 /badgescreditsaccreditation/.

Ewert, Stephanie, and Robert Kominski. 2014. *Measuring Alternative Educational Credentials: 2012.* Washington, DC: US Census Bureau. Accessed at https://www.census.gov/hhes/socdemo/education/data/files/p70-138 .pdf.

Fain, Paul. 2014. "Badging from Within." *Inside Higher Education,* January 3. Accessed at https://www.insidehighered.com/news/2014/01/03/uc-daviss -groundbreaking-digital-badge-system-new-sustainable-agriculture -program#.UsdCH-PmByA.email.

Hickey, Daniel. 2014. "Introducing the DML Design Principles Document Project." Humanities, Arts, Science and Technology Alliance and Collaboratory. Accessed at http://www.hastac.org/blogs/dthickey/2012/10/08 /introducing-dml-design-principles-documentation-project.

Higher Learning Commission of the North Central Association. 2013. "Background Information on Direct Assessment Competency-based Programs." Accessed at https://www.ncahlc.org/Monitoring/direct-assessment -competency-based-programs.html.

Johnstone, Sally M., and Louis Soares. 2014. "Principles for Developing Competency-Based Education Programs." *Change* 46(2): 12–19, doi: 10.1080 /00091383.2014.896705.

Labi, Aisha. 2014. *Closing the Skills Gap: Companies and Colleges Collaborating for Change.* London: The Economist Intelligence Unit.

Laitinen, Amy. 2012. *Cracking the Credit Hour.* Washington, DC: New American Foundation and Education Sector. Accessed at http://higheredwatch .newamerica.net/sites/newamerica.net/files/policydocs/Cracking_the _Credit_Hour_Sept5_0.pdf.

Lumina Foundation. 2013. *Strategic Plan 2013–2016,* accessed at http://www .luminafoundation.org/goal_2025.html. See also http://www.lumina foundation.org/goal_2025/goal2.html#sthash.TdPd9Rzj.dpuf.

McCarthy, Mary Alice. 2014. *Competency-Based Education, Alternative Credentials and the Role of Federal Policy.* (lecture) WCET Leadership Summit, Salt

Lake City, Utah, May 7–8. Accessed at http://wcet.wiche.edu/wcet/docs /webcasts/2014/CompetencyBasedEducation/CBESlides.pdf.

Nagel, David. 2014 "Feds Call on Universities for Ideas for 'Experimental Sites,' New Learning Technologies." Campus Technology, January 15. Accessed at http://campustechnology.com/articles/2014/01/15 /feds-call-on-universities-for-ideas-for-experimental-sites-new-learning-technologies.aspx.

Roberts, Verena. 2014a. *Proposal: Flexible Learning Pathways for UBC Integrating Formal and Informal Learning.* Accessed at https://docs.google.com/docu ment/d/1AMgeIMIJiEFqIACpzVz0T3i7SwaJPyzd7RxUIm9sk4k/edit.

Roberts, Verena. 2014b. "Research and Badge System Design Call." March 26, openbadges.org. Accessed at https://openbadges.etherpad.mozilla.org /CCMarch26.

US Department of Education. 2011. *Meeting the Nation's 2020 Goal: State Targets for Increasing the Number and Percentage of College Graduates with Degrees,* March 18. Washington, D.C. Accessed at http://www.whitehouse.gov /sites/default/files/completion_state_by_state.pdf.

Access, Innovation, and Our "Sputnik Moment" in Postsecondary Attainment

■▌

Cathy A. Sandeen

This year, the year of UPCEA's centennial, we are in the midst of an era that will require the sort of intense focus and determination and innovation that our country demonstrated in the 1960s when President Kennedy challenged the nation to put a man on the moon, an audacious goal for the scientific community. Only this time our goal is to return the United States to preeminence in postsecondary educational attainment, a goal that is much more complex, much more challenging than putting a man on the moon. We need to confront this challenge not for the purposes of showing the world what we can do or so we can move up in the international rankings but because we must help more Americans achieve a higher level of education to enable them to earn family-sustaining wages, engage in civil society, and create a robust workforce, as well as to reduce economic and social inequity and, most importantly, because it is our moral imperative—it is the right thing to do. It is also the reason we are here, ultimately the reason we have devoted our careers and our lives to higher education.

Professional and continuing education has played an important role in postsecondary attainment for more than a century and will be called upon in the future to increase its contribution. Understanding the broader landscape is an important first step. This essay will provide a snapshot of the postsecondary landscape at the point of UPCEA's centennial, including major drivers of change, current areas ripe for innovation, areas of

---

Cathy A. Sandeen is Chancellor of University of Wisconsin Colleges and University of Wisconsin Extension, on the UPCEA Board of Directors, and recipient of multiple awards.

caution, and how the professional and continuing education community is making and can continue to make enormous contributions.

Our Audacious Goal

The United States historically has had one of the most highly educated populations in the world, but we have fallen behind. Over the past decade, the proportion of the population with a postsecondary degree has increased far more significantly in other advanced economies than in the United States, particularly among young people. According to the Organization for Economic Cooperation and Development (OECD), only 43 percent of young Americans age 25–34 currently hold an associate's degree or higher. Contrast that with Korea at 64 percent. The United States now ranks twelfth among the thirty-seven OECD countries (Organization for Economic Cooperation and Development 2013, 2). We have a difficult time tracking graduation rates due to the large number of students who drop out, stop out, or transfer. However, according to the National Center for Education Statistics, our national six-year graduation rate in 2012 was 59 percent for first-time, full-time students—not a stellar achievement.

For decades, the United States benefited from a robust manufacturing sector, one where high school graduates and even high school dropouts could prosper, earning a family-sustaining wage. That has changed. Well-paying manufacturing jobs have been replaced by minimum wage jobs in the services industry, mainly food service and retail. However, 65 percent of US jobs are projected to require some level of postsecondary education by 2020, compared with 28 percent in 1973 (Carnevale, Smith, and Strohl 2013, 15). On a social level, postsecondary attainment has always been an important means for providing social equity and economic mobility to US citizens and that continues to be true today.

There is a huge gap to fill between our current attainment and what is needed for the workforce of the future. We must develop the means to provide quality education at a larger scale than ever before. Most national attainment goals envision 60 percent of the population achieving a postsecondary degree, credential, or certificate by 2025. See, for example, Complete College America, the Bill & Melinda Gates Foundation, and Lumina Foundation, among others (Russell, 2011). The White House goal is even more ambitious: by 2020 America will once again have the highest proportion of college graduates in the world (Obama Administration n.d.). It's important to note that postsecondary attainment in this context includes not just four-year degrees but also the completion of two-year degrees and high-quality certificates with labor market value.

Drivers of Change

Demographics

Diversity has nearly always been a major characteristic of the US population, but we are becoming even more diverse and on multiple levels. This diversity is a source of extreme strength for our culture and economy, but it presents educators with multiple challenges.

Four states—California, Hawaii, New Mexico, Texas—and the District of Columbia are currently majority-minority. An additional nine states had majority-minority toddler population as of 2012 (Frey 2013). Not only will many of the students coming to us be first-generation college students, they will be first-generation Americans as well. For a large number, English is not their first language.

Besides ethnic and racial diversity, elements of diversity among our student populations include older students, working students, students with family obligations, veterans, students with learning and other disabilities, and students with different learning styles, different levels of preparation, and different goals. Students come to us with risk factors that impact their ability to persist and complete degrees. Some of these include having to attend part-time, working, having family obligations, and having attended multiple institutions. We know first-time full-time students are in the minority, and most students, roughly 75 percent, are considered nontraditional students who confront a variety of these risk factors.

Globalization

We currently live in a much more globally connected world and acknowledge that we must educate our students to thrive in such an environment. We also acknowledge the fundamental role of postsecondary education in supporting US competitiveness in a global economy. Recruitment of greater numbers of international students to our institutions, especially recent increases in international undergraduates and the ability of online education to stretch beyond borders, have increased the multicultural component of our classrooms and the overall student and teaching experience.

Technology and Ubiquitous Information

The average smartphone has more computing power than the Apollo spacecraft that made it to the moon, and no aspect of our lives has been untouched by technology. This is also the case in higher education. We function in a world with broad and robust access to information. Colleges and universities are no longer repositories of information that organize and deliver this information to students and the public. Instead, students come to us already exposed to or having actively interacted with various sorts of information. This dynamic has changed the nature of the student-faculty and student-institutional relationship in fundamental ways. We are now curators of information, and our major goal has shifted to helping students analyze, evaluate, and manage the universe of information that surrounds us.

Consumerism

Economic forces as well as ready access to information over the Internet have fostered an increasingly consumer-oriented culture. Brand is becoming less important as a signal of product quality in a world where both expert and peer reviews are readily available and often take precedence over brand. Higher education is not immune from this influence. We have lived with ranking systems for decades, but when the president of the United States talked about getting "the most bang for your educational buck" in his 2013 State of the Union address, educational consumerism moved even more front and center. Students have brought their consumerism to campus, consulting ratings and reviews for academic programs and faculty in making choices. Brand is arguably still important for top-tier institutions, but the general trend away from brand superiority opens opportunity for a broad range of other institutions.

Accountability

Consumerism and economic pressures have increased the level of accountability imposed upon higher education as never before. Government funding has decreased for public institutions, requiring students and their families to bear a greater burden of their educational expenses. Private institutions have limited ability to increase the tuition they charge. Students are departing from our colleges and universities without degrees, and they still must repay what they have borrowed. The pressure is on for higher education to show results for its efforts in terms of student learning, completion, and employment. Academic culture is not accustomed to this level of scrutiny, but there is no sign of this pressure abating any time soon.

Innovation in Higher Education

Greater innovation in higher education is the clarion call of the day, as if this is something new and radical. In fact, the history of US higher education is marked by much admired innovations—most of these focused on increasing access and supporting economic development.

The Morrill Act of 1862, which created the land-grant universities with a mandate "to teach agriculture, military tactics, and the mechanic arts as well as classical studies so members of the working classes could obtain a liberal, practical education," established an important, new, innovative direction for higher education (Association of Public and Land-Grant Universities 2012, 1). This mandate subsequently served as the foundation for the Wisconsin Idea, "characterized by Charles R. Van Hise, President of the University of Wisconsin-Madison in 1904, as a pledge to make 'the beneficent influences of the University available to every home in the state'" (Schoenfeld 1975, 252).

Wisconsin, through its continuing education and outreach work as well as its cooperative extension division, was in the vanguard of universities creating new educational opportunities for the public through lectures, class study, and correspondence or home study. A decade after Van Hise made his pledge for community engagement there was sufficient momentum in the university continuing education movement to establish a national organization that today is the University Professional and Continuing Education Association (UPCEA).

In the one hundred years since the creation of UPCEA we have seen the development of new types of institutions or institutional sub-units, structural and curricular innovations including organizing curricula into majors and general education requirements, the establishment of student affairs professionals, and the development and growth of online education.

Innovation today continues to evolve around the core values of access and economic development, but the focus tends to be more on the level of technology and the individual learner than on organizational structure and public policy. Innovations are very much linked to and influenced by the drivers of change discussed above.

Big Data and Predictive Analytics

Our interactions in an online environment, particularly the collection of behavioral clickstream data (privacy concerns aside), has fueled a new area of innovation in postsecondary education that holds tremendous promise in helping us meet our attainment goals. Similar to Amazon and iTunes using algorithms to customize product offers based on previous purchases and shopping behavior, we are making progress in understanding more about the factors that influence learning, persistence, and completion. The enormous amounts of such data collected by massive open online course (MOOC) platforms during their heyday in 2012–2013 brought renewed attention to this potential.

Formed in 2011, the Predictive Analytics Reporting (PAR) Framework is one example of a systematic approach, "a collaborative, multi-institutional effort that brings together two-year, four-year, public, proprietary, traditional, and progressive institutions to collaborate on identifying points of student loss" (WICHE Cooperative for Educational Technologies, n.d.). Innovation also abounds right now in the development of technology-enhanced interventions to influence positive student behaviors, technologies such as early warning systems, automated feedback, and course schedule optimization. These and similar initiatives are showing promise in identifying key friction points in student progress and in measuring the effects of specific interventions.

Personalization

The holy grail of big data and predictive analytics is the personalization and customization of education targeted at the individual learner level. Will we be able to truly customize a student's experience to enhance learning, engagement, and completion? One can envision a system that would understand a student's learning style, preparation, and specific learning challenges and automatically target content and format to that individual student. Customization could go beyond the course level to providing real-time feedback and reminders to keep them on track toward completion, again customized in terms of frequency and level of detail to the needs of that student. These systems would constantly adapt by tracking progress toward desired outcomes. Although education is much more complex and critical than online marketing and commerce, we can see a future where customization based on real-time data will be an important tool in advancing educational goals.

Faculty Role

Innovation and changes in the faculty role within US institutions is not a new phenomenon. For example, over time, faculty have seen much of their advising role shift to student affairs professionals and their own institutional governance responsibilities increase (Sandeen 2014, 2). Nationally, the aggregate proportion of part-time and adjunct faculty far exceeds that of full-time tenured and tenure-track faculty, a trend that has slowly evolved over the last forty years.

Changes in the faculty role—particularly the teaching role—are evolving more quickly in recent times due in large part to the growth of online education. Faculty are commonly charged with the complete spectrum of teaching—instructional design, content sourcing, delivering the course content, designing assessments, administering assessments, mentoring students, and assigning final grades. Despite their deep disciplinary knowledge, most faculty do not have formal training in the majority of these teaching functions. An increasing number of institutions have unbundled or disaggregated these teaching roles and have hired specialists (usually non-faculty, presumably at a lower cost) to perform specific functions like instructional and assessment design. Western Governors University is notable in this regard, but an increasing number of institutions are adopting a similar approach. Such changes are not without controversy, but these innovations seem to be taking hold as long as they can demonstrate measureable improvement in educational and attainment goals.

Competency-Based Approach

Competency-based education (CBE) is another example of a "new" innovation that is not so new, but which has been in the spotlight recently because of its potential to serve the postsecondary education needs of today's students. Some CBE programs have existed for decades. The regional accreditation sector has been driving a shift from inputs to student learning outcomes in evaluating institutional quality for almost as long.

In essence, CBE focuses on what students can prove they know or can do. Competencies are defined student learning outcomes that can be measured and assessed. CBE is a distinct alternative to our current system of awarding degrees and credentials based on time and credit hours even though the time-based system is currently hardwired into US. higher education policy and Title IV student financial aid law.

In a credit-hour-based model, time to complete a class or program is held constant and the learning varies if we assume a score of 70 percent, or sometimes even less, qualifies for a passing score. In a competency-based model, student learning is constant, that is, all defined competencies must be mastered to a predetermined level, and time is variable. A student can progress quickly or slowly given their particular life circumstances. Such a system provides the flexibility needed by many non-traditional students who must work while attending school or for those students who choose to progress quickly in order to save time and money. Within this model, assessment of competencies is a key component.

Credit for Prior Learning

Closely related to competency-based education is the notion of credit for prior learning or CPL. CPL is a means for validating and providing academic credit for formal college-level learning that did not take place in a college or university setting. Major forms of CPL are credit by examination (e.g., AP and CLEP exams), course evaluations (e.g., the ACE credit recommendation service), and portfolio review (e.g., CAEL).

CPL has existed at least since the 1950s with the advent of the American Council on Education's military evaluation service, which provides transcripted academic credit recommendations that veterans can petition institutions to accept as transfer credit. These tools have become increasingly important in a competency-based and cost-conscious environment. By acknowledging and validating formal and documented prior learning, students are not required to spend the time and money to repeat learning they already have acquired. This is an important motivator for the large number of older students with some college but no degree who would benefit immensely from completing a degree or credential.

New and Alternative Credentials

Nondegree credentials, particularly certificate programs, have existed alongside degrees for decades, but mainly as a form of additional education and professional development in certain fields. Certificate programs are achieving increased attention as a valid form of postsecondary education in and of themselves, especially to the extent that they can lead to well-paid entry-level jobs and serve as a stepping-stone to further education.

Some of the more novel alternative credentials that have emerged in the past few years are digital badges or microcredentials. Originally focused on the youth and K-12 context and sponsored mainly by the MacArthur Foundation and the Mozilla Foundation, digital badges adapted gamification principles to document and motivate learning. More recently, the higher education community has begun to explore how digital badges might integrate into traditional curricula and programs.

Digital badges provide an open technology infrastructure that allows badge issuers to define outcomes, criteria, and assessments that an earner must complete in order to earn a particular badge. Many education technology companies are developing platforms where a badge earner can store these digital credentials in order to make them accessible for future employers and graduate school admission processes.

Although standards and criteria are still evolving, we are seeing a growing interest in adapting the badge or microcredential concept for use within higher education. For example, badges can be used to define granular competencies that scaffold to a full course, program, or degree. They can be used to validate learning achieved in cocurricular activities and programs. Badges are already being used as a way to document and record professional development achievements. Certain badges are being considered as part of admission processes, similar to other extracurricular activities and college-level learning achievements. The strength of the badge concept is the ability to see beyond the surface, to understand the learning outcomes and criteria for issuance that are transparently embedded in the badge's technical infrastructure.

Business Model

How institutions receive revenue for the value they provide is the essence of the business model question. Currently, revenue typically comes in the form of tuition, state or endowment support, research funding, and auxiliary services. The value provided is seen as the credential itself. Cross-subsidizations are very common. For example, subsidizing smaller, specialized upper division classes and providing graduate student support through high-enrollment introductory courses is a well-entrenched practice at many institutions. Unraveling this practice would be difficult. Developing means to generate additional revenue through self-support degrees and services is a common strategy at many institutions, but these activities supplement rather than alter the prevailing business model.

Recently, some fairly radical innovations in business model have emerged, closely tied to online and competency-based education and aligning with core values of access and affordability. For example, a subscription tuition model where students pay a set fee for a semester or term, during which they can "consume" as much education as they desire within that interval, has been adopted at a few institutions. Unaccredited education providers, such as StraighterLine, have emerged as well to provide low-cost lower division general education and developmental education courses for which articulation agreements have been negotiated to increase the transferability of the credit. Some institutions have formed partnerships with online service providers to deliver online programs on behalf of the institution on a revenue-sharing basis. Still others have struck deals with large national or global employers to be the sole source for degree programs for the firm's employees in exchange for a substantial discount.

Even more disruptive is the self-curated or DIY degree movement, the idea that some individuals will bypass degrees completely and instead aggregate a variety of certifications and other evidence of learning into something akin to an artists' portfolio that will be accepted by employers as valid job preparation in place of a degree. Weise and Christensen refer to this trend as "modularized industry-validated learning experiences" and view this as a potential disruption circumventing institutions and the accreditation process (2014, 27). The jury is still out on the probability of adoption of such extreme measures, but unless and until we see greater public investment in higher education, the business model is one area where innovation is likely to continue to expand.

Professional and Continuing Education and the "Sputnik" Challenge

Although the sections above are focused on large national trends in post-secondary education, it is easy to see the many threads of connection with—and opportunities for—the professional and continuing education (PCE) sector to contribute toward national attainment goals. Since the earliest days, PCE leaders have known that learning does not stop with earning a degree. For both personal and professional reasons, learning continues through a lifetime. Today, with industries and jobs that are continually evolving and changing, the opportunity to stay current and engaged is evermore critical. The PCE sector also realizes that postsecondary education is not just degrees, but encompasses a range of credentials, including the category of high-quality certificates with labor market value, that are part of the attainment conversation today.

PCE leaders are natural innovators. At many campuses the continuing education division is an incubator for ideas and programs some of which are eventually adopted as traditional programs on campus. PCE was an early adopter of online education and continues to embrace new technology-enhanced pedagogy to provide access and flexibility to students. PCE was an early adopter of competency-based education and, due to this expertise, is playing a key role in the development of this approach to education and credentialing.

PCE divisions are not "cities on the hill" but are directly and closely engaged with real life in the surrounding community, region, and usually the state. Leaders find themselves on the road, meeting with other leaders from industry, government, community groups, and other institutions, forming collaborations and partnerships to benefit students. PCE leaders are adept at connecting with employers to understand workforce and economic development needs and to design academic programs to prepare a robust and competitive workforce.

Being mostly (or entirely) self-supporting may have been viewed as a disadvantage in the past, but it is clearly an advantage now. PCE units are not locked into one business model and have the flexibility and agility to explore new configurations. PCE leaders have been at the forefront of forging productive partnerships with private industry, including service providers to support academic programs.

Professional and continuing educators have always understood there are different pathways to education. No one size fits all. They have always known that nontraditional students are the majority of students and that helping this large and diverse student segment earn degrees and credentials is serving the nation. Finally, the PCE community is university-based. The sector operates with business discipline and from an entrepreneurial perspective, knowing the true north of academic quality and the importance of fit within the culture of its home institutions.

The inherent qualities of the PCE sector—quality, access, flexibility, innovation, workforce connection, and accountability—are exactly what national leaders from government, think tanks, associations, and foundations say are necessary for US higher education to meet the attainment challenge. Today, at UPCEA's centennial, we are at an inflection point, a critical time when PCE divisions are no longer viewed as a satellite or appendage to a college or university but are seen as essential capacity the institution must deploy.

Future Challenges

Even with all these strengths, there are two areas where PCE divisions might focus some attention as they move into their second century as a profession. These two areas are integration and enhancement of both liberal arts skills and global/multicultural skills.

US higher education has had a strong workforce development orientation at least since the Morrill Act, and the majority of PCE divisions have followed suit, focusing on programs that would help someone obtain employment or progress in his or her career. However, we should not forget our liberal arts roots. Higher education was built on the foundation of liberal education—a broad curriculum spanning art, history, literature, mathematics, philosophy, sciences, and social sciences, intended to prepare an individual to think for himself or herself, engage in civic life, and continue to learn through a lifetime.

The current focus is on more vocationally oriented education that will lead to a post-graduation job, but what about the student's *next* job. The currently promoted, hyper-vocationalized, credentialist orientation will not help us develop the nimble workforce required for the coming century. We need people who have both specialized knowledge and underlying competencies such as communication and critical thinking skills, analytical ability, creative problem solving, teamwork, and global cultural awareness, all of which allows a person to continue learning and adapt over time. That is a crucial ability in a world where most good jobs will constantly change as technologies continue to evolve. Employers desire these traits and complain that our graduates lack these skills.

While many PCE divisions offer high-quality liberal arts degrees, these are often separate from the more narrowly focused professional programs. Can we do a better job of proactively integrating broad liberal arts skills as part of all our programs? Can we develop the means to measure and validate mastery of these skills? Should we participate more fully in the conversation about the vital importance of these skills?

Creating a globally competitive workforce is also central to our nation's postsecondary attainment goals. Global competitiveness is important, but this issue is inherently layered and nuanced. We live and work in an increasingly globally connected world, and jobs of the future will require people to connect and work effectively with global and multicultural teams. Local domestic workforces are and will continue to be increasingly multicultural. With increased immigration, greater enrollment of international students, especially in online programs, our students are increasingly global and diverse. Student veterans bring extensive and unique international experience. On some campuses, students in PCE classes may be the most diverse classes at the institutions. Are we taking full advantage of the learning opportunities this diversity provides? Are we proactively creating opportunities for students to learn about other cultures from each other? Are our faculty primed to inject a global and multicultural dimension into class content, assignments, and projects? Requiring one class in multiculturalism is not as effective as weaving content and experiences throughout an entire curriculum.

These questions about integration of liberal arts skills and multiculturalism are taking place throughout higher education and should be embraced by the PCE community as well. Addressing our nation's "Sputnik moment" is not only about the number of degrees and credentials awarded, but the quality and sustainability of learning that has taken place. Broad liberal arts skills and embracing diversity have been the "secret sauce" of US higher education in the past. We cannot ignore this as we also focus on student completion.

"Houston, We Have a Problem"

Our nation's postsecondary attainment goals are profound. We have never before attempted to provide postsecondary education to such a large proportion of our population. These attainment goals are every bit as challenging and complex—perhaps even more so—than putting a man on the moon and bringing the team back to earth. Meeting our goals will take the collective knowledge, energy, innovation, focus, and determination of the entire higher education community. It will take every single one of the four thousand or so postsecondary institutions performing at an optimum level. It will take a high level of rapid innovation and a data-informed orientation.

The professional and continuing education sector is a vital member of this team. The long tradition of access, innovation, and data-driven discipline within the sector are exactly what is needed in the days ahead. It is my most fervent hope that we will look back on this moment in time as a fitting inflection point for a profession at its centennial. I also hope that just like our country's achievements in space, we will look back in awe at what we have accomplished and will reap additional benefits for generations to come.

References

Association of Public and Land-Grant Universities. 2012. *The Land-Grant Tradition*. Accessed at http://www.aplu.org/document.doc?id=780.

Carnevale, A. P., N. Smith, and J. Strohl. 2013. *Recovery: Job Growth and Education Requirements through 2020*. Washington, DC: Georgetown Public Policy Institute. Accessed at https://georgetown.app.box.com/s /tll0zkxt0puz45hu21g6.

Frey, W. H. 2013. "Shift to a Majority-Minority Population in the U.S. Happening Faster than Expected." Brookings Institution. Accessed at http://www.brookings.edu/blogs/up-front/posts/2013/06/19-us-majority -minority-population-census-frey.

Obama Administration. n.d. "Higher Education." The White House. Accessed at http://www.whitehouse.gov/issues/education/higher-education.

Obama, Barak. 2013. "Remarks by the President in State of Union Address," February 12. Accessed at http://www.whitehouse.gov/the-press -office/2013/02/12/remarks-president-state-union-address.

Organization for Economic Cooperation and Development (OECD). 2013. *Education at a Glance 2013*. Accessed at http://www.oecd.org/edu /United%20States%20_EAG2013%20Country%20Note.pdf.

Russell, A. 2011. "A Guide to Major US College Completion Initiatives." (policy brief) American Association of State Colleges and Universities, October 2011. Accessed at http://www.aascu.org/policy/publications/policymatters /2011/collegecompletion.pdf.

Sandeen, C., ed. 2014. "Unbundling versus Designing Faculty Roles." *Presidential Innovation Lab White Paper Series*. American Council on Education. Accessed at http://www.acenet.edu/news-room/Documents/Unbundling-Versus -Designing-Faculty-Roles.pdf

Schoenfeld, Clay. 1975. "The Wisconsin Idea Expanded, 1949–1974." In Allen G. Bogue and Robert Taylor, *The University of Wisconsin: One Hundred and Twenty-five Years*. Madison: University of Wisconsin Press.

WICHE Cooperative for Educational Technologies. n.d. PAR Framework Executive Summary. Accessed at http://wcet.wiche.edu/wcet/docs/par /PARMemberBenefits103013.pdf.

Weise, M. R., and C. M. Christensen. 2014. *Hire Education: Mastery, Modularization and the Workforce Revolution*. Boston: Clayton Christensen Institute. Accessed at http://www.christenseninstitute.org/wp-content/uploads /2014/07/Hire-Education.pdf.

PART IV

Audiences

Look over the shoulder of any college or university continuing education registrar or registration clerk and you will be impressed by the diversity of the continuing education student body on many measures. Reflecting the traditional breadth of continuing education offerings, their market responsiveness, and historic relationships with diverse audiences, continuing education students follow many pathways to higher education: by occupation, as in military education; by age, as in the robust activity targeting older adults; or by nationality, as in the increasingly diverse ways in which students of all nationalities are integrated into American or Canadian higher education. To appreciate this diversity, it is worthwhile to have a historic accounting as well as a snapshot of the present. This section illustratively targets several audiences for a much closer look.

James P. Pappas provides a sweeping look at voluntary military education from George Washington at Valley Forge to our current engagements in the Middle East and the role of a major public university in being of service to our military personnel. Geraldine de Berly shifts our attention to international education and reflects on the roles played by specialists in university provision of international education, while also elaborating on the challenges and opportunities for its expansion. Judith Potter and Maia Korotkina, still within the ambit of international students, target the immigrant audience, particularly in Canada, providing a careful analysis of the opportunities and barriers for immigrants in their drive to acquire the skills that will support them in a new national setting. James M. Shaeffer and Sarah K. MacDonald shift our attention to another burgeoning population of continuing education students, the over-65 adult. They define the population in a brief look at demographics and then, usefully, contrast a historical review of programs for older adults with an exploration of the opportunities that present themselves in response to an increasing need. With Mary B. McIntire's essay on fund-raising we change the prism through which we have been viewing the audience for continuing education from student to donor. McIntire provides a practical view of the challenges and opportunities that present themselves to leadership of continuing education, as well as the university, in the development and implementation of a fund-raising role. Finally, George Irvine looks at structural support for building new programs, new audiences, or new capacities through the development of organizational partnerships.

Voluntary Military Education from the Perspective of Continuing Education

∎∎

James P. Pappas

Introduction

Continuing educators have historically sought to provide educational access and opportunity to those who cannot attend traditional campus residential programs. Military personnel are quintessential working adult students who are typically place- and circumstance-bound. Voluntary military education falls under this broader context of providing access and accommodating those who need specialized workplace programs. Voluntary military education also offers both a unique first chance for soldiers wishing to complete a college degree and a viable second chance for those who may have made earlier attempts to complete a degree but fell short due to deployments, work demands, family issues, or other competing priorities. These adult students face significant work-life balance issues and are the core of many of our programs, both degree and non-degree. Because of that, military students are a vital continuing education audience that should not be taken for granted and for whom we should do even more.

Today, voluntary military education includes undergraduate and graduate degree programs to equip service members for their assigned duties and to prepare them for professional lives after separating from the armed services. It includes, too, noncredit and certificate training programs, and it embodies a cluster of complex concerns and problems that each state, and sometimes even each higher education institution, must

James P. Pappas is Vice President for University Outreach, Dean of the College of Liberal Studies, and Professor, Departments of Educational Psychology and Liberal Studies, University of Oklahoma, past president of the UPCEA, 1996–1997, and a recipient of the Bittner and Nolte Awards.

resolve: tuition assistance, credit for military-provided training, counseling, on-base course delivery, government regulations, Department of Defense contracting, and many others. The audience for military education can also include veterans of armed services and the spouses and family members of service men and women. Military education has become a core part of the lives of millions of service members who engage in it and of thousands of higher education personnel who administer it. Moreover, in countless US colleges and universities, it has become a vital mission involving billions of dollars and untold hours of effort to deliver programs within the United States and overseas.

A Brief, Selective History

General George Washington certainly did not envision the enterprise that would emerge when, in 1778, he directed his chaplain to provide reading, writing, and arithmetic instruction to his troops convalescing at Valley Forge. He had perceived the challenges faced by illiterate soldiers and sought a practical remedy. To address the problems of literacy, Washington's faculty members were clergymen, and the curriculum they prescribed was the Bible. Nearly a century later, following the close of the Civil War, another future president, James Garfield, then a US congressman, argued for legislation to establish "post schools," which would educate enlisted men in patriotic history, all in an effort to ameliorate crime and vice among soldiers. Throughout the nineteenth and even into the twentieth centuries, a debate raged regarding whether enlisted personnel should engage in formal education and whether the government should provide it. Amid this rise and fall of political and legislative support, military education was transformed into a monumental government initiative that far surpassed the simple literacy training advanced by Washington.

With the announcement in 1878 of the formation of evening schools for soldiers, the War Department made advances in providing military personnel with an opportunity for a decent education. Significantly, the purpose of these evening schools was not merely to retool soldiers for their military work but to help them return to civilian life as "more intelligent" citizens.

In 1891, Captain Allen Allensworth presented a paper, "Military Education in the US Army," at the National Educational Association conference in Toronto, Canada. A former slave, Allensworth was a visionary who may well have been able to foresee what General Washington did not, for he advocated that the army provide vocational programs to soldiers, championed improvements in education as a means of making the military more efficient, and sought equality for blacks in the service.

By the mid-twentieth century, advances in voluntary military education had accelerated, and American colleges and universities stepped forward to assume greater responsibility for the education and training of US soldiers. In 1942, more than fifty years after Captain Allensworth's paper was presented, a key contract was signed between the War Department and Indiana University that would provide financial support for school and college teachers who would select and create materials for independent study courses to be offered at the US Armed Forces Institute. A year later, more than 500 colleges and universities had devised policies and procedures to use the American Council on Education's Sound Education Credit for Military Experience: A Recommended Program. The University of Maryland, an early leader in developing educational programs for military personnel, began offering classes in Europe in 1949. My own institution, the University of Oklahoma, was by 1944 offering more than 150 college and seventy-five high school courses to men and women in the armed forces in conjunction with the US Armed Forces Institute. Other institutions, public and private alike, played equally significant roles.

Certainly the watershed moment in military education history occurred in June 1944, just weeks after the Normandy invasion, when President Roosevelt signed the Servicemen's Readjustment Act, better known as the GI Bill, which provided among other things educational benefits for veterans as an award for honorable service. Less than three years later, the War Department would establish tuition assistance for military personnel enrolled in civilian colleges and universities during off-duty time. Since 2009, veterans have been able to transfer their GI Bill benefits to dependents.

With advances in program development and delivery came the formation of various groups to support a burgeoning military enterprise and to help establish quality control measures. Servicemembers Opportunity Colleges (SOC), formed in 1972, is a consortium of nearly 2,000 colleges and universities that follow established criteria to meet the higher education needs of military personnel. These criteria include residency requirements, credit awards for military training and experience, nationally recognized testing programs, and transfer credit.

Defense Activity for Nontraditional Education Support (DANTES) was established in 1974 to support both the Department of Defense's off-duty, voluntary education programs and its educational functions.

The Council of College and Military Educators (CCME) emerged as a result of education services officers gathering in the early 1970s to discuss how best to serve the needs of military personnel seeking a college education. Now worldwide in scope, CCME addresses the constantly changing educational landscape as the armed services partner with colleges and universities. Annual symposia offer forums to explore the rising costs of education within the context of declining military budgets, the increasing dependence on outsourcing and contracting in the education services community, and the implications of these developments on the services, the institutions, and military students.

Many other groups have played instrumental roles in contributing to the military education enterprise, including regional organizations such as the Council on Military Education in Texas and the South (COMETS), the Florida Advisory Council on Military Education (FL ACME), the Council on Military Education in South Carolina (CO-MESCO), and others.

The 1970s and later proved to be a prolific period in the creation of distance initiatives for the delivery of military education. As a means to gain accreditation and recognition for Air Force–delivered training, the Community College of the Air Force (CCAF) was developed in the early 1970s particularly to address the needs of noncommissioned officers. Today, CCAF has approximately 400,000 students and is the largest multicampus community college in the world. Another innovation, launched in 2001, eArmyU was established to enable enlisted soldiers to work toward a college degree or certificate online. This program provided distance learning support services to about 64,000 soldiers before it was shut down by the army in 2012. There are myriad other innovative military education programs, including Navy College PACE, which provides ship-bound sailors with opportunities to earn technical or college degrees through various options, and Credentialing Opportunities On-Line (COOL), which equips US Navy service members with information about civilian licensure and certification and helps prepare them for exams and training. An army COOL program provides the same services for US Army service members.

Veterans Programs

Today, one million veterans nationwide are using some form of educational benefits provided through the Department of Veteran Affairs. For those who served at least thirty-six months of active duty after September 10, 2001, 100 percent of their tuition and fees are covered under the Post-9/11 GI Bill. The significant change between veterans of the present era and those of the post–World War II era is that 25 percent of them are female, and 47 percent of student veterans are married and/or have children. Thirty-six percent of all higher education institutions (75 percent of four-year public schools) have a student-run military or veterans group on campus, and nearly 40 percent of public four-year institutions offer academic advising specifically for military or veteran students. Stories from students who have taken advantage of GI Bill benefits to further their education are pervasive.

Following the September 11, 2001, terrorist attacks, the Post-9/11 GI

Bill was inaugurated to extend educational and other benefits to men and women who served in the armed forces during Middle East conflicts. Campuses across the country found themselves needing to gear up to take in record numbers of veterans.

Every campus accommodates veterans in different ways, but many colleges and universities provide Veterans Upward Bound, a free US Department of Education program designed to help veterans refresh their academic skills and give them the resources and confidence needed to complete a college degree.

Higher education institutions in every state offer facilities and services for former military personnel. Oklahoma is no different, and its programs are exemplary. For instance, Oklahoma State University maintains a veterans lounge where student veterans can study and relax. At the University of Oklahoma, we provide a network of trained faculty and staff members who volunteer to provide specialized assistance to students who have served in the military. The University of Central Oklahoma houses a veterans affairs office to provide support to veterans and their dependents. Each state provides similar variants at its institutions of higher education.

Mindful of veterans' contributions to national security and preserving American freedoms, Congress passed a bill in summer 2014 requiring public universities to offer veterans in-state tuition. This tuition break addresses some but not all of the concerns faced by veterans. Some veterans confront colossal hurdles after suffering debilitating injuries during military service. It is one thing for able-bodied veterans to participate in educational programs; it is quite another for veterans with cognitive or physical disabilities to learn new skills through technical training programs or return to college for degree completion or to begin a degree program from the beginning. Some universities have stepped up to help disabled veterans. For instance, according to *Inside Higher Ed*, the University of Pittsburgh devised "a college transition program for disabled veterans interested in STEM disciplines" (Tyson 2014). Supported by a grant from the National Science Foundation, this program equips veterans not merely in science, technology, engineering, and math classes; it puts disabled veterans in a laboratory environment to work on applied projects that will help other disabled veterans—for example, developing a low-cost power wheelchair. In effect, these veterans are learning new in-demand skills and assisting others facing the same or similar challenges. Other institutions are replicating this innovative program with programs of their own.

America is a nation of interest-serving groups. One group that has taken a leadership role for veterans is the Student Veterans of America (SVA). This organization has been particularly committed to helping veterans return to college and complete academic degrees. One means of accomplishing this goal has been SVA's Million Records Project, which provides academic outcomes and progress data for policymakers, service providers, higher education institutions, and the public. These data promise to aid legislators and others to evaluate current programs for veterans and to devise new initiatives to ensure that veterans are successful as they participate in postsecondary education.

Of course, not all is rosy among some veterans, who all too often experience the bureaucracy of government and educational institutions. Red tape, new rules, restrictions on some programs, and significant cutbacks in programs—these problems certainly frustrate veterans hoping to use education to jumpstart a new career or make an effective transition from military to civilian life. Due to recent problems in Veterans Administration health facilities, Congress and other policymakers have become sensitized to the needs of America's veterans and will almost assuredly address shortcomings in educational programs aimed at helping veterans.

Student Experiences

The transformational impact of a college education on the life of a member of the military can be documented quantitatively, but it is the unique stories of these individuals that stir us. The stories I know come from our own students.

Five years ago, Daniel was deployed onboard the *USS Rodney M. Davis*, supporting narcotics interdiction on behalf of the US Coast Guard. During this time he completed his undergraduate degree from the College of Liberal Studies at the University of Oklahoma (OU). Today, he works as a university student adviser assisting military students pursuing higher education. According to Daniel:

> Starting my degree while on deployment really gave me a unique understanding of the needs of our active-duty service members after having been one myself. The college recognized the importance of developing education programs to meet the needs of our military members and allowed me to earn a bachelor's degree and begin pursuing a master's degree, all while being enlisted. I am excited and optimistic about what the future holds for military students, and I would encourage other interested individuals in the military to consider pursuing a degree. The Coast Guard gave me the confidence and discipline to achieve a higher education and the university provided the opportunity to reach those goals. I have no doubt my degrees are going to greatly expand my career future.

Tamara was an educational site representative at a military installation in southwest Oklahoma, where she oversaw a student body made up of active-duty soldiers and civilians. To better serve her students, she decided to go back to college herself to get a second master's degree in international relations from OU's graduate program designed for military personnel.

> It really helped me to understand my students' needs, both their educational and service-related needs. I have since been promoted to program director of engineering and geosciences continuing education programs. I am excited about the new things I am working on, and I credit my second graduate degree for making that possible. I'm positive that my new position and the opportunity that awaited me would not have been possible without obtaining my graduate degree. I would encourage every individual in the military to consider pursuing an advanced degree. The benefits are great and the cost is affordable, especially because of the options that exist through Chapter 33 of the GI Bill. Military personnel should make use of their benefits—they earned them. And my experience is that a graduate degree makes a big difference.

Samantha, a major in the US Air Force, was the first lead solo pilot for the USAF Air Demonstration Squadron, known as the Thunderbirds. She was only the second woman to fly with any military high-performance demonstration team.

> I was attracted to OU because of the dual degree option of human relations and international relations. I didn't want just a master's degree; I wanted a master's degree that would propel me forward as a leader, manager, subordinate, and person. The degree I chose afforded me this opportunity. I liked the range of classes that were offered in the human relations degree program. I also enjoyed the combination of online classes and actual classroom lectures. It enabled me to get the best of both worlds with the structured environment in the classroom, which helped me to focus on school, and the freedom of the online programming that allowed me to work with my schedule. My degree has already provided me with so much. I reflect on my classes quite often in my job and refer to my books for advice in certain situations. I took fifteen credit hours at a time while working full time, but I set a goal when I began the process

and wanted to achieve it. I had one year to try to finish the
human relations part of my degree, and I was able to do
that with a little dedication and determination.

Faculty Experiences

The impact of the college experience on military students is mirrored
in the exemplary experience of one of our faculty members. This faculty
member is an OU professor, assistant vice president of Outreach, and a
member of the National Guard with two tours of Afghanistan under his
belt. He also teaches on a regular basis for our graduate degree program
serving military bases in the United States and Europe. He noted:

> My first introduction to our military program came when
> I met an army captain during a field training exercise at
> Fort Hood several years ago. I noticed he was wearing an
> OU ring, and I asked him about it. He told me that he re-
> ceived his Master of Public Administration degree through
> OU without setting foot on campus. He went on to explain
> that due to transfers and deployments, he would not have
> been able to earn a graduate degree. He is now a proud
> Sooner. Since then, I have had the privilege to teach for
> this program. It is an honor for me to serve, in a small way,
> those who serve our country in the armed forces. My expe-
> rience has been rewarding each time. I find the students to
> be very engaged and very busy. I have been impressed with
> their commitment to continuing education and how they
> balance the many demands on their time. I've gained an
> appreciation for these students. I often gain new insight as
> their world experience is quite a bit different from the stu-
> dents I typically teach on campus. Many of them have dealt
> with the harsh realities of war. Some students have worked
> in many levels of government and have held significant po-
> sitions of leadership in the military, and they bring these
> experiences to bear in class. Their discussions can be lively
> while providing fresh perspective.

The Future

In significant ways, the future of voluntary military education lies in hands
other than those of higher education administrators. Federal efforts to
trim military spending, including base closure and realignment (BRAC)

and the drawdown of troops and overseas sites, have an understandable effect on the numbers of service members to whom continuing educators can provide educational programs. And significantly, the Department of Defense's consideration of reductions in tuition assistance will play an even greater part in whether military education can be provided at the same level as in the past. Of course, there will always be educational programs for the military, and to that extent continuing and higher education will have a role.

Technology will be ever more important in the provision of military education programs. With the deployment and mobility of service members, convenient access to education is essential, and the future will doubtless unveil many new means for course and program delivery. Continuing education will need to be nimble, prepared to take advantage of these new avenues and play roles in devising new ways to equip service members with the education they require in the twenty-first century and beyond.

Concluding Comments

Military personnel provide significant service to the nation, often at tremendous personal sacrifice and risk, and institutions of higher education must respond to such sacrifice. Colleges and universities have a great responsibility to provide military personnel and veterans with access to higher education.

Voluntary military education provides service members with special skill sets and broad educational competencies to help them do their work better—whether it is managing better (e.g., a degree in human relations to develop their interpersonal skills), budgeting better (to improve the management of military resources), or giving them specific job-related capacities in particular fields, such as criminal justice or health care administration. Continuing education simply makes them better at their military jobs.

As their comments have strongly acknowledged, military students and faculty who teach them are often meaningfully changed by the experience. Being around them and their excitement at events such as graduation is infectious. No greater work-related thrill matches presiding over a college graduation ceremony held at one of the US bases around the world. It is a privilege when we as faculty and administrators can celebrate with these students as they earn a degree after maintaining an up-tempo work schedule, pursing knowledge while at risk, and dedicating considerable effort to evening or online classes. Graduation ceremonies allow everyone attending to share the pride that the service man or woman feels as a result of his or her accomplishment, something that is often taken for granted by our traditional residential students. The shout-outs to parents and relatives, the beaming smiles of pride of supervisory officers and colleagues, and the invigorating walk across the stage create a memorable experience.

When I teach a class on a base, I am always reminded of the first military graduation ceremony I attended. During the event, I stepped forward to hand a diploma to a young officer of color and congratulated him on his degree. After the ceremony, as I mingled with the crowd at the reception, I was introduced to his father and mother, who had come from the States to see him graduate and to be with his wife and several children. The young man himself, though pleased, was quite reserved about having obtained the degree. The father, however, who was closer to my age, was effusive and excited. He held up his young grandchild, who wore a small university sweatshirt, and proudly announced that this child was a next-generation Sooner. I learned that the young officer was the first member of his family to attend college. And now he had completed his master's degree with our institution. His superior officer indicated to me that the advanced degree would help him in his promotion boards, and his wife was already talking about potential careers he might pursue after his discharge.

Our ability to provide these opportunities both within the military setting and after retirement are what continuing education should be about—helping students transform their lives and contributing to the educated citizenry of our nation.

References

Tyson, Charlie. 2014. "Healing War Wounds." *Inside Higher Ed*, August 12. Accessed at https://www.insidehighered.com/news/2014/08/12/disabled -veterans-college-transition-program-pursue-stem-develop-assistive.

Note: Special appreciation goes to Clinton "Andy" Anderson, whose monograph, *Remembering Those Who Have Made a Difference in United States Military Voluntary Education*, was consulted for this essay. Thanks also goes to Grey Edwards, whose conference presentation on military education at the International Adult Education Conference in Romania, 2014, helped frame some of the ideas contained in the essay.

Continuing, Professional, and International Education

Converging Skill Sets

■▌

Geraldine de Berly

Introduction

The mobility of students across continents has affected higher education in the United States, which in 2013 had some 820,000 international students (Farrugia and Bhandari 2013). Many incoming international students study in intensive English programs, attend professional development programs, or matriculate into degree programs housed in continuing education (CE) units. Further, these units' agility, delivery capabilities (technological and physical), and access to multidisciplinary expertise enable them to provide significant programming for international education.

Continuing and international education professionals are surprisingly similar in nature. They are committed to access, engagement, flexibility, varied delivery formats, responsiveness, assessment, evaluation, and borderless education. They have arrived at their profession from multiple disciplines: academia, business/corporations, nongovernmental organizations (NGOs), and government entities. Many are career changers and have thus leveraged transferable skills. Many have their origins in self-funding organizations and as such have excellent financial grounding in both the generation and administration of budgets, price points, and their impact upon enrollment. Finally, these professionals are ever vigilant for external funding opportunities and are adept at grant development.

Geraldine de Berly is Senior Associate Dean, University College, Syracuse University, UPCEA Global Associates chair, and recipient of an international leadership award.

Many continuing education units are stand-alone entities. Their administrators are mandated to bring significant return on investment to their institutions (UPCEA 2012, 76). They must be a credit to their home institutions and consequently are sensitive to quality delivery of programming at affordable rates and as such, must be efficient, at times parsimonious, always innovative, and consistently entrepreneurial. They must be willing to take risks but remain compliant. They must cooperate with multiple campus units, be politic in their negotiations, find ways to share costs without engendering the enmity of their collaborators, and they must be able to scale up or down with little notice.

Senior International Officers (SIOs) generally (but not always) oversee international education offices and rely on central administrative funds, as they tend to be responsible for services, programs, and institutional relationship building that do not generate revenue per se. These may include study abroad, admissions, intensive English programs, outreach, and contracting (Association of International Education Administrators, n.d.).

Seemingly, there is an overlap between the skill sets that continuing and professional education (CPE) deans and directors and SIOs demonstrate. Since many CPE units have international programs in their portfolios, it is worthwhile to consider the competencies related to international programming and activities more closely, as an understanding of these might contribute to better job descriptions, professional development, hiring decisions, and allocation of human capital.

UPCEA International Education Activity Survey

In order to determine some of the skill sets required by CPE deans and directors for successful international education activity, a survey was distributed to 329 institutional representatives based in US institutions who were members of the University and Professional Continuing Education Association (UPCEA, 2012). In total, 129 individuals replied to the survey, with 60 respondents (47%) having international education as part of their portfolios qualifying them to complete the survey. The survey sought to identify the range of responsibilities of CPE leaders engaged in international programs.

Specifically, as it relates to international programs, the survey covered areas of responsibility, types of programming, growth targets, and skill sets and experience of those responsible for international programs.

How Engagement in International Education Impacts CPE

Several respondents saw the increase in international activity as supporting the global missions of their universities. Others considered education a global enterprise. Adding to diversity on campus and opportunities for more short-term programs to "extend lifelong learning opportunities beyond the traditional campus through innovation, collaboration, and flexibility" were also seen as outcomes of international education. Such views are consistent with distance education practitioners' vision of the opportunities worldwide. Reed Scull, associate dean of outreach at the University of Wyoming notes:

> Leaders of lifelong learning and extended education organizations may well be faced with an unprecedented opportunity to innovate programmatically and expand educational access. Through the application of DE [distance education] methodologies many of us are already accustomed to using, we may now be able to find many untapped opportunities to provide our nontraditional learners experiences to strengthen their credentials with authentic internationalized learning opportunities that might intellectually engage, increase sensitivity, and even add skills and knowledge that are attractive to potential employers. (2014)

Continuing Professional Education Profile

The survey requested titles, as in some cases both continuing education (extension) and international or global responsibilities are reflected in the names of the positions. A third of the respondents held director titles: 21 percent held either associate or assistant vice president/provost or dean titles, with another 11 percent holding both. The majority of respondents (84%) had special contract programming (e.g., management, business, government, and academic preparation) as the most common service provided, followed by managing visiting international students (57%), engaging in international recruitment (50%), and overseeing intensive English programs (49%). Most also offered a dual or joint degree program either as part of CPE offerings or in partnership with campus departments.

Nearly all of the respondents indicated that their growth strategy included expanding international offerings, with a majority indicating a 6–10 percent expected increase. Others had a very ambitious 16–20 percent target increase, and a similar number had a more modest expectation of a 1–5 percent increase.

International and/or Foreign Language Knowledge

Concerning international experience, 31 percent of the respondents had five years or less; 23 percent had six to ten years experience; 26 percent had eleven to twenty-five years experience; and 20 percent had more than twenty-five years of international experience. However, the majority (54%) had not lived outside of the United States, with a significant number (87%) born in the United States, and 58 percent did not speak a language other than English. This would indicate that the bulk of the international experience was likely related to program development. Nevertheless, 46 percent had lived outside the United States, and 42 percent did speak a language other than English.

Skills and Knowledge Needed to
Work Effectively in International Education

Essential, helpful, and *not necessary* were the three rating descriptors asked of respondents to assess which skills/knowledge were required to succeed in international education activities.

For the 60 CPE respondents who had international experience, the skills seen as essential were intercultural competence (88%), cross-cultural communication (84%), organizational and leadership skills (79%), and adaptive skills (79%). Entrepreneurial skills were seen as essential or helpful (98%), while knowing a second or third language was deemed essential by 18 percent and helpful by 67 percent. Economic and geographic understanding of the targeted regions was deemed essential by 63 percent of the respondents and helpful by another 33 percent.

Skills that were considered essential by most but not all the respondents (in the range of 46–65%) were knowledge of foreign education systems, writing skills, project management, and negotiation skills. Considered less essential, particularly by the less experienced, was the need for substantial travel and/or experience working outside the United States. Finally, for the entire group, knowledge of export and intellectual property regulations was seen as helpful but not essential. What is perhaps most telling regarding the ranking of relative importance of the various skill sets is to consider respondents' perceptions by experience segment, that is, the level of significance attributed to experience in international education and having lived abroad. Those with more experience valued these highly, and those without experience found it helpful but not essential. Not surprisingly, those who had not lived outside of the United States and did not speak another language did not consider a second language an essential skill (but did describe it as helpful).

Senior International Officer Skill Sets

In 2007, NAFSA created a task force on skills and competencies of the international education leadership community which surveyed thirty-five highly experienced senior international officers (SIOs) using the Delphi technique to determine critical skills and knowledge for senior campus international leaders from all types of higher education institutions (e.g., public and private, community colleges, undergraduate, and research institutions; Lambert et al. 2007). The purpose of the survey was to identify a skill set, understand the SIO profile, and use the profile in designing professional development. The survey grouped initial responses into five categories: (1) personal qualities, (2) background knowledge, (3) specialized knowledge, (4) functional skills, and (5) specialized skills. In the second and final round of the survey, degree and importance were assigned to the various categories based on frequency counts. Deemed very important were strategic planning, cross-cultural skills, leadership, communication, overseas experience, change management, conflict management/negotiation, teamwork, flexibility, knowledge of international education, administrative experience, detailed knowledge of the home institution, ethics, energy/passion, policy development, and project management (ibid.).

It is not surprising that there is overlap in the skill sets demonstrated by CPE leaders and those displayed by SIOs. It supports the thesis put forth here that there are parallel skill sets and knowledge required of CPE leaders engaged in international education. Further, those are transferable skills. Sheila Thomas, statewide dean of extended education for California State University, commented:

> Continuing education leaders are assuming responsibility for important areas, such as international programs and advancement, and increasingly critical duties within academic affairs offices. The skills essential to successful continuing education administration are equally desirable in other areas of the university. (2013)

Critical Issues Facing Continuing, Professional, and International Education

The domestic nontraditional audience is no longer the minority but rather the majority; consequently, the market is expanding as is the competition. Many of the critical issues facing continuing and professional education are not peculiar to CPE or international education per se. They include the digitalization of education, the soft versus hard skills discussion along with workplace readiness, the importance of T-shaped individuals (breadth of knowledge and depth of expertise), homogenization of education, flexible formats (within established parameters, e.g., seat time or its equivalent), faculty buy-in, developing cutting edge programs which may have limited shelf life, intellectual property issues, and open courseware. International audiences also have concerns about access, bandwidth, price point (as do domestic audiences), English proficiency (depending on the country), length of study, and certificates (credit and noncredit) versus degrees. These are issues and opportunities simultaneously.

Opportunities

In the area of graduate education, many countries have the upgrading of their faculty across disciplines as a major educational goal, creating opportunities for comprehensive research institutions to provide the needed expertise. For example, the Putin initiative is to dramatically raise the international rankings of selected Russian universities by funding graduate study abroad ("Russia Announces New Investments in Higher Education and Study Abroad" 2014; Snytkova 2014; Smith 2014). Kansas State University dean of continuing education Sue Maes was instrumental in securing the Go Teacher Project (initiated in 2012), which has brought 427 Ecuadorian English teachers to its campus and an additional 405 teachers to the campuses of its project collaborators (Kansas State University 2014). The teachers are improving their English proficiency and acquiring training at a graduate level in language pedagogy and linguistics.

CPE units are particularly well placed to quickly respond to requests for proposals (RFPs) from government entities (such as those noted above) in the form of short- and/or long-term courses and programs in or out of country, delivered and/or enhanced by the use of compelling technologies.

The Organisation for Economic Cooperation and Development (OECD) report *Trends Shaping Education 2013* notes that the impact of education upon an aging population will affect voting patterns and consequently public policy. The need for health literacy will increase. People working longer will need skills and education to sustain employment. Pedagogical conventions will need to be adaptable and creative to engage older learners. Enabling access will be a priority. These patterns are evident in highly developed countries but are also true of less-developed countries with increasing aging populations. Global surveys on older persons' experience of aging indicate that their financial security and ability to work are a concern (United Nations Population Fund 2012, 3, 24–25).

Persons interviewed for the UNFPA report describe the difficulties that older people encounter in finding productive employment, often as a consequence of age discrimination, and also of general high levels of unemployment, health problems, and a lack of qualifications or poor working conditions. When applying for jobs, they are often told they are too old. In some cases, those working for the government are forced to retire. Some felt their qualifications were not sufficient or that they should not have expected to be employed while the younger generation also faces unemployment (ibid., 4).

Consequently, major opportunities exist for CPE within the international arena for academic, professional, and/or workforce development projects. Institutions can leverage their strengths in a number of disciplines either on their own, given their access to internal expertise, or through collaborations across campus as well as with other domestic and international institutions. Many higher education institutions, particularly comprehensive universities, have the resources available to impact some if not all eight United Nations Millennium Development Goals: (1) eradicate extreme poverty and hunger; (2) achieve universal primary education; (3) promote gender equality and empower women; (4) reduce child mortality; (5) improve maternal health; (6) combat HIV/AIDS, malaria, and other diseases; (7) ensure environmental sustainability; and (8) global partnership for development (United Nations 2014). Institutions with programs, research centers, faculty, and students working in these areas can provide intellectual and technological responses, thereby offering research and training opportunities as well as global interaction.

A collaborative, solution-based approach is deeply rooted in many CPE units; therefore, CPE leaders can identify areas where they can contribute, pool their expertise and resources, and meet educational objectives while contributing to the global good and addressing institutional priorities.

As CPE leaders consider program development, they must determine the major challenges and solutions for the future. Institutions generate strategic plans for three to five years yet must be cognizant of how quickly the landscape changes. Economies can falter and public policy changes; consequently, decisions as to how students spend disposable income and organizations build budgets are affected by the environment. Five-year projections with changing circumstances are probably too far out when a CPE unit is responding to immediate market forces; to wit, the California 2009 budget crisis and the 2014 budget surplus certainly radically altered the higher education landscape for the state over a five-year period. The dramatic turn of events in Ukraine impacted our colleagues attending a UPCEA-sponsored forum on Russia and Ukraine in February of 2014. The forum had been planned in preparation for a trip to the region in the fall of 2014. While the forum was underway, the Ukrainian government experienced a revolution. The trip had to be reconsidered thereby highlighting the need to understand the political realities in country when planning an international engagement.

The strength of many CPE units is in their wide variety of programs across disciplines (hard and soft sciences, humanities, technical areas) that allow them to draw upon their considerable internal resources (as well as those of the university as a whole) to address problems, respond to proposals, and participate in solutions. Ironically, it is in this very variety that challenges are imbedded.

CPEs provide the nontraditional student access to education through flexible and broad programming. The skills to manage continuing education effectively include working with faculty, staff, and administrators to develop new programs as well as adapting existing curricula and their delivery to changing needs. It is necessary to utilize enrollment management principles and strategic planning. It means understanding and working with turf issues and institutional protocols. It also means discovering who the movers and shakers are on (and off) campus and collaborating with them to rally the stakeholders toward agreed-upon objectives without alienating others. Externally, there are multiple relationships to be nurtured at the local, state, national, and international levels.

Innovative Programming

Most continuing education entities must respond to local, regional, and international markets and are committed to engaging with the community by providing appropriate and need-specific programming. The flexibility demonstrated by CPE units complements the type of flexibility needed when working with an international audience.

CPE units already offer transition programs, largely in the STEM fields, sponsored by corporate entities as well as professional preparation (noncredit and for-credit certificates and degrees). They encourage academic departments to provide classes in the evenings and on weekends and in accelerated formats that enable working students, many with families, to manage their studies. Additionally they work with academic departments (or as a stand-alone unit) to convert conventionally delivered courses to online or blended formats, enhancing accessibility. This expertise in course options positions CPEs to deliver programs internationally. By having online capabilities or even hybrid approaches (e.g., the US faculty delivers face-to-face in country for a short period), cost can be mitigated. (This is very attractive to countries willing to invest in higher education but mindful of maximization of funds.)

In addition, the CPE units are able to discount tuition for cohorts (domestic or international). This has an advantage in a competitive market, notes Cindy Elliot, assistant provost for strategic partnerships at Fort Hays University:

> Students know that a degree from an American institution,
> combined with real-life business skills, will be highly valued
> by multinational and local companies. Plus, they will have

improved their English language skills, which are sought-after skills for many employers. Professors that teach at American colleges often have strong connections with businesses across the country and can help students find full-time jobs or internships. What's more, students who hold an American degree can expect to earn nearly twice as much as those holding lesser certifications in their own country. An American college degree is quite a valuable commodity. (2012)

Development of International MOUs

Expanding recruitment internationally is also a way to increase revenue while adding to the cultural mix. Institutional strengths, faculty interests, and developing relationships in particular geographic areas as a result of a focused effort lead to successful collaborations. Memoranda of understanding (MOUs) need champions from both institutions (home and abroad) who develop programs, exchanges, and solve problems. Activities undertaken that fit the institution and, therefore, contribute to mutually intellectual pursuits are the most likely to succeed. CPEs are ideally positioned to pursue international training projects both in country and abroad while collaborating with schools and colleges as they explore new markets.

Conclusion

CPE leaders all have the responsibility to sustain their enterprises, usually with varied programming directed at local and regional audiences. Nevertheless, broadening the institutional reach beyond the immediate location to national and international audiences is an objective many share— and with which some have had notable success. Skilled and experienced CPE leaders, working with SIOs or who are SIOs, are well positioned to succeed within the international realm.

References
Association of International Education Administrators (AIEA). n.d. "What Is an SIO?" Accessed at http://www.aieaworld.org/what-is-an-sio-.

Elliot, Cindy. 2012. "Some Things Don't Change: The Global Draw of American Higher Education." The Evolllution: Illuminating the Lifelong Learning Movement. Accessed at http://www.evolllution.com/opinions/some-things-dont-change-the-global-draw-of-american-higher-education/.

Farrugia, C. A., and R. Bhandari. 2013. *Open Doors 2013 Report on International Educational Exchange.* New York: Institute of International Education.

Kansas State University. 2014. Go Teacher Fact Sheet. Accessed at http://global.k-state.edu/dayofecuador/docs/Go%20Teacher%20Fact%20Sheet.pdf.

Lambert, S., R. Nolan, N. Peterson, and D. Pierce. 2007. *Critical Skills and Knowledge for Senior Campus International Leaders.* Washington, DC: NAFSA. Accessed at https://www.nafsa.org/uploadedFiles/delphi.pdf?n=8208.

Organisation for Economic Cooperation and Development (OECD). 2013. *Trends Shaping Education 2013.* Accessed at http://www.oecd.org/edu/ceri/trendsshapingeducation2013.htm.DOI: 10.1787/22187049.

"Russia Announces New Investments in Higher Education and Study Abroad." 2014. *ICEF Monitor,* July 23. Accessed at http://monitor.icef.com/2014/07/russia-announces-new-investments-in-higher-education-and-study-abroad/.

Scull, Reed. 2014. "Breaking Down the Barriers to International Education: Distance Learning Opportunities for Adults." The Evolllution: Illuminating the Lifelong Learning Movement. Accessed at http://www.evolllution.com/distance_online_learning/breaking-barriers-international-education-distance-learning-opportunities-adults/.

Smith, Beckie. 2014. "Russia Gives Top Universities $300m for Global Rankings Boost." *PIE News,* July 28. Accessed at http://thepienews.com/news/russia-gives-top-universities-300m-global-rankings-boost/.

Snytkova, Maria. 2014. "Russia Will Send Its Geniuses Abroad." *Pravda,* January 15. Accessed at http://english.pravda.ru/society/stories/15-01-2014/126594-russia_genius-0/.

Thomas, Sheila. 2013. "The Importance of Continuing Education Leadership in Public Higher Education." The Evolllution: Illuminating the Lifelong Learning Movement. Accessed at http://www.evolllution.com/opinions/importance-continuing-education-leadership-public-higher-education.

United Nations. 2014. "Millennium Development Goals and Beyond 2015: Overview." Accessed at http://www.un.org/millenniumgoals/beyond-2015-overview.shtml.

United Nations Population Fund (UNFPA). 2012. "The Voices of Older Persons," in *Ageing in the Twenty-First Century: A Celebration and a Challenge* (pp. 1–25). Accessed at http://www.unfpa.org/webdav/site/global/shared/documents/publications/2012/UNFPA-Report-Chapter4.pdf.

University and Professional Continuing Education Association. 2012. *2011 Salary, Staffing, and Structure Survey.* Washington, DC: Author.

Immigration and University Continuing Education

Reflections on Our Future Role

▐▌

Judith Potter and Maia Korotkina

Introduction

As university continuing education units in Canada and the United States attract an increasing number of immigrants each year, the intent of this essay is to reflect upon the profiles and motivations of this segment of our learner population. Considered nontraditional because of age, international qualifications, cultural capital, and simultaneous work/family/study commitments, foreign-born students—like their native counterparts—turn to our institutions in an effort to acquire transferable language and professional skills to further their career development or transition into another occupation. Indeed, newcomers tend to "embark in formal education and training to validate, recycle, enrich or change their occupational profiles . . . [and] remain active in the labour force while pursuing further education" (Adamuti-Trache 2010, 145). Contrary to their North American–born peers, however, immigrants face distinct short- to medium-term challenges in integrating into the labor market, particularly when they arrive in their host country without a job offer, as is the case for most permanent residents in Canada. For them, the customizable, practical, flexible, and accessible nature of continuing education programs provides promise for offsetting those challenges. In a context where employers award more credibility to local than international credentials, and where navigating the local labor market may carry its own

Judith Potter is Dean of Continuing Studies, McGill University, and on the UPCEA Board of Directors. **Maia Korotkina** is Career and Transition Advisor and Workshop Facilitator, McGill University School of Continuing Studies.

set of cultural puzzles, our academic and vocational offerings facilitate the transfer and upgrade of professional skills. That being said, as their presence in our classes increases, we must recognize that their needs exceed the acquisition of skills; for newcomers with permanent residency status and open work permits in particular, immigrant- and occupation-specific employability training and network-building activities should be integrated into our offerings to optimize the classroom-to-workplace transition.

Immigration Models and the Canadian Context

Canada and the United States have long featured among the most coveted destinations for highly qualified workers from around the globe. Although their interest has remained constant, the landscape of expectations has evolved. Whereas political and security concerns in many source countries during the '80s and '90s created a context in which the majority of economic immigrants left home without looking back, today a large proportion of the mobile skilled workforce seeks to expand professional horizons. Meanwhile, this increase in mobility coincides with other phenomena that, in the developed world, heighten the urgency in attracting these workers. Aging populations, combined with lower birthrates, are causing demographic concern and adding great pressure on the public purse, as a shortage of labor supply undermines succession planning on a national scale. Moreover, the development of new technologies and transformation of key sectors in the emerging knowledge economy create the need for an educated, skilled, adaptable workforce for which domestic supply does not suffice. In this context, economic immigrants are being welcomed for their palliative demographic and economic impact and supported by national policies seeking to facilitate their professional integration.[1]

The Spectrum of Immigration Models

The recruitment of qualified candidates on a global scale follows a range of ideological positions and administrative processes. Indeed, selective immigration models differ according to whether they seek to meet long-term socioeconomic objectives or fill immediate labor market shortages. Similarly, they may involve only government or imply more interdependent planning and processing among political, regulatory, and market authorities. Third, they can either be explicit (such as a points system that assigns a numerical value to an applicant's characteristics) or implicit (for instance, the granting of a temporary and restricted work permit with the possibility of converting this status into permanent residency down the line).

This administrative spectrum includes, at one end, a system linked directly to specific labor market needs. Such a selection process is de-mand-driven by employers, requiring them to be involved at all stages of the relocation process, including the recruitment, administrative funding, and settlement activities of international candidates. Such a system does not impose any abstract conditions or preferences for acceptable educa-tion and skill levels. Moreover, it effectively considers professional integra-tion to be the first and conditional step in acquiring permanent status.

At the opposite end, the human capital model relies solely on govern-ment efforts in the selection and admission process for immigrant intake. This selection model is proactive and focused on labor supply, premised on the notion of adaptability, that is, that "well-trained flexible individu-als . . . who have experience in the labour force should be able to adapt to rapidly changing labour market circumstances" (Hiebert 2006, 185). In this second system, permanent status is granted *before* the process of professional integration and is not contingent upon the latter's success.

American versus Canadian Contexts

Although most existing models tend to mix features of the two, the United States is considered to represent the demand-driven system, whereas the Canadian model has traditionally favored a more proactive, government-centered selection process that considers education, lan-guage skills, work experience, and so on, to be intrinsically valuable at-tributes. As a result, the discourse surrounding immigration in Canada—specifically the economic category—is that of a productive, relatively autonomous segment of the population whose professional integration post-immigration meets the *collective* interest.

This notion of immigrants being chosen or selected by the host coun-try is radically different from the American perspective, which tends to associate immigration with something experienced or endured, and by extension something to be restricted, unless preceded by a certain test of concrete labor market demand. In order for a foreign-born professional to settle in the United States, the only economic pathway is through a work permit, the H-1B visa. His or her profile must be appealing enough to an employer to warrant a series of financial and administrative efforts—and only after many years of this precarious situation and status renewals may the temporary worker become eligible for permanent residency (a green card) through the sponsorship of his or her employer (Ruiz 2013). Proportionally speaking, the select few who enter the country through this means are perceived as the exception to an otherwise burdensome influx of foreigners made up of American citizens' family members, ref-ugee claimants, and undocumented migrants. This majority then faces a set of reactive, somewhat reluctant settlement measures, and even those who speak out to defend them still refer to them as an "underclass" that will eventually "enter the mainstream" (White and Glick 2009).

In the case of Canada, the majority of the immigrant population falls under the economic category, annually and actively selected from a pool of hundreds of thousands of applicants. Although Canada likewise honors its family reunification and humanitarian commitments and also offers temporary work permit programs for in-demand occupations, its primary focus is on the points system selection process upstream. Canada first introduced the points system in 1967 and officially incorporated it as the assessment mechanism of the economic stream in its Immigration Act of 1976. During the '80s and '90s, it carried out a series of amendments that played with the idea of including labor market assessments, until abandoning it altogether in 2002 with a purer version of the human capital model in which all reference to current or projected business conditions was removed and language and education criteria proportionally rose in importance.[2] Through this model, for the past couple of decades a fifth to a quarter of a million new permanent residents have landed on Canadian soil every year.

It should be noted that current policy is gradually steering Canada's immigration program away from abstract long-term planning. Since 2008, priority processing has been introduced through ministerial instructions; the minister of immigration, upon consultation with the provinces, prioritizes the processing of certain occupational profiles to fill more immediate skill shortages throughout the country. Since this turning point, Citizenship and Immigration Canada has continuously moved toward more business involvement and more demand-driven intake, as demonstrated by the most recent development of the Expression of Interest program, in which local employers flag an international candidate's profile online for priority processing.

Nevertheless, as the underpinnings of the nation-building, proactive, government-driven model remain, and as most permanent residents studying in continuing education in Canada arrive under the points system, this essay considers the impact of these broad immigration policy choices on labor market trajectories of the foreign-born. More specifically, it argues that as long as internationally trained professionals continue to arrive in Canada with a long-term perspective of resettlement and career transition, university CE units in Canada can play a key role in facilitating their professional integration.

Indeed, as the following section explains, the criteria and process by which the immigrant population in Canada is selected have important implications for the composition of the local labor market, that is, the sheer number of foreign-born candidates among job seekers (specifically at the skilled and highly skilled levels), the employment barriers they face post-immigration, and, in turn, the frequency and rationale with which they turn to university continuing education (UCE). As the US reality is radically different, largely due to the fundamental difference in immigration models and policies, the role of UCE for newcomers to the United States is left for another discussion.

Barriers to Professional Integration

To the extent that Canada's immigration model has sought to attract an educated, skilled, linguistically competent, motivated workforce, statistics show that it has been successful. According to Statistics Canada, over the last decade an average of 240,000 foreign-born people immigrated to Canada (with permanent residency status) on an annual basis; the foreign-born now account for 23 percent of the Canadian population. Over 56 percent of these individuals hold a university degree, and 49 percent of doctorate holders and 40 percent of those with a master's degree were born outside of Canada. With respect to language proficiency, Citizenship and Immigration Canada noted that in 2008, only 28.3 percent of immigrants (all categories combined) spoke neither English nor French upon arrival—down from 45.9 percent in 2002. More striking still, in the economic immigrants' category, only 8.7 percent spoke neither of the official languages. In the case of Quebec, according to the Labour Force Survey of 2006, 56 percent of all immigrants admitted to the province belong to the economic immigration category (which includes skilled workers and business persons; Zietsma 2007). In more recent data, this number increased to 65 percent and is projected to be closer to 70 percent for following years (Ministère de l'Immigration et des Communautés culturelles du Québec 2012). Of these individuals, 70.8 percent indicated fluency in French. In addition, over three-quarters (78.3%) of newcomers arriving from 2006 to 2010 had at least fourteen years of schooling.

Overall, therefore, as noted by Maria Adamuti-Trache in opening a discussion on the university training sought by highly skilled immigrants during their first years in Canada, "immigration policy has reached its goal of recruiting highly educated immigrants who are expected to contribute to Canada's economic growth and global competitiveness" (2011, 62). And yet, their labor market outcomes do not meet those expectations. For decades now, a multitude of studies, articles, reports, and testimonials have been denouncing the scope and complexity of the challenges immigrants face in professional transitions. Many highlight the nonrecognition of foreign credentials and the depreciation of work experience acquired overseas (ibid.; Boyd and Schellenberg 2007; Ferrer and Riddell 2004). This in turn creates a vicious circle where employers require that immigrants obtain Canadian work experience and local references to reassure them of the validity and value of qualifications. Others observe that the lack of proficiency in occupation-specific English and/or French language and the cultural nuances of communication are standing in the way of successful workplace integration (Zietsma 2007; Shellenberg and Maheux 2007). Others still point out the reluctance toward diversity in the workplace, noting disadvantages experienced primarily by women, visible minorities, and slightly older newcomers (Chicha 2009; Cousineau and Boudarbat 2009). These three obstacles, added to the lack of clear and comprehensive information on settlement and integration services, lack of awareness of local job search practices, and restricted access to established networks and the hidden job market, have resulted in alarming phenomena of unemployment and underemployment among qualified immigrants.

To illustrate, between 1980 and 2000 incomes of immigrant men decreased by 13 percent, whereas those of native Canadian men increased by 10 percent (O'Shea 2009, 16). In the case of immigrant women, although they actually gained 6 percentage points during this same period of time, this increase is largely inferior to that observed for native Canadian women. And among the university-educated—the very demographic that has traditionally been awarded the highest number of points—the gap between immigrants and Canadian-born workers continues. According to labor market data released in December 2013, university graduates who have been in Canada five years or less are more than four times more likely to be unemployed than their Canadian counterparts. In fact, "Canadian-born high-school grads have a better shot at a job than university-educated recent immigrants: 7.1 percent unemployment, compared to 11.9" (Paperny 2014). Equally critical, this does not account for the countless numbers of immigrants who are underemployed (Galarneau and Morissette 2004). A Statistics Canada report of April 2014 notes:

> Among university-educated immigrants who did not graduate in Canada or the United States, 43% of women and 35% of men worked in occupations requiring a high school education or less. In comparison, the same rates for the Canadian-born and for immigrants who graduated in Canada or the U.S. varied between 15% and 20%. (Uppal and LaRochelle-Côté 2014)

To summarize the above, the professional integration obstacles faced by tens, if not hundreds of thousands of immigrants admitted on an annual basis can be grouped into the following six categories:

1. nonrecognition of foreign credentials and experience and the related requirement of Canadian work experience;

2. language proficiency and communication issues;

3. persistence of discriminatory practices;

4. lack of clear and comprehensive information about the existence and relevance of integration services;

5. lack of familiarity with local job search norms and practices; and

6. lack of access to professional networks and direct contact with employers.

Some of these obstacles may be explained by a legitimate process of competency assessment, the time needed to adjust to a new cultural environment, and the responsibility for much of this adaptation resting on the autonomous shoulders of internationally trained professionals. Nonetheless, many of the barriers listed point to a *heightened perception of risk* on the part of regulatory bodies and employers in admitting an individual with a profile unlike their own. However understandable the human tendency to seek the familiar, this is also the same situation that has long given rise to the proverbial taxi driver with a PhD—a phenomenon that likewise undermines the intended economic impact of selective immigration policies.

Landscape of Existing Services in Canada

Over the past decade reports of issues immigrants face prompted a major concerted effort to identify and implement solutions to address them. Indeed, within the context of this common concern, a variety of labor market actors have sought to improve immigrants' career prospects.

Government, Professional Bodies, and the Nonprofit Sector

With respect to the selection process, consultations have been conducted with public and private bodies involved in labor market trends to align the points system with more concrete prospects of professional integration.[3] Free language courses in English and/or French for beginners or intermediate-level learners have been offered to all permanent residents for up to six months after arrival. To accelerate and facilitate the recognition of qualifications, preliminary credential assessments by assigned governmental partners have become mandatory throughout the past year for all economic applicants seeking to settle in all territories and provinces except Quebec. Meanwhile, in the case of the francophone province, a document attesting to the comparable quality of education completed outside of Quebec has been offered as an optional service to immigrants who wish to reassure employers of the equivalency of their academic qualifications.

Moreover, pertaining to regulated occupations and enforced by special commissioners at the provincial level, collaboration between policy makers, professional orders, and academic institutions has resulted in a host of new tools to better recognize foreign credentials. Commendable and fruitful initiatives have been undertaken in recent years to minimize the observed "brain drain" by improving access to information predeparture, developing mutual recognition agreements with professional orders from a variety of source countries, reviewing application requirements, creating bridging courses, and implementing special permits designed to facilitate and accelerate the recognition process for foreign-trained applicants.

In terms of the third obstacle noted above, that is, discriminatory employment practices, the enforcement of the Employment Equity Act, albeit not pertaining only to immigrants, has had a positive impact on levels of awareness among employers at the hiring, retention, and succession planning stages. Furthermore, in an effort to sensitize and encourage employers, subsidies and support programs have been created to facilitate a first work experience for newcomers. Pan-Canadian and regional programs to support entrepreneurship among immigrants have also been elaborated to provide start-up funding, mentoring, and follow-up to encourage this alternative pathway.

At the same time, a great number of initiatives to better inform and prepare immigrants for the job market have been integrated into online and in-person information resources and training programs throughout the country.[4] Workshops and employment counseling services, especially when given in partnership with federal and provincial ministries of immigration, allow immigrants to be informed sooner and better of local job search norms and practices, of access to loans and bursaries for accreditation or further postsecondary study, of the existence of mentorship and/or internship programs, and so on. Arguably, the biggest challenge today is to make sure that immigrants are aware of the multitude of services available to them; more valuable still, it is to consolidate this host of tools into a clear and comprehensive roadmap.

Academic Institutions

In recent years, an increasing number of academic institutions have also responded to the call by developing programs and services that help immigrants tackle the obstacles outlined above. In particular, initiatives to date have sought to alleviate the first and second barriers, namely, the nonrecognition of foreign credentials and discounting of internationally acquired work experience and the persistence of language and communication difficulties.

To facilitate the transition into regulated occupations, some universities have elaborated bridging programs in collaboration with regulatory bodies and professional associations. These offerings specifically target foreign-trained professional candidates and often include a combination of academic credentials assessments, skills upgrading courses, professional exam preparation support, mentoring, and sometimes even internships. Some of the notable programs in the Canadian context include:

- Internationally Educated Engineers Qualifications Bridging (IEEQB) program at Ryerson University's G. Raymond Chang School of Continuing Education in Toronto;

- Qualification in Pharmacy (QeP) program at Université de Montréal;

- Licensing International Engineers into the Profession (LIEP) program at University of Toronto's School of Continuing Studies;

- Master's degree in engineering, concentration in design and management of Canadian engineering projects at École de technologie supérieure in Montreal;

- Bridging Project for Internationally Educated Teachers (IETs) at the University of Alberta's Faculty of Education;

- Bridge to Canadian Nursing (BCN) program at Mount Royal University; and

- Internationally Educated Physiotherapists Exam Preparation Programme (IEPEP) at the University of British Columbia's Faculty of Medicine in Vancouver.

Similarly, other institutions expressly reserve a number of places in regular programs for internationally trained candidates, such as Queen's University Faculty of Education in partnership with the Ontario College of Teachers. Meanwhile, other universities highlight the transferability of internationally acquired qualifications by offering bridging courses into alternative occupations, for example, Ryerson University's Project Management Bridging Certificate for Internationally Educated Professionals and HEC Montréal's Microprogramme for Immigrant Engineering Entrepreneurs.

In terms of language proficiency and intercultural communication, many postsecondary institutions provide English and French as a second language offerings designed specifically for newcomer adults, such as the Workplace Communication in Canada (WCC) program at Ryerson University's School of Continuing Education, the two certificates of proficiency—English/French for Professional Communication at McGill

University's School of Continuing Studies, and English for Professional Purposes at University of Toronto's School of Continuing Studies.

Through the commendable efforts postsecondary institutions in Canada have undertaken in the course of the past decade, they are increasingly becoming the skills resource that governmental bodies hope—and internationally trained professionals expect—them to be. But for most internationally trained professionals, this only encompasses a third of the barriers they must overcome.

Continuing Education: Becoming a Resource for Skills, Information, and Networking

Newcomers who follow professional bridging programs are likely to learn about other integration services available in their communities from instructors and peers, thus avoiding the fourth barrier. They may also obtain assistance with overcoming the fifth obstacle through integrated workshops covering local job search norms and practices. In fact, the advice that they may receive through advanced, occupation-specific training may be even more valuable and more pertinent to their needs and profiles than information communicated to a broader audience through government and nonprofit organizations. To a certain extent, then, in addition to being a skills resource, academic institutions may become an information resource for immigrants as well.

That said, the majority of the tens of thousands of immigrants who attend UCE programs in Canada every year are not necessarily seeking admission into a regulated occupation. Instead, as research has shown that postsecondary education (PSE) obtained in Canada is an especially effective means of enhancing adult immigrants' position in the labor market, their PSE participation has emerged as a strategy to overcome professional adversities, in particular for those who have completed university education in their countries of origin (Adamuti-Trache 2011, 70). In fact, according to Adamuti-Trache's study, in an attempt to increase the relevance and worth of the experience accumulated in their native countries, within four years of arrival, 46 percent of adult immigrants participate in PSE. And whether immigrants aim for a career in fields like accounting, finance, management, logistics, communications, marketing, or international business, continuing education units seem particularly appealing because of the relatively accessible, shorter-length, flexible, practical nature of their programs. In this context, as newcomers pursue courses in a heterogeneous environment with native Canadian peers, their awareness of the network of organizations and resources available to them tends to be much poorer, as does their ability to navigate the cultural nuances of North-American communication, in particular in networking and interview settings. Yet, despite this knowledge gap, "very rarely have immigrants been identified as a group with specific needs in postsecondary institutional policies" (Adamuti-Trache 2010, 162; also see Sinacore, Park, Mikhail, and Wada 2011, 181, 184; Canadian Council on Learning 2007). In the absence of integrated employability services that appreciate their human capital and address their specific preoccupations, immigrants' labor market outcomes still risk falling short. Even when the skills gap is closed, the job readiness level may still be too low to provide them—and the academic institutions from which they graduate—with the job placement rate they expect.

Furthermore, with respect to the last and perhaps most poignant obstacle for newcomers, attending a local university represents the promise to access a professional network specific to their occupation. It is with this key prospect in mind that many internationally trained professionals, particularly in unregulated occupations where the transition is less clear, turn to UCE. While updating or upgrading their skills, they seek to improve their confidence, assess the transferability of their prior qualifications, attend career-related events, and hopefully obtain their first work experience in their adopted country through an internship, so that by the time they graduate, they have overcome most of the barriers which they faced upon arrival. As it stands, however, internship offerings through UCE units in Canada are still quite sparse, and career-related events through university-wide career planning centers rarely correspond to midcareer professional profiles (Sinacore et al., 183). Understandably, these centers' primary target audience is undergraduate students—culturally at ease, locally established, with little to no work experience in their field. This is a drastically different demographic than the thirty plus, internationally trained, experienced individual most often studying part-time or even online, potentially juggling multiple work and/or family commitments, and trying to get a foothold in his or her new home. Their profiles are different, and so are their needs.

As discussed earlier, because of the selective immigration process through which they acquire permanent residency, internationally trained professionals constitute the cream of the crop in the student population of Canadian UCE units. For the economy, they represent a skilled, motivated, adaptable, autonomous, multilingual labor pool; for our academic institutions, too, they are hardworking, committed, aspiring individuals in need of a mere additional boost. Through our accessible, flexible academic offerings, we have already become the skills resource to which they turn to increase transferability of qualifications. By expanding our services to integrate employability training and conduct employer-outreach activities specifically for continuing education students, we can position ourselves as their information and networking resources as well. And in turn, through their ensuing successes, our expanding service offer is likely to carry the promise of a mutually beneficial relationship.

Conclusion

Without doubt, all of the efforts and initiatives outlined herein—whether through government, professional orders and associations, nonprofit organizations, or academic institutions—attest to a growing awareness that responsibility for immigrants' successful integration is shared among newcomers and the host society—but this is not just a responsibility. In their own efforts to maximize their chances, recent immigrants increasingly turn to short-term, part-time university programs to complete bridging courses, improve language levels, increase understanding of economic trends and job search practices of their host country, and to access a professional network—in short, to obtain local diplomas and connections for increased credibility in the labor market. Indeed, today they represent an ever-growing proportion of the student population in our institutions. This is an enormous opportunity for university continuing education to position itself as the top-of-mind resource for this distinct clientele in the education market by building further on what is already established. In fact, as this article has sought to argue, this target audience deserves priority attention: our relatively small investment in facilitating their transition through employability training and network-building activities will provide a disproportionate return of resources, engagement, and reputation.

Notes

1. In fact, as Bonikowska, Hou, and Picot argue, these integration policies will in turn affect how attractive the destination country appears: "To the extent that well-educated immigrants are becoming increasingly sought-after by traditional immigrant-receiving countries, their relative (to host country workers) outcomes could influence the choice of host country among individuals considering migration, and therefore the self-selection of individuals who choose to immigrate to Canada in the future" (2011).
2. The national immigration policy in Canada extends to all but the province of Quebec, which holds almost exclusive authority to select its economic migrants and implement measures to aid their settlement and integration. This autonomy came as a result of a series of negotiations begun in the late '60s, characterizing much of the '70s and '80s, and culminating in the devolution of constitutionally shared powers through the Canada-Quebec Accord of 1991. Nevertheless, as its immigration policies have tended to echo the spirit of federal initiatives—with the exception of greater emphasis on the French language—Quebec's immigration model and outcomes run parallel to Canada's track record. In the context of this article, they will therefore be amalgamated.
3. The nonprofit sector in Canada includes a mobilized network of local and

provincial organizations that offer immigrants settlement services, information, language courses, job search assistance, civic engagement, community building and social activities, and other resources to facilitate their integration; most of these services remain accessible for up to five years after arrival.

4. Some of these information resources and programs are even offered pre-arrival, both in the source countries and online, such as through the federal CIIP (Canadian Immigrant Integration Program) and Quebec's SIEL (Service d'intégration en ligne).

References

Adamuti-Trache, M. 2010. "Is the Glass Half Empty or Half Full? Obstacles and Opportunities That Highly Educated Immigrations Encounter in the Segmented Canadian Labour Market." PhD thesis, Department of Educational Studies, University of British Columbia.

Adamuti-Trache, M. 2011. "First Four Years in Canada: Post-Secondary Education Pathways of Highly Educated Immigrants." *Journal of International Migration and Integration* 12(1): 61–83.

Bonikowska, A., F. Hou, and G. Picot. 2011. "Do Highly Educated Immigrants Perform Differently in the Canadian and U.S. Labour Markets?" *Statistics Canada.* Accessed at http://www.statcan.gc.ca/pub /11f0019m/11f0019m2011329-eng.pdf.

Boyd, M., and G. Schellenberg. 2007. "Réagrément et professions des médecins et ingénieurs immigrants." *Tendances sociales canadiennes, Statistics Canada* 84: 2–11

Canadian Council on Learning. 2007. *Post-Secondary Education in Canada: Strategies for Success.* Accessed at http://www.ccl-cca.ca/pdfs/PSE/2007 /PSEFullReportENLR16july08Bookmark.pdf.

Chicha, M.-T. 2009. "Le mirage de l'égalité : les immigrées hautement qualifiées à Montréal." *Fondation canadienne des relations raciales.* Accessed at http://www.cc-femmes.qc.ca/documents/MTChicha_MirageEgalite.pdf.

Cousineau, J.-M., and B. Boudarbat. 2009. "La situation économique des immigrants au Québec." *Relations industrielles* 64(2): 230–249.

Ferrer, A., and C. Riddell. 2004. "Education, Credentials and Immigrant Earnings." *Canadian Journal of Economics* 41(1): 186–216.

Galarneau, D., and R. Morissette. 2004. "Immigrants: Settling for Less?" *Perspectives on Labour and Income* 5(6). Statistics Canada Catalogue no. 75-001-XIE. Accessed at http://www.statcan.gc.ca/pub/75-001-x/10604/6921 -eng.pdf.

Hiebert, D. 2006. "Skilled Immigration in Canada: Context, Patterns and Outcomes." In B. Birrell, L. Hawthorne, and S. Richardson, eds., *Evaluation of the General Skilled Migration Categories* (pp. 182–223). Canberra: Commonwealth of Australia.

Ministère de l'Immigration et des Communautés culturelles du Québec. 2012. *Portraits statistiques : L'immigration permanente au Québec selon les catégories d'immigration et quelques composantes, 2006–2010.* Accessed at http://www.micc.gouv.qc.ca/publications/fr/recheches-statistiques /Portraits_categories_2006_2010_1.pdf.

O'Shea, E. 2009. "Missing the Point(s): The Declining Fortunes of Canada's Economic Immigration Program." *Transatlantic Academy Paper Series.* Accessed at http://www.gmfus.org/doc/TA_OShea_web.pdf.

Paperny, A. M. 2014. "Immigrant Unemployment: The More Education, the Bigger the Gap." *Global News,* January 14. Accessed at http://globalnews .ca/news/1074811/immigrant-unemployment/.

Ruiz, N. G. 2013. "Immigration Facts on Foreign Students." Brookings, Metropolitan Policy Program. Accessed at http://www.brookings.edu /research/interactives/2013/facts-on-foreign-students.

Schellenberg, G. and H. Maheux. 2007. "Perspectives des immigrants sur leurs quatre premières années au Canada : Faits saillants des trois vagues de l'Enquête longitudinale auprès des immigrants du Canada." *Tendances sociales canadiennes, Special edition,* Statistics Canada, April 2007: 2-36.

Sinacore, A. D., J. Park, A. M. Mikhail, and K. Wada. 2011. "Falling through the Cracks: Academic and Career Challenges Faced by Immigrant Graduate Students." *Canadian Journal of Counselling and Psychotherapy* 45 (2): 168–187. Accessed at http://eric.ed.gov/?q=continuing+education +immigrants&id=EJ930797.

Uppal, S., and S. LaRochelle-Côté. 2014. "Overqualification among Recent University Graduates in Canada." *Insights on Canadian Society,* Statistics Canada, April. Accessed at http://www.statcan.gc.ca/pub/75-006-x/2014001 /article/11916-eng.pdf.

White, M. J., and J. E. Glick. 2009. "Achieving Anew: How New Immigrants Do in American Schools, Jobs, and Neighborhoods." Russell Sage Foundation. Accessed at http://eric.ed.gov/?q=continuing+studies+immigrant +&ff1=dtySince_2005&id=ED524057.

Zietsma, D. 2007. "Les immigrants sur le marché canadien du travail en 2006: premiers résultats de l'Enquête sur la population active du Canada." *Série d'analyses de la population active immigrante,* Statistics Canada. Accessed at http://www.statcan.gc.ca/pub/71-606-x/71-606-x2007001-fra.pdf.

Older Adult and Lifelong Learning

Programs, History, and Recommendations

█▌

James M. Shaeffer and Sarah K. MacDonald

> The object of all education is to teach people to think for
> themselves . . . a man who is educated in the truest sense
> may even be unable to read or write, for an educated man is
> a man who is capable of thinking about what he sees.
>
> —JAMES STUART, 1871

This quote, from Adrian Barlow's wonderful book, *Extramural: Literature and Lifelong Learning*, comes from James Stuart's address to the Leeds Ladies' Educational Association entitled "University Extension." Barlow goes on to suggest that this lecture may have been the "starting point for extramural studies in any modern sense" (Barlow 2012, 18). It is interesting to note that, according to Barlow, this concept may have its roots in 1112 when the Lincolnshire Abbey of Croyland "sent monks out across the Fens to give lectures in local barns" (ibid., 16).

While not a recent phenomenon, most colleges and universities recognize that learning doesn't end with formal education and that learning has no boundaries in terms of age. This recognition has resulted in the creation of offices and programs that cater to the needs of adult students. This essay will review current and anticipated demographics showing not only the growth in the older adult populations but also the diversity of this group. We will explore a short history of programs and offices that

James M. Shaeffer Sr. is Dean of the College of Continuing and Professional Development, Old Dominion University, and past president of UPCEA, 2011–2012. **Sarah K. MacDonald** is Interim Senior Director for Outreach and Engagement, James Madison University, and a UPCEA associate committee chair.

were developed to respond to the needs of older adult students and conclude with a discussion of possible future directions for lifelong learning institutes.

Demographics

The older adult student population, 65+ years of age, continues to grow. The Administration on Aging reports that there were about 43.1 million older adults in the United States in 2012, representing an increase of 7.6 million or 21 percent since 2002. While this is significant growth for this population, the US Census Bureau's report *The Next Four Decades: The Older Populations in the United States 2010–2050* predicted that by 2050 the number of Americans age 65 and older will more than double to 88.5 million.

Much of this growth is the result of the baby boomer generation coming of age. Another important factor is that life expectancy has increased. For example, in the United States, "in 2011, persons reaching age 65 had an average life expectancy of an additional 19.2 years (20.4 years for females and 17.8 years for males). A child born in 2011 could expect to live 78.7 years, about 30 years longer than a child born in 1900" (US Department of Health and Human Services 2012, 2). The result is that not only are there more older adults but the range in age, due to increased life expectancy, is more diverse and thus the need for a larger range of learning experiences.

The range of age is only one example of the growing diversity of this population. One area in particular where we will see diversity is in the attainment of higher education in this population overall. In 1965, 24 percent of the older population had graduated from high school, and only 5 percent had at least a bachelor's degree. By 2010, 80 percent were high school graduates or more, and 23 percent had a bachelor's degree or more. The diversity in educational attainment also affects the need for a range of programming that meets the interests of older adult students, which can range from self-improvement to international experiences to community service programs.

Adding to the diversity of this population is an increase in how long older adults are staying in the workforce. In 2013, 8.1 million (18.7 %) Americans age 65 and over were working or actively seeking work, representing approximately 5 percent of the US workforce.

Clearly the older student population will continue to grow, and the educational needs of older adults have become more diverse with the growing diversity in the age, educational attainment, and work status of those in this group.

Brief History of Programs

The first older adult education program in the United States was established in 1962 and was called the Institute for Retired People (IRP). Like others that came after,

> it was founded by a group of retired school teachers, mostly women, who prevailed upon the New School to provide space for a program designed to accommodate women and men interested in intellectual and social interaction in an academic environment. The New School obliged by providing classrooms and helping the group to organize themselves and arrange their course offerings and manage their curricular affairs. (Shinagel 2012, 23)

Shinagel estimated that there are approximately five hundred lifelong learning institutes operating in North America and suggested that "in the best tradition of American individualism, each such institute is the creation of a distinctive group of retirees, hosted by a college or university, with a special culture and sense of mission" (ibid., 28).

Another lifelong learning program is Elderhostel. In the summer of 1975, five colleges and universities in New Hampshire offered the first Elderhostel programs to 220 "pioneer" participants. From this pioneer beginning, Elderhostel quickly expanded, and by 1980 (relying almost entirely on word-of-mouth promotion), more than 20,000 older adults participated in programs in all fifty states and most Canadian provinces. In 1981, Elderhostel offered its first international programs. In 2004, Elderhostel launched Road Scholar, expanding the number of international programs they offered and increasing the range of topics and formats offered in the United States and around the world ("The History of Elderhostel and Road Scholar").

Another significant influence on lifelong learning programs has been the Osher Institute. In 2001, the Bernard Osher Foundation, reflecting their support for a "national lifelong learning network for seasoned adults" provided an endowment grant to the University of Southern Maine to "improve and extend its excellent programs," and the name Senior College was changed to Osher Lifelong Learning Institute (OLLI). Sonoma State University, a member of the California State University system, was also given a grant. Due to the success of these programs the foundation expanded its reach nationwide and at present supports 118 lifelong learning programs on university and college campuses across the country, with at least one grantee in each of the fifty states and the District of Columbia. There is considerable variation among the Osher Institutes, but the common threads include noncredit educational programs specifically developed for adults age 50 and older, university connection and university support, robust volunteer leadership and sound organizational structure, and a diverse repertoire of intellectually stimulating courses.

Future Possibilities

The future for lifelong learning institutes at colleges and universities looks particularly bright, given demographic projections as well as changes in technology, opportunities for research, and decades of work on cognitive processing. The doubling of the older adult population as a result of the aging of the baby boomer generation offers untold opportunities for lifelong learning organizations; however, not all of those senior citizens will be able, willing, or motivated to participate in lifelong learning activities. According to one cognitive model, seniors can be divided into three categories in terms of intellectual functioning: "optimal cognitive aging" (20–30%); "normal cognitive aging" (50–60%); and "high-risk cognitive aging" (15–20%) (Powell 2011). Predictably, the group identified as having optimal cognitive aging tend to be already members of lifelong learning institutes, driven by curiosity, intellectual capacity, and tenacity to seek opportunities to expand their horizons. The group identified as having normal cognitive aging tends to need more encouragement to open their minds to new experiences. Participation in a lifelong learning institute could greatly benefit this group, leading to a more active and rewarding retirement. Interestingly, if 60 percent of Americans over 65 in 2050 fall into this group of those considered to have normal cognitive aging, that alone would be an estimated 53.1 million people, which is greater than the current (2010) total of all older adults. The potential to reach a vastly expanded number of participants bears serious consideration and is a valuable opportunity for lifelong learning institutes in particular and continuing education in general. The rewards these potential participants could reap include intellectual stimulation, a supportive community, enhanced self-esteem, and spiritual renewal, all of which can help lead to more productive and meaningful lives that contribute to society (Lamb and Brady 2005).

However, we must consider carefully that while these changing demographics lead to a larger pool of potential members or participants, the conditions of their lives are also changing, and we must adapt to that. Our traditional image of seniors retiring to a lifestyle of relaxation and leisure is changing along with changing technology, economic conditions, and expectations. While older Americans now live longer and with better physical function than in previous generations, they also face financial burdens, which can lead to some working longer than they might have otherwise. Kidahashi and Manheimer (2009) describe five typologies of

positive life models in later life: Traditional Golden Years, what we traditionally think of as retirement; Neo Golden Years, where an individual
seeks self-fulfillment and discovery but retires from paid work; Second
Career, individuals who retire from one career (including the military)
and then take up a second career; Extension of Midlife Career, individuals who choose to continue working in their chosen field either for financial or identity/satisfaction reasons; and Portfolio Life, individuals who
balance two or more of the other lifestyle typologies, perhaps working
part time in their chosen field and volunteering at something that has
personal meaning for them. This leads to several implications; for example, some older Americans may need more career and professional training, either to enhance their current position and marketability or to begin a new one entirely, than was traditionally the case. This could shift the
balance of lifelong learning programming away from enrichment toward
professional skills. It also has implications for logistics such as program
scheduling and delivery methods; seniors who are working even part time
may not be able to come to campus in the middle of the day.

Changes in technology, including online and hybrid learning, computer skills, and tools for marketing and communication, also impact lifelong learning institutes both broadly and deeply. While not many lifelong
learning institutes are currently offering courses online—citing the critical nature of the supportive community that their face-to-face programs
provide and nurture as the primary reason—this is another area that
represents significant potential (Cardale and Brady 2010). That sense
of community has been shown to be critical to the mission and success
of these programs (Brady, Cardale, and Neidy 2013). However, rather
than seeing online programs, courses, and resources as a substitute for
in-person learning, we could consider ways to enhance that experience
and sense of community by offering deeper, richer, and continually updated resources. Courses could certainly be taught online, and as more
people who have worked with technology for the last few decades of their
work life retire, their comfort level with that technology will increase.
But courses could also be offered in blended and hybrid models that still
support face-to-face interaction, as well as increasing access for members
who may be homebound, have disabilities that make it difficult to participate in person or need screen readers, or are geographically located at a
distance. Other options include videoconferencing to satellite campuses
or community colleges, interactive video, local-access television, and mobile applications. Technology also impacts the way lifelong learning institutes market their courses and programs; many are working to encourage
online registration and e-mail marketing; a subset of their population
does not have e-mail or computer access, but that is also changing. One
institute experimented with increasing the number of members who use
e-mail (thereby decreasing marketing and postage costs) by encouraging

members without e-mail to sign up for their basic computer skills course (Cardale and Brady 2010).

A final recommendation for the consideration of the future of lifelong learning institutes is the development of scholarly research on their participants, programs, and impact. Very little research exists currently; the majority of the publications available are anecdotal in nature, and many researchers have called for more (Lamb 2011; Brady, Cardale, and Neidy 2013; Hansen and Brady 2013). Given that lifelong learning institutes are most commonly attached to colleges and universities, the value of considering their programs, activities, and outcomes from a research perspective is evident and could help increase support for their further growth and development. Hansen and Brady (2011) give an excellent overview of research methods, including basic methods of both qualitative and quantitative analysis, that offer an "action research" perspective on lifelong learning. Lifelong learning programs could also consider partnering with departments on campus such as social work, gerontology, education, psychology, or others; with the growth in the population of older adults, this could create a fertile research agenda for both lifelong learning institutes and academic departments. Finally, older adults might consider participating in other research on campus related to aging but not necessarily lifelong learning as research subjects.

Lifelong learning offers a rich perspective, new opportunities for engagement and social impact, and a deep and abiding sense of community for both the older adults and the campus community that surrounds them. As continuing educators, we should continue to advocate for and support these programs, as well as consider new opportunities, modalities, and futures for them.

References

Barlow, A. 2012. *Extramural: Literature and Lifelong Learning.* Cambridge, England: Lutterworth Press.

Brady, E. M., A. Cardale, and J. C. Neidy. 2013. "The Quest for Community in Osher Lifelong Learning Institutes." *Educational Gerontology* 39(9): 627–639.

Cardale, A., and E. M. Brady. 2010. "To Talk or to Text: Is That the Question?" *LLI Review* 5 (Fall): 15–18.

Hansen, R. J., and E. M. Brady. 2011. "Solving Problems through Action Research." *LLI Review* 6 (Fall): 82–90.

Hansen, R. J., and E. M. Brady. 2013. "Research in the Osher Lifelong Learning Institute Network." *Journal of Continuing Higher Education* 61(3): 143–150.

"The History of Elderhostel and Road Scholar." Road Scholar. Accessed at http://www.roadscholar.org/about/history.asp.

Kidahashi, M., and R. Manheimer. 2009. "Getting Ready for the Work-ing-in-Retirement Generation: How Should LLIs Respond?" *LLI Review* 4 (Fall): 1–8.

Lamb, R. 2011. "Lifelong Learning Institutes: The Next Challenge." *LLI Review* 6 (Fall): 1–10.

Lamb, R., and E. M. Brady. 2005. "Participation in Lifelong Learning Insti-tutes: What Turns Members On?" *Educational Gerontology* 31: 207–224.

"Osher Lifelong Learning Institutes." The Bernard Osher Foundation. Ac-cessed at http://www.osherfoundation.org/index.php?olli.

Powell, D. H. 2011. *The Aging Intellect.* New York: Routledge.

Shinagel, M. 2012. "Demographics and Lifelong Learning Institutes in the 21st Century." *Continuing Higher Education Review* 76: 20–27.

US Census Bureau. 2014. *The Next Four Decades: The Older Population in the United States 2010–2050.* Accessed at http://www.aoa.gov/Aging_Statistics /Profile/2013/2.aspx.

US Department of Health and Human Services. 2012. "A Profile of Older Amer-icans: 2012." Accessed at http://www.aoa.gov/Aging_Statistics/Profile /2012/docs/2012profile.pdf.

The Power of Fund-Raising
for Continuing Education

Mary B. McIntire

Overview

Most of us who have been in the field of continuing higher education for
a decade or more have experienced at least one comprehensive capital
campaign at our institutions. Fewer of us have had our continuing education schools included in the goals and activities of these campaigns. I
have made several presentations for UPCEA regarding fund-raising over
the last decade, and almost no one has reported having extensive experience in fund-raising within his or her institution. Typically, continuing
education is expected to pay its own way through enrollments and to return significant funds to its institution. The prevailing belief of university
administrations seems to be that continuing education should not compete with the academic core but rather further the core goals by increasing resources. Although hundreds of higher education institutions claim
the threefold mission of teaching, research, and community outreach,
resources go primarily to teaching and research. It is not surprising that
many CE professionals view their efforts in the same light as their parent
institution does: we see ourselves as entrepreneurs, producing educational products to be purchased by the public.

For at least some institutions, continuing education is becoming a part
of fund-raising. In an informal survey of approximately twenty continuing education deans at Association of American Universities institutions,
eight responded, and only one had taken part in a university-wide capital campaign. However, seven had attracted program funding, two had
raised capital funding for new or remodeled space, two had attracted gen-

---

Mary B. McIntire is Dean, Susanne M. Glasscock School of Continuing Studies,
Rice University, and on the UPCEA Board of Directors.

273

eral purpose annual funding, and one had brought in some endowment funding. Four responded that continuing education has been included in general university solicitations, and four had either a part-time or full-time development officer assigned to them. Although one respondent feared being viewed as "cannibalizing" donations from other parts of the university, others had a more positive response, for example: "Development is more than raising money—the importance of telling our story and raising friends is critical to our success." "Fund-raising for selected programs serving deserving audiences is the main goal for our efforts. Helping the underserved is a logical part of my job."

I would argue that both the parent institutions and many CE schools themselves have historically underestimated the significance of what continuing education accomplishes in strengthening and maintaining the social fabric of our communities. Continuing education can and should be a civic driver and the leader of an institution's community outreach. On its own, it can attract resources for educational outreach that ultimately benefit both society and the university.

In some ways continuing education, like its parent institution, resembles both a business and a nonprofit. In his monograph *Good to Great and the Social Sectors*, which focuses on nonprofit organizations, Jim Collins points out that the input of business is money (a resource for achieving greatness) and the output is also money (a measure of greatness). For traditional nonprofits, on the other hand, money is only an input, not a measure of greatness. A superior performance and adherence to mission are the significant outputs. Collins describes higher education institutions as business/nonprofit hybrids because they attract funds through donations and also generate revenues through tuition and other means. Because we in continuing education use our resources to create and build profitable programs that produce money for our parent institutions, we too have a business function. That is not to say that many of our moneymaking programs do not also produce social good—often they build the workforce and transform lives. Yet when we seek and receive external funding for crucial but not necessarily profitable programs, we act much like a traditional nonprofit. Continuing education, like our parent institutions, should both make money and produce social good. But to have an impact on our communities we, like our institutions, must also attract resources. Yes, we should be entrepreneurs and aggressive in using sound business strategies. We must use the methods and measurements of business, including accountability and, for many of our programs, profitability. But I also believe that we are in a unique position to create a multiplier effect of social good that may even exceed the effect of the larger institution on our local and regional communities. Our access to large populations beyond traditional college students, our experience in collaborating across our campus and with other institutions and associations beyond our campus, and our expertise with technology in teaching equip us to effect social good in a powerful way. For some of this good to occur and be sustained, we need resources.

Although we are under constant pressure to generate income, my experience with CE leaders has taught me that we are among the most idealistic, mission-driven people on any campus. I suspect that much of the tension between CE units and central administrations is that CE leaders see as our mission to create social and civic good while many of our superiors do not share that vision—even though those superiors speak frequently and publicly about the importance of educational outreach and responsibility to the community. To put it another way, we might want to be business/nonprofit hybrids, but our institutions want us to be businesses only. What potentially complicates and makes this situation both more interesting and more heartening is that donors want to support many of the programs that CE leaders want to offer. Philanthropy research underscores the idea that giving is a choice, and fund-raising experiments increasingly show that donors are motivated to give, and give more, to specific projects than to unrestricted funds, much to the dismay of some university administrators. This trend is an advantage to CE units because measurement and demonstrating success is standard practice in our operations.

What programs do we offer—or could we offer—that require and deserve external funding? Many of us offer K-12 teacher preparation and professional development, STEM learning for students and teachers, programs for counselors, and early literacy education. We may be helping veterans with career change, strengthening nonprofits and social services, expanding opportunity in the workforce, enabling adults or disadvantaged students to become successful through certificate or degree completion or the acquisition of new skills, providing a rich experience for senior citizens, and furthering personal development. Scholarships for nontraditional students, the expansion of programs to reach wider numbers within our communities, seed money for new certificate and degree programs that meet a local need, and programs that provide the outreach component for government grants secured by researchers on our campuses are all worthy of support. All in all, we can and should be drivers of success for the future of our communities.

History of Continuing Education at Rice University

What is now the Susanne M. Glasscock School of Continuing Studies at Rice University began as a small office in 1967 with a one-time grant from the university of $10,000. From the beginning we experienced financial difficulty, and our efforts were complicated by the university's ban on our offering courses for college credit. Our real growth did not begin until we received a $40,000 gift in 1975 from a local bank to support a yearlong series of courses in honor of the nation's bicentennial. Our series dovetailed with the bank's sponsorship of Alistair Cooke's popular *America* series on local television. For several years following, the bank also funded a series of lectures called *Living Texas*. Other early fund-raising included $250,000 from a local individual and $50,000 from other donors in 1986 for remodeling an inherited building for administration and classrooms.

In the last fifteen years, however, we have raised nearly $45 million through grants and gifts. Like many other CE schools, we have received federal grants, including nearly $2 million from the National Science Foundation and the Department of Education. We have also received $1 million from a local foundation for K-12 initiatives, several hundred thousand from annual fund drives and special events, more than $1 million to establish our Center for Philanthropy and Nonprofit Leadership, $1.5 million from a corporate foundation in support of our early childhood literacy program, and more than $25 million for a new building. Finally, our school was generously endowed in 2005 by a local couple who had been taking our personal development courses for many years. Although federal grants have been helpful and welcome, our fund-raising efforts have been aimed primarily at foundations and, to a much greater degree, individuals, which will be the focus of this essay.

Our success at attracting external funding did not happen overnight but was the result of establishing and maintaining relationships with donors over a period of years as well as offering programs of interest to individuals and foundations. By far, the greatest number and size of gifts came from individuals, aligning with current research. According to Giving USA (a publication of the Lilly Family School of Philanthropy at Indiana University), 72 percent of the $335.17 billion contributed in the United States in 2013 came from individuals, 15 percent from foundations, 8 percent from bequests, and 5 percent from corporations. These percentages, fairly consistent over time, mirror our experience. Many of the donors to our building campaign had given more modest donations to us in previous campaigns, which illustrates an important point in fund-raising: if people give and are pleased with the results, they most likely will continue to donate. This holds true for foundations also, which often give multiyear grants after seeing success with an initial grant. Foundations are legally required to grant 5 percent of their corpus annually, and many fund local and regional projects that strive to improve their communities. Funding from corporations is more difficult to obtain as it is often tied to their marketing strategies or to the interests of their CEOs or employees. Large corporations often have foundations, too, and funding decisions may be made locally and regionally, although they are often made nationally, as was the case with our $1.5 million gift to support early childhood literacy.

Creating Friends for the School

Special Events

As one fund-raising officer once said, "The best 'special event' is two people successfully asking a third person for a donation." Many nonprofits hold too many special events, ranging from galas, dinners, and luncheons to golf tournaments. Often these involve silent or live auctions, which are staff-intensive activities that, although good for raising friends, are chancy for raising funds. A successful event for a CE school should accomplish multiple objectives: raise the profile of the school to the greater community, educate donors to the value of the school's mission, engage top instructors with the school, attract financial support, and, of course, celebrate success.

As early as twenty years ago, we began celebrating five-year anniversaries, which we found to be a reasonable length of time between events. Our easiest and most successful events have been what we named Continuing Conversations, simple dinners with no auctions where tables sold for varying amounts from $3,000 to $10,000. Popular faculty members agree to lead table discussions within their area of expertise (e.g., "The Cubists," "Thomas Jefferson's Monticello," or "How Nanotechnology Improves Our Everyday Lives"), thus this event is very much in keeping with our educational mission. The formal program is a short but powerful statement on the value of the school, including videos of our impact on individual students and the community. Both times we have held this event, we sold all available tables, the first time with no marketing other than a letter to friends of the school and "frequent flyers," people who have taken many courses with us. We have raised a few hundred thousand dollars in this way, and many of the attendees have since made gifts to our building and program funds.

Annual Fund Drives

When your CE participant database is filled with thousands of names, how do you determine who might have the interest and the means to contribute? One way to identify potential major donors is to test the waters through an annual solicitation. For noncredit programs, sending solicitation letters to frequent flyers can be a relatively easy way to gauge support. A simple, well-crafted letter, which can be adapted to work with different segments of the audience, can result in individual gifts in the hundreds or thousands of dollars. Prompt thank-you letters are essential, preferably handwritten. Continued engagement is key: follow-up letters outlining how gifts are being put to use keep donors informed and create stakeholders in the CE unit. Inviting donors to lectures that are not filled to capacity or to events that are already planned also leverages those events as friend/fund-raisers and gives staff an opportunity to get to know these donors, a strategy the fund-raising professionals call stewardship or cultivation. Thus the annual fund drive, whether it is across the entire unit or targeted to certain program support, can be an effective first step in major fund-raising. Further, because these donors are not likely to be engaged with other parts of the campus, they may become CE donors exclusively. Ultimately, potential donors should have had a history of meaningful interactions with the school before a major gift is requested. We also found that donors of major gifts (a minimum of $50,000 at Rice) usually had more than one connection to us, for example, as a student, faculty member, previous donor, friend of other major donors, friend of the dean or other staff, Rice alumnus, and/or an advocate for one of our programs. The more connections, the more likely the donor would make a gift.

Advisory Boards

Many CE schools maintain one or more advisory boards—boards that advise the school in general as well as boards that advise individual programs. Our school-wide board was created in 2005, and its twelve members understood clearly before joining the group that their charge was to serve as a resource by sharing their advice and expertise and acting as a sounding board for significant new program initiatives and strategic planning, to serve as ambassadors for the school, to assist in fund-raising or introduce the dean and development director to individuals who might financially support the school, to help build the case for support of a new building and other fund-raising goals, and to serve two- or three-year terms and attend two or three lunch-hour board meetings annually. Senior school staffers attend meetings and often give short reports on their programs. The advisory board has proven to be invaluable in many ways. Among the initial members were two Rice trustees, three trustees emeriti, and three instructors. Their work ranged from helping us significantly in strategic planning to donating funds for our new building and, very important, to helping us secure gifts from other community leaders. Every member contributed, from a few thousand to millions of dollars, although in their charge they were not specifically asked to make a donation. All gave in one or more of the three W's: work, wisdom, and wealth. This board is now being enlarged; some members have stepped off and others remain. New program-related committees with new charges are being formed, and these will vary as to whether fund-raising is a stated goal.

Making the Case for Support

As stated earlier, convincing the institution's administration may be the most challenging part of getting a project off the ground. It is crucial to have advocates, including (if possible) board of trustee members, advisory board members, students, alumni, and faculty. Because the development office often has daunting fund-raising targets to meet, central development officers can also be allies because they recognize the attractiveness of continuing education programs to donors' interests. An advantage for continuing education is that because it is usually the one school totally engaged in educational outreach, it is a strong contender for the portion of a university campaign earmarked for outreach. We were not included in Rice's previous (and essentially only other) campaign, which was very centrally controlled and not completely successful. From our perspective, Rice was more enlightened in its recent campaign by expecting all deans and schools to participate in fund-raising.

Before we moved forward with our building campaign, we were asked to rework our strategic plan to include program growth and budget projections. Clearly, any administration would want to see from any CE school increased income and contributions. We made the case that we could increase the monies returned to the general university fund if we had greatly increased classroom availability, that is, we needed a new, larger building dedicated to continuing education.

In our campaign, we received hundreds of donations from first-time donors to Rice, broadening the university's base of support and strengthening its brand as a good community neighbor. Every one of our staff members made an individual donation, proving internal support. We also received gifts from alumni and others with whom we had had a relationship for many years and who were unlikely to make a gift elsewhere during the campaign. We even received gifts in the hundreds of thousands from longtime supporters of the university who also made multimillion-dollar gifts to other schools and projects in the recently completed billion-dollar capital campaign. Our experience supported the argument that we did not reduce the success of the overall campaign for the university.

Whether a modest request for funding or a multimillion-dollar project, making the case for support is essential. Seen by fund-raisers as a necessary tool, the case statement is a persuasive, brief document that explains the need for funding to a variety of audiences (internal and external), the importance of the donor's support, and the benefits that will result. It becomes the document that is left with the potential donor at the time of a visit, so crafting a strong argument for support is crucial.

Repetition is also important. We included contribution envelopes and fund-raising advertisements in course catalogs for several semesters, maintained eye-catching and informative campaign pages on our website, hung a large banner on the side of our building to mark our progress, and even distributed handouts in classes. It would have been difficult for any of our stakeholders to be ignorant of our campaign. Finally, repetition should not end with the gift. Prospects who become donors cannot be thanked too often or by too many people involved.

Role of the Dean

Individuals with the means to contribute major gifts want to give to successful programs, but they also want to give to those they consider their peers. Often, this means they want to be assured that their gift—specifically the intention of the gift—has the support of both university leadership and people they consider their peers. It is therefore crucial to have upper administrators, board members, and community leaders engaged with continuing education. As the chief academic officer of the school, the dean also plays a strong role. Donors are more likely to respond positively to a dean rather than a development officer, to a president rather than a dean, and to a peer or friend above all. All philanthropy is based on trust—trust in the quality and mission of the program, trust in the integrity of the leaders, trust in the person who asks for a donation. What the dean in particular has to foster that trust is knowledge of the school and its value, a commitment and passion for the school's mission, and the academic credentials to represent the school. In early stages of fund-raising, the dean will probably spend a few hours a week in visits and lunches and writing letters and reviewing proposals. As fund-raising ramps up in a major campaign, the time spent might rise to two or three days a week. Thus, it is essential to have a strong school administrative team to support the day-to-day work, so that the dean can focus externally. Finally, the dean is the public face of the school. The more the dean is a recognized and established figure, the more successful he or she will be in making the connections necessary for support. Fund-raising is largely personal. People, after all, give to other people.

Role of a Development Officer

Rice's current development office structure involves directors (part time or full time) in the schools who are paid by the development office but who also report to the school dean. This can be a delicate balance but works well at Rice. Ultimately, the development officer keeps the process running, a function that cannot be managed well by a dean or staff member with no connection to the central development office.

When we held our first annual fund drives and even when we attracted our endowment gift in the early 2000s, we did so without our own development officer. For several years following, we were assigned a part-time officer. Only when we entered the campaign for the building in January 2011 did we have a full-time development officer as well as the ongoing help of the central development office. Our development professional was crucial to our success. She had the major responsibility for maintaining and growing our portfolio of donors and potential donors, communicating with and representing our interests to the central development office, arranging and attending visits with donors and prospects, and planning building-related events (groundbreaking, topping off, and grand opening). She kept all the trains running, not a simple feat. Our campaign raised more than $25 million in essentially two years, drawing more than four hundred gifts including thirty-one named spaces (starting at $50,000).

Another role of the development officer is ensuring that the school's database of donors is current and correct. Robust databases are essential for keeping track of donors, gathering and updating information about donors and prospects over time, and recording gifts and acknowledgments. Some institutions have one large database into which all information from schools or divisions must flow. Others, such as Rice, have multiple databases (continuing education, the business school, various institutes, and so on) in addition to the development office/alumni affairs database. One advantage of the single large database is that information can be more accurate and complete, for example, showing all of the affiliations a particular individual may have. On the other hand, a database is only as good as what is entered into it and the lack of ownership may inhibit frequent updates. Additionally, it is difficult for any one part of the university to assert control over its part of the database if all of the others who are in fund-raising mode have access to that information.

At the Glasscock School we have always treated our database of students as confidential information. We do not sell the information nor do we give it away to others who might want to use it. In the recent campaign, we did provide the development office with a list of several hundred people who had taken multiple courses with us over time. The development office had the list vetted to give us a rough estimate of the gift-giving capacity of those individuals (property values and other publicly available numbers). Whatever the system, an effective development officer can argue the case with the central development office for the school to be assigned certain donors and prospects. In our experience, we won some and lost some. Ultimately, though, effective development offices practice donor-centered fund-raising, meaning that the donor's interest determines the recipient of the gift. As a result, we received many gifts from donors assigned to others.

Role of Volunteers and Friends

As mentioned, our advisory board (all volunteers) and other friends of our school were central to our success. Those who know us well and appreciate our efforts often worked behind the scenes to secure gifts we may not have gotten otherwise. The Glasscocks, both as donors and friends of the school themselves and as highly respected community leaders committed to the school, played a major role. Instructors were also very helpful. One longtime photography teacher volunteered his time to help us raise $100,000 for a student art gallery in the new building. He secured lead donors among his current and past students, who helped persuade other students to donate. Alumni and students from our Master of Liberal Studies program volunteered their time to raise $50,000 to name a classroom. Additionally, friends of the dean gave substantial amounts or helped secure gifts from others. Friendships should not be abused in a fund-raising campaign but also should not be overlooked. Do not hesitate to ask for help.

Lessons Learned

Quite simply, fund-raising is hard. Sitting across from a prospective donor, making the first request for a gift, is the most difficult. Keep in mind that continuing education is worthy of support. One of the most frequent reasons people do not give is because they are never asked outright. People who are sought for major gifts are accustomed to being asked, so discomfort on the part of the seeker is unnecessary. And with a seasoned development officer and some practice, asking becomes easier. Expect risk. At the beginning of our $25 million campaign, we had no idea if we would be successful. Expect some disappointment. We had a proposal for $2 million to a local foundation which left us waiting for a year and then turned us down. On the other hand, some gifts will arrive unsolicited and unexpected. For example, a couple who had already made a significant gift asked us later if they could give $2 million to name our auditorium. There are low moments, exciting moments, and even beautiful moments. At its best, philanthropy gives the donor great joy—it truly can be greater to give than to receive. Finally, be as thankful for a modest gift as for a larger one; the relationship established is a fine thing, a demonstration that your school has touched someone's life and that someone wants to give back.

Suggested Readings

Burk, Penelope. 2003. *Donor Centered Fundraising*. Hamilton, Ontario: Cygnus Applied Research, Inc.

Burnett, Ken. 2002. *Relationship Fundraising: A Donor-Based Approach to the Business of Raising Money*. San Francisco: Jossey-Bass.

Ciconte, Barbara L., and Jeanne Jacob. 2009. *Fundraising Basics: A Complete Guide*. Sudbury, MA: Jones and Barlett.

Fredricks, Laura. 2010. *The Ask*. San Francisco: Jossey-Bass.

Grace, Kay S. 1997. *Beyond Fund Raising: New Strategies for Nonprofit Innovation and Investment.* New York: John Wiley and Sons.

Williams, Karla A. 2013. *Leading the Fundraising Charge: The Role of the Nonprofit Executive.* Hoboken, NJ: John Wiley and Sons.

References

Collins, Jim. 2001. *Good to Great and the Social Sectors.* New York: HarperCollins.

Giving Institute. 2014. *Giving USA: The Annual Report on Philanthropy.* Chicago: Giving USA Foundation.

Partnership Capital and Continuing Education

Can It Be Accrued and Spent for Greater Impact?

■■

George Irvine

How important are organizational partnerships to professional and continuing education (PCE) units in our twenty-first-century knowledge economy? If organizational partnerships are increasingly important to the successful implementation of a PCE unit's strategy, what kinds of organizational partnerships make the most sense to pursue? And which skills should PCE professionals develop in order to nurture partnerships that generate value to the organizational partners involved and the broader community? This brief essay suggests preliminary answers to these questions by exploring the implications of recent research on network theory and organizational connectivity for professional and continuing education.

To my mind, this research indicates that PCE units that have the ability to conceive of and nurture mutually beneficial organizational partnerships both on and off the campus will be more successful in our networked, knowledge-based society than those that do not. I define this partnership creation ability as *partnership capital*, building on Robert Putnam's (1993) groundbreaking concept of social capital as the underpinning of successful democratic societies. It is my belief that partnership capital could well become a core organizational ingredient of an engaged, impactful, and profitable PCE unit in the twenty-first century. In this essay, I will first explore salient research and thinking about network theory and connectivity from fields of urban affairs, organizational

George Irvine is Assistant Director, Organizational Learning Solutions, Division of Professional and Continuing Studies, University of Delaware, and a UPCEA committee chair.

development, and public administration, then consider the implications of this research for PCE units and introduce partnership capital as a useful concept to help PCE units develop their partnering and collaborative capabilities. I close by suggesting specific employee development and organizational steps a PCE unit could take to develop its partnership capital in order to transform itself into a twenty-first-century *networked organization.*

Network Theory: The Imperative of Organizational Connectivity

Network theory, as put forth by the urban affairs scholar Manuel Castells (2000, 2008) among others, argues that society is going through a fundamental and profound transformation due to the rapid development and diffusion of information and communication technology (ICT). There are three principle contours to Castells's new network society. First, in the network society, an organization's productivity and competitiveness are measured by its capacity to use knowledge and information to create additional, value-laden knowledge and information (Castells 2000, 155). Second, the network society's economy is global, with important economic activities upon which we rely on a daily basis, such as financial markets and supply chains organized on a global scale (154). Third, this new economy is based on networks comprised of whole or parts of organizations in all sectors—public, private, nonprofit, and educational—not on the discrete organizational units of the twentieth century, that is, states, agencies, companies, universities, and so on. Organizations form temporary and permanent networks with other organizations and units at the sub-organizational level (such as divisions and teams) in order to remain competitive but also to reap the full rewards of the ICT advances that enabled the creation of the networks in the first place. For Castells these networks across organizational structures and sectors are the unit of analysis and the value-generating catalysts of the network society.

Castells's contentions about the network society's impact on public administration are relevant to other bureaucratic organizations such as educational institutions. At the level of public administration, Castells identifies three coordination challenges facing the network state—organizational, technical, and political (Castells 2008, 88). Organizationally, a public agency created and based on the territoriality and the authority of a nation state must restructure itself to address the growing need to form networks with other state agencies and social actors. Technically, agencies must embrace the use of ICT even though it may initially disrupt work and allow greater access to information across and outside the agency, which cannot be controlled as easily. Politically, agencies will lose bureaucratic autonomy and control as they enter into networks with other agencies and organizations. The bureaucratic, hierarchic organizational structures of the twentieth century will be diminished by the formation of horizontal networks within and across organizations. For Castells, an organization in the twenty-first century *must* partner with other organizations in dynamic networks if it wishes to survive in the network society. If it does not, it will be eliminated by those that do (Castells 2000, 156). There is no middle ground in his analysis.

Scholars from business administration (Berman and Korsten 2014) and public administration (Agranoff 2012) provide supporting evidence and nuance to Castells's bold contentions. For example, Berman and Korsten's survey of 1,700 CEOs and senior public sector leaders finds that these leaders believe it is imperative, as Castells argues, for organizations to form partnerships and networks with other organizations in order to remain competitive. Such partnerships allow the firm to jointly develop new products and services, reach their customers in novel ways, and enrich their creativity. In addition, they found that when looking to hire talent 75 percent of the senior public and private sector leaders surveyed consider the ability to collaborate within and outside an organization as critical. In addition, the authors found that openness and collaboration was associated with the high-performing organizations in their study and that such organizations know how to change to become more open and collaborative. They also found that the surveyed leaders believe that social media will be the most important way to engage customers and partners in the next five years. Finally, the surveyed leaders believe that radical innovation requires extensive partnering with other organizations. The perceptions of the surveyed leaders support Castells's contention that the ability to collaborate, connect, and derive value from networks is at the core of the twenty-first-century network society.

Some public administration scholars remain skeptical about the extent to which networks are indeed transforming public agencies (Pollitt and Bouckaert 2011, 20). Other scholars, such as Agranoff (2012), have researched how much organizational networks matter to the public sector managers working with them daily. Agranoff's research is important since it provides insights into the extent to which collaborative management via participation in organizational networks is indeed transforming public organizations. Agranoff finds that the imperative for public agencies to network is growing but that twentieth-century bureaucratic organizational structures persist. Castells is correct about networks changing bureaucratic organizations—just not to the extent that he claims. Agranoff concludes:

> Today's wicked policy problems . . . and intergovernmental overlays guarantee that managers must engage other governments and nongovernmental organizations. The payoff is that public management networks have a lasting collabo-

rative effect, as they build collective capacity for subsequent collaborative solutions and teach managers the essential skill of collaboration. (619)

This "essential skill of collaboration" that Castells theorized about and Agranoff researched is particularly important for PCE units to learn.

So, just what is this essential skill of collaboration? Agranoff and Mc-Guire's (2001) review of the research on the management of organizational networks in the public and nonprofit sectors identify four management behaviors that are distinct from traditional management behaviors. These network management behaviors are:

1. *Activation* of a network by selecting the appropriate partners with the right resources for the desired goal, and the related *deactivation* of a network if its performance is sub-optimal.

2. *Framing* the network's operational rules and partners' perceptions of the network in order to allow the network to do good work.

3. *Mobilizing* the partners' initial and ongoing commitment to the network particularly in regards to resource contributions.

4. *Synthesizing* the network by creating the "conditions for favorable, productive interaction among network participants." (300)

These four management behaviors all require a high degree of communication and people skills, what organizational development scholars call *emotional intelligence,* or the ability to interact well with colleagues in and outside of an organization to advance a particular agenda. One could certainly argue that these four collaborative management behaviors have always been important for managers to possess, but the rise of the network society makes it imperative for managers to learn and use these behaviors in order to maintain organizational competitiveness and vitality.

The Network Society's Implications for Professional and Continuing Education Units

Castells argues that our twenty-first-century society is now connected and networked to an unprecedented degree and that if an organization does not become networked it will decline. Berman and Korsten's survey results indicate that senior public and private sector leaders worldwide recognize the imperative for their organizations to use ICT to connect and collaborate internally and externally in order to create value-laden products and services. Agranoff's research illustrates how public and nonprofit managers are making sense of and using networks in their daily work, and that indeed the ability to collaborate is essential for managers in the twenty-first century. In addition, Agranoff's research indicates that most managers work with organizational networks but still within bureaucratic agencies, in a kind of hybrid bureaucratic-networked organization. Agranoff's findings hint that public and nonprofit organizations may have more time to change than Castells suggests but that organizational networks are on the rise because they provide collaborative solutions to complex problems. It follows from these findings that the future trajectory of professional and continuing education *must* take into account organizational partnerships and networks and the ability to collaborate both inside and outside the university. PCE units will have to have the capacity to build and sustain organizational networks because the society in which they are embedded and whose problems they seek to address through education is itself increasingly networked.

I believe that the research on the rise of the network society and its associated management behaviors has two important implications for PCE units. First, PCE units should develop their employees' collaboration skills so that the unit is better positioned to form value-laden organizational partnerships and, in turn, thicker organizational networks. This will require hiring employees with communication and emotional intelligence skills. It will require providing existing employees with professional development programs to develop their collaboration skills. In addition, it will require familiarizing employees with the ongoing development of ICT and its impact on the unit's operations. If ICT is the key causal factor of the network society's rise and the key enabler of network formation, then PCE professionals need to be both aware of and comfortable with ICT.

Second, PCE units should consider flattening their organizational structures to give managers of its various departments (marketing, registration, student advising, workforce development, etc.) the authority and the opportunity to create short- and long-term partnerships with other campus-based and off-campus organizations. Such partnerships form the basis of organizational networks. Some of these partnerships may be for discrete training programs, others might be for research into workforce development needs in the community, and still others may deal with effective social media marketing. The traditional, hierarchic organizational structures of twentieth-century educational bureaucracies—in which authority and decisions flow down from the executive level while reporting on educational outputs flows up from the line managers and employees—are not as conducive to creative partnership and network creation.

However, there is no single prescription for a PCE unit to transform itself into a networked organization. Prior to starting such a transformation, each unit will have to consider its particular organizational structure and cultural legacies, its ability to operate entrepreneurially, its room for maneuvering separately from central university administration, and its staff's appetite for change. I would like to suggest, however, that there is a concept which can guide PCE units as they transform into networked organizations and that is the concept of partnership capital.

Partnership Capital: Essential for PCE Units

What I call *partnership capital* is the accumulated ability of organizations in a given polity (city, state, region, country) to form *mutually* beneficial (to the organizations involved) and *collectively* beneficial (to the polity as a whole) partnerships within narrow or wide, single or multisector networks. The focus of the concept is on the degree to which the organizations (PCE units in this case) recognize the imperative to partner and know how to partner with other organizations. To my mind, an organizational partnership between two or more organizations is the building block of the thicker organizational networks described by Castells. In other words, a network is the thicker web formed by discrete but connected organizational partnerships. My hypothesis is that just as the concept of social capital helped scholars, policy makers, and practitioners understand the individual, citizen-level connections that make for a healthy, democratic polity, the concept of partnership capital can help us understand how organizational-level connections make polities more or less effective at delivering services in the network society. If my hypothesis is correct, then PCE units need to improve their ability to partner with other PCE units, government agencies, nongovernmental organizations, and businesses in organizational partnerships in order to achieve their strategic goals.

It is worthwhile exploring a little further the relationship between collaboration skills, organizational partnerships, and organizational networks. PCE professionals need the four collaboration skills described by Agranoff and McGuire (2001), discussed above, to form mutually beneficial organizational partnerships between two or more organizations to achieve a given near- or long-term strategic goal. Without these skills, no partnership can form or succeed. Once established, these organizational partnerships form the building blocks of thicker organizational networks which have the potential of delivering greater value to the partners involved and the broader community. To some degree, it is easier to conceptualize the creation of a partnership because we are familiar with this term from business and other social situations, whereas forming a network can seem to be a more amorphous undertaking. It is for this reason that I prefer the term *partnership capital* rather than *network capital*, though one could certainly argue that the latter term has greater theoretical utility.

Partnership capital can be leveraged for the benefit of a PCE unit, other units in the university, and the broader community. For example, two years ago my PCE unit formed an internal organizational partnership with our university's college of business and economics, forming a joint venture to offer customized executive and management education programs to area organizations. Both units carefully negotiated the terms of the partnership, particularly with regard to start-up costs and revenue sharing (activation); developed the educational programs and services by leveraging each unit's faculty, instructors, and credit and noncredit courses (framing and mobilizing); and built a communication and reporting process to ensure that both partners could monitor the joint venture's outreach, programming, and revenues (synthesizing). This joint venture has allowed both university partners to provide businesses and organizations in our region with greater educational value than either could have done independently. By collaborating, we strengthened our internal partnership capital and increased our ability to provide more and better educational services to our clients. One of our services includes networking organizations (both clients and others) together via roundtable events on strategic human resource management. In addition, clients serve on our program advisory committee, helping us match our programs to local employee development needs. Admittedly, our joint venture has not yet built a formal, thicker organizational network, but such a network among university and nonuniversity organizations focused on workforce development and policy issues is now in the realm of the possible.

What then should a PCE unit do to develop its partnership capital? A good starting point is to develop their employees network management behaviors in order to be better positioned to nurture and benefit from organizational partnerships and networks. PCE professionals need to know how to activate, frame, mobilize, and synthesize organizational partnerships and networks. A part of this could be to empower and encourage employees to join existing professional networks or form new ones via social media, UPCEA, and local community organizations (such as chambers of commerce, United Way, etc.).

Second, embracing ICT and its possibilities appears to be a significant contributor to the accrual of partnership capital. It is ICT that allows for the high degree of communication, teamwork, and, hopefully, trust among organizational partners within a network. It also allows for the extension of knowledge from the PCE unit to its stakeholders via distance education, for example. Further, it enables efficient processing of information within the PCE unit, which benefits staff and students alike. ICT cannot be an afterthought but rather needs to be at the center of a PCE unit's operations and strategic implementation.

Third, PCE unit leadership might consider the extent to which its use of organizational partnerships on and off the campus is central or peripheral to its organizational strategy. If organizational partnerships are conceived of as nice but not imperative, it may be time to reconsider how existing and future organizational partnerships can help a PCE unit better implement its strategy. PCE leaders could ask themselves the question, "Can I achieve my goal through a mutually beneficial organizational partnership (which may already exist but may need some additional resources) rather than using only my unit's resources and talent?"

Fourth, take small steps toward the goal of accruing partnership capital and becoming a networked organization. Historically, the university as a societal organization does not respond well to rapid changes, which may in part explain its resilience in the face of wars, depressions, social upheaval, and generational changes. Incremental but steady change into a networked organization through the accrual and expenditure of partnership capital will allow the twenty-first-century PCE unit to maintain its fit within the change-averse university culture yet still help catalyze change in that same university culture ultimately for the benefit of multiple stakeholders—students, staff, faculty, and the community. The network society is already upon us, so becoming a networked organization is the least that the PCE unit can do for itself, its home university, and its local and global community.

References

Agranoff, R. 2012. "Inside Collaborative Networks: Ten Lessons for Public Managers." In J. Shafritz and A. Hyde, eds., *Classics of Public Administration*, 7th ed. (pp. 610–621). Boston: Wadsworth Cengage Learning.

Agranoff, R., and M. McGuire. 2001. "Big Questions in Public Network Management Research." *Journal of Public Administration Research and Theory* 11(3): 295–326.

Berman, S., and P. Korsten. 2014. "Leading in the Connected Era." *Strategy and Leadership* 42: 37–48.

Castells, M. 2000. "The Contours of the Network Society." *Foresight* 2: 151–157.

Castells, M. 2008. "The New Public Sphere: Global Civil Society, Communication Networks, and Global Governance." *Annals of the American Academy of Political and Social Science* 616: 78–93.

Pollitt, C., and G. Bouckaert. 2011. *Public Management Reform: A Comparative Analysis—New Public Management, Governance, and the Neo-Weberian State*, 3rd ed. New York: Oxford University Press.

Putnam, R. 1993. "What Makes Democracy Work?" *National Civic Review* 82: 101–107.

PART V

Metrics and Marketing

Critical core functions of continuing and professional education are dependent upon metrics for assaying the extent to which we have achieved success—increasingly important in the new policy environment. Data, as well, are critical to the measurement of marketing's success in reaching, recruiting, and retaining students.

On a practical level, Emily Richardson provides a guide to the several tools available for achieving new insights into performance as well as measuring potential for activities within continuing education. James Campbell and James L. Narduzzi use their combined multi-decade experience with marketing to reflect on the history and current state of the practice, focusing on the fascinating role and impact of technology. Jim Fong and Noreen Mack conclude the section by tracing marketing's roles over the past twenty-five years, drawing attention to the shifting nature of marketing from communications and the four P's—product, price, place, promotion—to social media and CRM software, while speculating on the nature of the practice in the future.

Measuring the Success of Professional and Continuing Education Units

■■

Emily C. Richardson

Calls for greater accountability from the policy-making and governance community have combined with the changing demographic and goal profile of today's learners to make documentation of student academic success a priority. With the increasing visibility of the post-traditional student in higher education generally, it is becoming increasingly important that campus distance and continuing education leaders propose alternative ways to measure success that go beyond traditional measures and success criteria. "Being proactive in defining and using excellence measures is likely to be more satisfying and productive than waiting until accountability and performance measures are defined and imposed by others—more often than not by groups which have a considerably more restricted view of what constitutes excellence than will administrators, faculty and staff of the institution/program" (Ruben 1999, 8).

So the question must be asked whether we as professionals in the online and continuing education space are doing enough to measure how well our students are doing? A study published in 2013 by the University Professional and Continuing Education Association (UPCEA) Center for Research and Consulting in conjunction with InsideTrack, a student coaching company, and reported on in an article in *Inside Higher Education*, stated "a whopping 77 percent of institutions do not know the graduation rate for their adult students" (Fain 2012, 1). The article notes that the Western Association of Schools and Colleges (WASC) met with professionals who handle adult students to help create a template for tracking and measuring adult student performance.

Emily C. Richardson is Dean, Hayworth School of Graduate and Continuing Studies, Queens University of Charlotte, and on the UPCEA Board of Directors.

These sources demonstrate that both the government and accreditors are looking at retention, persistence, graduation rates, and hiring success for traditional students. Brent Ruben states that "there is little argument about the value of assessment, measurement, and the use of the information that results therefrom, but the question of what should be measured and how that information should be used has been more problematic" (1999, 1). Adults are the new face of higher education, and we must supply the metrics to enable others to see that we are succeeding with them when it comes to degree completion.

This essay will first look at the movement toward the use of metrics in higher education, and how both efforts initiated by Malcolm Baldrige and the balanced scorecard concept have resulted in higher education developing metrics to measure not just inputs but also outcomes. Then there will be a discussion about key performance indicators (KPIs) that are used by the traditional university and often displayed in the form of a dashboard. Finally, we will look at what needs to be accomplished by the professional and continuing education experts to ensure that we are all on the same page as we move forward on measuring what matters.

Defining Benchmarking and Its Purpose

Schuler defined benchmarking as "a structured approach for looking outside an organization to study and adapt the best outside practices to complement internal operations with new, creative ideas" (1998, 40). Jackson and Lund (2000) explain that benchmarking involves a comparison of practices, performance, and process among organizations or industries. Doerfel and Ruben, in an article in *New Directions for Higher Education* that was dedicated to the overview of benchmarking as well as dashboard indicators for higher education, noted: "Whereas comparison is a time-honored tradition, the term *benchmarking* and the application of the concepts to organizational assessment and innovation is a more recent development" (2002, 14).

Three types of benchmarking practices in higher education were listed by Upcraft and Schuh (1996). Internal benchmarking refers to making comparisons between units (enrollments for engineering versus enrollments for public health), competitive benchmarking refers to identifying best practices of direct competitors, and generic benchmarking involves looking at other organizations employing similar practices and procedures.

These types of benchmarking are something that many UPCEA members perform on an annual basis, looking at the comparisons internally while filling out and then using the annual management survey to compare results across members nationally. The 2012 management survey, published in the 2013 Center for Research and Consulting report *Research That Matters*, specifically answered the questions:

1. What does the typical continuing education unit look like based on size, type of institution (public/private), and region?

2. How do units differ based on staffing, salary, structure, budgeting, and other factors?

3. How are units organized based on size, type of institution (public/private), region? (Fong, Hansen, Simpson, and Sibley 2013, 109)

Benchmarking is done by continuing education and higher education to provide a context for our own progress and achievements. But it is also done for the purpose of innovation. It forces an organization to look at its results, gaining insights from others. It is the feedback loop of benchmarking that provides the ideas and often the motivation for the profound change that is necessary.

Doerfel and Ruben point out the paradox that comes when looking at our competitors for comparison. "At the core of external benchmarking lies an incongruity: organizations often look to their competitors for models of best practice" (2002, 12).

It is proposed by Cox, Mann, and Samson (1997) that collaboration will occur more readily if the initiator is a third party, such as UPCEA with the management survey. As a continuing educator it is easier to share the unit's benchmarks with an association who holds the information closely versus opening up the information to direct competitors in the local market.

Frameworks for Higher Education

The American Society for Quality website offers the following history and purpose of the Malcolm Baldrige award:

[It is] an award established by the U.S. Congress in 1987 to raise awareness of quality management and recognize U.S. companies that have implemented successful quality management systems. Awards can be given annually in six categories: manufacturing, service, small business, education, healthcare and nonprofit. The award is named after the late Secretary of Commerce Malcolm Baldrige, a proponent of quality management. The U.S. Commerce Department's National Institute of Standards and Technology manages the award, and ASQ administers it.

The framework for the award is built on organizational excellence, cutting across seven categories:

1. Leadership: how upper management leads the organization, and how the organization leads within the community.

2. Strategic planning: how the organization establishes and plans to implement strategic directions.

3. Customer and market focus: how the organization builds and maintains strong, lasting relationships with customers.

4. Measurement, analysis, and knowledge management: how the organization uses data to support key processes and manage performance.

5. Human resource focus: how the organization empowers and involves its workforce.

6. Process management: how the organization designs, manages and improves key processes.

7. Business/organizational performance results: how the organization performs in terms of customer satisfaction, finances, human resources, supplier and partner performance, operations, governance and social responsibility, and how the organization compares to its competitors.

In 2001 University of Wisconsin–Stout was the first higher education institution to receive the National Baldrige Award. Numerous other institutions of higher education have used the framework to analyze their operation and in many cases apply for the award. Since then we have seen an increase in the principles being applied to regional accrediting standards. "The Baldrige principles and the standards of the accrediting association have been extremely influential in their respective spheres, and there is a natural and growing compatibility between them" (Ruben 2007, 9).

In addition, the extension of the Baldrige award to the excellence in higher education (EHE) model expanded the criteria to include colleges and universities. The EHE model includes seven dimensions of organizational functioning: leadership, strategic planning, external focus, information and analysis, faculty/staff and workplace focus, process effectiveness, and outcomes and achievements. "Collectively, the categories and the many interactions between them define a systems framework that can be used to conceptualize and analyze the workings, effectiveness, strengths and improvement needs of a higher education department, program or institution" (Doerfel and Ruben 2002, 17).

An additional framework used by many colleges and universities is built upon the concept of a balanced scorecard. As described by Kaplan and Norton, "the Balanced Scorecard translates an organization's mission and strategy into a comprehensive set of performance measures that provides a framework for a strategic measurement and management system" (1996, 2).

"Traditionally, business has measured performance using a financial accounting model that emphasizes profitability, return on investment, sales growth, cash flow or economic value added" (Ruben 1999, 1). For those of us in continuing education, financial measures are often the easiest for us to discuss or to use to make our case about the contribution of our unit. However,

> the general conclusion is that financial indicators alone are limited in their ability to adequately represent the range of factors associated with organizational excellence. Accounting-based measures, for instance, may not capture key elements of an organization's mission, customer satisfaction and loyalty, employee satisfaction and turnover, employee capability, organizational adaptability or innovation, environmental competitiveness, research and development productivity, market growth and success, and other important company-specific factors. (Ibid., 2)

Many traditional measures are input based—thus not providing useful information on what our institutions contribute, on the value of our programs courses and institutions. Consider the power of discussing economic capacity for a continuing education unit or the customer satisfaction with course offerings as true measures of our worth.

Dashboard Indicators for Higher Education

"A Dashboard Indicator (DI) is a quantitative measure providing a snapshot of a particular metric that represents a critical issue of concern for an institution or corporation" (Allen 2007, 1). In some cases these are also presented as KPIs.

Jeffrey Seybert, director of the National Higher Education Benchmarking Institute, provided the following purposes for dashboards in a webinar hosted by ZogoTech:

- To communicate current information about major indices of organizational performance to primary stakeholders

- To provide information to assist in evaluation of organizational performance

- To provide a comprehensive analysis of how the organization's achievement of its strategic objectives leads to effectively carrying out its mission and vision

- To provide information about organizational performance compared to appropriate benchmarks (2010, 3).

It is important to know that dashboard indicators must be processed in the context of:

- Prior data (e.g., the growth or depletion of resources over time, such as the increase of tuition costs compared year-by-year)

- Targeted data (e.g., a targeted goal for a particular measure or quantity, such as enrolling 2500 new freshmen in 2014); or

- Correlated data (e.g., the ratios or other expressed relationships between data points, such as the percentage of minority students who enroll and also listed the university as their first choice institution) (Allen 2007, 1).

Seybert recommends that the information must be timely, accurate, easy to understand, and represent the current state of the organization. Research by Yonezawa and Kaiser (2003) recommends that dashboard indicators should be easy to understand, relevant to the user, strategic, quantitative, up to date with current information, and not used in isolation.

In 2012, Terkla, Sharkness, Cohen, Roscoe, and Wiseman published results of a study with the Association for Institutional Research from their analysis of sixty-six dashboards that they collected in the fall of 2005. The dashboards analyzed resulted in eleven broad categories that included financial indicators, admissions statistics, enrollment statistics, faculty data, student outcomes, student engagement, academic information, physical plant, satisfaction, research, and external ratings. They determined that the average number of indicators used was approximately twenty-nine, with the fewest used being three and the largest sixty-eight.

Ruben (1999) recommends five dashboard clusters that include teaching and learning, scholarship and research, public service and outreach, workplace satisfaction, and finances. Kirwan, in an article in *Change Magazine*, recommended the following consideration about what should be reported:

We also need to measure and report how higher-education institutions fare in meeting the "big three" core educational outcomes: the development of critical thinking, analytical reasoning, and written communication skills. First and foremost, we should do this because it will enable us to improve the quality of our educational offerings. But we also have an obligation to demonstrate to our paying customers the benefits they can expect to receive in knowledge and skills from our degree programs. (2007)

Dashboard Indicators for Continuing Education

So what should the key performance indicators be for continuing education? What should be on our dashboard? And most important, can we begin to define the terms that provide meaning such that comparisons can begin?

Let's take as an example the word *retention*. According to the online glossary provided by the Integrated Postsecondary Education Data System (IPEDS), retention is defined as follows:

> A measure of the rate at which students persist in their education program at an institution, expressed as a percentage. For four-year institutions, this is a percentage of first-time bachelors (or equivalent) degree-seeking undergraduates from the previous fall who are again enrolled in the current fall. For all other institutions this is the percentage of first-time degree/certificate-seeking students from the previous fall who either re-enrolled or successfully completed their program by the current fall.

But does this definition work for continuing education? Apparently not, because in a study by UPCEA and InsideTrack, when schools were asked to define *retention* for post-traditional baccalaureate students, multiple definitions were offered (Fong and Jarrat 2013). They are listed here, along with the percentage of schools that noted the specific definition.

- Enrollment in at least one course within a year 36%

- Enrollment in at least one course in consecutive terms 26%

- Enrollment combined with some measure of academic progress (course completion) 23%

- Enrollment in at least one course at a specific point in time (census date) 13%

- Other 3%

This is not surprising since many nontraditional students don't start in the fall like traditional students but rather at their convenience. This variance in definitions among continuing education units results in difficulty of comparison with KPIs.

In the same UPCEA study, individuals were asked what obstacles stood in the way of making progress on cross-industry benchmarking. The answers included lack of consensus on key definitions and metrics, insufficient coordination among industry stakeholders, and inadequate resources at the institutional level. "In addition, 61 percent cite cultural resistance to measurement and accountability as an obstacle to establishing effective benchmarks of performance for post-traditional baccalaureate student success" (Fong and Jarrat 2013, 3).

The same problem with definitions occurs with the terms *nontraditional student, persistence,* and *cohorts,* as discovered in conversations with colleagues in UPCEA. In each case, the context of the institution and the program can make a difference in how these terms are utilized.

There are, however, wonderful examples of continuing education units that have implemented dashboards. An example of a dashboard in use, is from the Professional and Liberal Education Division, part of the School of Arts and Sciences, at the University of Pennsylvania. Here is how Nora Lewis, the vice dean, explains their dashboard.

> We have a web-based enrollment dashboard that our computing applications people developed for us using QlikView. The dashboard is universally available to all full-time staff, and we expect folks to use it on a daily basis to pull data from the dashboard to inform requests, decisions, annual reports, etc.
>
> The dashboard has several tabs: Admissions, Enrollment data (headcounts, registrations), Course-level data, Academic progress, Financial (budget vs. revenue/expense year to date—still under development and access restricted to certain staff), and Demographic data on current students.
>
> The dashboard can roll up data on all programs across the division, and then you can click down to sub-divisions (e.g., all graduate programs, or all high school programs), and eventually to an individual program. It also tracks data historically and shows trend graphs over time, but again you can click down from the ten-year history to a single year, or to a single term in a year. (Personal communication, August 2014)

But keeping in mind the inherent difficulties across campuses and units, it may be better to begin discussion with what continuing education divisions should measure. Although many of these deal directly with credit-bearing programs, many can also be used for noncredit work. These recommendations come from peers in UPCEA, plus personal experience in continuing education. In mind is the need to capture information that will help us solidify the position of professional and continuing educators in the world of higher education and the concepts previously discussed in this essay. Where appropriate, definitions are offered as an initial means to get the conversation rolling toward finding definitions that will work for all units.

Enrollments

- Total number of students enrolled
  - Total credit
  - Total noncredit
  - Total by program/certificate/course
  - Number of full-time versus part-time
  - Number of total credit hours per semester/per year

- Number of new students enrolled in a given semester

- Yield funnel (number of prospects/applicants/admits/ enrollments)

- Retention (enrollment fall to fall; enrollment spring to spring; enrollment summer to summer)

- Persistence (enrollment in at least two academic periods within the year)

- Graduation (number of graduates per school/program/ average time to graduation)

Students

- Demographics of students
  - Females/males
  - Ethnic diversity

      ○ Geographic locations

      ○ Age breakdown (especially important if serving high school students, senior citizens)

- Student satisfaction measurement (internal survey or national survey, such as the Noel Levitz survey of student satisfaction)

- Tuition reimbursement

      ○ How many internal candidates are you serving?

      ○ How many students are receiving tuition reimbursement from their companies?

- Number of students inducted into Alpha Sigma Lambda

- Student engagement in activities, either university or unit based

Strategic Partnerships

- Number of articulations or corporate partners signed in a given year

- Number of education fairs attended (number of prospects/enrollments as a result of the fair)

- Number of alumni interactions

Faculty/Staff

- Number of faculty members (tenure/tenure-track/non-tenure-track/adjunct)

- Demographics of faculty

- Highest degree earned by rank

- Average class size

- Analysis of evaluations (new versus continuing faculty)

- Percent of full-time faculty on overload

- Number of staff (per student served in the unit)

- Satisfaction of both faculty and staff (internal survey)

Assessment of Student Learning

- General education outcomes

- Programmatic outcomes

- Capstone course outcomes

Financial Measures

- External funding (grants/scholarships/alumni giving/campaign)

- Tuition (credit/noncredit)

- Net percent either returned to the university or, in the case of self-funding, kept for future use

Incubation/Innovation

- New programs/certificates/courses developed (time to completion; success of program)

- Interdisciplinary efforts with schools and colleges that are internal

- Joint programs with community

A Call to Action

Although this is simply a listing of potential KPIs for continuing education, it becomes a call to action. Peter Drucker once stated, "If you can't measure it, you can't manage it," and this holds true today. As continuing educators we must begin to measure and share information to ensure that we are measuring the success of our units, our students, and our value to the academic community and the community as a whole. Ruben said, "One of the defining themes of contemporary organizational theory is the emphasis on information and measurement for assessing, tracking, and promoting organizational excellence" (1999, 1).

It was announced in July 2014 that five higher education organizations are working together to benchmark persistence and completion rates for non-first-time college students nationwide. The following quotes from the press release were published on the InsideTrack website.

"Our national goals for postsecondary attainment will only be reached if we effectively serve the millions of Americans who began their education, but never finished their degree," says Cathy Sandeen, vice president for education attainment and innovation at ACE.

In order to enhance student outcomes, decision makers need to be able to benchmark themselves and track their progress relative to their peers," according to Dave Jarrat, vice president of marketing at InsideTrack.

This measurement project is a start to what we can consider as benchmarks for adult students. But it is only the beginning. As a group of passionate and devoted continuing educators, we must join together and let the next decade become a time for measurement, during which we meet and agree upon not just what should be measured, but how the measurement will be collected and distributed to provide us all true benchmarks for the important work we do with nontraditional students.

References

Allen, J. 2007. Dashboard Indicators. Presentation, Widener University, Chester, PA.

Cox, J. R., L. Mann, and D. Samson. 1997. "Benchmarking as a Mixed Metaphor: Disentangling Assumptions of Competition and Collaboration." *Journal of Management Studies* 34: 285–314.

Doerfel, M. L., and B. D. Ruben. 2002. "Developing More Adaptive, Innovative, and Interactive Organizations." *New Directions for Higher Education* 118 (Summer): 5–28.

Fain, P. 2012. "Where Are All the Adults?" *Inside Higher Ed*, July 11. Accessed at https://www.insidehighered.com/news/2012/07/11/accreditor-will -require-colleges-stop-ignoring-adult-student-retention.

Fong, J., and D. Jarrat. 2013. "Measuring Post-Traditional Student Success: Institutions Making Progress, but Challenges Remain." Washington, DC: UPCEA Center for Research and Consulting. Accessed at http://www .insidetrack.com/wp-content/uploads/2014/10/post-traditional -student-success.pdf.

"Higher Ed Organizations Join Forces to Measure Success of Returning Students." n.d. InsideTrack New. Accessed at http://www.insidetrack.com /higher-ed-organizations-join-forces-measure-success-returning-students/.

"Integrated Postsecondary Education Data System Glossary." n.d. National Center for Education Statistics. Accessed at http://nces.ed.gov/ipeds /glossary/?charindex=R.

Jackson, N., and H. Lund, eds. 2000. *Benchmarking for Higher Education*. Buck-ingham, England: Society for Research into Higher Education and Open University Press.

Kaplan, R. S., and D. P. Norton. 1996. *The Balanced Scorecard.* Boston: Harvard Business School Press.

Kirwan, William E. 2007. "Higher Education's 'Accountability' Imperative: How the University System of Maryland Responded." *Change Magazine,* March-April. Accessed at http://www.changemag.org/Archives/Back%20 Issues/March-April%202007/full-accountability-imperative.html.

"Malcolm Baldrige National Quality Award." n.d. American Society for Quality. Accessed at http://asq.org/learn-about-quality/malcolm-baldrige-award /overview/overview.html.

Ruben, Brent D. 2007. *Excellence in Higher Education Guide: An Integrated Approach to Assessment, Planning, and Improvement in Colleges and Universities.* Washington, DC: National Association of College and University Business Officers.

Ruben, Brent D. 1999. *Toward a Balanced Scorecard for Higher Education: Rethinking the College and University Excellence Indicators Framework.* QCI, Center for Organizational Development and Leadership, Rutgers University. Accessed at http://dfcentre.com/wp-content/uploads/2014/05/Balanced -Scorecard-in-Higher-Education.pdf.

Schuler, R. S. 1998. *Managing Human Resources,* 6th ed. Cincinnati, Ohio: South-Western College Publications.

Seybert, Jeffrey A. 2010. "An Introduction to Dashboards in Higher Education: Graphic Representation of Key Performance Indicators." PowerPoint presentation, Transforming Higher Education webinar series, ZogoTech. Accessed at http://www.zogotech.com/demoFiles/presentations/intro _to_dashboards_in_higher_ed.pdf.

Terkla, D.G., J. Sharkness, M. Cohen, H. S. Roscoe, and M. Wiseman. 2012. *Institutional Dashboards: Navigational Tool for Colleges and Universities.* Association for Institutional Research, no. 123 (Winter). Accessed at http://files .eric.gov/fulltext/ED532862.pdf.

Upcraft, M. L., and J. H. Schuh, eds. 1996. *Assessment in Student Affairs: A Guide for Practitioners.* San Francisco: Jossey-Bass.

Yonezawa, A., and F. Kaiser, eds. 2003. *System-Level and Strategic Indicators for Monitoring Higher Education in the Twenty-First Century.* Bucharest, Romania: United Nations Educational, Scientific and Cultural Organization.

The More Things Change

Reflections on the State of Marketing in Continuing Higher Education

James D. Campbell and James L. Narduzzi

Plus ca change, plus c'est la meme chose.
—ALPHONSE KARR

All of us can readily identify the major changes that have occurred in society over the past several decades and, more important, the manner in which these changes have affected the way we conduct the business of continuing higher education. For example, the telephone has been replaced by e-mail, which is now the most prevalent way we communicate with each other in the workplace. Social media and the web now dominate how we market our programs and communicate with our various constituencies. Instruction, once delivered primarily face-to-face in a classroom setting, is now routinely delivered utilizing various digitally mediated formats, with online and blended learning models now accounting for a significant share of delivery. This list could go on indefinitely, and these few examples only scratch the surface of the changes that have occurred.

What's interesting to us, however, is what has remained constant. The demand for continuous learning, the profile of our students, the way we credential, the indicators of quality in terms of instruction, and the role continuing education plays on most campuses still emphasizes the same core values. These constants persist in spite of the fact that the pace of

James D. Campbell is Director of Marketing, School of Professional and Continuing Studies, University of Richmond, and a UPCEA committee chair. **James L. Narduzzi** is Dean and Professor, School of Professional and Continuing Studies, University of Richmond, and on the UPCEA Board of Directors.

change continues to escalate dramatically, particularly so when it comes to technology. One simple example makes the point: we all carry around in our pockets greater computing power than all of NASA had access to in 1969 (Kaku 2011). Reflecting on the above led us to a simple yet profound truth: while change is ever-present and occurring at breakneck speed, what matters in how we conduct business has remained relatively constant and is likely to do so into the foreseeable future.

Throughout our careers, we have seen a great temptation to focus on what's new. Our fear is that this can distract us from focusing on what's important. We believe that this is particularly relevant when it comes to marketing, where technology has perhaps exerted its greatest influence. The purpose of this essay, then, will be to explore the changes and the constants that exist as they relate to marketing in continuing higher education. Particular attention will be paid to best practices and identifying useful data points, with the ultimate goal of encouraging the long view in making daily business decisions.

What's Changed?

Communication and marketing to current and prospective students has undergone transformative change. The web was in its infancy not too long ago and has become the dominant way we communicate with our various constituencies. Somewhere in the neighborhood of one billion smartphones were shipped worldwide last year, more than double the number sold two years earlier ("Global smartphone shipments" 2014). Leveraging social media on these mobile devices has become the preferred vehicle for driving traffic to the web. And yet, the fundamental goal has never wavered: creating relationships.

Today, marketers and administrators will be hard-pressed to attend a conference that doesn't include a few sessions about customer relationship management (CRM) systems. But CRM is a fairly new trend in continuing and professional education although the concept has been around in the corporate sales world for many years.

CRM grew out of the database marketing movement in the 1980s. The concept was pioneered by Robert and Kate Kestnbaum, statisticians who used statistical modeling to analyze customer data and develop customized communication to other potential customers. Next came ACT!, contact management software (CMS) that revolutionized the organization and storage of customer data.

Goldmine and others also released contact management software throughout the late 1980s. As personal computer and server growth exploded in the 1990s, huge strides were made in CRM software development, led by Brock Control Systems, an innovator of early sales force automation (SFA) tools, which combined elements of database marketing and CMS to create an automated task management solution ("A Brief History of Customer Relationship Management" 2013).

As the concepts of CMS, SFA, and CRM were evolving over the last forty years, they all became synonymous with technology. But the idea of building and maintaining a relationship with a prospective customer involves more than just new technology. For many of us, our system may have included file folders, Excel spreadsheets, tickler files, written to-do lists, and a day planner or desk calendar. Not terribly long ago, when prospective students inquired about a program (on the phone in most cases), we entered their names onto a list. We mailed them a packet of information and followed up on the phone to make sure they received the information and to ask if they had any questions. We usually followed up with them periodically by phone and mail to remind them of approaching deadlines to assess their interest.

Today, with a CRM system, we do many of the same things, but most are automated, allowing us to be more productive and efficient. Productivity and efficiency aside, our CRM system also helps build stronger prospect relationships by allowing greater engagement; enhances internal communication by allowing marketing, recruiting, academic departments, and enrollment management departments access to the same data; facilitates better decision making by providing real-time data and reporting on our prospect pool; helps analyze the effectiveness of marketing campaigns by tracking lead sourcing; and paints a clearer picture of the decision-making process and patterns of our prospects by helping track conversion rates at all stages of the enrollment funnel.

A CRM system only works if we generate leads, and the strategies and tactics we use to generate leads has changed drastically and continues to change, particularly with the increased use of online advertising and digital marketing tools. Search engine marketing, including paid and organic searching, search engine optimization (SEO), social media advertising—including Facebook, LinkedIn, and Twitter—and digital display advertising weren't part of most marketers' vocabularies ten years ago.

Today, these are all considered integral components of an integrated marketing communications plan, regardless of the demographics of your target audiences. And for good reason: digital marketing provides tremendous reach, especially on a global scale, is extremely cost effective, and is highly measurable and trackable.

As we discuss updated statistics on web usage, social media, and digital marketing, it's always a bit alarming to think about how dramatically things have changed in such a short period of time. Although we think about the technology revolution spanning more than thirty years, technology usage and its impact on continuing and professional education has really exploded in the last five years.

The growth of the personal computer can be credited with starting the digital marketing revolution. In 1984, it is estimated that 10 percent of US adults used a personal computer and just 1.4 percent used the Internet. With the birth of the World Wide Web in 1989, usage began to grow. By 1990, personal computer use increased to 42 percent. By 1995, Internet access had grown to 14 percent of US adults, although 42 percent had never heard of the Internet and 21 percent were vague on the concept. Today 81 percent say they use a computer in some part of their daily lives (Fox and Rainie 2014).

Equally important has been the growth of the cell phone market and mobile connectivity. Today, 90 percent of US adults have cell phones; two-thirds use them to access the Internet; and one-third say their cell phone is their primary connection to the Internet. That's impressive growth from 2000, when just 54 percent of US adults had a cell phone. In 2007, Apple introduced the iPhone, and smartphone usage has grown dramatically since. Today, 58 percent of US adults own a smartphone, compared to 35 percent in 2011 (Fox and Rainie 2014).

Personal computers, smartphones, and tablets continue to drive consumers' online habits. On average, Americans spend more than sixty hours online each month, with more than half accessing the Internet each day (eMarketer 2013). In addition to checking e-mail, users spend their time researching products and services, accessing social media sites, shopping, streaming media, and playing video games.

Social media has become a true global phenomenon. Consider these recent statistics when you hear some colleagues referring to it as a "trend" or think it is limited by the age of the user:

- 73 percent of all Internet users are active on social media.

- 90 percent of 18- to 29-year-olds are active.

- 78 percent of 30- to 49-year-olds are active.

- 65 percent of 50- to 60-year-olds are active.

- In the 65-plus bracket, 46 percent are using social media.

- US users spend more time on Facebook than on any other website.

- 40 percent of users access social media from a mobile device. (Pew Research Center 2014)

Facebook, Twitter, and Google+ are the top three sites in terms of average monthly active users. But other sites like Instagram, Pinterest, and Reddit continue to add active users. Plus social media continues to become more integrated into our daily lives. More than one million web pages are now automatically connected to Facebook, and 47 percent of Americans say Facebook is their number one influencer of purchases, up from 21 percent in 2011 (Jones 2013).

Social media continues to create a complicated and ever-changing challenge for continuing education marketers. When you see these staggering usage numbers, it's easy to be tempted to jump on the "shiny object" bandwagon and have a presence on every social media platform. In the past, that approach was very common—think of the "all people, everywhere" strategy. Today, we better understand the communication preferences of adult learners and how people use and value social media, the web, and e-mail, particularly when researching products and services. This increased understanding allows us to craft better communication strategies instead of solely focusing on the delivery channels (Copeland and Routhier 2012).

As we've been reflecting on what's changed in continuing education marketing, we feel it's just as important to look forward and prepare for what's next and how that may affect our strategies and budgets. There's a growing focus on dynamic content, inbound marketing, and visually driven content, all of which will allow marketers to create and deliver more personalized experiences to the right audiences at the right time. In addition, consider these interesting marketing statistics and projections:

- It's projected that marketers will have spent $135 billion on digital marketing collateral in 2014.

- 78 percent of chief marketing officers think custom content will drive marketing in the future.

- By 2015, online advertising will make up almost 24 percent of the entire advertising market.

- Social media marketing budgets will double in the next five years.

- 60 percent of the population are visual learners.

- Inbound marketing generates 54 percent more leads than outbound marketing.

- 55 percent of marketers increased their digital marketing budgets in 2013. (WebDAM 2014)

It's clear to us that the next generation of marketing tactics will therefore look different than the last. But we are equally certain that the focus will remain on building and maintaining relationships. That emphasis will never change.

What's Remained Constant?

Although marketing tactics and tools have changed dramatically, marketing planning and strategies have remained very consistent. That became very apparent to us recently while planning the launch of several new degree programs.

Our planning process started the same as many others: asking questions and establishing goals with our internal clients.

> What are we trying to accomplish?
>
> What are our enrollment goals?
>
> How many inquiries do we have to generate to meet our enrollment goals?
>
> What are our key dates?

Next, the conversation turned to defining our target audiences.

> Are they primarily men or women?
>
> How old are they?
>
> What's their education level?
>
> How many year's work experience do they have?
>
> What's their income level?
>
> Where do they live and work?

After defining our target audiences, we developed a detailed communication plan to reach them. Although the tactics have changed dramatically, we still use an integrated communication strategy that includes traditional advertising vehicles, print materials, direct mail, and in-person recruiting events.

It is interesting to note that traditional advertising has remained a constant in most of our media and marketing plans. We continue to use a combination of radio, television, and outdoor advertising. We primarily utilize television and outdoor advertising to build brand awareness. Radio helps build brand awareness but also drives event registration, particularly for offsite programs in smaller markets. Although traditional advertising has changed much since the black-and-white television sets of the 1950s, statistics continue to show that it remains an important marketing strategy. According to "TV Basics," a publication of the Television Bureau of Advertising, statistics show that consumers value traditional media outlets, despite the incredible growth of DVRs, satellite and streaming radio, the iPod and iPhone, and online media streaming. Included among the most important findings are the following:

- Adults still watch four to five hours of television program ming per day, including DVR and on demand viewing.

- The higher education sector remains a top-ten spot television advertiser.

- On average, television reaches almost 90 percent of adults each average day.

- Radio reaches approximately 60 percent of adults each average day.

- More people learn about products they'd like to try or buy from TV commercials than from any other medium.

- Although more media are competing for people's time, television and radio are still the top two categories in consumer media usage. (Television Bureau of Advertising 2012)

Because we only offer seat-based degree programs, on-campus events remain an important part of our recruiting strategy. We typically host eight information sessions each year. Attendance has waned in recent years, but the impact of attending an information session on a prospective student's decision to apply and enroll remains high. We attribute much of this to the consistent role that relationship building and high-touch personal interactions have played in the recruiting, retention, and referral process over the years.

When asked how students hear about us, "from a friend or colleague" has consistently topped our list since we began collecting statistics many years ago. Regardless of where someone is in the enrollment funnel, there is nothing quite like a phenomenal experience to help ensure positive word-of-mouth marketing, and the importance of word-of-mouth has been consistently strong. National data supports the significance of word-of-mouth advertising. When asked what sources "influence your decision to use or not use a particular company, brand, or product," 72 percent claim reviews from family members or friends exert a "great deal" or "fair amount" of influence. Additionally, 92 percent of consumers worldwide trust recommendations from friends and family more than any other form of advertising ("Everything You Need to Know about Word of Mouth Advertising" n.d.).

Another marketing constant is the importance of print collateral. Don't misunderstand us. We no longer print tens of thousands of class schedules or catalogs. In fact, we don't print a class schedule or catalog at all for our degree programs. Instead, we have transitioned these on-line, which was a long process (and painful for some). We do still print program brochures. And we still mail (yes, US Post Office "snail mail") packets to prospects who request them. The print brochures and packets create an important engagement point for us. In particular, they allow us to provide information for prospects to share with those they consult in the decision-making process and help shape our brand.

Conclusion

There is perhaps no other facet of continuing higher education that has undergone a more dramatic transformation than marketing. Almost all of the tools currently available to us did not exist when each of us entered the profession. Our constituencies continue to broaden and diversify, adding a layer of complexity to our decision making as we are tasked with reaching audiences in a very crowded marketplace across the enrollment lifecycle and therefore regularly requiring us to utilize the full gamut of communication tools available. While sometimes daunting and always a complicated challenge, we believe that the most important constant in developing a successful marketing program is to focus on building rela-tionships. That simple fact has never changed.

References

"A Brief History of Customer Relationship Management." 2013. CRM Switch [blog post], September 12. Accessed at http://www.crmswitch.com /crm-industry/crm-industry-history/.

Copeland, T., and A. Routhier. 2012. *The Interactive Marketing Preferences of Adult Learners—2012.* Accessed at http://resources.plattformad.com /sites/default/files/2012-Interactive-Marketing-Preferences-Adult -Learners-DemandEngine.pdf.

eMarketer. 2013. "Digital Set to Surpass TV in Time Spent with US Media." Accessed at http://www.emarketer.com/Article/Digital-Set-Surpass-TV -Time-Spent-with-US-Media/1010096.

"Everything You Need to Know about Word of Mouth Advertising." n.d. Wom-mapedia. Accessed at http://www.wommapedia.org/.

Fox, S., and L. Rainie. 2014. *The Web at 25 in the U.S.* Pew Research Cen-ter. Accessed at http://www.pewinternet.org/files/2014/02/PIP_25th -anniversary-of-the-Web_0227141.pdf.

"Global Smartphone Shipments." 2014. *The Economist (US)*, February 1, 81.

Jones, K. 2013. "Growth of Social Media v2.0 [Infographic]." *Search Engine*

Journal, November 15. Accessed at http://www.searchenginejournal.com /growth-social-media-2-0-infographic/77055/.

Kaku, M. 2011. *Physics of the Future: How Science Will Shape Human Destiny and Our Daily Lives by the Year 2100.* New York: Doubleday.

Pew Research Center. 2014. *Social Networking Fact Sheet.* Accessed at http://www.pewinternet.org/fact-sheets/social-networking-fact-sheet/.

Television Bureau of Advertising. 2012. *TV Basics: A Report on the Growth and Scope of Television.* Accessed at http://www.tvb.org/media/file/TV_Basics .pdf.

"2014 Marketing Statistics Infographic: 20 Captivating Marketing Statistics." 2014. WebDAM. Accessed at http://www.webdam.com/2014-marketing -statistics-infographic/.

The Evolution of Enrollment Marketing from Creative Tactics to Integrated Strategic Processes

▌▌

Jim Fong and Noreen Mack

Introduction

Change is inevitable. Higher education, and especially continuing education, has likely changed more in the past decade than it did in the previous half century. The role and structure of the marketing department of the continuing education unit and those working in it have also undergone significant transformation. Not only is marketing dealing with new forms of communication (digital versus print) but also changing demographics and even an evolution in the institution's structure itself, from brick and mortar to brick and click. The role of marketing has shifted from a tactical or support function to a more strategic initiative. Competitive forces, evolution of electronic marketing technologies, developments in data mining and customer relationship management (CRM), along with the greater expectations for marketing metrics and accountability, are helping to reshape how marketing units are positioned within continuing education (Fong 2013).

Premillennial Continuing Education Marketing

Today, the success of continuing education programs hinges on many factors, with marketing being one essential and strategic piece. Without a

Jim Fong is the Founding Director, Center for Research and Consulting, UPCEA, and a recipient of the Robertson Award. **Noreen Mack** is Analyst, Center for Research Consulting, UPCEA, and a committee chair.

strong marketing effort, it is unlikely any continuing education program would survive for long in today's economy. However, two decades ago the situation was vastly different and market conditions were more favorable for successful continuing education programming. In the latter half of the 1990s there was population growth and also favorable aging patterns for continuing education.

These changes were fueled primarily by the baby boom generation (US Department of Commerce 1996). Over this time span, and with the turn of the century, came another population boom that has an impact on continuing education marketers today, the echo boom or the millennials, children of the baby boom generation. Parallel to these population shifts, the 1990s saw an evolution from mass marketing that was based primarily on broadcast and print media to a more integrated and strategic marketing approach. In an interview with, continuing education pioneer Dorothy Durkin of New York University, Durkin identified the shift early on from mass marketing to integrated or target marketing and the principles that would transform not only higher education, but business and industry worldwide (Ryan 1993). "The answers lie with the learners themselves, because the more we know about their learning needs, the clearer our marketing directions are."

Figure 1 shows that today's marketers rely more heavily on digital marketing tools than they did a decade ago (Fong 2014).

Figure 1: Distribution of the Continuing Education Department Media Budget

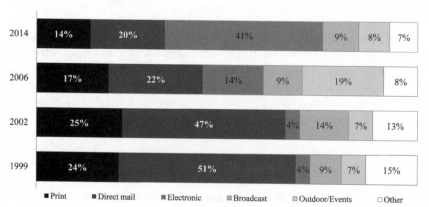

The marketing needs for continuing education two decades ago, as compared to today's needs, were far less complicated. Using the principle of the four P's of marketing—product, place, price, and promotion—the continuing education product or portfolio often consisted of credit courses offered in the evening or noncredit courses offered at a university or public venue. Online courses were just starting to take root, and few institutions offered distance education or correspondence courses, let alone full degrees, until the millennium. Those that did often took a leadership position in their marketing efforts. However, up until that point, the product was relatively easy to market; online classes were in their infancy, and the majority of classes were mainly campus based which resulted in marketing within service territories or more concretely defined regions. In fact, 1999 UPCEA research showed that 56 percent of continuing education units were focused on the region, while 26 percent said they served a national audience and 20 percent an international audience. Unless the program was noncredit, the price was fixed at whatever credit level the university set, and promotion was confined largely to direct mail and print. During this time, UPCEA continuing education marketers reported that direct mail was 51 percent of media expenditures and print was 24 percent (Fong 2000). During the latter half of the 1990s, cable television started to blossom and moved from analog to digital signals, and e-mail and the Internet were becoming more mainstream.

The result for continuing education units was a marketing department that was often labeled "Publications" or "Communications," with the core competencies being primarily copywriting, graphic design, public relations, and production. One could argue that marketing was more of an art than a science and was largely valued that way among many higher education leaders. Marketing was viewed as a tactic, often an afterthought of a program launch. After the program had been developed, only then would marketing be brought to the table to find a market or audience for the program and generate enrollments. No feasibility studies or market research were conducted. It was assumed that the market needed the course or program, that subject matter experts knew market demand best, and that advertising or marketing could generate the enrollments needed. If enrollments were minimal or insufficient to launch, the marketing department was often to blame and was urged to send out more brochures, postcards, and catalogs and/or place more advertisements. Marketing was often blamed for not getting collateral to the audience in time, not buying the right list, or not producing effective materials, despite a process that allowed multiple changes upstream from program or administrative staff and required approvals and acceptance of program stakeholders on list selection and marketing materials. Performance data and metrics, which could help institutions isolate success factors that could be repeated or problematic factors that could be avoided in future marketing efforts, were very rare. Durkin identifies the importance of growth metrics and the need to not only adopt performance metrics, but to also adapt or change them to illustrate clear trends (Durkin 2009).

With a changing market and a shift toward higher educational standards, evolving technology, and a relatively stable economy at the time,

generating enrollments through what would be primarily called advertising was largely successful for most institutions. It could also be argued
that a favorable supply and demand situation existed for continuing education. And a limited number of competitors within one's region often allowed all providers to achieve their enrollment goals with minimal
marketing or advertising efforts. The product was more in need by the
learner (and he or she would seek it out), which in turn required less
strategic marketing planning for continuing education. This is further il-
lustrated by the number of adults returning to college during this era. In
1980, 4.5 million adults age twenty-five or older returned to college and
in 1990, the number was 5.6 million. By 2001, this number had grown to
6.5 million (Aslanian 2001). Aslanian's research also cited the results of
a survey suggesting that a typical adult learner was forty years old, white,
and female. Her research showed that only 12 percent were nonwhite,
and in 2001 the effects of immigration and a global marketplace for education had not yet impacted the US market for continuing education.

During this era, continuing education did not need a stable of MBAs
to strategically lead the marketing department. It needed designers and
writers and production specialists. The job description for a marketing
professional in the 1990s required them to have a bachelor's degree,
preferably in journalism, business, marketing, communications, English,
or art. These individuals helped pave the way for programming with major events such as producing the complex and time-consuming continuing education catalog two or three times a year or buying a page in the
local newspaper to announce the current semester's evening offerings. If
an organization had a bigger budget, then radio and television were often part of the mix, and usually specialists or production companies were
hired to address this rare or episodic marketing event. If the organization
did not rely on broadcast media for its advertising, it was not uncommon
for a marketing department to have less than 1 percent of revenues devoted to media. Press releases were considered an inexpensive form of advertising with marketers hoping their announcements would be thought
worthy enough to print. Early in the 1990s, press releases would be phys-
ically mailed to media outlets or publications, as the Internet was in its
infancy. Today, with one click, one can send thousands of releases to news
sites, social media, or directly to publishers and editors.

Often forgotten in the media mix was the role of business-to-business
marketing or sales promotion. The academic culture of the 1990s neither
embraced nor respected the role of the salesperson within academia.
While rare within continuing education organizations during that era,
those who were more progressive realized the importance of a corporate
salesperson. Creating or funding the position became more of a challenge, as using the word *sales* in the job description was discouraged, and
many job descriptions in higher education lacked this competency. As a
result, and to appease the academic community, the salesperson was of-

ten given a title with the words *corporate relationship, client development, out-reach development,* or *relationship manager.* The position and function today is more valued and respected, as the higher education community has embraced the associated benefits. Today, one in four marketing leaders report that their marketing units have an individual with a sales responsibility as part of their job or in a full-time position (Fong 2014).

The Turn of the Century and the Rise of Digital and Integrated Marketing

Continuing education has seen a significant shift in emphasis since the turn of the century. As today's economy requires a commitment to life-long education, the focus has moved from primarily degree completion programs and enrichment opportunities to degrees and certificates providing critical thinking and global competencies in today's world. A tightened economy and reduction of state funding for many institutions fueled a race for online and global education. Further contributing to a more competitive marketplace was the rise of for-profit institutions and open-system universities. While open-system universities had lesser impact on marketing, institutions such as the University of Phoenix and Capella University invested heavily in marketing and enrollment management efforts. Traditional institutions such as the University of Maryland University College, Penn State and its World Campus, and New York University, along with other more progressive institutions in the traditional sector, also became models for adult and corporate learner-focused marketing.

Traditional institutions continued to spend 5 to 10 percent of gross revenues on marketing, while many for-profit institutions were spending 15 to 27 percent. As spending increased to advertise online programs, many institutions looked to the Internet for new marketing opportunities, as well as improving internal processes and conversion rates through improved customer relationship management (CRM) and enrollment marketing techniques. Institutions such as George Washington University and New York University became known as early innovators and for their investments in CRM systems.

While many institutions debated the merits of moving to online education, early adopting colleges and universities, such as Nova Southeastern University, New Jersey Institute of Technology, Colorado State University, and Champlain College, gained early market share in their niches and markets and made the case for more integrated marketing and investment into digital marketing tactics. Institutions such as the University of Minnesota, Northeastern University, and George Washington University also began staffing their communications and advertising units with more highly trained marketers and began building out full-service marketing units. Publications managers gave way to marketing directors. Many departments began building prospect databases or purchasing systems to manage leads more strategically. As marketing departments evolved through the early part of the new millennium, so did the role of the third-party marketing provider, which helped in this evolution, guiding them with prospect management systems, e-mail marketing, market research, and search engine optimization.

Ultimately, continuing education leaders saw more examples of marketing best practices throughout the field, not only from for-profits, but from peer institutions. As a result, many marketing budgets increased, more staff were added, and CRM systems were implemented. In 2004, UPCEA surveys showed that 42 percent of marketing departments had a database marketer or CRM leader on staff, and for many it was still a growing area (Fong and Bailey 2004). New leaders, often with MBAs or corporate marketing experience, were sometimes brought in to guide the continuing education unit through challenging but exciting times. This new breed of successful marketing leader had to be multidimensional—able to communicate the importance of marketing to continuing education leaders and faculty, transform the marketing department, mentor staff, and master new marketing techniques. They also wrote new job descriptions and filled them with positions that were often new to higher education, resulting in increased access to data and information and new technology innovations but also creating greater competitive pressures. These new positions included the electronic marketing specialist, database marketing analyst, marketing strategist, website developer, and market research analyst. Legacy staff were often reassigned to more functional roles within copywriting or creative services, or their skills were enhanced through increased professional development in new marketing. In other words, continuing education marketing in the early part of 2000 was becoming more complicated and scientific.

The new marketing department was no longer an advertising agency. Premillennial marketing plans often consisted of spreadsheets of anticipated media purchases and were not true marketing plans. With newly found resources and information and technology at hand, customer relationship and enrollment management began to take off and reshape marketing planning and accountability efforts. Effective marketing was less dependent on attractive advertising pieces, such as the multipage catalog, but more focused on driving inquiries and enrollments and improving return on investment. The evolution of CRM systems provided an underpinning for strategic marketing planning. Marketers were now beginning to store inquiry and prospect information centrally and often link it to specific marketing efforts as well as track performance based on programmatic spending and with specific media. This historical performance and financial information often became foundational for future marketing efforts. Real-time data and reporting was still rare, as systems during this time still required significant labor to produce meaningful reports.

If the data did not exist internally, then it could be collected through market research. Before the millennium, market research and gathering market intelligence and competitive information were rare, as many faculty-driven program ideas were strong enough to succeed in a less competitive but growing marketplace for education. Progressive institutions saw it as an obvious part of integrated marketing strategies and new program development processes. One in five of UPCEA members have full-time or part-time staff assigned to market research activities. They often have these staff not only to conduct activities such as customer surveys, market studies, environmental scans, or competitive intelligence but also to mine for data patterns in enrollment or inquiry data. Only about one in ten institutions surveyed today do not have in-house market research staff but instead outsource this function to specialized third-party market research providers or tap into these services through their marketing agencies, public relations firms, or learning management system providers. The profession of market research and intelligence has grown significantly over the past two decades.

The Evolution of the Enrollment Marketer

Today's marketing departments need a higher level of sophistication in order to survive. The 2014 UPCEA marketing survey showed the necessity for marketers to learn more about analytics, metrics, CRM, and social media. Some continuing education marketers are still struggling with e-mail marketing, paid search, and search engine optimization, all of which have been available for over a decade. A UPCEA Center for Research and Consulting study for a member institution showed that leading social media experts believed that social media is an ever-changing field with frequent new entries into the market (Fong 2012). Social media is no longer an option in continuing education marketing but rather a necessity, and yet just three in ten marketing leaders state that their marketing departments have a high level of competency in this area. In contrast, more than half say they have a high level of competency in print marketing. Not using social media as a marketing channel is a disadvantage to the institution, which competitors will certainly exploit.

Marketers, who have a history of being excellent multitaskers, have many responsibilities. Not only must they stay current and adapt to new technology, they must assess previous strategy for return on investment, identify target markets, and conduct program concept tests and postmortems on struggling programs. They must also identify revenue opportunities, strategies, and cost-saving marketing actions and manage the marketing scoreboard or key metrics. The 2014 UPCEA Marketing Survey shows that a marketing department is responsible for marketing many types of programs and services, many more than in the past.

Marketing departments are responsible for marketing 4.7 programs on average (Fong 2014). For example, in 1999, 44 percent of UPCEA marketers said they marketed summer programs, while today 78 percent say they do. Marketing departments usually market credit and noncredit programs; online degrees, courses, or certificates; summer sessions; and professional master's degrees, as well as programs targeted to international populations, precollege students, educators, and those in retirement or in the military.

As a result of continued change in education, technology, and marketing itself, marketers can no longer rely on just marketing one of the four P's (product, price, place, promotion), with the primary focus being promotion. With these new products (or programs), marketers are asked to understand more of the marketing spectrum. They're also asked to better market "place," with the most relevant and challenging being online programming. When staff are marketing online programs, effectively using digital marketing approaches can often be a reflection of the institution's ability to offer online programming and therefore must be executed properly.

In addition to noncredit courses and certificates, where price is flexible and the continuing education unit has greater influence, many institutions are bringing the marketplace into their credit programs. Greater emphasis is being put on not just setting the price, but also determining whether the market will bear the university's traditional pricing standards.

In comparison to the continuing education marketer of the 1990s, today's marketing leader has much more than design, copywriting, media buying, and production to manage. In addition to a leader's standard skills of planning strategically, mentoring and developing staff, and being able to communicate with leadership and faculty, today's leader also needs to be able to use digital as well as traditional marketing tactics. The leader needs to be able to assess competitive and industry conditions as well as apply analytics and market research in the decision-making process. In 1999, the average marketing staff consisted of 7.7 people with almost half (48%) of the staff being graphic designers, copywriters, editors, production people, or public relations staff. In 2006, the percentage of staff in these positions was 38 percent and is now 23 percent (Bailey and Erickson 2006). Even with the increased likelihood of outsourcing, the 2014 UPCEA Marketing Survey showed that the average marketing department has just over five full-time employees and just under one part-time employee equivalent today but has evolved significantly in its staffing mix (Fong 2014).

However, the breadth of marketing skill sets and knowledge has greatly expanded. These marketing employees often include a marketing director or leader, a marketing manager and assistant/coordinator, web developer, graphic designer, copywriter, and an e-marketing manager in charge of e-mail, search engine optimization, paid search, or other related tasks. At the University of Minnesota, over the past decade the dependence on creative staff has declined significantly with fewer full-time designers and copywriters and an increase in digital marketing specialists, social media managers, and content marketers. The University of Minnesota and Oregon State University have added staff who are responsible for enrollment management and the recruiting and advising of potential students.

Social media managers and coordinators are new positions to continuing education. A number of institutions have added these positions to their digital marketing and public relations functions. However, many organizations continue to struggle with this marketing channel. The 2014 UPCEA Marketing Survey showed that approximately one-third of the marketing departments had an individual, whether full-time or part-time, assigned to social media. Interviews with industry experts show that many organizations that have attempted to use social media continue to flounder and fail. Many have not adequately planned their communications cycle or have neglected to plan for two-way communication. For many institutions, social media has been an announcement of some event and not a dialogue for engagement. Successful institutions have leveraged the full technical capabilities of specific social media sites and created meaningful exchanges, such as one institution that provides direct inquiry to visitors and prospects asking questions about the institution and application processes, while others have created vibrant communities where alumni, current students, and faculty respond to visitor questions.

Social media may be more visible, but metrics, analytics, and enrollment management are the foundation; however, there are many factors that continue to evolve for the enrollment marketer. Mass media and print-based marketing in the 1980s and early 1990s by continuing education marketers evolved into targeted, database, or integrated marketing at the turn of the millennium. With the rise of technology came the dawn of the digital marketing era coupled with a more holistic approach to marketing and enrollment management. The phrase "enrollment marketing" has slowly evolved, blending the foundation of metrics, analytics, and customer relationship marketing with the development of not only marketing strategies but also advising and conversion tactics. While colleges and universities relied heavily on advertising, the discipline has now become a component of creative teams and design areas.

Enrollment marketing no longer focuses on the students in continuing education, as they have become so diverse, but draws upon a holistic approach that begins with understanding target markets and competition. It consists of developing marketing strategies and positions to nurture different types of prospects through application process and then to build a relationship with the graduate in the future for repurchase. In enrollment marketing, advising and customer service are now essential components. As seen with institutions such as the University of Minnesota and Penn State University, with the marketing and enrollment functions working more closely together, the ability to compete becomes much stronger.

While CRM is fundamental to strategic planning, it also plays a major role in communication with deans, directors, and faculty. Regular reporting or dashboard systems allow all parties to speak a similar language through the CRM and analytics process. Deans and directors seeing monthly or real-time reporting through evolved dashboard systems can better assess the progress of marketers. Faculty are focused on the success of their programs and can also measure progress through effective reporting. In addition, in a fully transparent organization, multiple stakeholders, including marketing, program managers, faculty, and finance can also see the success and struggles of specific programs and the impact of marketing. The ability to learn across the organization through the common language of marketing metrics allows diverse stakeholder groups to communicate more strategically and act more quickly in the planning and allocation of marketing efforts and priorities. However, marketers and others struggle with the maintenance and planning around CRM and enrollment management. Just 19 percent of those surveyed in the 2014 UPCEA Marketing Survey said their marketing departments had a high level of competencies in CRM.

Search engine marketing and optimization have become marketing staples for most continuing education operations. However, social media marketing and mobile marketing techniques are at the cusp of professional development initiatives for many marketers. Social media marketing will continue to evolve and be a critical tool in the marketer's toolbox. The challenge of social media will be mastering the tools and adapting to the changing needs of current and future adults. For example, in ten short years since the birth of Facebook in 2004, it has grown to 1.2 billion users registered on its platform. Few traditional media channels have the potential to reach this many consumers, and continuing education marketers struggle with the basics. While the platform is evolving into a strong channel to reach adults, many younger audiences have moved away from Facebook and onto sites such as Instagram, Twitter, and Pinterest. For marketers to master social media, all of these platforms plus LinkedIn, Google Plus, SnapChat, China's Baidu, and others require attention.

Technology has also created new challenges. Marketers must be prepared to address mobile marketing strategies. New challenges as a result include designing sites that can function on an array of devices. Marketers will need to make sure that they have staff who are prepared for mobile or have the resources to respond. With mobile marketing trends on the rise, the use and creation of video has become more important.

Marketing departments outside of continuing education have embraced this trend and have created positions that focused solely on mobile and computer video production. Some UPCEA marketing departments, such as Oregon State University (OSU), are also adding video production staff, while others are considering it. At OSU, with enrollments increasing over the past decade, the marketing department increased by eight individuals to thirteen marketing staff members, with one of these positions being a videographer and others in enrollment or advising (Fong and Dupont 2013). The 2014 UPCEA study showed that 10 percent of marketing departments have staff assigned to the video function of marketing.

Both social media marketing and the rise of mobile and video-based marketing are components of a larger marketing trend—content marketing. Many UPCEA marketing departments are becoming more knowledgeable in content marketing, realizing that their institutions do not always have to create new meaningful marketing messages but do have to become better at repurposing past content or using the content of others. The Content Marketing Institute defines content marketing as a "technique of creating and distributing valuable, relevant and consistent content to attract and acquire a clearly defined audience—with the objective of driving profitable customer action." Prevalent in the business-to-business world, it is becoming more accepted and utilized in higher education. It provides valuable information to the customer without "selling," and its objective is to change consumer behavior. The reaction by some institutions is to create the position, add responsibilities to existing staff, or, in the case of the University of Minnesota, to shift staff previously assigned to a creative function into a content manager position.

The lone marketing manager from the 1990s used to be able to do it all. Today's marketing department has evolved and is dependent on having a strong team or strategic outsourcing relationships in place, as the complexity of marketing has become much greater. Research has shown that many organizational models are in place within continuing education and extended university settings, which have an impact on the role of the marketing leader (Fong and Platteter 2013). The marketing leader needs to know the landscape of marketing and educational challenges to properly direct resources and develop strategies. The marketing leader needs to be respected as a supervisor by staff and valued by deans, directors, and faculty. Marketers and leadership have not always seen eye to eye, as they often speak two very different languages (Fong 2009). Past research has shown that marketing directors rate their performance on a number of competencies and responsibilities very highly, while their deans and directors rate them significantly lower, one of which is strategic marketing planning.

The Future for Marketers

The *Wall Street Journal* featured an article about what college may look like in 2023: "Over the next decade, technology may sweep away some of the basic aspects of a university education and usher in a flood of innovations and changes" (Kahn 2013). This has already begun, with the proliferation of online courses and degrees and the change in textbooks to digital content. Colleges and universities will combine resources by providing courses taught by rock-star professors to other institutions and by adopting other schools' courses and putting their own stamp on them. This is already taking place at University of California San Jose and University of California Sacramento, where students are taking engineering classes that were developed at the Massachusetts Institute of Technology. Despite the push to online, universities are opening up campuses or administrative offices outside of their traditional regions, such as Northeastern University's campuses in Seattle, Washington, and Charlotte, North Carolina, and Penn State's announcement of administrative office in San Diego, California (Spinelle 2013). How will marketing departments adapt to new changes in the learning environment as well as changes in marketing itself?

The role of a marketing professional, the evolution of online education, exponential growth of digital technology, and myriad other factors are changing and creating sometimes frightening but also exciting opportunities and challenges to the continuing education or enrollment marketer in the next decade. Search engine optimization and Facebook are no longer the hot topics, being replaced with mobile, personalized, and relationship marketing. CRM is not an option but a necessity. The 2014 survey shows that leaders see their greatest challenges as having to address declining enrollments with similar or shrinking budgets, increased competition, acquiring more resources, measuring return on investment and marketing performance, and a myriad of staffing and professional development challenges. Marketing departments will continue to change, as will marketing technologies, strategic outsourcing relationships, and staffing positions and responsibilities. Marketing leaders certainly have many opportunities and challenges in front of them.

References

Aslanian, C. 2001. *Adult Students Today.* New York: College Board.

Bailey, N., and K. Erickson. 2006. *Marketing Report.* Washington, DC: University Professional and Continuing Education Association.

"What Is Content Marketing?" Content Marketing Institute. Accessed at http://contentmarketinginstitute.com/what-is-content-marketing/.

Durkin, D. 2009. "Marketing Continuing Education." *Marketing Continuing*

Education. Accessed at http://dorothydurkin.files.wordpress.com/2012/09/marketingcontinuingeducation_042009_fp.pdf.

Fong, J. 2000. "Our Changing Marketing Departments: The State of CE Marketing." Presentation at UCEA Marketing Seminar, Savannah, Georgia, February.

Fong, J. 2009. "Improving the Relationship between Continuing Education Leadership and Marketing Directors." *Continuing Higher Education Review* 73: 153–162.

Fong, J. 2012. "Social Media End User Research," Internal Client Report. July 2012.

Fong, J. 2013. "Preparing Marketing for the Future: Strategic Marketing Challenges for Continuing Education." *Continuing Education in Colleges and Universities: Challenges and Opportunities,* no. 140: 89–100.

Fong, J. 2014. *UPCEA Marketing Survey.* Washington, DC: University Professional and Continuing Education Association.

Fong, J., and N. Bailey. 2004. "The State of Continuing Education Marketing: A UCEA Study." Presentation at UCEA Marketing Seminar, Savannah, Georgia, February.

Fong, J., and J. Dupont. 2013. "The Strategic Alignment of the Continuing Education Marketing Department." Presentation at UPCEA Annual Meeting, Boston, Massachusetts, April.

Fong, J., and S. Platteter. 2013. "The Continuing Education Organizational Marketing Chart." Presentation at UPCEA Marketing Seminar, Las Vegas, Nevada, November.

Kahn, Gabriel. 2013. "A Glimpse into the Future: College in 2023." *Wall Street Journal,* October 9, R7.

Ryan, Ellen. 1993. "Program the Market, Market the Program." *Currents* 19(2): 32–38.

Spinelle, Jenna. 2013. "Bringing Penn State to the World." *Town and Gown Magazine,* August 2013. http://www.statecollege.com/news/town-and-gown/bringing-penn-state-to-the-world,1375037/

US Department of Commerce. 1996. *Population Projections of the United States by Age, Sex, Race, and Hispanic Origin: 1995 to 2050.* Washington, DC: Author. Accessed at http://www.census.gov/prod/1/pop/p25-1130/p251130.pdf.

University Professional and Continuing Education Association Presidents

1915–1916 Louis E. Reber, University of Wisconsin

1916–1917 Hervey F. Mallory, University of Chicago

1917–1919 Charles B. Robertson, University of Pittsburgh

1919–1920 William D. Henderson, University of Michigan

1920–1921 John J. Pettijohn, University of Minnesota

1921–1922 Frederick W. Reynolds, University of Utah

1922–1923 Charles G. Maphis, University of Virginia

1923–1924 Richard R. Price, University of Minnesota

1924–1925 Harold G. Ingham, University of Kansas

1925–1926 Leon J. Richardson, University of California–Berkeley

1926–1927 William H. Lighty, University of Wisconsin

1927–1928 James A. Moyer, Massachusetts Department of Education

1928–1929 Thomas H. Shelby, University of Texas

1929–1930 Norman C. Miller, Rutgers University

1930–1931 Elmore Petersen, University of Colorado

1931–1932 Robert E. Cavanaugh, Indiana University

1932–1933 Theodore G. Grayson, University of Pennsylvania

1933–1934 Arthur M. Harding, University of Arkansas

1934–1935 Frank W. Shockley, University of Pittsburgh

1935–1936 Albert A. Reed, University of Nebraska

1936–1937 Frank M. Debatin, Washington University in St. Louis

1937–1938 D. Walter Morton, Syracuse University

1938–1939 Bruce E. Mahan, University of Iowa

1939–1940 Bert C. Riley, University of Florida

1940–1941 J. Orvis Keller, Pennsylvania State University

1941–1942 Russell M. Grumman, University of North Carolina

1942–1943 George B. Zehmer, University of Virginia

1943–1944 Robert B. Browne, University of Illinois

1944–1945 Charles A. Fisher, University of Michigan

1945–1946 Fessenden C. Lowry, University of Tennessee

1946–1947 Maurice A. Chaffee, Rutgers University

1947–1948 Robert E. Tidwell, University of Alabama

1948–1949 Knute O. Broady, University of Nebraska

1949–1950 Edward L. Keller, Pennsylvania State University

1950–1951 Julius M. Nolte, University of Minnesota

1951–1952 Lorenz H. Adolfson, University of Wisconsin

1952–1953 J. Walter Brouillette, Louisiana State University

1953–1954 Everett J. Soop, University of Michigan

1954–1955 Lloyd W. Schram, University of Washington

1955–1956 Roy R. Thomkins, Oklahoma State University

1956–1957 Ernest A. Lowe, University of Georgia

1957–1958 Ernest E. McMahon, Rutgers University

1958–1959 John R. Morton, University of Alabama

1959–1960 James R. D. Eddy, University of Texas

1960–1961 Thurman White, University of Oklahoma

1961–1962 D. Mack Easton, University of Colorado

1962–1963 Paul H. Sheats, University of California–Los Angeles

1963–1964 Howard R. Neville, Michigan State University

1964–1965 Stanley J. Drazek, University of Maryland

1965–1966 Alexander N. Charters, Syracuse University

1966–1967 Charles F. Milner, University of North Carolina

1967–1968 T. Howard Walker, University of Kansas

1968–1969 Stanley C. Robinson, University of Illinois

1969–1970 Nicholas P. Mitchell, University of South Carolina

1970–1971 Robert F. Ray, University of Iowa

1971–1972 Floyd B. Fischer, Pennsylvania State University

1972–1973 Armand L. Hunter, Michigan State University

1973–1974 Glenn A. Goerke, Florida International University

1974–1975 Lowell R. Eklund, Oakland University

1975–1976 John B. Ervin, Washington University in St. Louis

1976–1977 Paul E. Hadley, University of Southern California

1977–1978 Phillip E. Frandson, University of California–Los Angeles

1978–1979 William L. Turner, North Carolina State University

1979–1980 Grace M. Donehower, University of Nevada–Reno

1980–1981 Jean C. Evans, University of Wisconsin

1981–1982 Joseph P. Goddard, University of Tennessee–Knoxville

1982–1983 Quentin H. Gessner, University of Nebraska–Lincoln

1983–1984 Adelle F. Robertson, University of Virginia

1984–1985 Harvey J. Stedman, New York University

1985–1986 John C. Snider, University of Alabama

1986–1987 Hilton T. Bonniwell, University of Akron

1987–1988 Harold A. Miller, University of Minnesota

1988–1989 Mary L. Pankowski, Florida State University

1989–1990 Daniel W. Shannon, University of Chicago

1990–1991 Thomas M. Hatfield, University of Texas at Austin

1991–1992 Calvin L. Stockman, Grand Valley State University

1992–1993 Robert W. Comfort, University of Pittsburgh

1993–1994 Marcia Bankirer, Colorado State University

1994–1995 Miriam Williford, University of Massachusetts–Amherst

1995–1996 Edward G. Simpson, Jr., University of Georgia

1996–1997 James P. Pappas, University of Oklahoma

1997–1998 Gordon H. (Nick) Mueller, University of New Orleans

1998–1999 Sue C. Maes, Kansas State University

1999–2000 Thomas Kowalik, State University of New York–Binghamton

2000–2001 Wendell Smith, University of Missouri–St. Louis

2001–2002 Audrey S. Anderson, California State University–Fresno

2002–2003 John Ebersole, Boston University

2003–2004 Muriel Oaks, Washington State University

2004–2005 James Broomall, University of Delaware

2005–2006 Roger Whitaker, George Washington University

2006–2007 Barbara Scott, Southern Oregon University

2007–2008 Richard J. Novak, Rutgers University

2008–2009 Robert Wiltenburg, Washington University in St. Louis

2009–2010 Patricia A. Book, University of Northern Colorado

2010–2011 Judy Ashcroft, University of Texas at Austin

2011–2012 James Shaeffer, James Madison University

2012–2013 Thomas Gibbons, Northwestern University

2013–2014 Karen Sibley, Brown University

2014–2015 Bethaida González, Syracuse University

2015–2016 David Schejbal, University of Wisconsin, Extension

University Professional and Continuing Education Association
Member Institutions, Affiliates, and Associates

Alabama
Auburn University
Samford University
University of Alabama
University of Alabama at Birmingham

Alaska
University of Alaska Anchorage

Arizona
Arizona State University
Northcentral University
Northern Arizona University
Thunderbird School of Global Management
University of Arizona

Arkansas
University of Arkansas

California
Ashford University
Brandman University
California State Polytechnic University, Pomona
California State University, Bakersfield
California State University, Channel Islands
California State University, Chico
California State University, Dominguez Hills
California State University, East Bay
California State University, Fullerton
California State University, Long Beach
California State University, Los Angeles

California State University, Monterey Bay
California State University, Northridge
California State University, Sacramento
California State University, San Bernardino
California State University, San Marcos
California State University, Stanislaus
Everest College Phoenix
Fielding Graduate University
Fresno Pacific University
Life Pacific College
National University
Otis College of Art and Design
San Diego State University
San Francisco State University
San Jose State University
University of California, Berkeley
University of California, Davis
University of California, Irvine
University of California, Los Angeles
University of California, Merced
University of California, Riverside
University of California, San Diego
University of California, Santa Cruz
University of San Diego
University of the Pacific

Colorado
Colorado State University
Jones International University
Metropolitan State University of Denver
Naropa University
Regis University
University of Colorado at Boulder
University of Colorado Denver
University of Denver
University of Northern Colorado

Connecticut
Central Connecticut State University
Eastern Connecticut State University
Sacred Heart University
Southern Connecticut State University
University of Connecticut
University of New Haven

District of Columbia
American University
Catholic University of America
George Washington University
Georgetown University

Delware
Delaware State University
University of Delaware

Florida
Embry-Riddle Aeronautical University
Kaplan University
Northwest Florida State College
Rollins College
Saint Leo University
Stetson University
University of Miami
University of South Florida
University of West Florida

Georgia
Emory University
Georgia Institute of Technology
Georgia Southern University
Kennesaw State University
Mercer University
University of Georgia

Hawaii
University of Hawaii at Manoa

Iowa
Iowa State University
University of Iowa

Idaho
Boise State University
Lewis-Clark State College

Illinois
Chicago School of Professional Psychology
DeVry University
Dominican University

Eastern Illinois University
Lewis University
Loyola University of Chicago
North Park University
Northern Illinois University
Northwestern University
Southern Illinois University, Carbondale
Triton College
University of Chicago
University of Illinois at Chicago
University of Illinois at Springfield
University of Illinois at Urbana-Champaign
University of Illinois System

Indiana
Ball State University
Indiana State University
Indiana University-Purdue University Fort Wayne
Purdue University
University of Indianapolis
University of Southern Indiana

Kansas
Emporia State University
Fort Hays State University
Kansas State University
University of Kansas

Kentucky
Lipscomb University
University of Louisville
Western Kentucky University

Louisiana
Louisiana State University
Tulane University
University of Louisiana at Lafayette

Massachusetts
American International College
Bay State College
Berklee College of Music
Boston College
Boston University

Brandeis University
Bridgewater State University
College of Our Lady of the Elms
Curry College
Fitchburg State College
Framingham State University
Harvard University
Lasell College
Massachusetts College of Art and Design
MCPHS University
MGH Institute of Health Professions
Mount Holyoke College
Northeastern University
Salem State University
UMassOnline
University of Massachusetts Amherst
University of Massachusetts Boston
University of Massachusetts, Dartmouth
University of Massachusetts, Lowell
Wentworth Institute of Technology
Westfield State University
Worcester State University

Maryland
Goucher College
Johns Hopkins University
Morgan State University
University of Baltimore
University of Maryland Baltimore County
University of Maryland College Park
University of Maryland University College

Maine
Saint Joseph's College of Maine
University of Maine
University of Southern Maine

Michigan
Central Michigan University
Eastern Michigan University
Ferris State University
Grand Valley State University
Michigan State University
Oakland University

University of Michigan–Flint
Western Michigan University

Minnesota
Bemidji State University
Capella University
Metropolitan State University
Minnesota State University, Mankato
St. Catherine University
St. Cloud State University
University of Minnesota
Winona State University

Missouri
Columbia College
Missouri State University
Truman State University
University of Central Missouri
University of Missouri, Columbia
University of Missouri, St. Louis
Washington University in St. Louis

Mississippi
Mississippi State University
University of Mississippi

Montana
Montana State University, Billings
Montana State University, Bozeman

North Carolina
Appalachian State University
North Carolina State University
Pfeiffer University
Queens University of Charlotte
University of North Carolina at Charlotte
University of North Carolina at Greensboro
University of North Carolina at Chapel Hill
University of North Carolina at Pembroke
Western Carolina University

North Dakota
Minot State University
North Dakota State University
University of North Dakota

Nebraska
University of Nebraska
University of Nebraska, Lincoln
University of Nebraska, Omaha

Nevada
University of Nevada, Las Vegas
University of Nevada, Reno

New Hampshire
Granite State College
Southern New Hampshire University

New Jersey
Centenary College
College of New Jersey
Fairleigh Dickinson University
New Jersey City University
Ramapo College of New Jersey
Rowan University
Rutgers the State University of New Jersey
Seton Hall University
William Paterson University

New Mexico
University of New Mexico

New York
Adelphi University
Buffalo State College
Columbia University
Elmira College
Excelsior College
Fordham University
Long Island University
Marist College
New York University
Pace University
Purchase College, State University of New York
Sarah Lawrence College
State University of New York at Stony Brook
State University of New York Empire State College
State University of New York Institute of Technology
State University of New York Oneonta

SUNY College at Oswego
SUNY System Administration
Syracuse University
University at Buffalo–SUNY

Ohio
Kent State University
Miami University
Ohio State University
University of Akron

Oklahoma
Oklahoma State University
Tulsa Community College
University of Central Oklahoma
University of Oklahoma

Oregon
Linfield College
Oregon State University Extended Campus
Portland State University
Southern Oregon University
University of Oregon
Western Oregon University

Pennsylvania
Alvernia University
Chatham University
Delaware Valley College
Drexel University
Duquesne University
LaSalle University
Lehigh University
Millersville University
Misericordia University
Penn State University
Saint Francis University
Saint Joseph's University
Shippensburg University of Pennsylvania
Slippery Rock University
University of Pennsylvania
University of Pittsburgh
Washington and Jefferson College
Widener University

Puerto Rico
Universidad Metropolitana
University of Puerto Rico, Bayamon

Rhode Island
Brown University
Bryant University
Johnson and Wales University
New England Institute of Technology
Providence College School of Continuing Education
Rhode Island School of Design
University of Rhode Island, Providence Campus

South Carolina
Benedict College
Clemson University
University of South Carolina

South Dakota
Dakota State University
South Dakota State University
University of South Dakota

Tennessee
Austin Peay State University

Texas
Rice University
Sam Houston State University
Southern Methodist University
St. Edward's University
Texas Tech University
University of Houston
University of Texas at Austin
University of the Incarnate Word

Utah
Brigham Young University
Southern Utah University
University of Utah
. Utah State University
Utah Valley University
Weber State University

Virgin Islands of the United States
University of the Virgin Islands

Virginia
Bluefield College
George Mason University
James Madison University
Longwood University
Mary Baldwin College
Old Dominion University
Regent University
University of Richmond
University of Virginia
Virginia Commonwealth University
Virginia Polytechnic Institute and State University

Vermont
University of Vermont
Vermont Technical College

Washington
Bellevue College
Central Washington University
Eastern Washington University
Pacific Lutheran University
University of Washington
Washington State University
Western Washington University
Whitworth University

Wisconsin
University of Wisconsin, Eau Claire
University of Wisconsin, Extension
University of Wisconsin, Green Bay
University of Wisconsin, La Crosse
University of Wisconsin, Madison
University of Wisconsin, Milwaukee
University of Wisconsin, Oshkosh
University of Wisconsin, Stout
University of Wisconsin, Whitewater

West Virginia
American Public University System

Wyoming
University of Wyoming

International
McGill University
McMaster University
Memorial University of Newfoundland
Mount Royal University
Ryerson University
Simon Fraser University
Tecnologico de Monterrey
University of British Columbia
University of Guelph
University of New Brunswick
University of Northern British Columbia
University of Toronto
University of Victoria
University of Waterloo
York University

Affiliates
American Council on Education
California State University, Office of the Chancellor
DANTES, Defense Activity for Non-Traditional Education Support
Graduate School USA
Higher Learning Commission
Massey University
NAASS, North American Association of Summer Sessions
NASPA Student Affairs Administrators in Higher Education
Pontifical Catholic University of Chile
Roanoke Higher Education Center
Southwest Virginia Higher Education Center
University of Sydney
Western Veterinary Conference

Corporate Partners
Diamond
Blackboard
Platinum
Hobsons
InsideTrack
Jenzabar
Gold
Cooley LLC

Entrinsik, Inc.
Silver
Colloquy

Strategic Alliance Partners
JMH Consulting Inc
Thompson Coburn LLP

Corporate Members
12 West Capital
Augusoft
Burning Glass Technologies
Circa Interactive
Converge Consulting
Destiny Solutions
Ed4Online
Education Advisory Board
Educational Testing Consultants (ETC)
India Education Services Pvt Ltd
Iniciativa Tecnológica del Norte (INTENOR)
Jaxxon Promotions, Inc.
Millennium Integrated Marketing
MindMax
Parchment
Pearson
PlattForm
Ranku
Solomon EOS LLC
story+structure
StraighterLine
Triad Advertising
The Learning House, Inc.
W.I.T.S.
World Education, LLC
Xenegrade Corp